MANAGEMENT

An Organizational Perspective

MANAGEMENT

An Organizational Perspective

MARTIN J. GANNON
University of Maryland

LITTLE, BROWN AND COMPANY
Boston   Toronto

Library of Congress Catalog No. 76-26293

ISBN: 0-89463-012-1

THIRD PRINTING

Printed in the United States of America

ACKNOWLEDGMENTS

Chapter 1: The case study *Temporary Help* is based in part on Martin J. Gannon, "A Profile of the Temporary Help Industry and Its Workers," *Monthly Labor Review 97* (May 1974): 44-49. **Chapter 15:** Expanded and revised from Martin J. Gannon, "Entrepreneurship and Labor Relations at the Ford Motor Company," *Marquette Business Review* XVI, no. 2 (Summer 1972). Reprinted with permission.

Critical Incident, p. 282, no. 1: Published here for the first time with permission from the author, Richard H. Kirchmeyer.

Case Studies: State University Medical Center is published here for the first time with permission from the author, Carl P. Zeithaml. **Monitoring the Performance of Bank Tellers** is from Martin J. Gannon, "Employee Perceptions of Promotion," *Personnel Journal 50*, no. 3 (March 1971), p. 215. Reprinted by permission of Personnel Journal Inc., copyright March 1971. **The New Engineers** is published here for the first time with permission from the author, Daniel K. Donnelly.

Experiential Exercises: Motivation Feedback Opinionnaire is from "Motivation: A Feedback Exercise," John E. Jones and J. William Pfeiffer, eds., *The 1973 Annual Handbook for Group Facilitators*, pp. 43-45 (La Jolla, Calif.: University Associates, 1973). Reprinted by permission. **T-P Leadership Questionnaire: An Assessment of Style** is from J. William Pfeiffer and John E. Jones, eds., *A Handbook of Structured Experiences for Human Relations Training*, Volume I (rev.), pp. 7-12 (La Jolla, Calif.: University Associates, 1974). Reprinted by permission. **An Interpersonal Communication Inventory** is from Millard J. Bienvenu, Sr., "Interpersonal Communication Inventory," *Journal of Communication* (December 1971). Reprinted by permission of publisher and author. **Group Decision Making** is from Alan Filley, *Interpersonal Conflict Resolution* (Glenview, Ill.: Scott, Foresman and Company, 1975), pp. 139-143, as adapted from William H. Haney, *Communication and Organizational Behavior* (Homewood, Ill.: Richard D. Irwin, Inc., 1967), pp. 319-320. **Coaching and Goal Setting** is reproduced with permission from *Behavior in Organizations: An Experiential Approach* by James B. Lau (Homewood, Ill.: Richard D. Irwin, 1975 ©), pp. 261-264. **Role Playing: The Promotion Interview** is from Norman R. F. Maier, *Psychology in Industrial Organizations*, 4th ed., 1973, pp. 501-505, published by Houghton Mifflin Company. Reprinted by permission.

Dedicated to my wife Doris,
and our children Marlies and Reid

PREFACE

My basic objective in writing this book is to develop a model of management that integrates the two streams of thought in this field, economics and behavioral science, and the major schools within each stream. In addition, there are many other objectives that this book seeks to attain.

This book is based on ten years of teaching the introductory management course. The students who take this course usually have limited work experience; they have not been involved much, if at all, in the management of organizations. For this reason, one of my major goals in writing this book has been to do more than simply describe and analyze the work of managers. I have tried as well to convey a sense of what it is like to be part of a functioning organization in today's world.

As its title implies, *Management: An Organizational Perspective* views management as the complex set of activities by which managers establish, maintain, and improve successful organizations. These activities are seen as taking place within four dimensions: organization design, planning and control, behavioral processes, and decision making. Although the effective manager is seldom involved in all four dimensions at once, he or she must understand how each dimension affects the organization, and how all four dimensions relate to each other.

Chapter 1 describes and explains this organizational model of management, and three short case studies give students a chance to apply it to real organizations. Chapter 2 discusses the historical evolution of this model and provides students with some understanding of the classic problems that theorists and practitioners in this field have confronted. The model of management is then used as the framework for the next four parts of the book. The last part, Managerial Careers and Orientations, confronts the career questions that a manager typically faces, and the general questions he or she is likely to encounter in the future. It also contains a chapter on the fascinating topic of entrepreneurship. A chapter on the career of Henry Ford then allows students to see how the four dimensions of management functioned in the successes and failures of a well-known entrepreneur and manager.

Each chapter of this book begins with a set of performance objectives, so that the student can direct and evaluate his or her own study. Discussion questions following each chapter encourage the reader to think beyond the text, to apply the concepts introduced to real or hypothetical situations. Suggestions for further reading, also at the end of each chapter, indicate sources that can amplify the material. With the exception of a few recent books, I have used these suggested readings in either my basic undergraduate or graduate class; all are suitable for undergraduates. Students have consistently rated these readings as thought-provoking and interesting. At the end of the book, there is a glossary of terms that enables the student to focus on key concepts and definitions.

But to understand what it is like to be a manager, a student must do more than read. After every chapter (except in Part I) are several critical incidents, short cases to be analyzed by the individual student or discussed in class. Ordinarily, it is difficult to involve students actively in case studies, because of limited classroom space. To overcome this problem, a participatory method has been created specifically for the lecture hall: The Case Observational Method (see Appendix). In addition, longer case studies have been provided after Parts II and III and experiential exercises follow Parts IV-VI; all can be used with the Case Observational Method if desired. The experiential exercises include questionnaires on motivation, leadership, communication, and goal-setting; a group exercise on decision making; and one role play on the promotion interview.

Thus this course can be taught entirely by means of lectures, by a combination of lectures and participatory methods, or entirely by means of participatory methods. My preference is for the second option.

A student does not need background in specialized subjects, such as operations research or statistics, to use this text successfully. All quantitative material covered in this book is presented at a level that should be accessible to any introductory student. To help the student fully understand the quantitative material, short problems are included following chapters 5 and 13.

Throughout the text, I have tried to strike a balance between the presentation of concepts and their illustration. Although theory and research findings are highlighted, only a select number of studies are discussed in detail. Studies, examples, and case material all have been selected to illustrate a wide variety of organizational environments, not just the business corporations highlighted in many traditional texts. In addition, I have tried to indicate the increasingly important role of women and minority group members in management.

Professors may not want to attain all of the objectives this book seeks to achieve; the text is structured so that each can choose his or her own approach in teaching the course. In short, the book is set up to be flexible, adaptable to the needs and preferences of various instructors.

An instructor's manual and readings book are also available. The instructor's manual contains standard material, and also additional experiential exercises and lecture notes. The readings book, co-edited with Carl Anderson, follows the format of the text.

There are many individuals I want to thank for helping me with this book. My wife, Doris, provided the comfort and understanding that made the long ordeal of writing this book bearable. Our two children, Marlies and Reid, were deprived of many outings and trips during the past three years, but they were remarkably resilient and sympathetic. I also wish to thank Michael A. McGinnis, Assistant Professor at Shippensburg State College, Shippensburg, Pennsylvania, who wrote the original drafts for chapters 5, 6, and 13. As co-author of these chapters, Michael's help was indispensable. Bruce W. Steigerwalt, also of Shippensburg State College, provided assistance on the glossary of terms.

In writing this book, I was particularly fortunate to be a faculty member at the University of Maryland. Several of my colleagues stimulated me to extend my thinking about different aspects of the model and the book. Three of them—Carl Anderson, Frank Paine, and Craig Schneier—were particularly helpful, and I appreciate their efforts.

Several colleagues at other universities commented on all or part of the book, and I am grateful for the critiques they provided. The book has benefited immeasurably from their comments. They are: *James Agresta,* Prince George's Community College, *John R. Anstey,* University of Nebraska at Omaha, *Lloyd S. Baird,* Boston University, *Kathryn M. Bartol,* Syracuse University, *Orlando Behling,* Ohio State University, *Arthur P. Brief,* University of Iowa, *Roderick A. Forsgren,* University of Maine at Orono, *James E. Gates,* University of Georgia, *Paul J. Gordon,* Indiana University, *David R. Hampton,* San Diego State University, *Dorothy N. Harlow,* University of South Florida, *Lawrence G. Hrebiniak,* The Wharton School, *Fremont Kast,* University of Washington, *Ralph H. Kilmann,* University of Pittsburgh (Graduate School of Business), *Earl F. Lundgren,* University of Missouri at Columbia, *J. Timothy McMahon,* University of Houston, *Jack L. Mendleson,* Arizona State University, *Edwin L. Miller,* University of Michigan (Graduate School of Business Administration), *Edward J. Morrison,* University of Colorado, *Henry R. Odell,* University of Virginia, *Bernard C. Reimann,* Cleveland State University, *John E. Sheridan,* Wayne State University, *Robert D. Smith,* Kent State University, *Charles E. Summer,* University of Washington, *Henry Tombari,* The George Washington University, *Arthur H. Walker,* Bentley College, *Bert W. Weesner,* Lansing Community College.

The administrative staff of the College of Business and Management also lightened my work by making available scarce secretarial and clerical help when tight deadlines had to be met. I particularly appreciate the assistance of Dean Rudolph Lamone, Ginger Molvar, Suzie Allman, Alys Kerns, and Dorothy Vance.

This book has benefited from the large number of examples and case studies developed out of my experience as a consultant to a variety of organizations. I would like to thank all of the managers and organizations that have provided me with insights difficult to obtain in a strictly academic setting.

At Little, Brown & Company, several individuals provided assistance and moral support well above and beyond the call of duty. Among them are Basil Dandison, Chris Hunter, and Lynn Lloyd. I am particularly appreciative of the aid rendered by my two editors, Darrell Griffin and Carol Verburg. They patiently and skillfully helped me to sharpen the focus of both my organizational model of management and the entire book. I consider myself fortunate to have worked with this group.

Although many individuals have been helpful, I must take final responsibility for any errors or omissions.

At the back of this book, there is a short questionnaire that I would like you to complete and return. Any comments you offer will be taken into consideration in future editions.

M.J.G.

ABOUT THE AUTHOR

Martin J. Gannon (Ph.D., Graduate School of Business, Columbia University) is Professor of Management and Organizational Behavior, College of Business and Management, University of Maryland, College Park, Maryland. He has been the author or co-author of 50 articles that have appeared in the *Academy of Management Journal, Journal of Applied Psychology, California Management Review, Industrial Relations, Business Horizons, Personnel Psychology, Monthly Labor Review, Journal of Accountancy,* and other periodicals. Professor Gannon is President of the Eastern Academy of Management and Program Chairperson for the Personnel/Human Resources Division, Academy of Management, for 1977. He has been and is currently a consultant to a large number of organizations, including The Upjohn Company, National Science Foundation and Chemical Bank of New York; since 1971, he has been an advisor to the U.S. Civil Service Commission, Washington, D.C. Professor Gannon has been involved in management training for the Advanced Executive Programs at Columbia University, University of Maryland, U.S. government agencies, and International Temporaries in Madrid, Spain.

CONTENTS SUMMARY

CONTENTS

II ORGANIZATION DESIGN

3 The Hierarchy and Organizational Models   57

VI MANAGERIAL CAREERS AND ORIENTATIONS

MANAGEMENT

An Organizational Perspective

■Many activities can be studied under the heading "management," and they can be viewed in almost as many ways. This book takes an organizational perspective: managerial activities are seen as those that must be performed for an organization to function, rather than those performed by any individual manager. From this perspective, managerial activities fall into four dimensions: organization design, planning and control, behavioral processes, and decision making. All of the chapters in this book relate to these four dimensions.

Part I describes the organizational perspective and the four dimensions of management: what each dimension involves, and the relationships among dimensions as well as among specific activities. It will be useful to see how management has developed as a field of study, and particularly how tension between the two main streams of management thought has produced the integrated model that provides the framework of this book.

INTRODUCTION

I

A Model
of Management

1

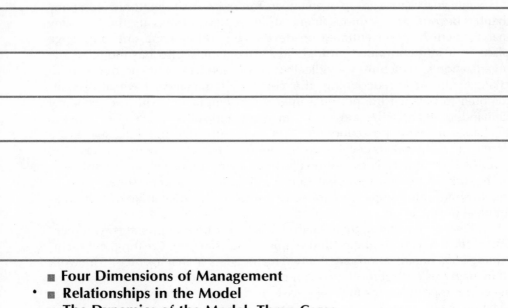

■ **Four Dimensions of Management**
■ **Relationships in the Model**
■ **The Dynamics of the Model: Three Cases**
■ **Summary**

Performance Objectives

1. To identify and define the four dimensions within which managerial activities take place: organization design, planning and control, behavioral processes, and decision making.

2. To understand the dynamics of the model showing the important relationships among these four dimensions.

3. To be aware of the distinction between the organizational perspective of the model and an individual manager's perspective.

Twenty years ago, a group of engineers formed a small electronics company that has become an enormous financial success. Over the years, the company management has concentrated on developing and carrying out long-range plans to insure continued profitability. Management also has modified the organization's structure periodically as its services and products have changed. In such redesigning, the company's managers have always attempted to balance the personal interests of employees with the technical demands of the organization. In fact, management still encourages employees to change any work procedure they consider ineffective and dull. Salaries are excellent, and workers receive group bonuses based on yearly profits. The level of productivity is exceptionally high; many managers and employees even work overtime without pay because their jobs are so personally satisfying. In short, this company operates very effectively and can be described as an ideal organization.

An ideal organization, then, might be seen as one that operates with maximum efficiency, profitability, and employee satisfaction. Creating and maintaining ideal organizations are the two major goals of management. The work of managers is critical for the construction of ideal organizations, since managers are responsible for making decisions that determine whether the organization is effective and efficient.

Managerial work consists of an extremely large number of activities, many of which do not appear to be logically related. When a visitor walks into a manager's office, he is sometimes overwhelmed by the diversity of activities taking place. For example, the manager may tell a subordinate over the phone to pursue a particular course of action; he may inform his secretary that he cannot attend an important meeting; he may sign some letters; he may interrupt the discussion to talk with another subordinate who needs an immediate answer; and, finally, after fifteen minutes he may turn his full attention to the visitor. For centuries, practitioners and scholars have attempted to describe the field of management in a manner that logically relates such diverse activities.

Four Dimensions
of Management

The historical evolution of the field of management, as well as the work of managers, includes four basic types of activities: organization design, plan-

Table 1.1   The Four Dimensions Within Which Managerial Activities Take Place

Organization Design

The *design* of an organization establishes its structure, provides a framework for its activities, and delineates lines of authority and responsibility. The appropriate design for a given organization depends on such factors as its technology and the external environment within which it functions.

Planning and Control

An organization's *plans* specify its goals and the means it will use to reach them. *Control systems* monitor the organization's implementation of its plans and pinpoint significant deviations from plans. In some situations, the control system contains an action device that automatically corrects such deviations. In other situations, managers must determine what corrective action is appropriate.

Behavioral Processes

The *behavioral processes* within an organization—motivation, leadership, group behavior, and communication—are the interactions between and among organizational members that enable the organization to move toward its goals.

Decision Making

Decision making is a problem-solving activity that begins and ends with an analysis of the performance of organizational members, organizational subsystems, and the entire organization (separately or together). It involves recognizing a gap between what is and what should be; identifying the problem; generating potential solutions; choosing an alternative; and implementing the chosen solution.

ning and control, behavioral processes, and decision making (see Table 1.1). In any organization, managerial activities take place within these four dimensions. Thus the perspective of this model is that of the entire organization rather than that of a single manager. A manager usually is not involved in activities within all four dimensions at any one moment. For example, managers do not constantly concern themselves with the design of the organization, although management in its entirety is vitally interested in this dimension. However, it is common for a manager to be involved periodically in each dimension. Some managers, some of the time, are simultaneously immersed in activities within two or more dimensions.

This model of management includes not only the four basic dimensions within which managerial activities take place, but also the relationships among them. As we will see, a manager's plans for an organization usually involve its design; his or her methods of control influence behavioral processes; and so on. Although some decisions are made in the isolation of the manager's office, their effects are felt much more widely, often in several areas of the organization.

This model effectively describes the managerial activities that take place in all or most organizations. Once they are learned and understood, a common body of managerial skills can be applied successfully to a variety of organizations, from business firms to government agencies to charitable institutions, even though some features of each type of organization are unique and require special study.

Organization Design

The first of the four dimensions of management is *organization design,* which refers to the way the organization is constructed. It includes issues such as lines of responsibility, authority, and communication within an organization, all of which are important for creating an efficient and effective structure within which organizational activities can take place. A typical design problem is to determine the *optimum span of control:* the proper number of subordinates each manager should supervise.

Even before management designs an organization, the founders must identify overall objectives. Typically, this general planning focuses on the establishment of goals in order of importance. The founders normally scan the

---

A Definition of Organization and Management

An organization comes into being when (1) there are persons able to communicate with each other, (2) who are willing to contribute action (3) to accomplish a common purpose. The elements of an organization are therefore (1) communication, (2) willingness to serve, and (3) common purpose. These elements are necessary and sufficient conditions initially, and they are found in all such organizations. . . .

The essential executive functions, as I shall present them, correspond to the elements of organization as already stated. . . . They are, first, to provide the system of communication; second, to promote the securing of essential efforts; and third, to formulate and define purpose.

Chester Barnard, *The Functions of the Executive* (Cambridge: Harvard University Press, 1966, originally published in 1938), pp. 82, 217.

external environment so they can understand the impact of outside forces, such as the degree of competition in the industry, existing or proposed governmental regulations, and the rate of technological change that will directly influence the marketability of their products. Thus, a certain amount of general planning must precede design, and management must design the organization before anything else can occur.

Many activities are part of organization design, such as determining the amount of responsibility that should be placed in each organizational position, constructing a formal system of communication among units, and developing procedures for handling employee grievances. These and similar managerial activities relate directly to the way the organization is constructed.

Planning

Planning essentially consists of two activities: setting the organization's objectives, and selecting the means to achieve them. These means can be described as strategies or tactics. *Strategic plans* or *strategies* involve the attainment of general, long-range objectives. *Tactical plans* or *tactics* focus on specific objectives that will contribute toward the general ones.

As has been suggested, even before managers design an organization, it is critical that they develop a strategic plan or set of plans to serve as a guide to its destiny. Such strategic planning usually identifies the services and products the organization will generate, and how it will market them. The Gillette Company was founded at the turn of the century by a door-to-door salesman who set as his company's initial objective the elimination of trips to the barber for the purpose of shaving. At that time, it was difficult to shave at home because the equipment was so elaborate. To reach the company's objective, Gillette developed a two-pronged strategy. First, he created the safety razor. However, he had no access to retail outlets through which it could be sold; so he decided to pursue a strategy of personal, door-to-door selling.

Strategic planning also occurs periodically after the organization has come into existence, primarily because the clients and markets may change. For example, the Gillette Company has continued to be profitable because it has developed many new strategic plans over the years to please its customers and outsell its competitors.

Tactical plans, which are generally designed to help carry out the general, strategic plans, are much more specific and short range: One tactical plan might be to reduce defective parts by 20 percent within one year. Although the organization's destiny probably would not be jeopardized if this plan were not accomplished, a significant number of failures with similar tactical plans could easily force management to take drastic measures.

Control

Once plans have been stated and implemented, the organization must develop control systems to check continually how well they are being carried out. *Control* can be defined as monitoring plans and pinpointing significant deviations from them. In some situations, the control system automatically corrects these deviations; in other situations, the manager must determine what corrective action is appropriate.

Like plans, control systems can be either strategic or tactical. *Strategic control* usually guards against a long-term loss of clients or markets. For a business firm, the profit statement over a period of years serves as a strategic control mechanism. If profits decline continuously, some major adjustments in either the firm's plans or its means of carrying them out may be necessary. In a religious order, the number of applicants over a period of years operates as a similar control mechanism, since the organization's existence would be threatened if only a few individuals wanted to join it. In all organizations there are strategic control systems that run parallel to strategic planning systems.

Tactical control systems are typically specific and short range. A tactical plan to reduce defective parts by 20 percent within one year might be accompanied by a control system that emphasizes close supervisory attention to each employee's work. In addition, management might penalize an employee who produces a significant number of defective parts.

As the discussion thus far suggests, control consists of two separate concepts. The first is the control of the entire organization and its major subsystems. For example, a budget is a control mechanism that monitors deviations from plans on an organizational basis; if an organizational unit exceeds its budget by a significant amount, its management must explain why this deviation has occurred. The second concept is the control of organizational members, for they must perform adequately if plans are to be completed successfully. Control of individuals includes the proper selection of employees, their job orientation and training, and the measurement of their performance. If employees perform adequately, they are usually given rewards such as promotions and salary increases. If they do not perform effectively, they may be given a warning or a demotion, or they may even be fired.

Because of the close tie between planning and control, these two elements can be considered together. The system of planning and control—the second dimension of management—is the *central* mechanism around which all of the other dimensions revolve, for planning influences all other activities.

Behavioral Processes

The third dimension of management involves the *behavioral processes* in organizations. Interactions within a group of workers, between workers and managers, and between two or more managers all affect—and are affected by—the organization's operations.

One of the most important activities within this dimension is *leadership,* for the manager must direct and coordinate the work of his or her subordinates. The *motivation* of individuals is also critical. If individuals are not motivated to work, the overall efforts and productivity of the organization will suffer. Another behavioral process is *group behavior.* When groups and units are functioning effectively, the probability increases that the tactical and strategic plans of the organization will be accomplished. Moreover, it is important that *communication* within and between groups is effective. If communication begins to break down, frictions can easily arise that hinder the achievement of plans.

Behavioral processes in the organization must be in balance if objectives are to be met. When they are not working smoothly, negative consequences such as a high rate of turnover and a low rate of productivity can easily occur.

Decision Making

The fourth dimension of management is *decision making,* which consists of recognizing a problem exists, identifying possible causes, developing alternative solutions, choosing among alternative courses of action, and carrying out the one chosen (see chapter 12).

Decision making is essentially a problem-solving activity that comes into play when the individual realizes the gap between what is and what should be is too great. If managers make decisions or take courses of action that do not maintain and improve the organization, the other dimensions of management quickly become irrelevant. If the decisions result in improved performance, the organization moves toward its ideal state of maximum efficiency, profitability, and employee satisfaction. Decision making is thus the key dimension of management and can even be thought of as synonymous with management (Simon 1960).

Relationships
in the Model

The relationships among the four dimensions of management are important. The model is dynamic, for it incorporates not only the various dimensions of management but the associations that exist among them. (See Figure 1.1.)

Figure 1.1   A Model of the Four Dimensions

Within Which Managerial Activities Take Place

The perspective is that of the organization rather than the individual manager. A particular manager may be involved only in activities within one or two dimensions at any given moment; however, management in its entirety is vitally interested in all four dimensions and the relationships among them. All of these dimensions are affected by the external environment, for example, competition and governmental regulation.

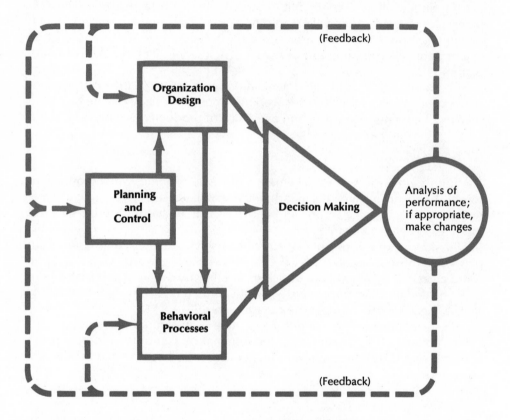

The Impact of Planning and Control

One frequent result of strategic planning is its influence on the design of the organization. When the Ford Motor Company decided to produce the Edsel during the 1950s, the strategic plan was to market a car for affluent buyers who wanted a unique possession. To persuade customers that the Edsel was indeed unique, top managers at Ford changed the company's organizational structure to set up a separate dealership for it. They reasoned that regular dealers could not provide enough personal service because they were selling several models of cars. But since the regular Ford dealers were not allowed to sell Edsels, they became hostile, even to the point of telling customers the Edsel was an inferior car. The result was the second largest financial catastrophe in recent business history, to the tune of $350 million.

Tactical planning also influences the design of the organization, although usually on a smaller scale. When too many tactical plans fail, management may create a new system for delegating authority, restructure work groups and units, or replace people with machines.

Planning also affects the behavioral processes that take place in an organization. When management alters its direction by developing a new strategic plan or set of plans, individuals are frequently upset because they fear they may be let go or given undesirable assignments. Similarly, if management constantly changes tactical plans, individuals can become annoyed about interruptions in their routines. When individuals become too upset, it is common for negative consequences to occur, such as high rates of absenteeism and low rates of productivity.

While control systems run parallel to planning systems, they can independently influence behavioral processes. For example, two companies may want to decrease defective parts by 20 percent within one year, but one of them may buy new machinery to accomplish this tactical plan while the other may tighten up its control of employees by closely monitoring their work. This tight control could easily make the workers uneasy and create difficulties between them and their supervisors. And, when such tight control sytems are implemented, the design of the organization normally becomes rigid and highly bureaucratic.

The Impact of Design

Inevitably, the design of the organization can affect the behavioral processes that take place within it. For example, management may design an organization so that a subordinate reports to two superiors. This practice can easily create behavioral problems if the subordinate cannot complete his assignments for both superiors. In this situation, the subordinate will probably experience role conflict and a sense of frustration. Or management may decide to save money by routinizing the work and replacing skilled workers with unskilled workers. Such a design change dramatically alters behavioral processes, for unskilled workers are characterized by higher rates of turnover and absenteeism; there is a much greater amount of friction in unskilled work groups; and informal leadership is more ineffective in the unskilled work groups (see Sayles 1958).

The Setting for Decision Making

All of the other dimensions of management directly influence decision making. In essence, the other dimensions provide a setting within which decision making takes place. For example, a company may develop a strategic plan of diversifying its product line, manufacturing several products instead of just one. This plan has obvious implications for managers in their role as decision makers, for they no longer can pursue courses of action that relate only to the sale of their original product.

It is difficult to separate planning and decision making before creating the organization. When the founders develop a set of strategic plans, they are also engaging in decision making as they eliminate undesirable alternatives. Later, once the initial plans are put into practice, the plans help to form a setting in which decision making takes place. If the founders or managers determine that changes in the initial plans need to be made, they are involved with the dimension of decision making, having decided that the gap between what is and what should be is too great.

The design of the organization also influences the decision-making scope of management. If a firm invests millions of dollars in new equipment that allows the organization to hire unskilled rather than skilled workers, management cannot even think about using its previous method of production or its former design. Managers must tailor their decisions to make the change to a

---

Dimensions in Which Managerial Activities Take Place

The manager's chief task, as we perceive it, is that of integrating organizational and human variables into an effective and efficient socio-technical system. On occasion, he carries out this task rationally and before the fact, attempting to blend an appropriate mix of these variables. More often, he finds that someone has already provided him with a recipe and that one of these sets of variables, organizational or human, is more or less fixed and he must adjust the other set to it. Typical here is the situation where goals and technology are set and the manager's task is that of fitting persons with an appropriate set of characteristics to them. On occasion, however, the opposite occurs—the manager has before him a group of people with given characteristics for whom he must design appropriate objectives and a structure through which these can be accomplished.

Most often, the manager finds himself in the midst of an ongoing socio-technical system, with concurrent—and frequently conflicting—requirements for adjustments of both organizational and human needs and characteristics.

Raymond E. Miles, *Theories of Management* (New York: McGraw-Hill, 1975), pp. 20–21.

new organizational structure as smooth as possible. Once the revised structure is functioning, managerial decisions must take it into account; courses of action that would have suited the former design are no longer appropriate.

Behavioral processes, too, critically influence decision making in organizations. When a group of decision makers experiences clashes of personality, it is difficult for them to coordinate their efforts. Behavioral problems among employees, such as a high rate of turnover or absenteeism, may even force managers to make decisions they consider relatively unattractive. For example, managers may delay the introduction of a new product when a high turnover rate occurs, for they must train new employees even before the production process can begin.

Analysis of Performance

For the organization to be effective, organizational members and organizational subsystems must perform at a satisfactory or superior level. To evaluate past decisions and gather information for future ones, managers must continually analyze the performance of organizational members, organizational subsystems, and the entire organization (either separately or together). If analysis indicates it is advisable, managers make changes within the dimensions of organization design, planning and control, and behavioral processes.

Analysis of performance is part of decision making. As the previous discussion indicates, decision making is a problem-solving activity; *analysis of performance* is the manager's means of determining that there is a problem, that the gap between what is and what should be is too great.

If an organizational member is not performing satisfactorily, managers typically use negative control techniques, such as a reprimand or a short layoff, to change his or her behavior (see chapter 6). To reinforce satisfactory performance, managers normally use positive control techniques, such as salary increases and promotions. In some situations, managers may try to improve the performance of an organizational member, whether satisfactory or unsatisfactory, by focusing on the dimension of behavioral processes. Sending the individual to a human relations training course or assigning him or her to a work group in which he or she feels comfortable are two such approaches. Managers rarely change the design of the organization to improve the performance of organizational members unless more than a few members are involved.

If an organizational subsystem or the entire organization is performing in an unsatisfactory manner, management typically tries to bridge the gap between what is and what should be by undertaking changes within the dimensions of organization design, planning and control, and behavioral processes. The managers may decide that they must develop a new set of strategic plans, if their competitors have taken a substantial amount of business away from their organization. Or they may feel the planning systems are operating effectively but the control systems are not efficient in signaling deviations from plans. They may determine that the organization is not properly designed. They may even decide that behavioral processes are at fault—the rate of employee turnover may be so high that the organization is understaffed and unable to manufacture its products efficiently.

Even if the performance of the organizational subsystems and the entire organization is effective, managers may decide that the gap between what is and what should be is too wide to insure continued or greater success. Thus analysis may indicate that some changes should be made within the dimensions of organization design, planning and control, or behavioral processes. For example, General Motors was very successful in 1920, although the Ford Motor Company dominated the automotive market. The top managers at General Motors could have been content with this success. Instead, they decided to undertake several major changes that led to the company's becoming the unchallenged leader in the industry.

Decision making, including analysis of performance, influences and is influenced by the other three dimensions of management, as shown in Figure 1.1 (see p. 12). Nearly every other managerial activity involves decision making in some way, and thus decision making is the key dimension of management.

The Dynamics
of the Model:
Three Cases

Three case studies illustrate the dimensions of the model and the relations among them. Since each case is unique, the model must be used selectively to analyze the important relationships among dimensions. The relationship between planning and organization design may be critical in one situation; in another setting, the relationship between organization design and behavioral processes may be most important.

Temporary Help

In the United States and Europe, a special type of temporary employment has become prominent since World War II. In the temporary-help industry, employees are sent on assignment by agencies set up to fill temporary vacancies in clerical, industrial, or professional jobs. The workers are employees of the agencies rather than of the organization in which they work. Their assignments generally are of short duration, and they may refuse any assignment.

The temporary-help industry has grown since 1946 from only a few thousand employees to approximately 3 million. A critical facet of this industry is its entrepreneurial spirit and high degree of competition. There are a few large firms such as Manpower and Kelly Girl; however, most are small. To compete against the giant firms, the small agency must develop a marketing strategy to differentiate it from its competitors.

International Temporaries hires bilingual clerical employees and places them in organizations where the use of two languages is essential. Mature Temps originally hired only "responsible" and "mature" workers, that is, 55 years of age or older. After Mature Temps became successful, it changed its strategy and marketing to emphasize that it provided workers with "responsible" and "mature" attitudes, regardless of age. Challoner Service, a London agency, operates a bus, equipped with telephone, radio, and portable typewriters, that cruises the financial district and drops off workers at a moment's notice after a call is received from a business firm. Some firms even provide temporary executives who will work for a year or more in such positions as traffic managers, controllers, and branch-bank managers. But 70 percent of the employees in the temporary-help industry are clerical. For a small entrepreneur to compete successfully in this part of the industry, it is important that he or she develop a strategic plan or strategic set of plans that will clearly mark the product as distinctive.

If an organization is initially small, it is important that its design be appropriate for its strategic plans. A typical small firm in the temporary-help industry has three major departments (see Figure 1.2). The personnel department, which includes the clerical workers, is run by a few supervisors who test job applicants and send them on assignments. In addition, the firm typically employs an accountant to handle the financial aspects of its work. But the most complex part of the organization is the subsystem for the sales representatives, since they must visit the business firms and convince them to use the distinctive services the temporary-help agency offers.

Usually the agency does not experience any behavioral problems with employees. The supply of workers who want temporary-help employment is typically quite large. Workers seldom interact with each other, so no conflicts within work groups can develop. In addition, if a business firm informs the agency that a particular individual is an ineffective employee, it is not necessary to fire him or her formally; rather, the agency simply ceases to offer work opportunities. Hence, the control of individuals is very easy and effective.

Figure 1.2   Design of a Typical Small Clerical Temporary-Help Firm

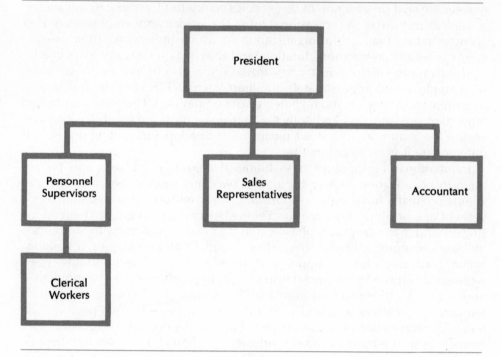

Since the agency is typically small, the major behavioral problems involve the relationship of the head of the agency with the sales representatives. The greater his or her length of service, the more important a sales rep becomes to the agency, as he or she is responsible for attracting the business that makes the company successful. Frequently the sales reps begin to realize their importance over time and start to demand better wages and treatment. The head of the agency usually will attempt to meet all reasonable demands.

Another critical behavioral process is the relationship between the agency and its customers. If customers become dissatisfied, the agency's future is jeopardized. In efforts to avoid this, some small agencies periodically take clients to dinner and send them gifts during the holiday season. At least one small firm has provided its best clients with a week's trip to Europe.

Questions. What factors, if any, do you think limit the ideal size for a temporary-help agency? How large could such an agency grow without having to change its design?

U.S. Civil Service Commission

In the latter decades of the nineteenth century, political corruption was rampant in the United States. This period was characterized by the famous phrase, "The Spoils System." For appointment to government jobs, competence was not as important as knowing an influential politician.

To combat this problem, President Chester Arthur established the U.S. Civil Service Commission in 1883. Although the commission now performs many diverse functions, its basic mission is to protect the merit system. Under ordinary circumstances, merit is the major standard by which applicants for jobs are evaluated, both before and after hiring. Over the years, the commission has compiled an enviable record in the area of merit hiring and promotion. Although it is relatively small (about 6,000 people), it has effectively accomplished its major objective.

The commission's Bureau of Inspection periodically sends teams of inspectors into various government agencies to monitor compliance with the merit principles. However, during the late fifties and early sixties, it became obvious that the Bureau of Inspection could no longer monitor the entire work force effectively, for its inspection teams could canvas only a very small percentage of government installations. At this point, the commission's top managers developed a series of strategic plans to help solve their problems.

The first major change was a new name for the Bureau of Inspection, which became the Bureau of Personnel Management Evaluation. Next came changes in the bureau's practices. In the Bureau of Inspection, inspectors served essentially as policemen, seeking out violations of the merit system. Evaluators in the Bureau of Personnel Management Evaluation now highlight both successes and failures of agency management in following merit principles. Hence, agency managers sometimes view the bureau in a friendly fashion, especially if the investigation places them in a favorable light. In addition, the bureau began to include members of the agency in its evaluation teams, which gave more legitimacy to their recommendations.

Still, the bureau could not handle all of its work; there were simply too many installations to monitor. To combat this problem, the commission changed its design; top management persuaded the president of the United States to establish internal evaluation teams within each agency. These internal teams now do most of the evaluating, although the commission still sends out evaluation teams on a piecemeal basis. Thus, the bureau serves as an overall control mechanism. If commission evaluators, on surveys they conduct by themselves, discover the internal agency teams are not doing their work correctly, the commission helps the agency to improve its capabilities.

The commission also developed some tactical plans that, along with the design change, aid internal evaluators in carrying out the bureau's strategic plan. A standardized questionnaire was constructed, and completed by 40,000 federal employees. When the internal agency evaluators investigate an installation, they can compare their questionnaire responses to this data base. If significant deviations occur, the evaluators automatically explore the issues that have been pinpointed.

The new system has not eliminated behavioral problems. In fact, the scope of such problems may have expanded, for the commission has created specialists within each agency whose knowledge is as great as their own evaluators. In such a situation, it is only natural that some disagreements will occur. Still, these disagreements have proved to be beneficial, for they have forced all of the evaluators to improve their techniques.

Finally, decision making has been significiantly affected by the setting the commission has created. When the top managers of the commission decide to develop new analytical techniques, or to emphasize particular areas, such as the improvment of equal employment opportunities within the federal work force, they must involve agency evaluators. The commission sponsors an annual two-day meeting during which emerging issues are discussed by all evaluators.

Question. Should the U.S. Civil Service Commission act primarily as a policeman or as a consultant in fulfilling its main function, the protection of the merit system?

Branch Banking

The banking industry has always been very conservative, partly because societies cannot tolerate a free-wheeling but unstable banking system. When banks are unstable, an entire country's future becomes perilous. For this reason, many regulations are placed on banking operations.

Between 1945 and 1969, the United States experienced its longest period of prosperity. During this time, some bank managements decided to shed some of their conservatism. Specifically, management of a New York bank developed a strategic plan to increase its customers by making them see banks as offering a larger variety of services rather than just a few specialized services (cashing checks, putting money into savings accounts, and making loans). Management wanted the bank to increase in size and keep pace with the growing prosperity in the United States.

Typically, a consumer selects a bank in terms of convenience—he or she frequents a branch close to home or place of work. For the average consumer, banks are interchangeable, since they all basically provide the same services.

This case study focuses on a large bank in New York City that operated 20 branches in 1958. By 1970 the branch-banking system had grown to 180.

To attract new customers, the bank started to provide specific services not available elsewhere. New customers received gifts; tellers provided specialized services such as the sale of baseball and football tickets; and interest rates on savings accounts were placed at the highest level the law would permit. One of the bank's most interesting ploys was to eliminate the distinction between checking and savings accounts. A customer who keeps a minimum balance in his checking account receives interest on it, so he or she has no need to open a savings account. Another important plan created "preferred" customers: If a customer uses the bank extensively over a period of three years, he then receives some special services free of charge, such as a free safe deposit box, and the bank backs his checks to a limit of $500 if he does not have enough money in his account to cover them.

Because of these strategic and tactical plans, the branch-banking system expanded at a spectacular rate. However, the control of organizational subsystems became troublesome. As the number of checks increased, it became increasingly difficult to process them efficiently. Many monthly statements were in error or sent out late, and the bank spent a lot of money on computer equipment to handle this problem.

Control of individuals also proved problematic. When the branches were small, tellers could process the work efficiently but pleasantly. When trade increased, branch management encouraged tellers to work faster. Inevitably, they began to make mistakes and could not account for some of the money. A conflict occurred between speed and accuracy, and, at the time of this writing, management has not developed a final solution to this problem.

The bank's success also created problems in its design. When the system contained only 20 branches, it was possible to coordinate their efforts from headquarters. By the time the system had increased to 80 branches, it became necessary to group them into regions. In effect, a new level in the organization was created.

Before the regions were established, it was possible to solve problems throughout the bank on an informal basis. Such solutions are difficult within the regional structure, for management at the headquarters level coordinates the efforts of branches and regions with a series of policies and rules that regulate everyone's activity. Hence, the authority of the branch managers has been severely restricted.

The success of the plans and the new design of the organization also created behavioral problems in the system. When the branches were small in size, employees felt a loyalty to them. The employees personally knew all of their customers and treated them in a pleasant manner In the new system, impatient customers who wait in long lines for service become merely numbers to managers and employees. Turnover of employees and managers has increased dramatically.

Within this setting, the managers or decision makers confront new and difficult problems. Previously, employees and managers had been trained informally; this is no longer possible. Additionally, the complaints of irate customers have become bothersome; in some branches, the branch managers spend as much as ten hours a week handling them. Although the bank continues to grow, top management has started to wonder about the optimum size of the system; some managers argue that the optimum level has already been passed.

In short, the spectacular success of this branch-banking system has been accompanied by many problems, several of which are extremely difficult to solve. This system has evolved from a small organization that operated informally into a giant that necessarily is somewhat impersonal. All decisions made within this new structure are heavily influenced by the changes that have occurred within the dimensions of planning and control, organization design, and behavioral processes.

Questions. What do you see as the major planning problems in this branch-banking system? How might they be solved?

Summary

A model has been developed in this chapter that includes the four dimensions within which managerial activities take place: organization design, planning and control, behavioral processes, and decision making. This model is dynamic in that it emphasizes the relationships among these four dimenisons.

Three dimensions—organization design, planning and control, and behavioral processes—provide a setting in which the fourth—decision making—takes place. Whether their decisions result in successful or unsuccessful performance, the managers must analyze the situation and decide what changes to make. When performance is unsuccessful, it is normal for managers to propose changes; even when performance is successful, managers frequently initiate changes to insure continued or greater success.

The perspective of this model is that of the organization rather than that of the individual manager. From this perspective, management is interested in all four dimensions, although a particular manager may be involved only in activities within one or two dimensions.

Discussion Questions

1. Think of an organization you have been a member of—a school or religious group, a club, or a business firm for which you have worked. How would you describe that organization's activities in terms of the management model developed in this chapter? Now describe an ideal organization, or what you consider to be an ideal organization, that is the same type as the one you just described. What are some of the major differences between the actual and the ideal organization?

2. The management model proposed in this book applies to business and government organizations. Do you think it also applies to other kinds of organizations such a volunteer groups, friendship groups, work groups, the family, the church, and the school? Why or why not?

3. Do you think it is possible for a single manager to be effective in all four dimensions of management? Why or why not? Do you think it is possible for an organization to perform effectively if it neglects any one of these dimensions? Why or why not?

4. Why is it important for the analysis of performance to come out of the interactions between the dimensions of management and to link them together by means of a feedback loop?

5. Why is the management model proposed in this chapter dynamic rather than static?

6. How would you evaluate the effectiveness of your management class in terms of the four dimensions of management?

Suggested Readings

Barmash, Isadore, ed. *Great Business Disasters.* New York: Ballantine Books, 1973, 302 pages, paperback.
 This short and inexpensive paperback contains a series of case studies

focused on some of the outstanding business disasters in recent history. The student learns to appreciate management by examining these failures. RCA's $500 million venture into computers, the $350 million Edsel fiasco at Ford, the Penn Central collapse, and other failures are highlighted in an interesting and entertaining fashion. This book is a perennial favorite with students.

Mintzberg, Henry. *The Nature of Managerial Work.* New York: Harper & Row, 1973, 298 pages, available in hardback or paperback.
This readable book summarizes the research on the work and activities of managers. The emphasis is on what managers actually do, not what they should do.

Historical
Development
of Management

2

- **Classical Management**
- **Human Relations**
- **Integrated Perspective**
- **Summary**

Performance Objectives

1. To understand capitalism and its need for hierarchical organizations.

2. To understand the major theories within the two main streams of management: behavioral science and economics.

3. To be aware of major historical figures in management, such as Weber, Fayol, Taylor, and Mayo, and to be aware of their contributions to the field.

4. To trace the development of the integrated perspective on management from the tension between the two main streams of management.

5. To know how other management theories—contingency and systems theories in particular—are included within the framework of the integrated model of management.

27

It is often difficult for an outsider to understand the conflicts among writers within the same discipline. Sometimes these struggles become so intense that the person rather than the theory is attacked. In fact, one of the more entertaining aspects of reading professional journals is to come across a statement such as: "Theorist X has spent a great many years researching a topic that has no intrinsic value. In addition, his method of proof is of questionable validity."

Like many disciplines, the field of management is characterized by numerous points of view and arguments over them. And, as in most disciplines, each point of view has its own advantages and disadvantages.

According to the *systems* viewpoint, an organization is a system that consists of subunits or subsystems which not only interact with one another but also are heavily dependent upon one another (see Barnard 1938). For this reason, it is important to comprehend the nature of the interactions and interdependencies among the subsystems. For example, two subsystems may be heavily dependent upon one another if they must share machinery, personnel, and space. Further, the organization is an open system that interacts with its external environment and is heavily dependent on it for its existence. Some of the external environmental forces that affect the organization include the degree of competition in the industry, laws, and social norms. To understand the functioning of an organization within the systems framework, it is necessary to pinpoint the specific external environmental forces that impact on the subsystems and the interdependencies between them.

The systems approach has now been extended into the *contingency* approach to management (Woodward 1958 and 1965; Lawrence and Lorsch 1967). According to this approach, the type of management that is successful in a given organization is primarily dependent or contingent on: (1) the kind of technology that is used to create the final good or service of the organization; and (2) the degree of external environmental or market uncertainty the organization faces. Hence there is no "one best way" to manage. Rather, the style of management should be appropriate for the kinds of problems that an organization faces.

As we will see in this chapter, the integrated perspective on management that is put forth in this book incorporates both the systems and contingency viewpoints. This perspective examines and identifies organizational subsystems and the impact of external forces on them, and it also recognizes that these and other factors interact in different ways in different situations.

Historically, numerous different approaches have contributed to the development of current management thought. These are sometimes considered to fall into three major streams or viewpoints in the management literature: classical management, quantitative management, and behavioral management (Donnelly, Gibson, and Ivancevich 1975). *Classical management* essentially reflects the perspectives of practicing managers at the turn of the twentieth century who grappled with the complex problems of organizing enterprises; *quantitative management* focuses on the application of quantitative methods of analysis, such as operations research and statistics, to organizational problems; and *behavioral management* centers on the solution of human problems in organizations.

As Miner (1973) has shown, these three steams actually constitute only two streams—economics and behavioral science (see Figure 2.1). Both classical management and quantitative management can be seen as part of the economic stream, since these two areas are primarily economic in orientation. The second stream, behavioral science, is concerned with the approaches and techniques of behavioral science, and it focuses on human elements in the study of management.

This chapter highlights the historical tension between the economic and behavioral science streams, out of which an integrated perspective on man-

Figure 2.1   Major Schools and Streams of Management

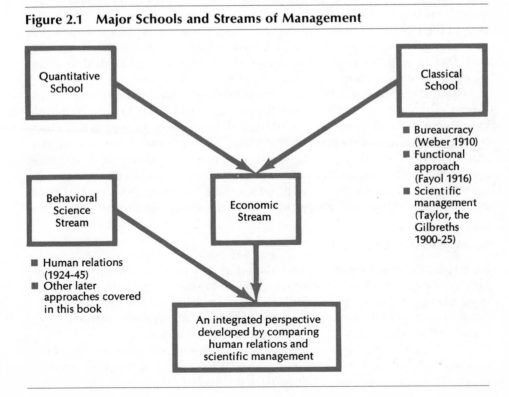

agement emerges. This integrated approach includes the four basic dimensions of management that are the framework for this book: organization design, planning and control, behavioral processes, and decision making. Although there are many schools of thought within the two streams of management, only one significant and representative school within each stream is treated in depth in this chapter. For the behavioral science stream, *human relations* will serve as the representative school. For the economic stream, the representative school will be *classical management*.

Classical

Management

The birthdate of the field of management is in dispute. Some writers feel management is as old as the first organized society; others date it from the time of the industrial revolution. Nevertheless, there is general agreement that the field of management, as it is currently recognized, began between 1880 and 1900. During this period, the approach now known as classical management became prominent.

Within the school of classical management are three major subdivisions: Weber's bureaucracy, Fayol's functional approach, and Taylor's scientific management (Thompson 1967). Although all three are discussed in this chapter, the final, integrated perspective on management comes from a comparison of the third, scientific management, with human relations. Both scientific management and human relations have exerted enormous influence on management theory and practice, and the contrast between them should bring into focus the integrated perspective stressed throughout this book.

Max Weber and Capitalism

Until recently, Max Weber was not treated as a member of the classical management school. Weber, a sociologist, was only secondarily interested in applied management problems. Still, he was similar to other members of the classical management school who were concerned about these problems, as is evident when the works of Weber and Fayol are compared.

Weber is a giant figure in the history of modern social science. His influence was so great that he is generally considered a major founder of modern sociology. He was an interesting individual: a distinguished professor, the head of the German Red Cross during World War I, and a tireless worker who sometimes went without sleep for several days. Throughout his busy life, he maintained an avid interest in the study of capitalism and its growth.

Weber's analytical starting point is unusual in the history of management (Weber 1930 and 1947). Unlike others who were concerned with the applied and daily problems that beset organizations and managers, he initially focused his attention on *capitalism*. This form of economic and social organization features the private ownership of goods, private investment, and a free market that determines prices, production, and the distribution of goods.

Weber's initial question was: What makes modern capitalism—the form that has arisen in Western Europe and the United States since the fifteenth century—so different from other preceding forms of economic organization? Capitalism in elementary forms had existed in older societies, such as China in 4000 B.C., but Weber felt modern capitalism was radically different. A great amount of economic activity throughout society, thousands of individuals employed by one large organization, complex trade agreements that span several countries—such conditions were not prevalent in other capitalistic societies.

Preconditions for Capitalism. To answer his initial question, Weber set out to demonstrate that certain preconditions were necessary for capitalism to evolve into its modern form. A major precondition was a skilled labor force, so a middle class could arise. In the absence of a middle class, there would be only a few rich individuals and the masses of the poor, a combination not likely to generate much economic activity. By the fifteenth century, a skilled middle class had arisen in Western Europe, trained and protected by the craft guilds, which were the forerunners of modern craft unions.

Another precondition for large-scale capitalism was an appropriate method for keeping track of business transactions. This was provided by *double-entry accounting*, a detailed listing of a firm's assets and liabilities. In the thirteenth century, Italian businessmen developed this system, which allows firms to plan wisely for the future because all transactions, both sources of income and expenses, are laid out in detail. Double-entry accounting provides an effective visual representation of what the firm is doing and should be doing in order to survive.

Just as double-entry accounting was critical, an effective legal system was necessary to handle disputes between business firms. The legal system common in fifteenth-century Europe was particularly suitable for capitalism, since there was a definite bias in it toward the ownership of private property, the payment of debts, and the punishment of individuals who violated the rights of others.

After a historical investigation of a large number of former and ongoing societies, Weber concluded that most of them held profit making in low esteem. Partly for religious reasons, individuals in such societies were not motivated to accumulate private property and other forms of wealth, and without such motivation, modern capitalism would not be possible. But when the Protestant Reformation began in Europe, there was a decided shift in opinion concerning the pursuit of profit. Protestant theologians basically argued that worldly success was an outward sign of God's favor. Weber coined the term *Protestant Ethic* for this fusion of worldly success and religion. This belief encouraged the acquisition of material resources, both for individuals and corporations—a critical precondition of capitalism.

Bureaucracy. Weber also felt modern capitalism had to employ a unique organizational structure suitable for its needs. As a final ingredient of capitalism, he argued that *bureaucracy* was critical.

The key concept of bureaucracy is *hierarchy,* the ranking of individuals in terms of power. When an individual comes into the organization, he or she is assigned a particular position. An immediate superior has *power* over this individual, that is, the ability to give commands that he or she must accept. The individual, in turn, has power over his or her own subordinates. An individual reports to only one superior in order to avoid confusion and role conflict, so there is a *unity of command* throughout the hierarchy.

Weber was aware that bureaucratic organizations had existed before the fifteenth century, for example, in the Catholic Church and in the Roman army. However, only with modern capitalism did bureaucracy become the dominant model for business and governmental organizations. Previously, business and governmental structures were essentially a direct reflection of a society's social structure, as they still are in developing countries. Typically, an individual was born into a particular social class, and this determined the kind of job he or she could expect to obtain. But the bureaucratic organization is divorced from society, and relationships become impersonal, with rewards based on efficiency rather than familial connections. In fact, Weber believed the emphases on expertise, education, and bureaucracy in business and government would eventually lead to a society in which class distinctions would be blurred.

For employees to feel committed to this impersonal organization, they must not view their work merely as a job, but as a career. The hierarchy typically establishes a definite number of positions through which each individual can advance in terms of promotions, pay increases, and greater responsibilities. These rewards are the motivating elements that generate a high degree of efficiency and commitment from organizational members.

The Protestant Ethic: The Fusion of Religion and Worldly Success

I say you ought to be rich; you have no right to be poor. . . . I must say that you ought to spend some time getting rich. You and I know that there are some things more valuable than money; of course, we do. Ah, yes. . . . Well does the man know who has suffered that there are some things sweeter and holier and more sacred than gold. Nevertheless, the man of common sense also knows that there is not any one of those things that is not greatly enhanced by the use of money. Money is power; money has powers; and for a man to say, "I do not want money," is to say, "I do not wish to do any good to my fellowmen." It is absurd thus to talk. It is absurd to disconnect them. This is a wonderfully great life, and you ought to spend your time getting money, because of the power there is in money.

Greatness consists not in holding some office; greatness really consists in doing some great deed with little means, in the accomplishments of vast purposes from the private ranks of life; this is true greatness.

From the "Acres of Diamonds" speech given at least 4,000 times by the Reverend Russell H. Conwell, the first president of Temple University, Pennsylvania. In Agnes Rush Burr, *Russell H. Conwell and His Work* (Philadelphia: John C. Winston Co., 1917), pp. 414–15.

Although the nature of the work completed by large organizations may be simple and/or unskilled, the bureaucracy, to be efficient, requires that positions be specialized. Each person must know what he or she is supposed to do and must perform at a minimum level of competence. The most significant role distinction is between line and staff. A *line* manager or employee, for example, a vice-president of production, is directly engaged in producing the final product. A *staff* officer or employee, for example, a vice-president of personnel, advises and assists the line officers. For Weber, the distinction between line and staff was critical, because the complex nature of the hierarchy in a large organization demands that roles and functions be as clear and simplified as possible.

Another aspect of bureaucracy that Weber considered vital was record keeping. When proper records are kept, the firm is able to generate a moving picture of its historical activities so that corrective actions can be taken if deviations become evident over time. Weber would have approved of sophisticated, computerized, management information systems that have become popular since World War II, since the volume of records that can be handled efficiently has increased tremendously.

Weber discussed other aspects of bureaucracy but those just mentioned are the most essential: hierarchy, unity of command, career orientation, distinction between line and staff, record keeping, and impersonality. These elements provide the organization with a structure that can be highly productive.

Bureaucracy

The following may thus be said to be the fundamental categories of rational legal authority:

1. A continuous organization of official functions bound by rules. . . .
2. A specified sphere of competence. . . .
3. The organization of offices follows the principle of hierarchy. . . .
4. The rules which regulate the conduct of an office may be technical rules or norms. In both cases . . . specialized training is necessary. . . .
5. . . . it is a matter of principle that the members of the administrative staff should be completely separated from ownership of the means of production or administration. . . .
6. . . . there is also a complete absence of appropriation of his official position by the incumbent. . . .
7. Administrative acts, decisions, and rules are formulated and recorded in writing. . . .
8. Legal authority can be exercised in a wide variety of different forms.

Max Weber, *The Theory of Social and Economic Organization*, ed. Talcott Parsons and trans. A. M. Henderson and Talcott Parsons (New York: The Free Press, 1964), pp. 329–33.

Moreover, they were especially well suited to the large-scale economic activities that began in the fifteenth and sixteenth centuries. Even today, although more complex organizational structures appropriate for modern problems have replaced bureaucracy in many instances, its essential features are still important. Admittedly, an excessive amount of bureaucracy can lead to inefficiency. An organization may emphasize record keeping so much it begins to drown in its own paperwork. Still, a bureaucracy is vastly superior to an organization where an individual's status and position are determined by accidents of birth.

In summary, Weber began his analysis of modern capitalism by examining the preconditions that made it possible. Bureaucracy is a critical element because it provides a structure that can generate a high rate of efficiency. All of the preconditions discussed existed in fifteenth-century Europe; thus, modern capitalism was born.

Henri Fayol and Administrative Practices

As we have seen, Max Weber was basically a social theorist who was not concerned about the specific problems of real organizations. Henri Fayol was the direct opposite, for his theories grew out of his years of experience as a successful businessman in the coal-mining industry in France. His contributions are contained in one small book, *General and Industrial Management* (1916), where he presented the principles he felt a manager should use to guide an organization. Although he expressed them as facts, he did not regard them as final, since he had never tested them in a scientifically rigorous fashion. If conditions had changed, he would doubtless have accepted modifications in his ideas.

Although Weber and Fayol are contrasting figures in the history of management, they agreed on many major issues. Both emphasized the concept of unity of command, where each subordinate reports only to one superior. But Fayol is distinctive in that he believed that management is a specialty in its own right, and that an individual can learn to become a successful manager. Fayol held that the basic foundations of this specialty are the *principles* and *functions* of management.

For Fayol, there are 14 principles that a manager should follow. Although many of these are now primarily of historical interest, others are still current and useful for practicing managers. One is the *parity principle:* the amount of authority an individual possesses should be equal to his responsibility. If the gap between authority and responsibility becomes too large in an organization, employees will not know exactly what to do.

Fayol also felt there is an *ideal span of control,* an ideal number of employees a supervisor can manage effectively, within each section or level of an organization. A first-line supervisor in charge of production employees might be able to handle 20 to 30 subordinates, for the work at this level is usually standardized. At the top level in the organization, the chief executive might reasonably be able to handle 5 or 6 immediate subordinates.

Fayol, like Weber, realized that bureaucracies tend to become rigid because communications pass through a large number of superiors before plans can be implemented. To eliminate this problem, he proposed that *bridges* be constructed throughout the hierarchy (see Figure 2.2). If someone in one part of the hierarchy wants to communicate with equals in other sections, he should do so directly rather than relaying the message to his superiors. If superiors were constantly transmitting the messages of subordinates, they would have trouble completing their own work. Fayol observed that an overly formal pattern of communication is a frequent cause of rigidity in bureaucracies such as governmental organizations.

Finally, Fayol argued that a manager must perform certain essential functions in an orderly manner in carrying out his administrative practices and principles of management. The manager must set plans, and he must then organize, direct, coordinate, and control activities. Fayol thus is generally regarded as the founder of the *functional approach* to management. (Although the dimensions of management discussed in this book resemble Fayol's func-

Figure 2.2 Fayol's Bridge

The dotted line from F to G represents a bridge. In a rigid hierarchy, F would have to send his message through D, B, A, C, and E. The bridge allows equals in different parts of the hierarchy to communicate directly.

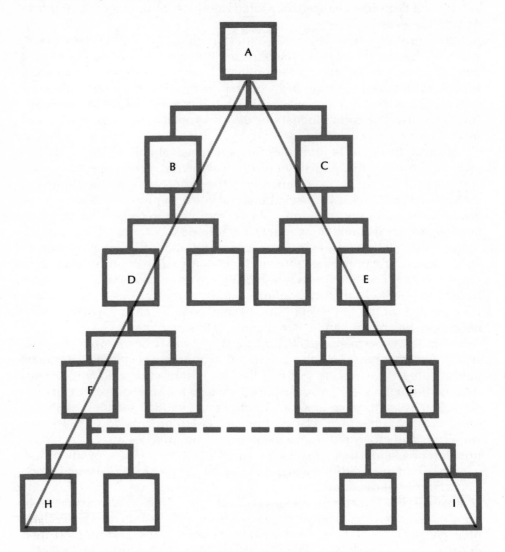

From Henri Fayol, *General and Industrial Management,* trans. Constance Storrs (London: Pitman, 1949), p. 34. Reprinted by permission of Pitman Publishing Ltd.

tions in some respects, our model takes an organizational rather than individual perspective; it emphasizes the dynamic relationships between dimensions; and it describes activities in terms of an open rather than a closed system.)

In short, Fayol was an experienced manager with such a wealth of information that he was able to construct a valid set of managerial functions and principles. Some of these are still important to practicing managers. But Fayol's major contribution was his point that management is a specialty and that an individual must be schooled in its various functions and principles to be successful as a leader. Although Fayol did not believe his principles were the only approach to management, he was bold enough to describe and advocate the administrative practices that had made him and other managers successful.

Frederick Taylor and Scientific Management

Both Max Weber and Henri Fayol analyzed organizations from the top down. Power flows down from the chief executive through the hierarchy; positions are arranged so that unity of command is achieved; and each individual has responsibility equal to his authority. But Frederick Taylor, the main figure in the history of scientific management, viewed organizations quite differently (Taylor 1911). To him, the starting point in analyzing an organization is the *operative* (lowest) level in the hierarchy, where the actual producing is done.

Improving the Worker's Productivity. Taylor believed the major problem in American industry was "goldbricking." Operative-level employees were, consciously or unconsciously, conspiring against employers by working well below their capacities. No standards had ever been set in most jobs for how much work employees ought to produce. To raise the level of productivity and eliminate the problem of goldbricking, Taylor developed an approach, scientific management, which is deceptively simple. He believed there is an ideal way to perform any job. The goal of *scientific management* is to use scientific methods to establish a standard for completing a job in the ideal manner.

In his writings, Taylor presents an extended example of scientific management that has become famous in the history of management. To demonstrate the importance of scientific management, he needed an employee who would submit to his instructions completely. The job he selected for study was handling pig iron. The pig-iron handler bends down, picks up a 92 lb. pig of iron, walks a few feet or yards, and then deposits it on the ground or on a pile. Taylor observed that the pig-iron handlers averaged about 12.5 tons per day. He also noticed that a particular pig-iron handler named Schmidt was performing an adequate job according to that standard, although he was strong enough physically to do much more work. Taylor reasoned that Schmidt was an energetic individual who could be significantly motivated by money:

> "Schmidt, are you a high-priced man?"
> "Vell, I don't know what you mean." [Conversation at this point lasts several minutes.]
> "Well, if you are a high-priced man, you will do exactly as this man tells you tomorrow, from morning until night. When he tells you to pick up a pig and walk, you pick it up and walk, and when he tells you to sit down and rest, you sit down. You do that right straight through the day. And what's more, no back talk. Do you understand that?"
> Schmidt started to work, and all day long, and at regular intervals, was told by the man who stood over him with a watch, "Now pick up a pig and walk. Now sit down and rest. Now walk, now rest . . . ." He worked when he was told to work, and rested when he was told to rest and at half-past five in the afternoon, had his $47\frac{1}{2}$ tons loaded on the car. And he practically never failed to work at this pace and do the task that was set him during the three years the writer was at Bethlehem. (Taylor 1911, pp. 46–47)

Motion Study. Taylor primarily relied on the stopwatch, for he focused on the amount of time it takes to complete a particular job. For this reason, he is usually called the father of time study. However, two other researchers, Frank and Lillian Gilbreth, began to emphasize the ideal motions required to perform a job in an optimal fashion. These researchers developed the concept of a *therblig* (Gilbreth spelled backwards), the basic element in on-the-job motion. According to the Gilbreths, there are 17 therbligs. To pinpoint the therbligs suitable for a particular job, the Gilbreths photographed the worker in action and then observed the film in slow motion.

The Gilbreths used motion study successfully in many different situations. In one interesting study, they analyzed the work of stone masons. This work is skilled and has a centuries-long tradition. Nevertheless, the Gilbreths noticed that each stone mason became tired because he had to bend continually to pick up his bricks, which were arranged in a small pile before him. To eliminate wasted motions, the Gilbreths constructed a special, adjustable stand for the bricks. Productivity rose 200 percent.

In short, many of the experiments conducted by advocates of scientific management proved highly successful. It was typical for productivity to double and, in some instances, to increase by 500 to 600 percent. Needless to say, American industrialists became very interested in this approach.

Resistance to Scientific Management. But there was a vicious reaction against scientific management. Humanitarian newspaper columnists accused Taylor of treating the human being like a machine, for the scientific management school emphasizes that the worker must submit totally to instructions if the job is to be performed most efficiently. The job is considered constant; the worker is viewed as variable in the sense that his behavior is molded to the job's requirements. Labor unions, too, opposed scientific management, primarily because it would restrict them during collective bargaining. If the employer knows how many units each worker should be able to produce, it is hard for the union to justify large wage increases.

There is some truth in the criticisms leveled against scientific management, although, in retrospect, it is hard to understand the wave of antagonism that greeted this new approach. In a congressional investigation of Taylor in 1913, he openly stated that the individual who would best meet the requirements of scientific management would be someone akin to an ox. Nevertheless, Taylor defended his position by showing that productivity would increase and salaries of both managers and employees would rise. In addition, Taylor introduced some practices that could be considered humanitarian: He pioneered in the use of rest pauses or coffee breaks, although his motivation was not humanitarian but pragmatic, since he discovered that the unskilled worker tires less and works more efficiently if given a rest pause.

Problems of Application. Scientific management has been absorbed in a modified form in industry. The fears of humanitarians and labor unions have proved largely unfounded. But several obstacles have arisen to the approach as Taylor envisioned it. First, scientific management requires the complete cooperation of the workers whose jobs are being measured. Such cooperation is rare, for workers know they will be forced to meet new standards and they slow down when an engineer begins to pace their jobs.

Second, and more importantly, the tools of scientific management are imperfect. Two engineers who examine the same job independently sometimes differ by as much as 80 percent as to how much time a worker should need to perform a given job cycle.

Third, as Taylor and his followers knew, the ideal application of scientific management requires violating the principle of unity of command. In Taylor's system, an employee would be responsible to several supervisors, each one examining one small part of the employee's job. Although this system can work in selected instances, it is difficult to use in many industrial situations because of its complexity.

Fourth, and perhaps the most basic problem with scientific management, is the internal inconsistency of the system. One of Taylor's essential principles was cooperation. Everyone would benefit financially if the ideal method for performing a given job were found, but discovering it required full coopera-

The Essence of Scientific Management

Now one of the very first requirements for a man who is fit to handle pig iron as a regular occupation is that he more nearly resembles in his mental make-up the ox than any other type. The man who is mentally alert and intelligent is for this very reason entirely unsuited to what would, for him, be the grinding monotony of work of this character. Therefore the workman who is best suited to handling pig iron is unable to understand the real science of doing this class of work. He is so stupid that the word "percentage" has no meaning to him, and he must consequently be trained by a man more intelligent than himself into the habit of working in accordance with the laws of this science before he can be successful.

Frederick W. Taylor, *The Principles of Scientific Management* (New York, Harper, 1911), p. 59.

tion between management and labor. However, once they had pinpointed this ideal method, Taylor vested all power in the hands of management, for the worker was constantly monitored. Specialization was the objective; the worker, who should cooperate voluntarily, became a machine who exercised very little freedom or responsibility. In such a situation, a worker might very well give up his freedom and subsequently find he had gained nothing. It was common at the turn of the twentieth century for management to give each worker high pay for each unit he produced until the average rate of productivity in a work group increased by 50 percent or more, at which time there was a significant reduction in the rate of incentive pay.

In summary, Taylor believed the operative or worker level in the organization is critical, and that a standard should be established for every job, based on the most efficient method of completing the work. Although he was aware of the importance of cooperation between management and labor, the techniques he used essentially rendered the worker a machine-like entity who did not participate in organizational decisions that directly influenced his job.

Human

Relations

The human relations school represents the other main stream of management thought, the behavioral science side. The human relations approach evolved out of a series of studies known as the Hawthorne Study carried out at the Hawthorne Plant of Western Electric between 1924 and 1932. (For an extended review of these studies, see Roethlisberger and Dickson 1939.) Like Taylor's, these studies and analyses focused on the operative level. However, as we have noted, the human relations school takes an opposite point of view to the teachings of scientific management.

The studies began in 1924, under the auspices of the Western Electric Company and the National Research Council of the National Academy of Sciences. The initial objective was to analyze the effects of illumination on the quantity and quality of production of employees at the operative level. The major hypothesis of the research was that an increase in illumination will result in an increase in productivity.

But some puzzling results began to emerge: Sometimes a *decrease* in illumination resulted in an *increase* in productivity. At one point, the investigators selected two workers for intensive study, and decreased the illumination from normal to 0.06 of a footcandle, an amount of light approximately equal to that of an ordinary moonlit night. Even then, the two workers maintained their previous levels of efficiency. They even stated that they were less tired than when working under the normal lights.

The Hawthorne researchers eventually explained these puzzling results by proposing that the intrusion of an investigator into the normal working world of employees caused a subtle and perhaps unconscious change in their behavior. In effect, the employees enjoyed being studied, which nullified the negative effects that would normally accompany reduction of light in the work area. This phenomenon was dubbed the *Hawthorne Effect:* The study of a human being automatically changes his or her behavior.

The Test-Room Experiments

In 1927 Elton Mayo and a group of social scientists associated with the Harvard Business School took over direction of the Hawthorne studies. They analyzed a group of five female workers who were assigned to a special test room so that the normal working environment of the plant would not influence their behavior.

During these experiments, the researchers concentrated on two major factors that could reasonably influence productivity:

1. Increased wage incentive. In the small group, the women could clearly see the relationship between the incentive plan and wages. They worked under a standard group piecework system: Each worker received the same wage, calculated in terms of the average number of units the five-member work group produced. It is difficult for the employees to understand and appreciate the relationship between a group piecework system and productivity if the group or plant is too large.

2. The informal and considerate style of supervision that was exercised in the test room. The researchers theorized that the considerate style of supervision would minimize the employees' fear of management and increase their job satisfaction, thus raising productivity.

In one stage of the experiment, the researchers varied only the wage system. Specifically, they set up a group piece-rate incentive system for the five workers that was separate from the plant-wide incentive system. Productivity rose 12 percent. The researchers then put a new group of five workers in the test room, who were paid under the group piece-rate incentive system that applied to all workers in the plant. However, the researchers did vary one factor: they stressed human relations by using a considerate supervisor who allowed the workers to make many of their own decisions, such as the length of their rest pauses and their workday. Productivity jumped 16 percent.

Based on these results, the researchers partially agreed with Taylor that money is important, for the change in the wage system appeared to bring about a 12 percent increase in productivity. But they argued that the human relations approach may be more important, since its effect seemingly brought about a 16 percent increase in productivity. The researchers consequently proposed that any organizational change, such as the use of a considerate supervisor or a new wage system, affects job satisfaction and productivity through employee attitudes: When employees feel an organizational change, such as a new wage system, is being introduced to obtain more work for less money, job satisfaction and productivity will not increase, but when management is genuinely interested in their welfare, they will react positively to an organizational change and increase their rate of productivity.

The Observation-Room Study

In the final stage of the Hawthorne study, the researchers centered their attention on the social structure of the work group. To complete this study, they placed an observer in a test room where 23 male operatives worked. His job was to observe the behavior of the workers and, at the same time, keep records of their productivity.

Some of the major findings were (Roethlisberger and Dickson 1939):

1. The workers set their own production standard, which was well below what they could have accomplished.
2. There were sizeable differences in status between subgroups in the work test room.
3. The workers exercised social control to insure strict adherence to status differences and the group's level of productivity. This control was harsh, and it

included sarcasm, name calling, ostracism, and ridicule. Even minor physical assaults were employed by the group. If an individual did not adhere to the group's mode of behavior, he was "binged" on the arm with a piece of steel.

4. The group had specific ideas as to the way a worker should conduct himself: (a) You should not turn out too much work; if you do, you are a "rate buster." (b) You should not turn out too little work; if you do, you are a "chiseler." (c) You should not tell a superior anything to the detriment of a fellow worker; if you do, you are a "squealer." (d) You should not try to act important.

The most important and clear finding in this study is that the informal relations in the work group influence attitudes, which then affect the individual's level of productivity. This informal organization did not correspond to the role descriptions of the bureaucratic or formal organization.

Integrated
Perspective

Both the scientific management school and the human relations school influenced the practice of management in a decisive fashion, even though they represented opposing points of view. The integrated perspective used in this book draws from both. On many points, the tension between the two schools has produced a more workable alternative than either school offered. To see how the integrated perspective developed, it is useful to look at the effect of the tension between the schools of scientific management and human relations on each of the four dimensions of management discussed in chapter 1: organization design, planning and control, behavioral processes, and decision making. Within these four dimensions, there are ten subdivisions or elements, as shown in Table 2.1. Each element is examined in a separate chapter in this book.

Organization Design

There are two elements within the dimension of organization design: (1) organizational models that serve as a guide for constructing organizations; and (2) the major influences on design, which are technology and external environmental uncertainty.

Table 2.1   The Four Dimensions and Ten Elements Within Which Managerial Activities Take Place

	Scientific Management	Human Relations	An Integrated Perspective
I. Organization Design			
Organizational models	Variation of bureaucracy: functional or divided foremanship. Hierarchy is still essential. Organizational structure is more important than attitudes.	Variation of bureaucracy: participative management. Hierarchy is still essential. Attitudes are more important than organizational structure.	Both bureaucratic and nonbureaucratic models are important. Importance of the hierarchy may be greatly deemphasized. Both attitudes and organizational structure are equally important.
Major influences on design: technology and environmental uncertainty	Of minor importance.	Of minor importance.	Of major importance.
II. Planning and Control			
Planning	Primarily at the operative or worker level. Short range and specific.	Of minor importance.	Planning throughout the organization. Both short range and long range.
Control	Primarily at the operative level. Short range and specific.	Of minor importance.	Concerned about the entire organization. Both short range and long range.
III. Behavioral Processes			
Motivation	Economic Man: motivated by money.	Social Man: motivated by attitudes formed through interactions in the informal group.	Complex individual: motivated by a variety of factors.

Table 2.1   (Continued)

	Scientific Management	Human Relations	An Integrated Perspective
Leadership	Of minor importance.	Favors considerate supervisor and participative management.	Emphasizes traits of leader, nature of task, and other situational factors.
Interpersonal and group behavior	Focuses primarily on the individual employee. However, the work group can undercut management by setting low production standards.	Focuses on interaction between: (a) employees in a single work group (b) supervisor and work group	Focuses on interaction between: (a) employees in a single work group (b) supervisor and work group (c) two or more adjacent work groups (d) organizational levels (operative, middle, and upper levels)
Communication	One-way communication: superior to subordinate.	Movement toward two-way communication between superior and subordinate.	Genuine two-way communication between superior and subordinate.

IV. Decision Making

	Scientific Management	Human Relations	An Integrated Perspective
The nature of decision making	One best way: time and motion study.	One best way: human relations techniques.	There is no "one best way."
Decision-making techniques	Time and motion studies.	Testing hypotheses.	Statistics, operations research, and other quantitative techniques.

Both the scientific management school and the human relations school treated bureaucracy as the model that should be used to construct organizations. Both accepted the need for a hierarchy; however, each modified the traditional hierarchy in a different way. The organizational model proposed by scientific management specified that *divided* or *functional foremanship* is critical; that is, the work of each employee is so specialized that it must be examined by several foremen, not just one. The human relations school emphasized participative management and a democratic style of supervision within the bureaucratic organization: At least on some issues, employees were to participate in making decisions. Whereas Taylor and his followers believed that the method of structuring the organization and the job is more important than the attitudes of workers, the human relations school argued that formal design of the organization is less important than the attitudes workers form through their interactions in informal groups.

The integrated perspective on management uses nonbureaucratic as well as bureaucratic models in exploring organizational behavior. For some work, such as factory-type employment, the hierarchy is relevant. A rigid hierarchy is much less crucial in other situations, such as in a research organization whose work force is highly educated. In either case, the integrated perspective holds that organizational structure and attitudes should receive equal consideration; although the design of the organization is important, it is also critical to examine the attitudes of individuals who work within its structure. Problems can arise from either source—organizational structure or attitudes.

From the perspective of the integrated management model, technology and external environmental uncertainty are the major influences on the design of the organization. *Technology* in this context refers to the means used to produce a final good or service. An organization's success may hinge on application of the proper technology. For example, management may be losing money because of its wage bill, which can be significantly reduced if machines replace workers. *External environmental uncertainty* refers to the degree to which the organization is influenced by outside forces. For instance, the passage of a new law may compel management to change some of its practices; increased competition from other firms may lead management to invest a great amount of money in advertising; and the departure of key executives to other firms that offer better financial opportunities may necessitate a revision in the salary schedule of the organization.

The schools of both scientific management and human relations downgraded the importance of technology. They completed their studies in factory-type organizations and did not focus on other types of technological situations such as white-collar work; hence, many of their conclusions apply only to factory-type work, which is declining in importance in the United States and Europe.

Neither the school of scientific management nor the school of human relations emphasized the importance of external environmental uncertainty in the explanation of organizational behavior. Rather, both schools centered their attention on the work that took place at the operative level, a focus that impeded their understanding of the fact that outside forces often determine behavior in an organization.

Planning and Control

The scientific management school emphasized planning and control, but only at the operative or worker level. Plans were specific and short range; industrial engineers established production goals and monitored the workers rigidly to increase efficiency.[1] The human relations school also dealt with planning and control at the operative level, but to a much lesser extent. Management allowed the workers to participate in setting production goals; managers exercised control by means such as a democratic style of supervision and a group incentive plan.

The integrated management perspective emphasizes specific and short-range planning and control systems, but it also stresses the importance of general and long-range planning and control. From the integrated perspective, management should highlight the use of planning and control not only at the operative level but throughout the entire organization.

Behavioral Processes

In many situations, behavioral processes that take place in an organization are of obvious significance. A motivated work force is typically satisfied and productive; an effective leader can energize his employees to produce more efficiently; the relations that occur within and between groups can determine individual attitudes; and an effective communication system can eliminate misunderstandings. In this book, the focus is on four major behavioral processes or elements: motivation, leadership, group behavior, and communication.

Motivation. In scientific management, motivation was of minor significance. The only motivation of any consequence is economic—the higher a worker's salary, the greater his or her productivity. If management knows the ideal

---

[1] Fayol and the members of the functional school emphasized general and long-range planning and control systems not stressed by the advocates of scientific management. However, Fayol did not highlight the importance of short-range planning and control systems.

method of structuring a job, it does not really matter if the worker is motivated or satisfied; he or she must perform at the level set by management.

The human relations school placed more importance on motivation and constructed a much more sophisticated theory. A worker's motivation is affected by the attitudes he or she forms as part of a work group within the organization. In some instances, the worker is even unaware or only dimly aware of the importance of the work group and the motivation he or she derives from the informal relations within it.

The integrated management perspective holds that the individual is complex and motivated by a variety of factors. Although money and informal relationships are important, other factors are also significant, such as the nature of the task and the feeling of accomplishment an individual achieves when he or she has completed it.

Leadership. Leadership, another behavioral process, was not a prominent aspect of scientific management. If the work of an individual is highly subdivided so that it can be monitored by several functional foremen, the power of supervisors is all that matters; leadership is not necessary. In contrast, the human relations school stressed the significance of leadership: If the supervisor is considerate and gets along well with his or her subordinates, workers' attitudes become positive and productivity probably will increase.

The integrated perspective also emphasizes that leadership is critical. However, different types of leadership are appropriate to different situations, depending on factors ranging from the characteristics of the leader to the nature of the work. An autocratic style of supervision may be effective in a factory, while a democratic style may be successful among professionals.

Group Behavior. A third behavioral process, group behavior, received only limited attention from the school of scientific management. Taylor and his followers put the major emphasis on the individual employee: If the employee's work is highly subdivided, functional foremen can monitor it closely. Still, the supporters of scientific management did feel that group behavior could be decisive if it were not controlled by management and the functional foremen. Taylor argued that workers, as a group, frequently set low standards of production because they fear management will push them beyond their limits.

The school of human relations was very interested in group behavior, believing that interactions among employees in a work group, and between supervisors and their subordinates, were important. If the attitudes formed through these interactions were negative, productivity would probably decline.

The integrated perspective also considers group behavior of primary importance. This perspective highlights several interactions or levels of analysis: among employees in a single work group; between a supervisor and his or her subordinates; between two or more adjacent work groups; and among organizational levels (operative, middle, and upper). Problems of cooperation can occur if any of these interactions becomes tense.

Communication. Communication, the final element within the dimension of behavioral processes, is basically one way, from the superior to the subordinate, when an organization uses scientific management. Taylor wanted the employee's cooperation so he could determine the best method for performing the job. However, once Taylor had ascertained the best method, he expected the subordinate to obey all orders completely. The school of human relations began to move toward two-way communication, since the considerate supervisor did respond to the questions and needs of the subordinates. Still, the superior essentially controlled the communication process in that he determined the extent to which employees could participate in decisions affecting their work. According to the integrated perspective, genuine two-way communication between superior and subordinate is not only desirable but necessary. Without genuine communication, misunderstandings that inhibit cooperation can easily arise.

Decision Making

Decision making is the key dimension of management, for poor decisions can easily make an organization ineffective and may lead to its total failure. Within this dimension are two identifiable subdivisions or elements: the nature of the decision-making process an organization employs, and specific decision-making techniques.

The schools of both scientific management and human relations put forth definite ideas about decision making, for example, that there is "one best way" to run an organization and make decisions. In the scientific management school, the one best way was to use time and motion studies to produce the ideal design for a job; in the human relations school, it was to use democratic supervision and participative management.

The integrated perspective holds that there is no "one best way" to make decisions. Rather, the methods selected to solve any problem are dependent or contingent on the situation and the problem. In some situations, the scientific management school's emphasis on organizational structure is appropriate; in other situations, employee participation as advocated by the human relations school is suitable. In still other situations, new and radical approaches need to be devised. Management must examine each problem individually and handle it on its own merits.

The other element of decision making concerns the techniques each school employs. Until the twentieth century, managers operated essentially in an intuitive fashion; that is, they based their decisions on their feelings rather than on a systematic analysis of alternatives and facts. The school of scientific management changed this focus by introducing systematic analysis of jobs. The human relations school later supplemented this approach with its use of statistics and the testing of hypotheses.

From the integrated perspective, any decision-making technique that helps a manager assess facts and alternative courses of action is valid. Hence, applied disciplines such as statistics and operations research are essential in the modern organization. This perspective thus includes systematic analysis of jobs and the testing of hypotheses, but it also stresses many other decision-making techniques developed to solve managerial problems.

Summary

This chapter has examined the differences between the two major streams of management, economics and behavioral science. In terms of the management model developed in chapter 1, the school of scientific management, which represents the economic stream, emphasizes planning and control at the operative level. In particular, scientific management stresses the importance of time and motion study in its quest to develop the ideal method of completing a specific job. Supervisors closely monitor the work of the employee, which has been fragmented and routinized. The school of human relations, representing the behavioral science stream, highlights the significance of behavioral processes. The attitudes of employees influence their behavior and level of productivity. In turn, the informal relations in a work group determine the attitudes that employees exhibit. Both streams of management seem to devote an equal amount of attention to organization design and decision making.

The integrated perspective on management consolidates the two streams of management, drawing from each and from the tension between them. In the remainder of the book, the four dimensions of management and the ten elements within them constitute the framework for the various parts and chapters.

Discussion Questions

1. This chapter has presented a discussion of differences between the schools of scientific management and human relations. What are some similarities of these two approaches?

2. In engineering firms, engineers are typically assigned to projects for several weeks or months. Upon completion of a project, the engineers are usually assigned to other projects that require their expertise. In such firms, whose theory should managers follow—Fayol, Weber, Taylor, or Mayo?

3. Scientific management is still popular. Where do you think it is primarily used? Why? Where is scientific management not likely to be used? Why?

4. Do you think societies develop particular kinds of organizations that are a direct reflection of the kinds of problems they face? Why or why not?

5. The key concept of bureaucracy is hierarchy. Can an organization be truly nonbureaucratic in the sense of having no hierarchy at all?

6. Are the four elements within the dimension of behavioral processes—motivation, leadership, group behavior, and communication—independent of one another? Why or why not?

Critical Incidents

NOTE: *These critical incidents can be used by the whole class with the case observational method (see Appendix), or used for thought and discussion by individual class members.*

1. Top management of the Shaw Company, which manufactures toys, has decided that its foremen are becoming ineffective. The average length of service for foremen is 20 years. For most of that time, the company's productivity has been high; within recent years, however, it has been falling, and the supervisors are not developing new approaches to raise it.

To combat this problem, the company has decided to send all of its 75 foremen to a week's human-relations training program held outside the plant. The objective of this program is to develop a new style of leadership among foremen to help increase the productivity of their employees.

Questions: Do you feel this solution is likely to work? Why or why not?

2. The Winston Company, a medium-sized insurance company with 10,000 employees, has an abnormally high turnover rate, so it hires a large consulting firm to survey the employees and pinpoint the problems that are bothering them. The consulting firm constructs a detailed questionnaire to examine many job-related issues such as attitudes about pay, supervision, challenging work, and fringe benefits. All of the employees complete this questionnaire. The consulting firm then summarizes the major findings and publishes them in an attractive booklet, giving a copy to every employee. In this booklet, the consulting firm indicates that management is initiating changes in accordance with the employees' responses and wishes.

Questions: Do you feel this is an effective approach? Why or why not? Can the company do anything else to increase the effectiveness of the survey? Could the consulting firm have created a Hawthorne Effect? Why or why not? If the consulting firm did create a Hawthorne Effect, were the results positive or negative?

3. In a graduate-level finance course, the instructor bases the final grades solely on a group project to be completed at the end of the semester. There are only six students in the class, and they have all worked on the same project. As is common in such situations, some students have worked harder than others; in fact, one did practically nothing. After reading the final paper, the instructor tells the six students to assign their own grades. However, since the quality of the various parts of the paper is uneven, the instructor tells the students they must assign the following grades: one A, one B, two C's, and two D's.

Questions: Do you agree with this instructor's approach? Why or why not? How do you think Mayo and Taylor would respond to this approach?

Suggested Readings

Baughman, James, ed. *The History of American Management.* Englewood Cliffs, N.J.: Prentice-Hall, 1969, 252 pages, paperback.

> *This book is somewhat difficult to read, but students have consistently enjoyed it. Some of the important topics covered here are rarely examined elsewhere, such as the use of control procedures in the railroad industry during the 1880s and the development of modern financial reporting practices.*

Cochran, Thomas. *Business in American Life: A History*. New York: McGraw-Hill, 1972, 402 pages, paperback.

> *This book is recommended if the curriculum does not include a course on business and economic history. Cochran is a historian who has written an excellent and readable introduction to business and economic history in the United States. The book gives the student an excellent background for understanding management problems.*

George, Claude. *The History of Management Thought*. 2d ed. Englewood Cliffs, N.J.: Prentice-Hall, 1972, 223 pages, paperback.

> *George provides a survey of management thought that spans the spectrum from ancient civilization to modern times.*

■ To operate effectively, management must work within an organization whose design is compatible with the types of tasks to be completed. Until the end of World War I, design was a minor managerial issue, for almost all organizations were structured as centralized, rigid hierarchies. In most situations, the president and a few key subordinates made all major decisions and allowed most subordinates to exercise little if any responsibility. Only in the past 50 years has management realized the importance of organization design in the attainment of success. Recently many new designs and approaches have been developed to handle the unique problems that particular organizations face.

Part II examines some models management can use to structure or restructure organizations. But what determines the type of design that is suitable for a particular organization? The two major influences on design, technology and external environmental uncertainty, are considered in light of the way they can shape an organization's structure and performance.

ORGANIZATION

DESIGN

II

The Hierarchy
and Organizational
Models

3

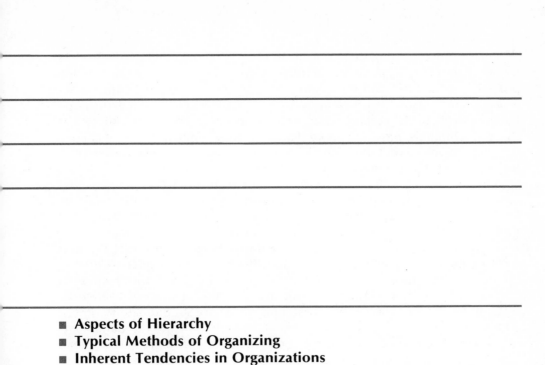

- **Aspects of Hierarchy**
- **Typical Methods of Organizing**
- **Inherent Tendencies in Organizations**

Performance Objectives

1. To appreciate the importance of hierarchy in the planning and construction of organizations.

2. To understand the basic concepts underlying the construction of organizations, such as line versus staff, span of control, and unity of command.

3. To describe the typical methods of constructing organizations.

4. To be aware of inherent tendencies in organizations directly associated with the concept of hierarchy.

It may seem obvious that an organization must be designed properly if it is to be effective. Still, managers frequently disregard this dimension when problems occur. One reason they do is that it is much easier to change other aspects of management—for example, to appoint a dynamic leader in the hope that improving behavioral processes will correct the problem. The structure of the organization is frequently more difficult to alter, since this type of change typically involves redefining jobs, changing the reporting relationships between individuals and units, and even eliminating some units.

However, as the integrated model presented in this book indicates, the design of the organization is an important issue for managers. If the organization's design is not appropriate for the work to be performed, behavioral problems can easily result and the effectiveness of the decision-making system can be seriously undermined. These possibilities confirm that the four dimensions within which managerial activities occur are strongly related; a problem within one dimension frequently creates difficulties within another.

Hierarchy is a critical concept in organization design. It refers to the existence of levels of power so that some individuals are subordinate to others, with reward systems in which some individuals earn more money than others, and status systems in which some individuals receive more respect than others. In designing an organization, managers typically emphasize the importance of the hierarchy and of the relationships among individuals and organizational units that it establishes.

Even if an organization's founders do not wish to create a hierarchy, it tends to arise inevitably. Some French companies were organized on the basis of cooperative ownership and management after World War II. However, chaos and conflict occurred as individuals tried to avoid the dull jobs, which tended

Organization Design

Organization is not an end in itself but a means to the end of business performance and business results. Organization structure is an indispensable means; and the wrong structure will seriously impair business performance and may even destroy it. Still, the starting point of any analysis of organization cannot be a discussion of structure. It must be the analysis of the business. The first question in discussing organization structure must be: what is our business and what should it be? Organization structure must be designed so as to make possible the attainment of the objectives of the business for five, ten, fifteen years hence.

Peter Drucker, *The Practice of Management* (New York: Harper and Brothers, 1954), p. 194.

to predominate. This forced the members to create hierarchies. If they had not done so, the organizations probably would have become ineffective.

This chapter focuses on critical aspects of the hierarchy that are important in organization design. There is also a discussion of the typical methods of designing organizations, all of which relate directly to the concept of the hierarchy, and an analysis of some inherent tendencies in organizations that are associated with this concept.

Aspects
of Hierarchy

A number of critical concepts in the management literature relate directly to the hierarchy and organization design: line and staff distinction; centralization and decentralization distinction; span of control; unity of command; and coordination.

Line and Staff Distinction

As was suggested in chapter 2, *line* personnel are those directly involved in producing the final good or service of the organization, for example, a vice-president of production or a worker who actually makes the product the firm sells. *Staff* personnel advise and assist the line personnel in accomplishing their work, for example, a vice-president of personnel or the personnel interviewer who actually hires the workers.

When an organization is small and uncomplicated, all or most of its managers and employees are line personnel. The small temporary-help agency described in chapter 1 includes a president, sales representatives, and supervisors who hire employees and monitor their assignments. All are line personnel, for they are involved in the production of the final service in this organization: the performance of the temporary-help employees. Usually the president hires an accountant on a part-time basis to take care of his books; the accountant is a staff person who merely goes over the books to make sure they are in order.

Growth. As an organization matures, it usually begins to increase its staff personnel. This occurs because of the complexity of the work: it is no longer

possible to use only line personnel. Some common examples of staff employees in large organizations are those in research, personnel, training, and industrial relations. Usually the staff functions are under one jurisdiction or
vice-presidency that is separate from that of the line organization.

Power. A staff executive can exercise a great amount of authority and responsibility within his or her own department. However, the basic function of staff
personnel is to advise and assist line personnel, and staff work is normally
treated as less important than line work. Top staff officers in some large corporations earn $100,000 or less, while their line counterparts receive nearly a
million dollars. In most decision-making situations, line officers merely listen
to the advice of staff officers and then make their own decisions.

However, some staff officers are often more powerful and important than
line personnel. In one medium-sized railroad company, the personnel director
wielded enormous influence, since the president usually accepted his recommendations concerning the promotion of both line and staff executives; thus,
he was able to make a large number of decisions that did not officially fall
within the scope of his duties. Similarly, a vice-president of industrial relations
wields a great amount of power in an organization that is troubled by labor-
management difficulties.

Many executives work in a staff function early in their careers and later
transfer to a line function. An individual who possesses a master of business
administration degree (MBA) in finance may do financial research for the first
few years of his career and then transfer to a line position in which he actually
makes financial decisions that influence production of the organization's final
good or service.

Individuals, such as researchers, who stay in staff positions for their entire
careers generally have different attitudes and orientations from their line
counterparts, even though both have the same ultimate interest in the organization's success (Dalton 1950 and 1966; Filley, House, and Kerr 1976). These
differences are understandable in that staff are usually subordinate to line
personnel. If staff personnel also engage in research or professional activities,
they tend to be less committed to the organization and to spend more time on
outside activities such as publishing research results in scholarly journals than
their line counterparts. Friction between line and staff thus seems inevitable.
In one large company, friction became so intense that management trans-
ferred its staff specialists in research and development to a new location, away
from the hostility of the production personnel (Woodward 1965).

Top managers have recognized the friction between line and staff, and have
sometimes established "dual ladders" of promotion: one for staff and the
other for line. However, because staff personnel are usually paid considerably

less than their line counterparts, the dual ladder has proved so disappointing that the ambitious staff executive frequently tries to transfer into a line position.

Centralization and Decentralization

The degree of *centralization* in an organization is the extent to which decision-making power is concentrated in the hands of one or a few people or positions. *Decentralization* refers to the power delegated throughout an organization. Centralization and decentralization, although they appear to be opposites, are actually two ends of a continuum. In practice, it is virtually impossible to achieve complete centralization or complete decentralization.

In a decentralized organization, individuals at the lower levels can make some critical decisions without checking with their superiors. Even then, however, the top managers in the organization exercise some control over the kinds of decisions that individuals at the lower echelons can make. In a centralized organization, the top managers usually make the strategic decisions, but it is nearly impossible for them to monitor every decision at lower levels.

At the turn of the twentieth century, a sociologist named Robert Michels studied the problem of centralization by examining the organizational structures of political parties in Western Europe, after which he put forth his famous Iron Law: "Whoever says organization, says oligarchy" (Michels 1915). According to Michels, all organizations tend to become centralized in that major decisions are made by a few individuals—an oligarchy. The political

---

Modern Organizations

Modern man is man in organization. He not only spends one-half of his waking day contributing to the cooperative effort of an organization, but he also occupies the other half watching television, reading books, or going to a theatre to be entertained—all output of the cooperative effort of men in organizations! It is no small wonder then that man should find the genesis, growth, and evolution of organization a fascinating study. . . . The contemporary student of organizations encounters difficulties in comprehending all of this. For him, organizations are more like life: they display no one outstanding regularity nor any singularly striking anomaly. Instead, a variety of events and processes present themselves, waiting to be understood and incorporated into a coherent conceptual framework.

Peter Schoderbek, Asterios Kefalas, and Charles Schoderbek, *Management Systems* (Dallas: Business Publications, 1975), pp. 107–8.

parties Michels studied had very different philosophies and objectives (for example, Democrats and Communists), but they all tended to use a highly centralized organizational structure in which only a few individuals decided on courses of action that influenced all the members.

In large organizations, Michels' Iron Law frequently applies, since a small number of top executives usually make the major overall decisions. Even so, it is possible and desirable for the lower echelon managers to make decisions about their own specific problems. If the lower echelon managers constantly referred their problems to the top managers, it would be difficult for the organization to complete its work. Decentralization thus adds considerable flexibility to an organization. For this reason, decentralization seems to be appropriate when an organization operates in a highly competitive and con- stantly changing environment in which executives must respond quickly to the problems that confront them. Still, decentralization may create problems if individuals in the lower levels cannot exercise authority responsibly. A middle manager who exceeds his budget by $500,000 may force top managers to cut back on services needed in other parts of the organization.

In short, there is an inevitable tension between centralization and decen- tralization in an organization. Some large organizations such as Westinghouse have emphasized decentralization at one point during their existence and centralization at another. When work is not being accomplished, manage- ment opts for a change in hierarchical relations, and this change frequently takes the form of more or less centralization.

Span of Control

As was suggested in chapter 2, there seems to be an *ideal span of control,* an ideal number of subordinates a superior should supervise, within each section or level of the organization. Although the exact number is difficult to deter- mine, it can be estimated.

When a superior manages the work of too many subordinates, he or she frequently is unable to spend enough time with each of them. Further, the subordinates tend to become inefficient, since the superior cannot effectively control and coordinate their work.

Joan Woodward studied the relationship between technology and the ideal span of control in 100 British firms (Woodward 1965). She classified the firms in terms of three types of technology. A company with *unit technology* spends a great amount of money on labor costs relative to capital investment in equipment; an example might be a custom-made furniture maker. With *mass production,* the organization spends a great amount of money on labor, but it also invests heavily in capital equipment or machines, as with an automobile manufacturer. An organization using *process* or *automated technology* does not spend much money in labor costs, but it does invest a large amount of money in capital equipment, for example, an oil refinery or chemical plant.

Woodward found that a first-line supervisor had approximately 23 subordinates in a successful unit-technology organization; 49 employees in a successful mass-production organization; and 13 employees in a successful automated organization. As an organization moved away from its ideal figure, it tended to become unsuccessful. Although Woodward reports that a similar relationship between type of technology and success holds at the upper levels in an organization, she does not mention any specific figures.

Robert House and John Miner (1969) have also investigated the ideal span of control by reviewing the literature on small-group research and other types of behavioral investigations. Like Woodward, they conclude that the type of technology is critical in determining the ideal span of control. Their review suggests that the ideal span of control is likely to be in the range of 5 to 10 under most circumstances. However, they feel that the larger spans, about 8 to 10, are most appropriate at the highest, policy-making levels of an organization, for managers need a large number of different ideas and inputs before they can make decisions that influence the entire system.

In industry, practices vary widely (Dale 1952; Janger 1960; and Simonds 1969). Janger (1960) found that the number of key subordinates reporting directly to a company president in 80 large organizations ranged from 1 to 24. This range is large if, as indicated above, the ideal number at the highest levels of the organization is between 8 and 10. However, it may be that ongoing organizations respond to organizational problems by developing spans of control suitable for their distinctive activities.

Unity of Command

Classical management theorists like Henri Fayol have argued that there should be a *unity of command* in a hierarchical organization. That is, there should be only one leader and one plan for activities having the same objective. This principle appears sensible, since an individual will tend to experience anxiety and run into conflicting priorities if he reports to two or more superiors who give him conflicting commands. A large-scale study of 725 employees confirms this (Kahn et al. 1964). Thirty-nine percent of the respondents reported being worried at "some time" that they would not be able to fulfill conflicting demands, and 15 percent reported the problem was very serious. Further, individuals experiencing conflicting demands mentioned that their trust in the superiors who imposed the pressure was reduced and that their own effectiveness was impaired.

However, other research suggests that organizations can successfully violate the principle of unity of command in many situations. In fact, certain kinds of organizations operate best with a flexible structure in which there is open and constant violation of unity of command. A common illustration is a firm of research engineers that develops new techniques and products, where an engineer may be working on more than one product at once, each under the direction of a different superior. The work demands that job specifications be flexible, for individuals must respond quickly to external competitive pressures and the internal need of the organization to develop several products.

Coordination

Coordination—the development of cooperative relationships between individuals and groups whose work overlaps—is one of the most pressing problems organizations face. The production department's work overlaps with that of the sales department; if production is not producing enough goods to honor commitments made by sales, tension can easily develop.

Henri Fayol attacked the problem of coordination by creating *bridges:* channels by which organizational peers or equals can communicate directly with one another without relaying messages through their superiors (see chapter 2). When subordinates communicate directly, they speed up the communication process and usually coordinate their efforts more effectively, since they can work out any problems and misunderstandings by themselves. For example, engineering draftsmen frequently complete work for engineers, but neither the draftsmen nor the engineers typically bother their superiors about the assignment. If a draftsman has available time, he will complete the work of any engineer who requests his services.

Linkages. Another approach to coordination has been suggested by Chester Barnard (1938), who argues that an organization should consist of units of ten members or less. Barnard feels this small size will help create a pleasant atmosphere in which individuals can interact comfortably and be productive. To coordinate the work in an organization, the leaders in interdependent units should then form into an executive unit that will direct all overlapping work. Barnard believes executives are unique in that they always belong to two groups: a working group they supervise, and an executive group that coordinates the overlapping activities between two or more working groups, as shown in Figure 3.1.

More recently, Rensis Likert expanded on Barnard's approach by suggesting that *linking pins* be established within the traditional hierarchy (Likert 1961 and 1967). Each individual designated as a linking pin would be a member of

Figure 3.1   Barnard's Unit Concept

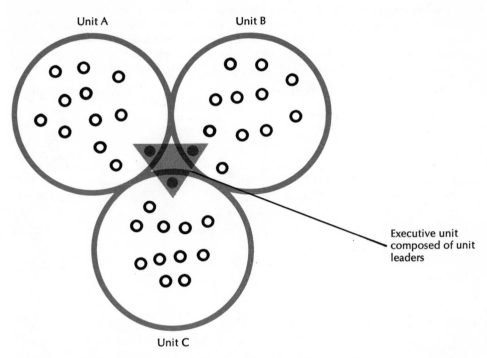

Unit A

Unit B

Executive unit
composed of unit
leaders

Unit C

Based on Chester Barnard, *The Functions of the Executive* (Cambridge: Harvard University Press, 1966; originally published in 1938).

both his own work group and another work group whose activities overlap with those of his own group. Consequently, he should understand the special problems of both units with which he is associated. The linking pin would then be charged with the task of coordinating the work of the two units. The coordination of overlapping work should thus become easier, since work groups would be linked together within the traditional hierarchy, as shown in Figure 3.2.

Office of the President. In a large corporation, the chief executive frequently has difficulty coordinating the work of subordinates; he or she may be over-burdened by the amount and variety of the work to be performed. To correct this situation, some large corporations have established an *Office of the President,* consisting of two or three co-equal chief executives who divide the work and coordinate their efforts. Sometimes this approach is very successful,

Figure 3.2 Likert's Linking Pins

On the left are traditional organizational structures; on the right are the same structures rearranged according to Likert's linking-pin function. The linking pins (colored circles) are the individuals who provide communication and coordination among groups through membership in more than one work group. Ultimately the entire organization would be linked, both vertically and horizontally, by such individuals.

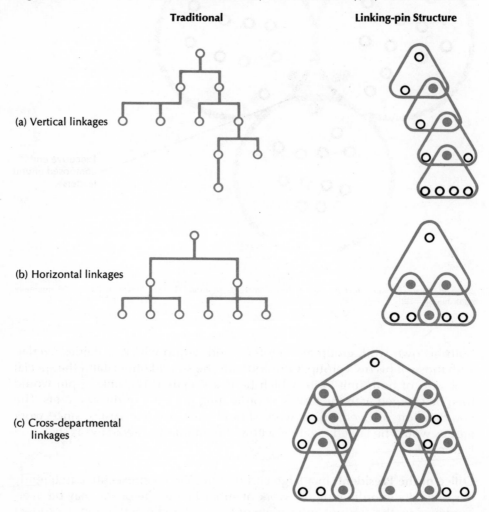

From Raymond Miles, *Theories of Management*, p. 87. Copyright © 1975 by McGraw-Hill Book Company. Linking-pin structure adapted from Rensis Likert, *New Patterns of Management* (New York: McGraw-Hill, 1961). Reprinted by permission.

especially if one chief executive simply cannot handle the volume of work. At the same time, there is an inherent danger in this approach, for the co-equal executives may fight among themselves when they apportion areas of responsibilities. Companies such as RCA and Ford have used an Office of the President, but they eliminated it after one chief executive became dominant.

Committees and Task Forces

In most organizations, each individual is responsible for performing a given job within the hierarchy. However, there are many activities that fall outside the scope of duties of any one individual. For this reason, organizations rely heavily on committees and task forces.

Committees. Usually an organization has a number of permanent *standing committees,* each formed for a specific purpose. For example, finance committees exist in many organizations to handle the allocation of resources to various departments. Standing committees are important because they provide a stable structure by which routine or recurring activities can be handled efficiently.

However, standing committees can also slow down activities, since all work that is specific to their jurisdictions must be processed through them. Because the members have full-time jobs in other areas, they often cannot schedule a meeting until they can find a time that does not conflict with their regular work. Even after meetings have been scheduled, members may fight over minor points in a project proposal, although they may unanimously agree with its thrust. For example, the U.S. Senate operates a number of standing committees in which members frequently attempt to direct a project so that it benefits the citizens who elected them to office.

Sometimes projects are delayed for years because standing committees create so much red tape. For example, five years may elapse from the time a new course is proposed until it is approved at a university, primarily because so many standing committees at various organizational levels must review the project.

As one alternative to a standing committee, organizations often create an *ad hoc* committee, a temporary committee, to complete a particular objective, after which it disbands. The use of *ad hoc* committees allows the organization to respond to problems as they surface, without being weighed down by the excessive red tape that can be generated by too many standing committees.

Task Forces. Task forces represent another approach organizations use to complete a particular objective. Like a temporary committee, a *task force* is set up to accomplish a specific objective, after which it disbands. However, it differs from a temporary committee in that its members are drawn from the various departments whose work overlaps relative to the objective. If a task force were to develop a new method for rating employee performance, some departments that would appoint members are personnel, production, finance, and training. In addition, an individual assigned to a task force works on it for an extended period, sometimes part time but frequently full time. In this sense, the task force violates the concept of unity of command, since the individual is responsible to both the head of the task force and his regular superior. This violation is especially pronounced if an individual works on the task force only on a part-time basis.

There are many advantages to the task force. Since individuals from various parts of the organization are on it, they usually possess more specialized knowledge than if they were selected from only one department. Members also understand the viewpoints of their superiors relative to the objective. In addition, it is much easier to implement a plan that will affect various departments if each is represented in the decision.

Disadvantages. Task forces and committees can be ineffective if their members are not rewarded for outstanding work. Frequently a superior is totally unaware of the work that his or her subordinate has accomplished. Efforts also can be hampered if a superior assigns his least effective subordinates to the task force or committee because he needs his effective employees for his regular work. Such assignments could be viewed as punishment. However, some task forces and committees are critical, and when a superior feels the work is important, he or she will typically assign the most effective employees. In fact, a person's success is sometimes assured because of his or her outstanding performance on a critical task force.

Typical Methods
of Organizing

There are several typical methods for designing or redesigning an organization. All involve the concept of hierarchy, which must be considered before managers can undertake any specific project. These methods of organizing fall roughly into five topical areas: bases of departmentation, centralization and federal decentralization, conglomerates, project management and the matrix form of organization, and vertical and horizontal integration.

Bases of Departmentation

Setting up departments or distinct subunits allows an organization to divide its work according to the kinds of tasks it faces. It is also easier for individuals to identify with a small group or department than with the entire organization. Although there are many ways to construct departments, four methods in general use are by purpose or product, by function, by place, and by clientele. An organization can have recourse to more than one method.

By Purpose or Product. When an organization sets up departments in terms of the specific goods or services it produces, it is departmentalizing by *purpose or product*. A textile firm organized by product (see Figure 3.3) would have separate divisions for towels, sheets, bedspreads, and blankets.

A major advantage of departmentation by product is that each unit operates independently. If one department needs to be revamped or shut down for a time, the other units can still function effectively.

By Function. Another common method of departmentalizing is to construct the organization in terms of the basic *functions* it performs, with separate departments for finance, industrial relations, marketing, and so forth. Special-

Figure 3.3 Departmentation by Product

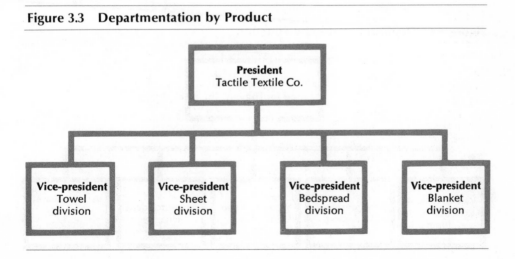

ists are grouped together, usually because they understand each other and can learn from each other when a problem occurs in their jurisdictions. Research chemists in a food products company (see Figure 3.4) are typically grouped together because they must interact to generate new ideas and fulfill their basic mission—the creation of new products. The food company also uses departmentation by function in the upper units of the organization for its marketing staff, industrial relations staff, and others.

If top managers structure the organization predominantly by function, individuals may identify too strongly with their respective departments, since everyone within a particular unit has essentially the same background. This identification is natural, for a specialist usually prefers to associate with other specialists in his or her area of competence. However, problems of coordination can easily occur if different departments begin to compete for scarce resources. In essence, the frictions that can arise in the functional organization are similar to those that occur between line and staff. In both instances, the general purpose of producing the final good or service can be adversely affected.

By Place. It is also common for an organization to departmentalize by *place,* with a department for each major region in which it is active. Some sales organizations operate in this fashion, as illustrated in Figure 3.5. Customer preferences may differ from one part of the country to another. Having a separate department for each section of the country allows each department

Figure 3.4   Departmentation by Function

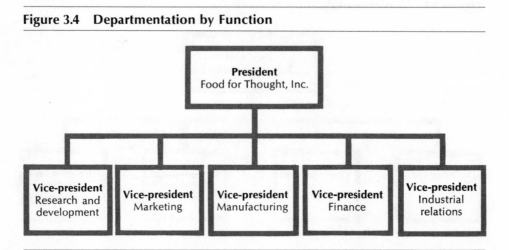

Figure 3.5 Departmentation by Place

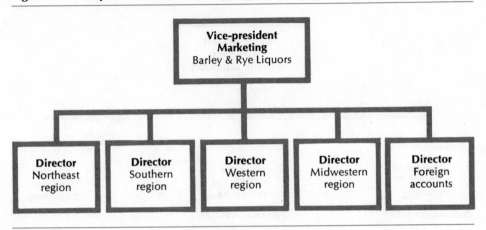

to focus on its own special needs and problems. Top managers frequently delegate a great amount of authority and responsibility to these departments, since the managers at headquarters are so far removed from local customer preferences that they cannot make effective decisions.

Usually departmentation by place is accompanied by a decentralized structure. Each department is allowed to make decisions tailored to the problems within a particular region. However, the advantage of decentralization can become a distinct disadvantage if top management is so far removed from activities in any region that it no longer understands its unique problems. In such a case, top managers can make incorrect decisions purely because they have a distorted concept of a particular department's work.

By Clientele. The fourth type of departmentation is by *clientele,* with each unit serving a different market or market segment. A cosmetics company might use several sales departments, one concerned with the general public, one devoted to wholesale dealers, and another focusing on sales to institutional buyers, like beauty salons (see Figure 3.6).

Centralization and Federal Decentralization

Until the end of World War I, centralized structures were typical, with departments organized by function. In the centralized functional organization, top managers made the decisions that were then implemented by functional specialists throughout the hierarchy.

At the turn of the twentieth century, the DuPont Company began to move

Figure 3.6   Departmentation by Clientele

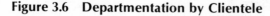

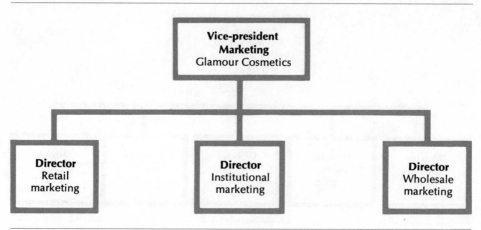

away from the centralized functional organization. An executive committee made the strategic decisions, but various subdivisions were allowed to exercise a great amount of responsibility and authority.

Federal Decentralization. In 1919 Alfred Sloan of General Motors developed the concept of *federal decentralization,* which is closely related to the DuPont approach. Federal decentralization is a combination of departmentation by function and by product (see Figure 3.7). At the headquarters level, specialists are grouped into identifiable departments by function. However, the various operating divisions are organized by product, such as Buick and Chevrolet. The operating divisions are self-contained; that is, all or most of the capabilities necessary to produce its final product are housed within each division's framework. Top management allows each unit to operate independently throughout a reporting period that may be as long as two or three years. If a division needs specialized services, the top managers provide them. They have direct authority over the functional specialists who work under the jurisdiction of the executive vice-president of the operations staff. For example, if the Buick division needs the help of design engineers to iron out difficulties in new models, the executive vice-president of the operations staff will ask the head of the design department to honor the request.

Integration. To integrate the efforts of the various subdivisions, top management frequently relies on two committees: the executive committee and the finance committee (see Figure 3.7). An executive committee consists of a small number of top managers who make the policies that guide the activities of the operating divisions. For example, the executive committee at General Motors in the 1920s decided to pursue a policy of changing styles of cars on an annual or biannual basis. This strategy was then put into action by the operating divisions of the company. A finance committee monitors the performance of the operating divisions; throughout a given reporting period, each division operates independently, and at the end, the finance committee evaluates its relative performance. If a particular division has become unprofitable or inefficient, the finance committee may initiate changes, such as recommending that a new head be appointed or decreasing the amount of financial support for the next reporting period.

A distinct advantage of federal decentralization is that the heads of the various operating divisions do not constantly check with top management. The managers respond to problems as they arise, since they are in charge of all activities within their divisions within a given reporting period. When used correctly, federal decentralization combines the best of both worlds: independence for the operating divisions, and coordination by top management through the executive and finance committees.

Frequently, federal decentralization is confused with geographical dispersion of units. They are not the same and do not always exist together. Even if a company has several plants distributed throughout a region or country, it can be highly centralized if all major decisions must be cleared through headquarters.

Conglomerates

An organization uses federal decentralization if its operating divisions are producing similar or related products. For example, all of the operating divisions at General Motors and Ford Motor Company produce automobiles or automotive parts. A *conglomerate*, in contrast, is a combination of two or more companies that produce unrelated products. Usually a conglomerate includes a large number of companies, but the essence of this form of organization is simply that the firms in it are unrelated.

A major advantage of conglomerates is that they are not subject to antitrust regulation, for they do not attempt to eliminate or reduce competition. In addition, a conglomerate is theoretically more flexible than any of its companies, for its top managers can transfer resources from one enterprise to another when they decide that changes must be made.

One problem with conglomerates is that it is difficult for top management to be familiar with the unique characteristics of all the industries under their direction, which can lead to poor decision making. This problem is compounded in that, when a conglomerate buys a new firm, it is common practice

Figure 3.7 Organization Chart of General Motors Corporation

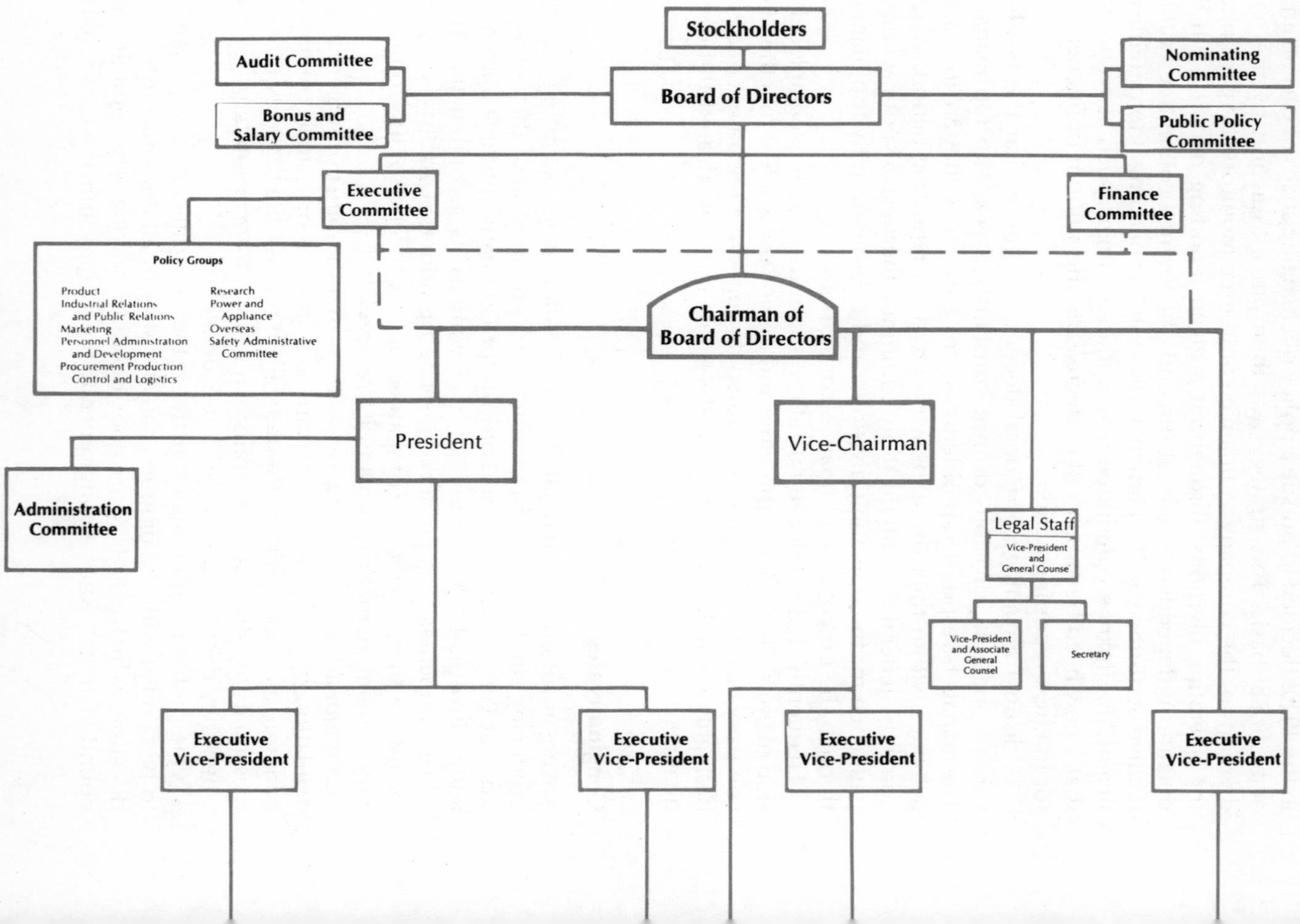

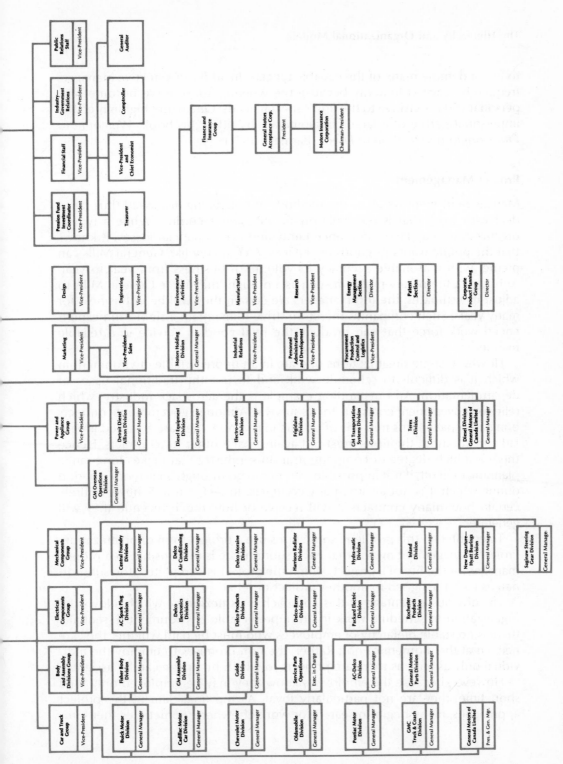

From *1975 General Motors Report on Programs of Public Interest* (Detroit, Mich.: General Motors Corporation, 1976), p. 8. Reprinted by permission.

to fire or demote many of the capable officers. In addition, effective managers frequently leave voluntarily because the working atmosphere becomes impersonal and insensitive to the firm's special needs. One writer highlighted the impersonal nature of a large conglomerate by titling his book: *Welcome to Our Conglomerate—You're Fired!* (Barmash 1971).

Project Management

Management employs all of the methods of organizing discussed thus far to deal with work that is relatively predictable and recurring. While a typical organization may face some uncertainty and even financial losses, it knows that the public wants its goods or services. A company like General Mills can predict with reasonable accuracy its volume of business from year to year. Although a temporary problem such as a drought may force General Mills to adjust its estimates, the top managers are certain they will be in business for many years. Such companies therefore strive to maintain a stable and experienced work force that can produce the final good or service in a reliable manner.

However, some organizations operate in an unpredictable environment in which it is difficult to schedule work and to use the traditional bases of departmentation. An outstanding example is the aerospace industry, which relies on government contracts for its survival. Although government contracts bring aerospace firms millions of dollars in revenue, they are awarded irregularly. In addition, the firms must bid against each other for contracts. Hence there is a high degree of competition in this industry that makes long-range planning difficult, if not impossible. A firm can go through an extended period during which it is not awarded any contracts. In fact, a firm is never entirely certain how many contracts it will receive or how much revenue they will generate.

To counteract this problem, some firms use a *project* form of organization. *Project management* means that each subordinate is responsible to a project manager for the life of a project. When the project is completed, the subordinate is either assigned to another project or let go.

The obvious advantage of this approach is its flexibility, which allows the organization to schedule work in an unpredictable environment. Essentially there is no stable hierarchy of employees who must be paid whether they are needed at the moment or not. Rather, the firm promises to employ the individual only as long as there are projects to which he or she can be assigned.

However, because the employees know they may be employed only for a short time, they are not particularly loyal. As the final date of the project approaches, many begin to search for work elsewhere. Sometimes their productivity becomes so low the project fails or falls short of expectations. In addition, the organization can easily waste a considerable amount of money in start-up time, since new employees must be hired at the beginning of each project. Usually these employees do not operate at peak levels of efficiency for some weeks or months, until they become familiar with the company's operations.

Matrix Organization

To eliminate the problems of project management, executives have devised a modified approach called the *matrix organization,* which is a combination of departmentation by function and by product. The product departments that carry out the projects are permanent or relatively permanent parts of the organization, and they draw on the resources and personnel of the functional departments to handle their different projects (see Figure 3.8). Both the product departments and the functional departments, such as engineering and manufacturing, report directly to the general manager.

The essence of the matrix organization is its use of dual lines of authority. The product manager has budgetary and overall responsibility for the successful completion of the project. However, the functional line managers have technical authority over the projects that each product department must finish. Each project is carried out by a product manager and a group of employees who are lent to the task by the functional line managers. When the project ends, the employees' superiors in the functional departments assign them to another project or activity. Employees in the matrix organization thus possess more job security than is possible under the pure form of project management.

The matrix organization is similar to federal decentralization in that both combine departmentation by function and by product. However, the subordinate does not report to two superiors under federal decentralization, while it is necessary for him to do so in the matrix organization.

A major problem in the matrix organization is its open violation of the principle of unity of command, for each subordinate reports to both a functional line superior and a product manager. This violation is extreme if the employee's functional superior assigns him or her to two or three projects simultaneously, since the employee must complete work for several superiors in a limited time. In that situation, it is almost inevitable that the subordinate will experience frustration, for he or she must please several superiors, all of whose evaluations can influence pay increases and promotions. Under these conditions, such negative consequences as a low rate of productivity and a high rate of absenteeism emerge (Kahn et al. 1964).

Figure 3.8 The Matrix Organization

Each product manager has budgetary and overall authority over the project being completed by his group (blue dotted lines); the functional managers have technical authority over each project (gray dotted lines). Thus, employees report to their product manager regarding their work on the project, and to their functional manager on questions of technical expertise and on routine matters such as salary and employee benefits.

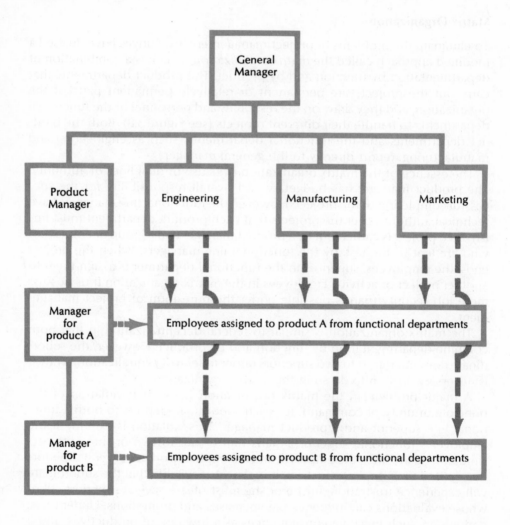

Another difficulty with the matrix organization is that product managers may struggle over the control of scarce resources. For example, two product managers may want the services of an outstanding engineer. Similarly, officers in the functional departments may fight with the product managers over the control of scarce resources. A functional line superior may not want a subordinate to work on a project simply because it will make his or her own work load heavier. Still, the matrix organization is suitable for an environment that is highly unpredictable (Galbraith 1973); in fact, it is hard to imagine another organizational structure that could work as well.

The matrix organization also can be modified for stable environments. A number of colleges of business and management now employ a modified version. A faculty member is responsible to his or her immediate superior within a particular discipline, such as accounting, marketing, or organizational behavior. The faculty member's performance is also evaluated by product leaders in the college in terms of his contributions to their programs—doctoral, master of business administration (MBA), undergraduate, and executive development and training. At the end of the year, the pooled judgments of a faculty member's immediate superiors and the leaders within each of the program areas of the college determine his or her future salary and promotion.

Vertical and Horizontal Integration

As suggested above, managers employ some methods of organization to reduce the amount of uncertainty that they face. For example, a conglomerate or a federally decentralized company can be highly successful even if some of its subdivisions are unprofitable. Two other methods of organizing have been devised to reduce uncertainty: vertical and horizontal integration.

Vertical integration is the construction of an organization so that it includes all steps in the production process, from the extraction of raw materials through the manufacture of the final product and its sale to the general public. A vertically integrated firm thus is not dependent on other organizations at any stage in the production process. This independence is invaluable in many instances, for numerous small firms have been forced into bankruptcy when they could not acquire critical supplies. Ernest Tenor Weir founded Weirton Steel Co. and made it a major success by integrating vertically, since he purchased his own deposits of iron ore and did not have to rely on the major steel companies for this critical item. Other small steel companies went out of business during periods of economic recession, because the major steel companies cut off their supplies of iron ore just when they needed them to survive.

If a company attempts to dominate a market at one particular stage in the production process, it is tending toward *horizontal integration*. The company is also flirting with antitrust laws, since its aim is to eliminate or reduce competition at that stage of the production process. A current political issue, for example, is whether laws should be passed to prevent the large oil companies, many of which are already vertically integrated, from becoming horizontally integrated as well by taking on uranium and solar energy interests.

Inherent
Tendencies
in Organizations

As this chapter has suggested, the hierarchy is the basic concept underlying the models managers use to construct organizations. Within the hierarchy, an organization and its members and subunits show certain inherent tendencies

An Inherent Tendency in Organizations?

Work expands so as to fill the time available for its completion. . . . Thus, an elderly lady of leisure can spend the entire day in writing and dispatching a postcard to her niece at Bognor Regis. . . . The total effort that would occupy a busy man for three minutes all told may in this fashion leave another person prostrate after a day of doubt, anxiety, and toil. . . .

From this description of the factors at work the student of political science will recognize that administrators are more or less bound to multiply. . . . Space will not allow of detailed analysis but the reader will be interested to know that research began in the British Navy Estimates. . . . The strength of the Navy in 1914 could be shown as 146,000 officers and men, 3249 dockyard officials and clerks, and 57,000 dockyard workmen. By 1928 there were only 100,000 officers and men and only 62,439 workmen, but the dockyard officials and clerks by then numbered 4558. As for warships, the strength in 1928 was a mere fraction of what it had been in 1914—fewer than 20 capital ships in commission as compared with 62. Over the same period the Admiralty officials had increased in number from 2000 to 3569, providing (as was remarked) "a magnificent navy on land."

C. Northcote Parkinson, *Parkinson's Law* (Boston: Houghton Mifflin, 1957), pp. 2 and 7.

in responding to pressures. These tendencies include forming political alliances, competing with each other, and increasing efforts to meet challenging goals.

Forming Political Alliances

The Hawthorne study described in chapter 2 demonstrated that informal relations in a group normally do not correspond to formal role prescriptions or a formal organization chart. This early finding has been extended by other researchers to incorporate the concept of the political nature of organizations. Melville Dalton (1959) views an organization as a series of cliques, with members attempting to provide benefits for individuals within their cliques that are not available to others. For example, one individual might be able to give the other members of his or her clique scarce resources such as comfortable offices, typewriters, and sophisticated audio-visual equipment.

Because of the impersonal nature of the hierarchy, it is often advantageous for individuals to form political alliances in which members typically can trust and interact comfortably with one another. They can also cover up mistakes for one another. Political allies additionally provide mutually beneficial information. To preserve these advantages, they frequently scrutinize closely the values of a new member in the organization before accepting him or her fully.

In short, political alliances help decrease the uncertainty individuals and groups face in an organization. They seem to be an inevitable by-product of the hierarchy.

The Tendency to Compete

Still, it is common for individuals in a group to be highly competitive. There are a number of factors over which they vie, such as promotions and pay increases. In fact, some research indicates that individuals have an inherent tendency to compete (Harlow and Hanke 1975). Two researchers have shown that uncooperative behavior in experimental studies tends to occur much more than would be expected by chance (Siegel and Fouraker 1960). This result obtains even when individuals can choose to cooperate and when it would be mutually beneficial to do so.

Behavior within the hierarchy is very complex. Groups are political systems that serve to protect their members; at the same time, individuals are highly competitive with each other, both within and between groups.

Working Toward Goals

Although these problems are significant, they are not insolvable. Management can link individuals and groups in the hierarchy by establishing goals toward which all members of the organization strive. The final inherent tendency in organizations is that individuals will increase their levels of performance to accomplish difficult but attainable goals (Locke 1968; Locke and Bryan, 1967). It is management's task to develop a series of goals that interrelate the work of individuals and groups.

There are many other inherent tendencies in organizations, some of which are examined in the later chapters of this book. Those tendencies discussed here relate directly to the concept of the hierarchy. To link members of the hierarchy, it is necessary to set common goals. If members of the organization see that working together toward a common goal benefits all of them, they are likely to overcome the tendency to compete.

Summary

The hierarchy is a critical concept in organization design. Most of the basic concepts within this dimension, including the distinction between line and staff, centralization versus decentralization, span of control, unity of command, and coordination, revolve around the complexities of hierarchical relations.

The concept of hierarchy also underpins the various approaches management can use to construct organizations. Some of the most important of these approaches focus on the bases of departmentation, centralization and federal decentralization, conglomerates, project management, the matrix form of organization, vertical integration, and horizontal integration.

Finally, some inherent tendencies in organizations occur within the hierarchy. Organizations are political systems in which groups strive to protect their own members. However, individuals are highly competitive with one another, both within and between groups. Thus, to link individuals and groups together, it is necessary to establish common goals that must be accomplished by members of the organization, for individuals will attempt to meet difficult but attainable objectives.

Discussion Questions

1. What are the similarities and differences between Barnard's unit concept and Likert's linking-pin concept? Do you think they are appropriate for different situations?

2. In what type of environment is a matrix organization appropriate? What problems would you expect to emerge when the matrix organization is used?

3. Organizations are political institutions; individuals have a tendency to compete; individuals will attempt to increase their level of performance to meet difficult but attainable goals. Do you think these three statements represent true tendencies in organizations? How are they related?

4. What are the main differences in the matrix organization, conglomerates, and federal decentralization?

5. Of the four bases of departmentation, which one involves friction between departments that is comparable to the friction between line and staff? Why?

6. Why are permanent committees created in an organization? What are some of the major problems that can occur when permanent committees are used? What is the difference between *ad hoc* committees and task forces? Why are *ad hoc* committees and task forces used in organizations?

Critical Incidents

NOTE: *These critical incidents can be used by the whole class with the case observational method (see Appendix), or used for thought and discussion by individual class members.*

1. A large state university has a total enrollment of 35,000: 5,000 graduate students and 30,000 undergraduates. This school has grown to its current size from 10,000 students in 1960. At that time, there were two major types of organizational units in the university: departments, such as chemistry and sociology, and colleges for professional schools, such as education and business. Each of the 40 departments and 10 colleges operated in a relatively independent fashion, since each worked directly with the university budget committee and controlled its own budget. However, the new chancellor now wants to integrate the efforts of all of the various departments and colleges. He has grouped them into 5 major divisions, each headed by a provost or chief officer. Also, he has appointed 4 vice-chancellors to advise him and help him administer the university. Hence, the 5 provosts are line officers who report directly to the chancellor, and the vice-chancellors are staff officers.

Questions: What are some of the advantages of the current organization design of this university? Of the previous design? What are some of the problems that may emerge under the current form of organization? How might the design be modified to eliminate these problems?

2. The Machon Company is a research and development firm in the electronics industry that has created several specialized items it sells to aerospace firms. This company has become very successful over the years because of the technical brilliance of its founder, Mr. Machon, who has always run the organizational activities very informally. However, the organization has grown dramatically in the past four years; there are now 400 engineers and scientists who are charged with the responsibility for developing new products, and 3,000 technicians who manufacture the specialized items. In addition, the company employs 80 salesmen. The three departments—research, manufacturing, and sales—operate independently.

In the past year, the research department has lost 10 of its best engineers, all of whom claim that they are in dead-end positions. This claim appears valid, since Mr. Machon's top associates are in their forties and have been with the firm since its founding. In addition, the sales department claims it cannot fulfill its orders because of the inefficiency of the production department.

Questions: Assume you are a consultant Mr. Machon has hired to redesign his organization. What are some of the problems you will probably face? How will you solve them?

Suggested Readings

Hutchinson, John. *Organizations: Theory and Classical Concepts.* New York: Holt, Rinehart and Winston, 1967, 178 pages, paperback.
   Hutchinson briefly reviews some of the major theories of organization and focuses on many of the concepts highlighted in this part and other parts of the textbook.

Parkinson, C. Northcote. *Parkinson's Law.* Boston: Houghton Mifflin, Sentry Ed. 1957, 115 pages, paperback.

This is a humorous but insightful treatment of problems that occur in hier-archical organizations. Students consistently rate this book as outstanding.

Perrow, Charles, *Complex Organizations: A Critical Essay*, Glenview, Ill.: Scott, Foresman and Company, 1972, 223 pages, paperback.
This is a sociological summary and critique of many of the most important theories of organizations. The basic proposition in this book is that the bureaucratic form of organization is far superior to all others.

Major
Influences
on Design

4

- **Organic and Mechanistic Structures**
- **The Impact of Technology on Design and Success**
- **The Impact of the Environment on Design and Success**
- **The Information-Processing Synthesis**

Performance Objectives

1. To describe the two major designs for organizations, mechanistic and organic.

2. To understand the impact of the two major influences—technology and external environmental uncertainty—on the proper design of an organization.

3. To be aware of important research that has shown a relationship among technology, design, and success, and among environmental uncertainty, design, and success.

4. To understand how all of the studies on technology and environmental uncertainty can be integrated by Jay Galbraith's approach, which sees an organization as an information-processing system.

Managers react to problems they must solve by using particular methods and models to construct organizations (see chapter 3). Companies in the aerospace industry, for instance, rely heavily on the matrix form of organization, because they must periodically establish new work groups to complete projects of relatively short duration.

This chapter focuses on specific organization designs managers can employ to achieve success. Researchers have identified two major factors—technology and external environmental uncertainty—that managers should consider when they design or redesign an organization. *Technology* refers to the means used to produce the final good or service of the organization (see chapter 2). An organization's technology includes, for example, its typewriters, assembly lines, and computers. *External environmental uncertainty* relates to the degree to which the organization is influenced by outside forces such as the passage of laws or the competition of other firms.

There are many possible ways to design or redesign an organization, and various types of structures an organization can take. This chapter analyzes these structures and examines the research studies that have related technology and external environmental uncertainty to design and success; it concludes by evaluating all of these studies in terms of their potential usefulness to the operating manager.

Organic

and Mechanistic

Structures

Two English researchers, Tom Burns and G. M. Stalker (1961), analyzed the organizational structures of 20 industrial firms in the United Kingdom. Their analysis suggested that there are two major types of organizational structures, mechanistic and organic. Essentially the *mechanistic* organization is highly bureaucratic, while the *organic,* its opposite, is flexible and responsive. Organizations exist along a continuum extending from mechanistic to organic. In real situations, it would be difficult if not impossible to identify an enterprise at one end of this continuum. However, it is possible to pinpoint differences between these two structures and to classify an organization as either more mechanistic or more organic.

In a sense, these two types of organizational structures represent the two major streams of thought in management—economics and behavioral science. A mechanistic organization focuses on efficient structure; an organic organization emphasizes the needs of employees within the structure. But the two types also can be compared in terms of some of the aspects of organization design discussed in chapter 3. There are seven important characteristics that differentiate the mechanistic from the organic organization (see Table 4.1). Three of these characteristics—division of labor, hierarchy of authority, and jobs and procedures—represent the traditional focus of the management field. The remaining four—motivation, style of leadership, group relations, and communication—reflect the behavioral processes highlighted in this book.

In the mechanistic organization, duties and responsibilities are divided by means of functional specialization. Everyone has a specialized role to play, and he or she typically works in a department that primarily or totally includes similar specialists. An example of functional specialization is the automotive assembly line, where workers perform routine jobs in which they are able to exercise only a very small amount of responsibility. In the organic organization, the division of labor emphasizes enlarging each worker's job so that the individual performs a variety of activities, and enriching it so that he or she also exercises significant responsibility. Top management of Volvo in Sweden has enlarged and enriched the work by deemphasizing the assembly line and allowing a work team to be responsible for the production of an entire car.

Table 4.1   Characteristics of Organic and Mechanistic Organizations

Characteristics of Structure	Mechanistic Organizations	Organic Organizations
1. Division of labor	Functional specialization or departmentation by function	Job enlargement and job enrichment
2. Hierarchy of authority	Clearly defined and centralized	Decentralized and participative
3. Jobs and procedures	Formal and standardized	Flexible
4. Behavioral processes		
a. Motivation	Primarily economic	Both economic and noneconomic
b. Leadership style	Authoritarian	Democratic
c. Group relations	Formal and impersonal	Informal and personal
d. Communication	Vertical and directive	Vertical and lateral consultative

A second feature that distinguishes mechanistic and organic organizations involves their hierarchy of authority. In the mechanistic organization, authority is clearly defined and centralized. Most individuals in the hierarchy operate in a limited sphere in which their authority is restricted. This feature is logically related to the concept of division of labor: The more specialized the work, the more clearly defined are the relative positions of individuals. In contrast, authority in the organic organization is decentralized, and individuals in the lower levels can make many decisions without double checking constantly with their superiors. In addition, most employees are involved in making decisions that directly influence their own work; hence the distinction between workers of various ranks tends to become blurred.

The specification of jobs and procedures used to complete the work is another feature that separates organic from mechanistic organizations. In a mechanistic structure, jobs and procedures are formal and standardized. Employees know exactly what procedures to follow in any situation, and what tasks are part of their jobs. In the organic organization, both jobs and the procedures for completing them are very flexible. When a problem occurs, the individuals directly affected attempt to solve it, regardless of the procedures specified in the official job classification system.

In the area of behavioral processes, motivation distinguishes mechanistic from organic organizations. To generate commitment from employees, leaders in the mechanistic organization rely primarily on economic motivation: Employees are paid a high wage to keep their productivity high. The organic organization uses both economic and noneconomic factors to motivate employees. While money is still important, other factors such as job enrichment and recognition from superiors for excellent performance are also highlighted.

In the mechanistic organization, the style of leadership is highly authoritarian. The leader's word is law, and the subordinate had better obey his or her commands. The opposite situation exists in the organic organization, for the leaders tend to be democratic and participative. As much as possible, the leader tries to involve his or her subordinates in any decision that will affect their position in the organization.

Mechanistic and organic organizations also differ with respect to interpersonal and group relations. In the mechanistic organization, communication is vertical and directive. That is, the superior gives commands to his or her subordinates (vertical) who are expected to respond to them immediately (directive). In the organic organization, communication is both vertical directive and lateral consultative. Superiors still issue commands to subordinates, but everyone also can communicate laterally with his or her equals when problems arise. Such communication is *consultative* because it does not involve giving orders to anyone else but, rather, exchanging opinions.

The Impact
of Technology
on Design and Success

There have been many studies of technology. However, only a few have emphasized the impact of technology on design and success. In this section, there is a review of three major studies in this area.

The Trist and Bamforth Study

Scientific management and human relations differ radically on the methods they use to motivate employees (see chapter 2). Proponents of scientific management favor mechanistic organizational structures: they would specialize the work to an extreme degree, but pay high wages to motivate the employee. From their perspective, individuals are primarily motivated by money. However, the human relations school favors organic structures, arguing that individuals are motivated by a variety of factors, only one of which is money. Advocates of this viewpoint believe job satisfaction is at least as important as financial rewards to an employee's productivity.

An important study that examined the impact of an extremely specialized organization design not only on job satisfaction but also on productivity was conducted by Eric Trist and K. W. Bamforth (1951) in England after World War II. While the results of this study do not resolve the critical argument between the schools of scientific management and human relations about the relative importance of money as a motivator, they serve as an important building block in the modern approaches now being advocated for the design of organizations.

The Problem. A major problem England has faced for many years is that its technology is aging. Because the Industrial Revolution originated in England, the country has had great difficulty both in building new technology and in winning the cooperation of labor unions in this endeavor. Normally the labor unions refuse to give up their traditional work privileges, such as *featherbedding*: using more workers than necessary to complete a job. In contrast, it is frequently argued that Japan and West Germany were lucky during World War II that their technologies were almost completely destroyed, because that forced them to create a new and efficient industrial order.

After World War II, the top management of large coal companies in England decided to modernize. To accomplish this objective, they introduced mass-production techniques for mining coal.

In England, coal mining has traditionally been done by teams of two to eight men. Each team operates independently in a specific section of the mine. Because each team is small and operates under dangerous conditions, cohesion among members tends to be high. In fact, members come to see one another almost as brothers, and they even assume responsibility for one another's families if anyone dies.

The mines in England have veins of coal of variable thickness. To modernize the process of extracting coal, the engineers in charge of the project installed a modified assembly line of approximately 50 workers and eliminated the use of the small, traditional work teams. This change gave each coal miner a cramped working space, only two yards by one yard. To complicate matters, some workers were not able to see the others in the tunnel and could converse with them only by shouting. Productivity declined dramatically.

The Solution. At this point, Eric Trist and other behavioral science researchers from the Tavistock Institute of London conducted long interviews with some of the miners. Trist's researchers found that many workers had developed the symptoms of extreme psychological stress and had begun to lose their sense of identity and masculinity. This last finding was especially interesting, since a coal miner is typically a strong, independent, and masculine individual (Goldthorpe et al. 1968).

To eliminate these problems, the researchers modified the assembly line. They rearranged the work processes so the miners could interact comfortably with one another, placing them close enough to each other to converse freely. Most importantly, the workers were encouraged to participate in decisions that directly influenced their work. For instance, the workers constructed a set of rules that controlled their salaries and their assignments to the mine's three work shifts. Productivity increased significantly, and the symptoms of psychological stress disappeared.

Sociotechnical System. The researchers began to view any organization as a *sociotechnical system:* one in which the formal demands of the organization should mesh with the psychological and social needs of the workers. In effect, the coal miners had worked for centuries in an organic organization, for the use of the small work teams allowed them to define their jobs and the procedures for completing them in a flexible manner. Because of the traditional method, the jobs of the coal miners were enriched in that each work team was solely responsible for extracting a specific amount of coal. In addition, there were several noneconomic sources of motivation, such as the cohesion of the work team.

When the engineers modernized the operations, they substituted a

Technology and Job Satisfaction

Robert Blauner has described in detail the devastating impact of the automotive assembly line on job satisfaction. This line is machine-paced, which means that the worker must complete his or her job cycle in a specified time. Typically the employee's job consists only of three or four simple motions that he or she can complete in a few seconds.

The workers feel *powerless,* since they must respond to the pace of the line. They also view their work as *meaningless,* since they do not understand the relationship between their jobs and the other activities in the organization (marketing, finance, etc). In addition, they feel *isolated* from other workers: The swift pace of the line inhibits even casual conversation. Finally, they see no *relationship* between their jobs and their overall goals in life: They work only to make money.

To combat these problems, most of these workers constantly daydream, either about setting up their own enterprises or sending their children to college in order to avoid the monotonous pace of the assembly line. Many also take up a hobby such as carpentry as an antidote to the boredom of their jobs.

Robert Blauner, *Alienation and Freedom* (Chicago: University of Chicago Press, 1964).

mechanistic organization (the assembly line) for the organic organization. The extreme form of the mechanistic organization precipitated a loss of identity among the coal miners and a decline in job satisfaction, both of which appeared to have an adverse effect on the level of productivity. While Eric Trist and his research team did not advocate a return to the traditional organizational structure, they did attempt to alter the modernized structure by means of participative management and redesign of the assembly line so it would become less mechanistic.

The Tavistock coal mining study does not hold that specialization per se is inefficient or evil. But it does argue that specialization or any other technology that disregards the needs of human beings will probably result in a significant decline in job satisfaction and productivity.

The Woodward Study

In 1965 Joan Woodward and her associates reported the results of a large-scale study of 100 English firms. This study is significant because Woodward was able to identify a relationship among the organizations' technologies, structures, and success. She found that the distinction between mechanistic and organic structures was important for understanding this relationship.

Woodward classified the 100 firms into three major groups according to type of technology (see chapter 3). Under the first type, *unit technology,* the organization spends a great amount of money on labor costs relative to capital investment in equipment, for example, with custom-made furniture that only highly skilled and well-paid workers can manufacture. The second type of technology is *mass production,* where the organization spends a great amount of money on labor but also invests heavily in capital equipment or machines, as on the automotive assembly line. The third type of technology is *process* or *automated technology,* where the organization does not spend much money on labor but does invest a large amount in capital equipment, for example, with an oil refinery or chemical plant.

Woodward rated each of the 100 firms studied according to an index of success consisting of such traditional measures as net income and percentage increase in market domination. Most successful unit-type firms were found to have an organic structure, and the unsuccessful unit-type firms generally employed a mechanistic structure (see Figure 4.1). This same relationship

---

Figure 4.1   The Relationship among Technology, Organizational Structure, and Success in 100 English Firms

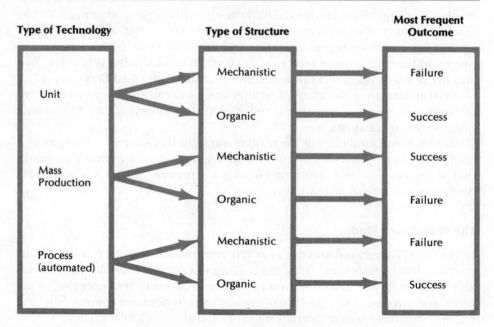

Type of Technology	Type of Structure	Most Frequent Outcome
Unit	Mechanistic	Failure
	Organic	Success
Mass Production	Mechanistic	Success
	Organic	Failure
Process (automated)	Mechanistic	Failure
	Organic	Success

Based on Joan Woodward, *Industrial Organization* (New York: Oxford University Press, 1965).

occurred in the continuous-process firms. However, the trend reversed in mass-production firms, for most successful companies were organized mechanistically, and the unsuccessful companies organically.

These findings suggest there is no "one best way" to organize a company. Rather, the approach that should be taken in designing an organization depends heavily on the technological system that underlies the production process.

Other research has generally confirmed Woodward's original findings (Harvey 1968). However, another research team in England that intensively analyzed the relationship between technology and organizational structure in 41 organizations only partially confirmed Woodward's original findings (Hickson et al. 1969). In effect, these researchers found that *size* seems to be a critical factor. If an enterprise is small, technology will directly affect structure, for it dominates the organization. Everything else—sales, marketing, accounting, and so forth—is a minor activity designed mainly to serve the technological requirements of the system. However, the influence of technology is weak in a large organization, for management must stress all activities to be successful.

While this revision of Woodward's approach is reasonable, it does not undermine the importance of technology, at least in a small organization. In addition, the top management of a large company could structure activities by breaking the organization into several independent subsystems. The impact of technology might then be expected to increase within each subsystem.

The Impact
of the Environment
on Design and Success

The second important factor that influences organization design is the degree of external environmental uncertainty. Three important studies in this area have been completed by Alfred Chandler, Tom Burns and G. M. Stalker, and Paul Lawrence and Jay Lorsch.

The Chandler Study

In 1962 Alfred Chandler, Jr. published a study that focused on the relationship between an organization's strategic plans and its design or structure. His conclusions were based primarily on historical analysis of 100 large companies. He also completed a detailed analysis of four companies: DuPont, General Motors, Standard Oil (New Jersey), and Sears, Roebuck. In this study, Chandler used historical documents, internal company records, correspondence, and interviews with some of the top managers in each of these four companies.

Chandler's major thesis was that the strategic plans of a company determine the type of organizational structure it does or should follow. Strategic plans, in turn, depend on the degree of certainty in the organization's environment. A successful organization in an industry that remains relatively stable in markets, raw materials, and production processes should not deviate from its strategic plans and should be structured mechanistically. If, however, environmental changes accelerate in the areas of market demands, availability of raw materials, or the use of new production processes, top management should alter its strategic plans through diversification into new product lines. This strategy of diversification decreases the probability that the organization will fail, since top management has spread its risk by relying on the success of several products. However, diversification should be accompanied by an organic organizational design, since top management must respond quickly to changes in the external environment that directly affect any of its product lines. Top management must meet the competition by allowing individuals and organizational subsystems to respond in a creative and responsible fashion, which would not be feasible in a highly centralized mechanistic organization.

The Burns and Stalker Study

As suggested by Chandler's study, top management in a mechanistic organization is typically not too concerned about designing or redesigning the organization if the firm is successful and exists in a stable environment in which it can predict its share of the market from year to year. However, since the world—and markets, sources of raw materials, and production processes—changes constantly, almost all firms eventually need to be redesigned to some extent.

Burns and Stalker conducted a study in 1961 to find out what kinds of redesign are successful when a firm with a stable technology and environment moves into new areas that are highly unpredictable and uncertain. They focused on 20 firms in the United Kingdom that were attempting to enter the electronics field. Previously, the firms had operated with similar traditional technologies in stable markets. However, the electronics field is highly competitive and dynamic, for inventions and innovations in processing work can dramatically and rapidly affect the firm's success.

Burns and Stalker's major finding was that an organic structure was most effective in the electronics field or, by extension, in any industry that operates in an unpredictable and competitive environment. A fluid and flexible structure is necessary for a firm to react instantly to any changes in its environment. If a firm used a mechanistic approach, its bureaucratic structure would slow down its response to competition and other environmental factors such as changes in regulatory laws and the tactics of labor unions.

The Lawrence and Lorsch Study

Based on the research of Chandler and Burns and Stalker, it seems clear that a mechanistic structure can be effective when conditions in an environment are certain but an organic structure is preferable when they are uncertain. However, these two studies do not deal with the specific techniques top management can use to change the design of an organization as it attempts to respond to environmental pressures. Lawrence and Lorsch (1967) examined this issue.

Degrees of Certainty. Lawrence and Lorsch selected three types of environment for analysis, defining them by such criteria as the changes in the number of inventions and number of firms within a particular industry over time. For each environment they chose a representative industry for study. One type of environment reflects a high degree of certainty. It is typified by firms in the container industry, where the technology is stable and sales are relatively predictable over time. Only a few innovations have been introduced into this industry in recent years, and only a few new firms have been created.

Within the food industry, the environment is moderately certain. Even though innovations do occur and each company's sales figures do change over time, the future is relatively predictable. General Foods and other large companies in this industry neglected the "natural food" mania for many years until they realized their new but small competitors were taking away many of their sales and customers. These large companies have successfully entered this area by producing their own natural foods, many of which have become very popular.

Finally, there is the highly uncertain or unpredictable environment, such as that of the plastics industry. Innovations occur rapidly, so a firm's position can change equally rapidly if it does not respond continually to the changing needs of its customers and the new approaches of its competitors.

Certainty and Structure. Within each of the three industries, Lawrence and Lorsch pinpointed one successful and one unsuccessful firm. They then compared the organizational structures of the successful firms to the unsuccessful ones (see Table 4.2).

Table 4.2 Design Strategies

Industry	Environment	Successful Organization Design
Container industry	Highly certain and predictable	Mechanistic structure
Food industry	Moderately certain and predictable	Movement toward organic structure: integrators or teams of integrators
Plastics industry	Highly uncertain and unpredictable	Organic structure: formal departments of integrators

Based on Paul Lawrence and Jay Lorsch, *Organization and Environment* (Boston: Harvard Business School, Division of Research, 1967).

In the container industry, with its highly certain environment, the successful firm used a mechanistic approach. According to Lawrence and Lorsch, the bureaucratic hierarchy, with its rigid specification of jobs and procedures, is an efficient way to coordinate the work. Since innovations are rare, the main worries of top managers are the quality of the goods they produce and the correct scheduling of deliveries so customers do not become dissatisfied. If coordination and communication begin to break down, managers can integrate their interdependent tasks by following bureaucratic rules.

However, the mechanistic organization and its hierarchy proved inadequate in the food industry's moderately certain environment. To solve problems of coordination, the successful firm relied on *integrators:* individuals charged with coordinating the work of interdependent departments or activities. These integrators cannot be classified as either line or staff personnel. Rather, they have enough authority to ensure that line managers whose tasks are interdependent work together toward the common goals of the organization.

The successful firm in the highly uncertain environment of the plastics industry had further formalized the work of integrators. To ensure that interdependent departments would coordinate their activities and respond quickly to environmental changes, the successful firm established formal departments of integration that both coordinated the work of interdependent units and monitored the external environment for any changes that might influence the firm's competitive position.

Lawrence and Lorsch found a tendency for organizations to move from a mechanistic to an organic structure as the degree of environmental uncertainty rose. Successful firms became *differentiated*—they created many departments to handle new problems—as the degree of external environmental uncertainty increased. To bring together new departments performing interdependent tasks as they respond to external environmental pressure, the successful firms relied heavily on integrators.

The Information-Processing
Synthesis

In 1973 Jay R. Galbraith attempted to integrate all of the studies concerned with the issues of technology and environmental uncertainty. However, his analysis shifted the focus away from technology and environmental uncertainty. To Galbraith, an organization is an information-processing system. Individuals and groups must coordinate their efforts if the organization is to be successful. But if the channels of information in the organization do not function effectively, it is frequently difficult or impossible to coordinate efforts. A firm may lose its bid for a major government contract because various departments such as production and finance fail to provide sufficient information to the task force set up to write the contract proposal. Or a firm may not respond adequately to a new competitor because its departments have only a partial understanding of the magnitude of the effort being made by the upstart.

Four Strategies

When an organization can no longer process information efficiently, communication and coordination break down. Thus, a firm that is experiencing difficulties must either reduce its need to process information or increase its capacity to do so (see Table 4.3). According to Galbraith, technology and environmental uncertainty must be evaluated in terms of their influence on the processing of information in an organization.

If a firm decides to reduce its need to process information, it can use two strategies. First, it can increase its use of *slack* or additional resources; that is, the firm can bring in additional resources—employees, materials, or whatever—so as to produce more without actually increasing its previous levels of performance. For example, if a firm is having difficulty meeting its deadlines, it

Table 4.3   Galbraith's Four Strategies to Process Information

A. To reduce the need for processing information:
1. Create slack or additional resources, e.g., increase the number of employees
2. Create self-contained units

B. To increase the capacity for processing information:
3. Invest in vertical information systems, e.g., computers
4. Create lateral relations that cut across lines of authority, e.g., the matrix organization

From Jay Galbraith, *Designing Complex Organizations*, p. 15. Copyright © 1973 by Addison-Wesley Publishing Co., Inc. Adapted by permission.

can increase the number of employees or the amount of time it assigns to each project. Second, the firm can divide its work into *self-contained tasks,* in which each work group has available all the resources it needs to perform its jobs. If groups are not interdependent and do not need to work together, the problem of coordination among them is eliminated or reduced. Of course, the costs of either of these strategies may be prohibitive.

If the firm decides to increase its capacity to process information, it also has recourse to two strategies. First, it can invest in *vertical information systems* that speed communication and coordination from one hierarchical level to the next. The firm's other alternative is to develop *lateral decision processes* that cut across lines of authority. If it opts for this strategy, it is moving from a mechanistic toward an organic structure, allowing workers to communicate with each other and deal with problems directly, without going through superiors. It can also use integrators: people who keep communications open between departments.

Seven Steps

If a manager decides to employ the strategy of creating lateral decision processes, he or she has recourse to seven steps that move the organization along the continuum from a mechanistic to an organic structure (Figure 4.2). The manager might implement each step in turn, from the most mechanistic to the most organic, until he or she irons out the organization's problems. He or she might stop after step 3 if coordination between individuals and groups improves significantly. Hence the manager determines when the organization has reached the ideal degree of organic structure, one that is appropriate for its goals.

First, when two departments whose tasks are interdependent are having trouble coordinating their work, their managers may reduce the problem by

Figure 4.2   Galbraith's Strategies to Create Lateral Relations

Cutting across Traditional Lines of Authority

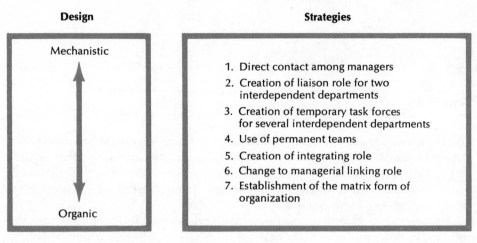

Design   Strategies

Mechanistic

1. Direct contact among managers
2. Creation of liaison role for two
   interdependent departments
3. Creation of temporary task forces
   for several interdependent departments
4. Use of permanent teams
5. Creation of integrating role
6. Change to managerial linking role
7. Establishment of the matrix form of
   organization

Organic

From Jay Galbraith, *Designing Complex Organizations,* p. 110. Copyright © 1973 by Addison-Wesley Publishing Co., Inc. Adapted by permission.

means of *direct contact.* Preferably this contact should be informal and face-to-face, for the managers should confront the problem directly, but in a nonthreatening manner. If this tactic fails, the organization can create a *liaison* role that links two interdependent departments. The next option is to set up a *temporary task force* to handle coordination among several interdependent departments. Members are usually drawn from all departments that will be affected by any course of action the task force recommends (see chapter 3). Once coordination improves significantly, the task force goes out of existence.

If this approach fails, the organization can establish *permanent teams* to handle the problem of coordination. As with a task force, members would typically be drawn from all departments whose work must be coordinated. Failure of the team approach would lead to the use of *integrators* charged with coordinating activities, although they would have no authority to make line managers accept their suggestions. If this does not work smoothly, the integrators can be placed in a *managerial linking role,* giving them power to force line managers to coordinate their work. If all these steps fail, the top managers can totally redesign the organization into the *matrix form.*

The beauty of Galbraith's information-processing approach is that it provides a practicing manager with a set of guidelines to follow in designing or redesigning his or her organization. While more research is obviously necessary to determine how well this approach works in practice, it does integrate and clarify many of the theoretical and practical issues basic to constructing effective and efficient organizations.

Summary

There are two major types of organizational designs—mechanistic and organic. The mechanistic organization is highly bureaucratic and rigid; the organic organization is informal and flexible. These two types represent the end points on a continuum; most organizational designs can be described as either "more mechanistic" or "more organic."

Two factors, technology and external environmental uncertainty, are important in determining whether an organization should use a mechanistic or an organic structure to achieve success. The Tavistock coal mining study indicated that an organization cannot easily substitute an extreme form of mechanistic organization for an extreme form of organic organization. From this perspective, an organization can be seen as a sociotechnical system, that is, one in which the formal demands of the organization should mesh with the psychological and social needs of the employees. Woodward's research indicates that successful organizations using unit or process technology generally employ an organic structure; and successful firms operating under conditions of mass-production technology usually rely on a mechanistic structure. However, Derek Pugh and David Hickson's research suggests that technology and design are related only in small firms.

Chandler's research on environmental uncertainty suggests that firms following a strategy of diversification find an organic structure is most effective for coordinating their various departments. Burns and Stalker's research generally confirms this finding. The research of Lawrence and Lorsch goes further by suggesting the successful organization in an uncertain environment is one that uses integrators, individuals charged with coordinating the work of interdependent departments or activities.

Jay Galbraith has integrated all of these ideas by defining an organization as an information-processing system. Technology and environmental uncertainty directly influence the flow of information in an organization. If the flow of information between individuals and groups whose work is interdependent becomes problematic, the organization can either reduce its need to process information or increase its capacity to do so. If the organization decides to reduce its need to process information, it can either create slack (additional) resources or establish self-contained units. If the organization opts for increasing its capacity for processing information, it can either invest in vertical information systems or implement lateral decision processes that cut across traditional lines of authority.

For the firm that decides to use lateral decision processes, the distinction between mechanistic and organic organizations becomes very important. According to Galbraith, a manager can take seven steps that move the organization along the continuum from a mechanistic to an organic structure. The manager can use these steps in sequence until he or she determines that the organization has achieved enough coordination to be successful. In sequence, these steps are: direct contact between managers; creation of a liaison role to link interdependent departments; use of temporary task forces to coordinate the work of several departments; substitution of permanent teams for task forces; creation of an integrating role or position whose incumbent does not possess the formal authority to force line managers to work together; use of an officer in a managerial linking role who does have the power to tell line managers how to coordinate their efforts; and, finally, construction of a matrix organization.

Discussion Questions

1. How is the ideal design for an organization that produces goods likely to differ from that for one that sells a service?

2. Is an organization in the public sector, such as a government agency, less susceptible to the pressures of environmental uncertainty than a privately owned organization? Is a nonprofit organization, such as a church, less susceptible than one run for profit?

3. What do Lawrence and Lorsch mean by an integrator? How might an integrator go about coordinating the work of two or more departments without actually being in charge of them?

4. In defining an organization as an information-processing system, has Jay Galbraith disregarded the issues of technology and environmental uncertainty? Why or why not? Do you think Galbraith's definition applies to all organizations?

5. Chandler's thesis is that structure follows strategy. What does this mean?

6. Both human relations and scientific management argued that their respective approaches were the "one best way" to run an organization (see chapter 2). How does Woodward's research agree and disagree with the position that there is "one best way" to organize and manage?

Critical Incidents

NOTE: *These critical incidents can be used by the whole class with the case observational method (see Appendix), or used for thought and discussion by individual class members.*

1. The following quotation is taken from an employee manual for one of the largest department stores in Chicago in the year 1857 (Shultz and Coleman 1959):

> The employee who is in the habit of smoking Spanish cigars, being shaved at the barber's, going to dances and other places of amusement will surely give his employer reasons to be suspicious of his integrity and honesty.

> Each employee must not pay less than five dollars per year to the church and must attend Sunday School regularly.

> Men employees are given one evening a week for courting and two if they go to prayer meeting.

Questions: What kind of design is this organization using, mechanistic or organic? Do you think an organization could be designed in this manner today? According to Woodward's analysis, would this or a similar approach be more appropriate for one type of technology than for others? Why or why not?

2. The National Weather Service has a unique organizational problem. Most weather forecasts are made from its national center in Miami and from its regional centers. Still, there are at least 400 small units spread throughout the United States, none with more than 15 employees. The local stations use the predictions provided by the national and regional centers, but they adjust them for local conditions. Employees in these small stations are constantly complaining that the headquarters and regional personnel neglect them completely. This complaint has some justification, for the stations are geographically isolated from one another. There is no doubt that these stations will survive, since weather forecasts have to be adjusted for local conditions.

Question: How would you redesign this organization to eliminate some of these complaints?

3. You are the president of the Melcher Company, which manufactures custom-made draperies. Your company, which employs 500 workers, is very successful. However, your personnel director recently completed a questionnaire survey of all employees that indicated job satisfaction is low. In addition, 20 of your best workers recently quit, and they will be hard to replace. If you lose any more of your better workers, you may find it difficult to produce enough drapes to keep your clients satisfied with your service.

Questions: How would you redesign your organization to reduce turnover? Should you try other ways to raise the level of job satisfaction among your employees? If yes, why? If not, why not? Would you give the same answers if your workers were unskilled?

Suggested Readings

Blauner, Robert. *Alienation and Freedom: The Factory Worker and His Industry.* Chicago: University of Chicago Press, 1964, 222 pages, paperback.
   Blauner discusses the relationship between technology and job satisfaction. See the description in this chapter.

Lawrence, Paul, and Lorsch, Jay. *Organization and Environment: Managing Differentiation and Integration.* Boston: Division of Research, Harvard Graduate School of Business, 1967, 279 pages, hardback.
   The authors describe the contingency approach to management. This book provides a good summary of management literature focused on the contingency approach. See the description in this chapter.

Woodward, Joan. *Industrial Organization: Theory and Practice.* New York: Oxford University Press, 1965, 281 pages, hardback.
   Woodward describes the relationship between technology, organizational structure, and success. See the description in this chapter. She also provides a series of enlightening case studies.

II CASE STUDIES

The Overly Successful Bank

In chapter 1, there is a description of a large New York branch-banking network. This bank has been so successful that it has grown from 20 branches in 1958 to its current size of 180 branches. However, its phenomenal success has created many problems, primarily within the dimension of organization design.

There are three major organizational levels in the bank: the main headquarters, nine regional offices, and 180 branches. Within each of the three levels, there are two kinds of officers. *Loan officers* are in charge of lending and financing activities. *Operations officers* handle the personnel activity of the system; they are primarily responsible for the integration and harmony of the workflow. The split between loans and operations is emphasized by the fact that branch loan officers and branch operations officers attend separate regional meetings every two weeks.

Throughout the system, the operations officers are subordinate to the loan officers. This subordination is especially pronounced at the branch level: all 180 branch managers are loan officers (see Figure 1). Within each branch, loan officers are responsible only to the branch manager. The chief operations officer in each branch oversees the activities of all employees and other operations officers.

The design of the branch-banking system is relatively simple and, at first glance, sensible. However, the design of the system creates problems that impede the decision-making capability of management.

Subordination of Operations Officers

Perhaps the most basic problem in the design of the system is that operations officers are always subordinate to loan officers, regardless of the issues involved. This is true at all levels in the organization: headquarters, region, and

Note: These cases can be used by the whole class with the case observational method (see Appendix), or used for thought and discussion by individual class members.

Figure 1   Simplified Organizational Structure of a Typical Branch Bank

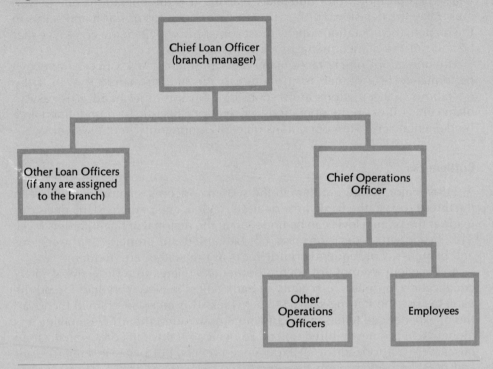

branch. Part of the reason for this is the bank's officer training program. When college graduates and MBAs begin to work for the bank, they are sent to a six-month training course that is primarily oriented to accounting and finance, which are of obvious importance in banking. At the end of the course, they receive either a passing or a failing grade. If they pass, they become loan officers; if they fail, they become operations officers. No matter what an operations officer does for the rest of his career with the bank, he is branded with inferior status because of his failure in the training course.

From the perspective of the employees, the operations officer is the leader of the branch, for he handles all requests for salary increases or promotions. But his position is constantly undermined by the fact that he cannot actually grant raises or promotions without the explicit approval of the branch manager. The branch manager is usually far removed from the employees; his purpose is generating new business for the branch, not monitoring personnel.

If the branch manager decides that a particular employee should not be given a raise or a promotion for budgetary reasons, it is the operations officer who must relay the decision. Further, in order to protect his position and status in the branch, the operations officer must somehow convince the employee that he and not the branch manager made the decision.

The operations officer faces many other problems. Any aspect of effective performance of a branch is attributed to the branch manager, even if the operations officer's efforts are responsible. On the other hand, it is easy to blame difficulties on the operations officer, since his role is so undefined. In a fundamental sense, the operations officer is a nonentity in the system.

Bottlenecks

Another major design problem in the system concerns relationships between the three levels in the bank: headquarters, region, and branch. Many decisions made at the branch level can be undercut at the regional or headquarters level. Also, headquarters decisions may not be carried out properly by the regions and branches. Consequently bottlenecks in the system are frequent.

An excellent example of such a bottleneck relates to a program of salary equalization for tellers. A scarcity of bank tellers in New York had forced the bank to raise the starting salary $15 per week. This increase strained the loyalties of experienced tellers, many of whom now found themselves making less money than the newly-hired tellers. To overcome this difficulty, equalization raises were authorized for all experienced tellers. But because some regions and branches put through their increases faster than others, several experienced tellers waited for two years or more for their equalization raises. This delay caused discontent and resulted in high turnover among the experienced tellers. Many branches began to receive an abnormal number of customer complaints because of the inexperience of the newly hired tellers.

In short, two major organizational design problems in the system are the inferior status of the operations officers and bottlenecks.

Question. Assume that you are a consultant to this bank. What design changes would you recommend to solve these two problems?

State University Medical Center

State University Medical Center is located in a small southern city. The center is affiliated with a university in the same town; the university's enrollment is approximately 24,000 students. Along with housing an 800-bed medical-surgical and psychiatric hospital, the medical center includes full teaching and research facilities for a medical school, dental school, nursing school, and other health-related professions. Both the state government and the university are extremely proud of the institution, and the people of the central portion of the state consider it a mecca of health care. Despite this success and popularity, as well as generous funding by the state legislature, the medical center faces constant financial difficulties. The teaching hospital, in particular, is unable to break even.

Faced with this general situation, Dr. Patrick Haines, previously the administrator of a large metropolitan hospital and president of a prestigious medical school, has entered the picture. Lured by an excellent salary, favorable climate, and the opportunity to test his abilities with this interesting challenge, Dr. Haines accepted the position of vice-president of Health Affairs at the university. The position places him in control of the administration of the teaching hospital and the College of Health-Related Professions.

As shown in Figure 1, the vice-president of the medical center is accountable for both its management and its budget. While the vice-president has essentially a free hand in internal administrative matters, both the university and the state legislature must approve all long-range plans and budgets. Thus the vice-president must be not only a manager but a politician. Because the medical center must obtain approval for major programs from both the university and the state legislature, it is subject to their rules, regulations, and priorities. The state legislature favors expenditures for health care, while the university prefers a budget structure supporting teaching and research. Dr. Haines prepared himself for extreme political and financial stress from outside the organization.

At the same time Dr. Haines found internal pressures significant. The educators and health care personnel directly below him in the hierarchy also have conflicting priorities, the former group emphasizing teaching and research and the latter group health care. Second, a sluggish bureaucracy is firmly entrenched in the organization. Most of the important individuals in the organization respect the bureaucracy, since it provides them with the resources they require. However, many individuals within the bureaucracy often foil well-conceived plans because they lack initiative or have no interest in the effective management of the institution.

Figure 1   Design of State University Medical Center

Solid lines represent formal lines of authority. Dotted lines indicate that the departments within both the hospital and the colleges use the same facilities and services.

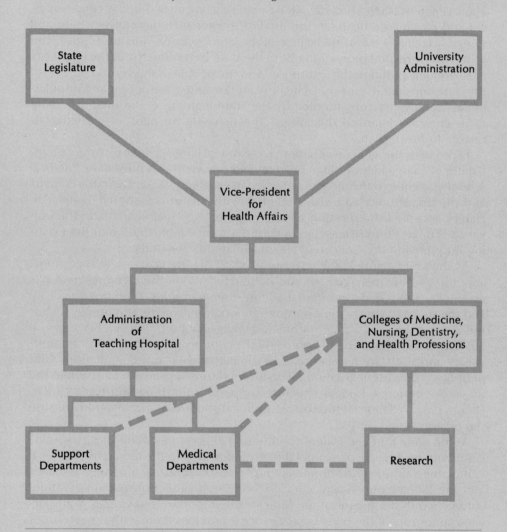

An example that illustrates both the external and internal problems facing Dr. Haines is the case of the purchasing agent for the medical center. Mr. William Saunders is approximately 55 years old, and a retired military officer (something common at the center); he handles the procurement of all items for the hospital, from nuclear radiation equipment to gauze pads. Many of his purchases are dictated by state specifications. However, he frequently buys exactly what every physician orders with no regard for cost. The result is that the budget allocation for purchasing usually runs out after only eight or nine months of the fiscal year, which contributes to the deficit and forces the medical center to borrow supplies from the local municipal hospital. Mr. Saunders neither has attempted to have state specifications changed to obtain cost savings he knows are possible, nor has used his influence to persuade physicians and educators to order less expensive items of equal quality. He is not, however, violating any rule or regulation, and he is executing his job properly in terms of the bureaucracy. Dr. Haines soon recognized that Mr. Saunders was not the exception as an employee at the medical center.

Questions. How would you redesign this organization? What specific problems would you try to eliminate? Construct the organizational chart for the revised structure.

■ When a new employee comes into an organization, he or she is frequently confused by the large number of activities that appear unrelated. How do interviewers in the personnel office know what applicants to send to the production manager? How can the warehouse crew tell when inventory is too low to suit the needs of the sales department?

If the planning and control systems in the organization are working effectively, the employee's confusion should eventually give way to an understanding of the relationships between his or her own work and that of others. The *planning system* determines what goals the organization and its subsystems pursue, and the *control system* keeps the organization moving toward these goals. All of the subsystems, and their employees, receive guidance from the planning system. At the same time, the control system monitors the performance of each organizational subsystem so significant deviations from plans can be pinpointed.

What happens when the subsystems of an organization fall out of step with each other, or a change in the external environment causes previous ways of meeting goals to lose their effectiveness? Change is constant in organizations; if the planning and control systems fail to allow for change, they will become obsolete. To combat this problem, organizations should be careful to introduce planned and systematic changes into their structures. This is the concern of the field known as organization development, or O.D.

GUIDING
AND MONITORING
THE ORGANIZATION
III

Planning

5

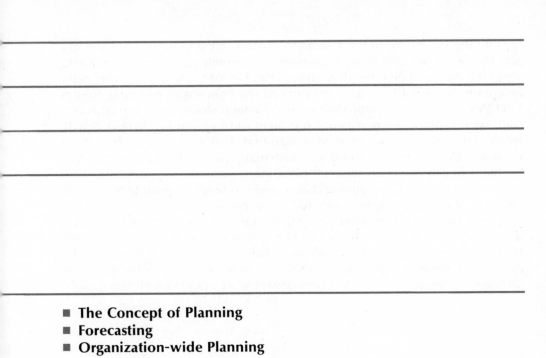

- **The Concept of Planning**
- **Forecasting**
- **Organization-wide Planning**

Performance Objectives

1. To understand the concept of planning and its importance in an organization.

2. To be able to distinguish between strategic and tactical plans, and between forecasting techniques and organization-wide planning techniques, and to know the purposes of each.

3. To comprehend the basics of, and know how to use, several planning techniques.

4. To learn how some planning techniques also function as control techniques.

Until the beginning of the twentieth century, most organizations did not plan their activities systematically. Rather, they merely reacted to the immediate problems and difficulties they faced. The DuPont Company was the major exception to this pattern, for it introduced the concept of planning around 1900. While a few other companies such as General Motors followed DuPont's lead, systematic planning was not prevalent until the end of World War II, when many companies started to realize that their success, and even their existence, depended on careful and systematic planning. These companies gradually began to create separate planning departments in their organizational structures. Today, planning is accepted not only as desirable but also as necessary if an organization wants to be successful.

In this chapter, there is an analysis of the concept of planning, and a discussion of some research on the planning function. Various forecasting techniques an organization uses to predict the future are also examined. Finally, the chapter focuses on organization-wide planning techniques that managers systematically use to coordinate the work of individuals and groups.

The Concept
of Planning

Planning involves two key aspects: developing the *goals* an organization seeks to attain, and deciding on the *means* to achieve them. It is not necessary for one person or group to perform both activities. In fact, it may be possible and even desirable for one department to define the organization's goals while other departments focus on the means to achieve them. For example, top managers may establish the goal of producing a new product within two years, and engineers in the organization may be responsible for developing the means to accomplish this objective. In all instances, managers should closely coordinate the development of goals and the creation of means to achieve them.

Development of Goals

Goals serve several useful purposes. Obviously, management must have an overall goal in mind before the organization even comes into existence. This and subsequent more specific goals help determine the organization's structure. Goals also provide a basis against which management can measure performance. In addition, they serve as a guide when management must make difficult decisions. For example, managers may decide to curtail production of a new product if sales within the first year fall short of expectations. Further, goals can link departments, giving them a target they can seek jointly rather than struggling with one another over scarce resources. Because of the importance of goals, top management typically sets the major objectives to be achieved throughout the organization.

To be useful, goals should satisfy two objectives: they should be explicit and they should not be in conflict. Top management can insure that goals are explicit by making them as clear and specific as possible. The goal "to improve customer service" does not define customer service; consequently, there is no way to measure whether the organization has achieved it. An explicit version of this goal would be "to provide next-morning delivery on 95 percent of all orders received from the Sales Department by 5:00 P.M."

If goals are in conflict, they cannot normally be met. Conflict is inherent in the goal, "to provide the highest quality at the lowest cost." Usually there is a trade-off between quality and cost; it is not possible to achieve both objectives simultaneously. A more consistent statement would be, "to produce a product of maximum quality subject to a selling price of $8.50."

Strategies and Tactics—The Means

Means to achieve an objective take two forms: strategies and tactics. *Strategies* are the means to accomplish the overall objective or objectives of the organization. *Tactics* are the means to attain specific objectives that relate directly to the overall objective or objectives. One of Polaroid's strategies for maintaining its dominance in instant photography was to develop the technologically advanced SX-70 camera system; submodel variations of the SX-70 are some of the tactics to achieve the overall objective.

An outstanding example of the interplay between strategies and tactics occurred in General Motors during the early 1920s. At that time, the Ford Motor Company dominated the automotive industry. Its success rested solely on consumer demand for the Model T, which was an all-purpose and inexpensive car. Top management at General Motors developed a strategy to appeal to all kinds of consumers rather than just the solid, middle-class American who was attracted by the Model T. They developed six lines of cars, which represented the company's tactics. In addition, top management established specific rules or guidelines that each of the six operating divisions was required to follow. The operating division that manufactured the lowest-priced car had to keep the cost between $450 and $600; the operating division that produced the highest-priced car had to stay within the range of $2,500 to $3,500 (Sloan 1963, p. 67). Even today, General Motors still uses this basic approach, although the company now produces five rather than six types of cars.

Long-Range and Short-Range Planning

Both goals and means can be part of either long-range or short-range planning. There is no general agreement about the length of time involved in long-range and short-range planning. In general, long-range planning usually involves a time horizon of at least one year, and a short-range plan rarely exceeds three years. The methods used for these two types of planning do not differ in principle; however, because of the difference in the time horizons, management does not expect its long-range plans to be as precise as its short-range plans.

Research on Planning

Research on planning has confirmed that it is vital to an organization's success. Stanley Thune and Robert House (1970) analyzed the planning function in 36 similar firms in 6 industries. Specifically, they compared companies that planned with those that did not, after which they concluded:

1. Companies that establish formal planning departments are more successful than those that plan only in an informal fashion.
2. Companies that establish formal planning departments perform more successfully after the system is instituted than previously.

In the Thune and House study, the impact of planning appeared to be overwhelming. The average performance of companies after formal planning was initiated increased by 38 percent in sales, 64 percent in earnings per share, and 56 percent in stock price.

Because of the importance of planning, it is not surprising that most organizations, even relatively small ones, do establish some type of formal planning system. A study of 93 companies, each with 2,000 or fewer employees, indicated that only 4 do not plan at all (Bacon 1971). The period covered by most companies' plans ranged from one to ten years, although the majority used a time frame of four to five years.

Given its importance, it is significant that planning one or two years into the future is generally highly accurate. More importantly, long-term plans of five years or more have proved reasonably accurate (Vancil 1970).

Forecasting

A problem central to planning in any organization is knowing what is likely to happen, both in the organization and in its external environment. In the governmental sector, a top manager who fails to anticipate future events can misallocate resources, attract adverse publicity, and even face removal from office. In the private sector of the economy, ineffective forecasting can lead to the selection of incorrect courses of action, unsold inventories, decreased profits, and, in some cases, the financial failure of the firm. While these examples are extreme, they do emphasize the critical role that forecasting plays for both the organization and the individual manager.

Essentially forecasting serves two general purposes. The first is to provide a basis for long-range planning. Areas influenced by forecasting include production planning, capital budgeting allocations (the apportioning of large sums of money to various projects), determination of overall personnel requirements, financial planning, and inventory needs. As might be expected, the second general purpose of forecasting concerns short-range scheduling decisions. Areas usually affected by short-range forecasts include production scheduling, adjustments in personnel actions, and procurement management (the determination of supplies an organization needs to function effectively).

The four basic purposes of forecasting are to predict future demand for the organization's goods or services; future *trends* in demand; future *changes* in trends; and the *magnitude* of changes in these trends. When forecasting is inadequate or inaccurate, the result is sometimes an outstanding failure to achieve one or more of these four purposes. The airline industry was forced to ground several airplanes in 1974 when forecasted passenger traffic did not materialize. Similarly, the recreation vehicle industry underestimated the effect of the energy crisis on demand and found itself swamped with thousands of unsold vans and campers. And the fashion industry underestimated the strength of customer resistance to maxifashions in the early 1970s to the extent that dozens of firms went bankrupt in the resulting downturn.

Types of Forecasts

Forecasts are of three major types. The *long-range forecast* refers to the long-term planning needs of the organization; the *short-range forecast* describes the firm's immediate needs; and the *rolling forecast* is constantly updated as the time for accomplishing an objective approaches and as new information becomes available.

To prepare a long-range forecast, managers examine information that has traditionally indicated changes in business and economic conditions in the distant future, for example, the general state of the economy. The *planning horizon*—the amount of time a long-range forecast predicts into the future—may vary from a few weeks to several years. However, a typical long-range forecast will estimate conditions six months to a year into the future. Quantities and product mixes are usually stated in general terms, for example, the number of tennis rackets customers will probably buy rather than the number within each model. The firm relies heavily on published and public data for its long-range forecasts, since many of the factors that influence long-range forecasts are external to the organization and cannot be controlled directly by it. Some organizations that publish these data are the U.S. Department of Commerce, the U.S. Department of Labor, and the U.S. Department of the Treasury. In short, the long-range forecast is tentative in nature and very sensitive to changes in external economic conditions.

Usually the short-range forecast is more detailed. The planning horizon for it typically ranges from a few days to a few months. The analyst examines recent business and economic conditions to establish estimates of the immediate market demand for the firm's product or service. Both products and quantities that seem likely to meet the demand are specified precisely. Such a short-range forecast is more dependent upon internal data, such as sales in previous years, than external data. In addition, the short-range forecast is sensitive to short-run changes, such as a strike at a customer's plant, a competitor's sidewalk sale, and even the weather.

The third type, the rolling forecast, integrates the long-range and short-range forecasts into one comprehensive forecast that is continually revised. If goals are not met or if conditions change, management alters its rolling forecast. Hence, the rolling forecast may include a general forecast for the distant future and more specific forecasts for short-run planning. Because of its flexibility, the rolling forecast accomplishes at least two purposes: it enables management to maintain a long-range overview of its operations and to make adjustments in operating plans within an overall perspective; and it allows management to plan and manage resources rather than constantly react to problems on a daily basis.

In general, the rolling forecast seems to be more useful than either long-range or short-range forecasting alone. This approach can include most or all of the specific planning techniques described in this chapter; it is flexible and sensitive to economic changes; and it can be used for short-range and long-range planning. The rolling forecast also encourages managers to focus attention constantly on how effectively their planning is working.

Long-Range Planning and Strategy

The first thing that can be said about a long-range plan is that having one is a step forward. Once made explicit, any long-range plan, whether applicable at the corporate, divisional, or regional level, can be evaluated quickly and improved. However, if no attempt is made to commit the plan to paper, there is always the danger that the plan is either incomplete or misunderstood.

Although it is unusual for a company to continue to grow successfully and to branch out into new ventures without a real understanding of its strategy, many firms are unaware of the strategy that underlies their initial success. This is why many established companies fail miserably when they attempt a program of corporate acquisition, product diversification, or market expansion. The one best place to identify, agree upon, and solidify the corporate strategy is in the long-range plan.

Leslie Rue, "The How and Who of Long-Range Planning," *Business Horizons* 16, no. 6 (December 1973): 23.

Specific Forecasting Techniques

Management can use many different techniques in preparing its forecasts. Some of these are highly subjective and *qualitative* in nature: that is, the organization relies heavily on the opinions of experts, consumers, and its own experienced managers. There are also several *quantitative* techniques, which allow the manager to specify his or her predictions in the form of numbers and equations. Effective forecasting typically requires a combination of qualitative and quantitative approaches. Opinion polling and the informal gathering of information are qualitative approaches to forecasting. Major quantitative techniques include barometric techniques, econometric models, and mathematical and statistical models.

Polls. When the research staff of an organization conducts an opinion poll, it frequently asks knowledgeable managers both within and among industries to assess future business conditions. Such a poll might ask managers to predict whether a recession will occur within 18 months. Or it could request customers to indicate the kinds and amounts of various products they expect to purchase in the near future. Some large organizations conduct periodic polls and publish them for national distribution. The Survey Research Center of the University of Michigan, for instance, conducts national surveys of consumers.

Within a firm, the research staff may conduct a poll among executives, the sales staff, or customers. While each group by itself will not provide a forecast top management can use to predict the future with complete certainty, all of them in combination can serve as the basis for an integrated forecast.

Informal Approach. Informal gathering of information can be as important as a systematic poll. The alert manager picks up useful data from periodicals, customer contacts, suppliers, trade shows, discussions with the sales force, and many other sources. The first indication of a change in future demand can often be gleaned from a casual comment in an informal conversation or a short article in a trade journal. Some experienced managers visit their colleagues in various regions of the United States periodically, partly because they want to find out what is happening elsewhere. This helps them acquire a sense of the state of the economy that is difficult to obtain any other way. An astute manager will capitalize on any reliable informal source of information.

Barometric Indicators. *Barometric indicators* are economic data that forecast the future state of the economy, such as the dollar amounts of sales for industrial raw materials, foodstuffs, and cotton. *Business Week* publishes a list of 33 indicators, and it has developed an overall index that includes the 12 leading indicators. This index is more predictive of the future state of the American economy than any one indicator. Each specific indicator may predict an event or change in the economy (a *leading* indicator), coincide with the event (a *coincident* indicator), or lag behind the event (a *lagging* indicator). While all three types of indicators are useful in forecasting, the manager is typically most interested in leading indicators, since he or she wants to know what will happen in the future. However, the overall index that contains all three types of indicators is much more reliable and valid than any one indicator in predicting the future.

Frequently managers develop their own set of economic indicators. For example, a large chemical manufacturing firm discovered that the rate of new home starts was an excellent indicator of sales for a particular chemical six months later. This relationship exists because the chemical is used in making roofing shingles. Hence, fluctuations in new home construction were felt six months later by the chemical manufacturer.

Econometric Models. Another form of forecasting involves *econometric models:* complex models of the United States economy that can be created only on a sophisticated computer. They are usually employed to predict the general state of the economy; however, some can predict the economic state of a particular industry or region of the country. Econometric models are very expensive to operate, and only large organizations such as government agencies and universities maintain them. But their results are, sometimes available by subscription from the forecasting organizations, and summaries are frequently reported in business publications such as *Business Week* and *Fortune*.

Mathematical Models. An organization that wants to predict the future sales volume of its various products often uses mathematical and statistical models to analyze past figures and trends. From these historical data, it can *extrapolate*—make an informed guess about—trends in the future. While the organization may put its mathematical model on the computer, it is not always necessary to do so. Some of these models include only five or six key variables, and the manager or analyst can solve them easily with the aid of a calculator.

The Delphi Technique. The *Delphi technique* is quite different from the other forecasting techniques discussed. Named after a Greek oracle, it is typically concerned with predicting long-run technological and market changes that will eventually affect the organization. The organization polls at periodic intervals a small number of experts. An oil company might poll 50 to 75 experts on a yearly basis in the area of natural resources to assess future energy needs. The organization usually guarantees these experts anonymity to ensure that they will be as candid as possible.

First, the experts are asked to complete a questionnaire on which they give numerical estimates of their opinions of the likelihood of specific technological or market possibilities occurring within a certain time. In the case of the oil company, the experts might be asked if they feel the United States can develop a new kind of fuel in the next 20 years that is competitive with oil as a source of energy. A summary of the results of this questionnaire survey is then prepared, usually in terms of some descriptive statistics. For example, 80 percent of the experts may believe the United States will not develop a new kind of fuel competitive with oil within the next 20 years. The organization gives this summary back to the experts, who are allowed to revise their earlier predictions if they wish. A summary is again prepared and sent to the experts, but they are now asked to justify their predictions if their responses deviate significantly from the others. Thus, if 80 percent of the experts still believe the United States will not develop a new kind of fuel competitive with oil in the next 20 years, the remaining 20 percent of the respondents are asked to indicate why they disagree. The organization then prepares a final summary of the results, which is given to top management.

Planning based on the results of the application of the Delphi technique is very tentative in nature, for the predictions are made within an extended time frame. Still, this technique provides an organization with a carefully considered prediction based on the opinions of experts, which can be valuable within this limited scope. It has proved to be helpful in many situations, for an organization's long-run success is partly determined by its reactions to the kind of technological and market changes the technique predicts. Thus, the Delphi technique has become not only popular but important in recent years.

Nominal Group Technique. Another important forecasting method is *nominal group technique* (NGT), which uses a structured group meeting (Delbecq, Van de Ven, and Gustafson 1975). Seven to ten individuals sit around a conference table, and each one writes ideas on the assigned topic on a pad of paper. NGT forecasting can be either short range or long range. A short-range forecast might focus on consumer demand for oil within the next six months. A long-range forecast might attack the issue of other fuels that could be developed as alternatives to oil within the next 20 years.

After a period that usually ranges from five to ten minutes, the participants share their ideas, one at a time, in a structured round-robin manner. A secretary or recorder writes all the ideas on a flip chart or blackboard in full view of the participants. A period of structured discussion follows during which all of these ideas are analyzed by the participants. This period is structured to insure that each idea receives an appropriate amount of attention. If the members of the group spend too much time on one idea, the secretary asks them to treat the other ideas. After the structured discussion participants rank-order each idea in terms of its relative probability of occurrence. The mathematically pooled results then become the group's decisions.

In principle, the Delphi technique and NGT are very similar, since they rely upon the judgments of experts to predict the future. However, the basic difference between them has to do with anonymity. When the Delphi technique is employed, the participants are anonymous; the open nature of NGT precludes anonymity. However, NGT allows the participants to interact while the Delphi technique does not.

Organization-Wide

Planning

The forecasting techniques discussed thus far provide the organization with general guidelines for averting potential problems. On the basis of such information, organizations can plan their projects in a systematic and specific fashion. *Organization-wide planning,* which directly or indirectly influences the actions of all or most individuals in the organization, helps management to coordinate the work of individuals and subunits whose activities overlap. Four of the organization-wide planning techniques managers employ are policies, planning-programming-budgeting system (PPBS), management by objectives (MBO), and program evaluation review technique (PERT).

Policies

A *policy* is a general guide that management employs to direct organizational activities. Within the guidelines or boundaries of a policy, a manager is allowed to exercise his or her judgment and discretion. Usually top management develops several policies to guide activities. Hence, policies constitute a planning mechanism in an organization.

Top management normally develops policies for activities within each of the functional areas of the organization. A personnel policy might be to pay employees at higher than prevailing rates in the industry; a marketing policy might be to advertise only in media specifically aimed at lawyers; and a financial policy might be to secure needed capital by borrowing from creditors who will extend long-term loans.

Typically policies are accompanied by *procedures,* which are plans that establish a customary method of handling future activities. Procedures differ from policies in that they are specific rather than broad guidelines which describe the exact sequence in which a particular activity must be completed. A company might develop a procedure whereby all advertising expenditures

---

The Need for Planning

Most organizations operate in an environment of change. They must be prepared to accept change as the inevitable consequence of operating in a dynamic world. The general political, economic, social and ethical philosophies in our country have promoted an atmosphere of freedom of change for the enterprise. In fact, continued success generally has demanded adaptation and innovation. This is in direct contradiction to many societies—both past and contemporary—in which political, religious, cultural, and other institutions placed major impediments in the path of economic and social progress.

Rapidly advancing technology has also emphasized the need for planning. Companies not abreast of current technology are in trouble over the short run. Moreover, companies unaware of the technical changes likely to occur over the next five to twenty years will be in a disadvantageous position.

Fremont Kast and James Rosenzweig, *Organization and Management,* 2nd ed. (New York: McGraw-Hill, 1974), p. 439.

must be approved by three different departments in the organization before any action can be taken.

Procedures, in turn, are normally subdivided into *rules,* which are the simplest types of plans. A procedure can be defined as a series of rules. A rule does not allow any discretion on the part of the individual. He or she must perform a given action in accordance with a specific rule. For example, a manager must complete particular financial forms before he or she can obtain approval for advertising expenditures. However, not every rule is directly related to a procedure or policy. "No smoking," for instance, is a rule not directly associated with any procedure.

PPBS

In 1962 the U.S. Department of Defense began to use the planning-programming-budgeting system (PPBS). This approach became very popular during the 1960s, especially in governmental agencies and educational institutions. It is particularly appropriate when an organization sponsors a series of independent projects that top management must support from a central fund of money.

The first and critical step in PPBS is defining the objectives to be accomplished (planning). Then managers design various programs to accomplish these objectives (programming). At this point, top management decides to fund some of these programs and eliminate others (budgeting). Top management subsequently allocates its financial resources from the central fund to the funded programs. The basic steps to PPBS are outlined in Figure 5.1.

A *program* in PPBS is all of the resources needed to accomplish a specific goal, much like a project in project management (see chapter 3). Under project management, or the matrix form of organization, management establishes a temporary team to complete a specific project, after which the team disbands. A program differs somewhat from a project in that a cost-benefit analysis is always undertaken; that is, the cost of each program is balanced against the anticipated benefits before the program is begun. (For a more complete explanation of cost-benefit analysis, see chapter 13). After the completion of a program, top management evaluates its effectiveness so as to refine the planning process and objectives for future activities.

PPBS is radically different from the traditional system of planning and budgeting. Under PPBS, the benefits of each program or project are evaluated against its specific costs, and funds are allocated to programs individually. The traditional method of planning and budgeting is to allocate resources by department or functional unit, after which the managers distribute resources

Figure 5.1   Steps in the Planning-Programming-Budgeting System (PPBS)

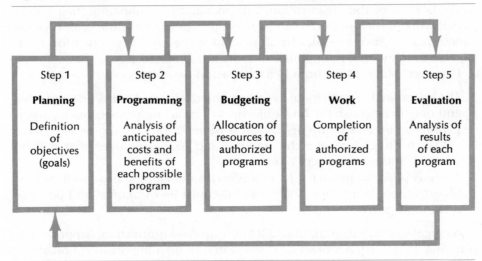

Step 1	Step 2	Step 3	Step 4	Step 5
Planning	**Programming**	**Budgeting**	**Work**	**Evaluation**
Definition of objectives (goals)	Analysis of anticipated costs and benefits of each possible program	Allocation of resources to authorized programs	Completion of authorized programs	Analysis of results of each program

to individual projects as they see fit. Thus, PPBS is frequently linked to the use of project management or the matrix organization, where projects are constantly being funded and terminated after a specific interval of time.

Although PPBS is primarily a planning technique, as its first step is the definition of an organization's objectives, it is also a control mechanism. As suggested above, the cost-benefit analysis is always completed before a program is funded, and in this way PPBS functions as a planning mechanism. However, management sometimes completes a cost-benefit analysis at each stage of a program, and PPBS then serves more as a control mechanism than a planning device. If the costs at a particular stage are much greater than anticipated, management can revise the program or terminate it early. In addition, management monitors future programs very closely if they are similar to previous programs that proved troublesome.

Management by Objectives (MBO)

Management by objectives (MBO) is similar to PPBS in that its first step is the definition of objectives or goals to be accomplished. Under MBO, top management typically defines four or five general objectives that it wishes to achieve within a given span of time such as two or three years. Managers throughout the hierarchy then refine these objectives into subobjectives that their particular units can accomplish. This refinement proceeds from the top to the bottom of the organization, with managers coordinating their objectives if work in their respective units overlaps. For example, the sales division cannot plan to increase sales by 50 percent if the production division is incapable of increasing the number of units it manufactures.

However, MBO differs from PPBS at least in two respects:

1. The subordinates participate in setting objectives, even if they do not have authority to establish the final objectives to be accomplished. Such participation can involve group discussion sessions of proposed programs, individual meetings between the superior and each employee that will be affected, and written suggestions.
2. There is periodic feedback to subordinates concerning how well various objectives are being met, difficulties that must be overcome, and possible revision of goals.

As suggested by these criteria, MBO constitutes a *motivational* approach to planning; that is, each individual is motivated to help the organization attain its objectives because he or she has participated in establishing them. Also, motivation is reinforced by periodic feedback of results so the successful completion of objectives can be shown clearly and problems can be corrected. Hence MBO is quite different from the other planning techniques discussed in this chapter.

Performance Evaluation. In addition to being used as a planning technique, MBO can be used in place of the traditional method of evaluating a subordinate's performance. Traditionally, a superior meets periodically with a subordinate and provides an overall evaluation of his or her work. Frequently managers seek to avoid this kind of meeting, for it typically means evaluating the subordinate's performance in terms of subjective criteria such as ability to interact effectively with others and degree of initiative. Usually managers have no real basis for judging subordinates by such criteria, and they may tend instead to emphasize negative factors, such as the subordinate's having been late for work twice in one month. As managers are not behavioral scientists trained to interview effectively, it is not surprising that subordinates often resent the confrontations that take place in such an evaluation session.

When MBO is used, the performance of a subordinate is evaluated only in terms of his or her accomplishment of specific objectives. Hence the discussion between the superior and the subordinate tends to be objective, unemotional, and helpful.

MBO in Action. Management by objectives has been used successfully in many organizations. The Bureau of Personnel Management Evaluation of the

U.S. Civil Service Commission instituted MBO because it was having trouble scheduling work in a traditional fashion. This bureau is charged with monitoring violations of the merit system in federal government agencies. The bureau sponsors several important projects, which previously were often interrupted and delayed when the staff had to complete irregular work created by the demands of politicians, large companies, and irate citizens. Hence it was difficult for the bureau to evaluate the effectiveness of its projects or the performance of its employees, for there was no logical connection between the regular projects and the irregular work that often interfered with them.

To solve this problem, the bureau's management introduced a simplified MBO system. After consultation with staff members, top management classified projects in terms of priority: (1) projects whose completion was absolutely essential; (2) projects whose completion was essential but which could be delayed if the irregular work became too urgent; and (3) projects whose completion was desirable but which could be completed when more essential activities had been accomplished.

Three regular projects were eventually established in one of the major units of the bureau after superiors and subordinates were allowed to express their feelings about the relative importance of each. Management and members of the staff considered Project A absolutely essential. Input from the members of the staff indicated they could probably complete Project A by August 1975 if the irregular workload did not become too burdensome. Management felt Project B was essential but not absolutely essential, but most of the staff members believed it also could be completed by August. Finally, management considered Project C desirable but not essential. If everything went according to schedule, December appeared to be an appropriate target date for the completion of Project C.

Management then provided the staff of this unit with a schedule of deadlines and a reporting sheet for each project similar to the one shown in Figure 5.2. Members of the staff could comment on any irregular work that delayed the completion of any of the three projects. This forced them to justify any delays by offering hard evidence that they were unavoidable. Management exercised control over the three projects by establishing deadlines that were definite but flexible. At the same time, management allowed the staff members a degree of independence, since they could delay the completion of a project if this course of action was appropriate.

Disadvantages of MBO. Although MBO has several positive aspects, there are many drawbacks to this planning process. An organization tends to hold more meetings after MBO is instituted, for many people must participate in setting the objectives. Such meetings interfere with getting the regular work done. In

Figure 5.2   Form for Evaluation of an MBO Project

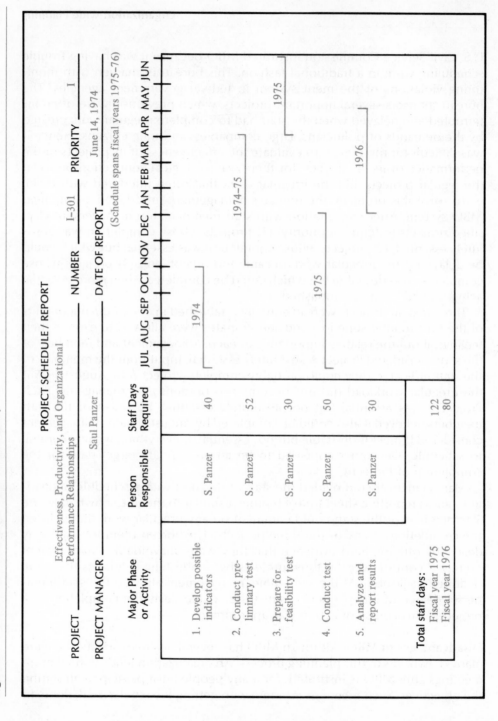

PROJECT SCHEDULE / REPORT

PROJECT _____ Effectiveness, Productivity, and Organizational
Performance Relationships _____

NUMBER _____ I–301 _____ PRIORITY _____ I

PROJECT MANAGER _____ Saul Panzer _____

DATE OF REPORT _____ June 14, 1974 _____

(Schedule spans fiscal years 1975–76)

Major Phase or Activity	Person Responsible	Staff Days Required	JUL AUG SEP OCT NOV DEC JAN FEB MAR APR MAY JUN
1. Develop possible indicators	S. Panzer	40	1974
2. Conduct pre-liminary test	S. Panzer	52	1974–75
3. Prepare for feasibility test	S. Panzer	30	1975
4. Conduct test	S. Panzer	50	1975
5. Analyze and report results	S. Panzer	30	1976

Total staff days:
Fiscal year 1975   122
Fiscal year 1976   80

addition, since the system usually requires specifying objectives and the tentative dates of their completion, the amount of paperwork may become irritating (see Carroll and Tosi 1973).

Such disadvantages are usually outweighed by the advantages. The major advantage of MBO is that it links together the motivational and planning systems in the organization. Since members of the organization actually participate in developing the objectives to be achieved, they are typically more committed to them. Hence the level of productivity in the organization normally rises. Because of the link between planning and motivation, many organizations have found MBO to be beneficial.

PERT

When a project consists of a number of interrelated steps or activities, the *program evaluation and review technique* (PERT) may make it easier to plan. PERT is the development of a plan that specifies the series of interrelated steps necessary to complete a specific project. It became widely known during the early 1960s because it was the major planning technique for the Polaris missile program. To build the Polaris missile, management developed an intricate plan that consisted of a series of interrelated steps, some of which could be completed simultaneously, and some of which had to be finished before others could begin.

In its most simple form, the technique consists of laying out or diagramming the flow of activities in a project in order to identify all the possible sequences of steps between the beginning and the end of the project. The longest sequence is the *critical path* which determines the completion time of the project. Once it is known, managers can focus on those particular activities that are likely to delay the project.

The first step in the PERT process is to identify every significant event that must happen for a project to be completed. After the identification of these events, called *milestones*, management must ascertain the *order* in which they must be completed and the *time* to be allotted to each of them. Each milestone is plotted on a PERT chart so the managers can pinpoint various possible sequences of milestones and the length of time it will take to complete each sequence. Managers then can calculate the total time that must be allocated for the completion of the entire project.

Let us assume that a rollerskate manufacturer is developing a new kind of skateboard, a project tentatively entitled "Project 81." The product manager must insure that Project 81 is completed rapidly so the new skateboard can go on sale well before other companies start introducing competitive models. Information gathered on this project from various corporate subunits has indicated that 11 milestones are critical for producing the new skateboard (see Table 5.1).

The 11 milestones are plotted on a PERT chart in such a way that the project manager can see which ones must be completed before others can be started (see Figure 5.3). It is not necessary for all twelve milestones to be placed one after the other. Usually different parts of the project team will be working on different milestones at the same time. For example, the production department will work on path A – E – I – K and path A – G – I – K, while the marketing department will focus on paths C – H – I – K and C – D – F – J – K. These two departments will be jointly responsible for path B – C – H – I – K.

Comparing the total time for each sequence or path indicates that the entire project will require 30 weeks, for the longest path is A – E – I – K (see Table 5.2). This sequence is called the *critical path*. (Strictly speaking, PERT is different from the critical path method (CPM) in that PERT employs three time estimates in the construction of the PERT chart—optimistic, average, and pessimistic—while CPM uses only one time estimate; but for practical purposes, there is little difference.) Any delay in completing the milestones in the critical path will stall the entire project by the length of the delay. If problems develop

Table 5.1   Milestones for Project 81

Milestone	Description	Expected Time (in weeks)	Preceding Milestone
A	Formulate product	6	None
B	Create packaging, structural design	4	None
C	Design package graphics	10	B must be completed 4 weeks before graphics are complete
D	Design promotional literature	5	C
E	Modify production equipment	20	A
F	Inform sales force	8	D
G	Procure raw materials	6	A
H	Procure packaging materials	12	C
I	Produce initial inventories	3	E,G,H
J	Inform middlemen	4	F
K	Ship to retailers	1	I,J

Figure 5.3 Project 81 PERT Chart

To determine the critical path for Project 81, it is important to identify all paths from the beginning to Step K. These paths are presented in Table 5.2. All times are expressed in weeks.

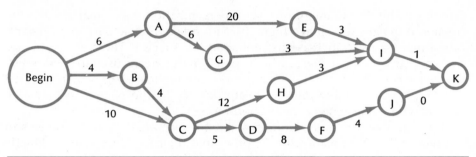

so that product formulation (milestone A) requires 10 weeks rather than 6 weeks, the critical path A – E – I – K will increase to 34 weeks (see Tables 5.1 and 5.2).

   If the critical path can be shortened significantly, it may no longer be critical. It might be possible to complete production equipment (milestone E) in 2 weeks rather than 20 weeks so the path A – E – I – K would become $6 + 2 + 3 + 1$ or 12, rather than 30. If this occurred, path C – D – F – J – K would become the critical path.

   While PERT is not a panacea for all projects, its value is great enough to make it a useful managerial tool in diverse organizational settings. In addition, PERT does function as a control mechanism, for managers can easily discover deviations from the time allotted to each milestone.

Table 5.2 Project 81 Paths

Path	Time (in Weeks)	Total Time
A – E – I – K	6 + 20 + 3 + 1	30
A – G – I – K	6 + 6 + 3 + 1	16
B – C – H – I – K	4 + 4 + 12 + 3 + 1	24
C – H – I – K	10 + 12 + 3 + 1	26
C – D – F – J – K	10 + 5 + 8 + 4 + 0	27
B – C – D – F – J – K	4 + 4 + 5 + 8 + 4 + 0	25

Summary

Planning is the development of goals an organization seeks to attain and the creation of means to achieve them. It is a fundamental activity in an organization that wants to increase its probability of success. There are two basic types of plans: strategic plans, which center on the means used to accomplish the overall objective(s) of the organization; and tactical plans, which are used to attain specific objectives that relate directly to the overall objective(s). Plans can be either long range or short range.

There are two kinds of planning techniques—*forecasting* techniques, and techniques that are *organization-wide* in that their use directly or indirectly affects the activities of most of the members of the organization. Forecasting techniques include polls, informal gathering of information, barometric indicators, econometric models, mathematical models, the Delphi technique, and nominal group technique. An organization's policies serve as an organization-wide planning guideline. Other organization-wide techniques are PPBS, MBO, and PERT.

Discussion Questions

1. Of the planning techniques discussed in this chapter, which one links the planning system to the motivational system? How? What are the advantages and disadvantages of this approach?

2. What is the relationship between forecasting techniques and organization-wide planning techniques? Are they interchangeable? Why or why not?

3. Why is PPBS frequently linked to discussions of project management or the matrix form of organization?

4. When can a planning technique be treated as a control technique? Of the planning techniques discussed in this chapter, which ones can be readily used as control techniques?

5. What are some of the critical factors an automobile manufacturer will consider in the formulation of a long-range forecast? In a short-range forecast?

6. What is the relationship between planning and control in a PERT system?

Critical Incidents

NOTE: *These critical incidents can be used by the whole class with the case observational method (see Appendix), or used for thought and discussion by individual class members.*

1. A basic problem managers face in running an art museum is juggling three goals. First, the museum wants to preserve the works of art it already possesses. Second, it seeks to collect new works, all of which cost a good deal of money. Third, it must educate the public so individuals will continue to visit it and also provide financial support. Often these goals conflict. For example, a manager of an art museum was complaining to the board of directors about the acute need for money to purchase new works. When a member of the board suggested the manager advertise to increase the number of visitors to the museum and bring in more money, the manager argued that the plan was not feasible: If too many people visited the museum, the probability would increase that its existing works of art would be damaged.

Questions: Of the planning techniques discussed in this chapter, which one would be most suitable for planning in this organization? Why? What other techniques might also be suitable?

2. A large agency in the federal government decided to introduce a management-by-objectives system. Both employees and managers were involved in the development of the goals their particular units would seek to attain, although top management eventually made the final decisions. Top management decided there were 305 goals that the organization and its subdivisions should seek to achieve. Then they established a department whose sole function was to track the completion of these goals.

Questions: Does this approach carry out the concept of MBO appropriately? Is MBO being used more as a control mechanism or a planning mechanism in this organization?

3. Multinational Motors is a large foreign manufacturer of automobiles. During the 1960s, Multinational had enjoyed an excellent rate of growth in the United States car market. By 1970 this company's sales were about 4 percent of total new car sales. Multinational planned on maintaining this share of the market through the 1970s. But beginning with the 1972 model year, this company's market share began to decline, hitting a level of 2.7 percent for the fall of 1973. During the 1974 and 1975 model years, sales increased dramatically, reaching 4.1 percent of domestic sales. This percentage would have been higher if the company had possessed greater assembly capacity. Beginning with the 1976 model year, sales again began to decline, leaving Multinational with heavy inventories of unsold cars and excess capacity in its manufacturing plants.

Questions: What are some reasons that might explain Multinational's shifts in market shares? Can Multinational's forecasting system be changed to take these reasons or factors into account? If yes, how? If no, why not?

Problems

1. Given the following PERT chart, identify the steps needed to complete the project. (All times are expressed in days.)
    a. Determine all paths and identify the critical path.
    b. What will be the critical path if A – E becomes six days? If D – G becomes ten days?

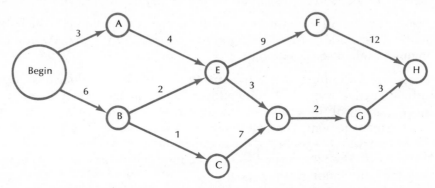

2. You have been assigned a project that has five milestones. The milestones, the expected time to complete each milestone, and the order of completion are given below.
    a. Construct a PERT chart of this project.
    b. What happens to the critical path if milestone D shortens to three weeks?
    c. What happens to the critical path if milestone D shortens to four weeks and milestone C increases to five weeks?

Milestone	Expected Completion Time (in weeks)	Preceding Milestone
A	5	None
B	8	None
C	2	A,B
D	10	B
E	3	C,D

Suggested Readings

Chandler, Alfred. *Strategy and Structure*. Garden City: Anchor Books, Doubleday, 1966, 580 pages, paperback.
> *This is a somewhat difficult but interesting book. See the description in this
> chapter.*

Drucker, Peter. *The Concept of the Corporation*. New York: John Day Company, 1972, (originally published in 1946), 297 pages, hardback.
> *This is a short and interesting study of the development of planning systems
> and organizational structure in General Motors. Drucker puts forth his be-
> lief that federal decentralization is the most suitable organizational struc-
> ture for large corporations.*

Sloan, Alfred. *My Years with General Motors*. New York: Doubleday, 1963, 472
pages, available in hardback and paperback.
> *Sloan has written a long but fascinating study of the creation and develop-
> ment of General Motors. If you are serious about becoming an executive in
> a large corporation, you should read this book.*

Control

6

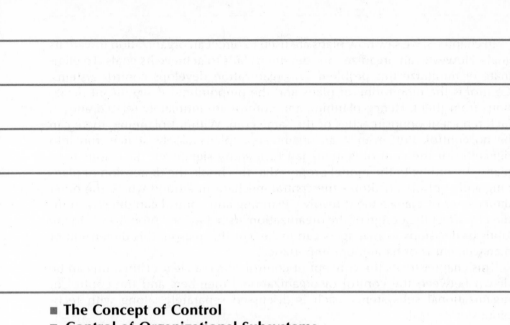

- **The Concept of Control**
- **Control of Organizational Subsystems**
- **Control of Organizational Members**

Performance Objectives

1. To understand what control is and how it relates to planning.

2. To understand the distinctions between feedback control and feedforward control, and between the control of organizational subsystems and the control of organizational members.

3. To be familiar with several control techniques, both positive and negative, and to know when to apply them.

In chapter 5, we saw how plans are used to direct an organization toward its goals. However, an organization sometimes fails to achieve its goals. To eliminate or minimize this problem, an organization develops control systems. *Control* is the monitoring of plans and the pinpointing of significant deviations from them. Hence planning and control are intimately related and, in fact, represent opposite sides of the same coin. Without planning, there can be no control. But, even if an organization plans wisely, it may run into difficulties if the control systems fail to identify significant deviations from plans. According to the model proposed in this book, the dimension of planning and control constitutes the central mechanism around which the other dimensions of management revolve. Planning and control can directly or indirectly affect the design of the organization, its behavioral processes, and the kinds of decisions its managers can make. For this reason, this dimension of management is of paramount importance.

This chapter treats the concept of control. Since a clear distinction can be drawn between the control of organizational members and the control of organizational subsystems, each is discussed separately, along with techniques of control.

The Concept

of Control

Control ideally involves four separate but interrelated activities (Porter, Lawler, and Hackman 1975). First, the organization must establish a standard or set of standards against which deviations from plans can be measured. Second, the organization must develop a monitoring device or devices to measure the performance of the individual or system. While one monitoring device may suffice, it is preferable to use two or more so that performance can be measured accurately. Third, the measurements obtained through different monitoring devices are compared to determine whether the current state is close enough to the planned state. Finally, the organization must employ *effectuating* or *action* devices to correct any significant deviations that have occurred. Sometimes the control system contains an action device that automatically corrects these deviations. In other situations the manager must decide what action is suitable for correcting these deviations.

Management might measure the performance of a factory worker by establishing several separate but interrelated standards; that is, he or she is expected to: (1) produce 100 units of a particular item per day; (2) have an error rate of 1 unit per 100 units; (3) be late for work an average of one day per month; and (4) be absent from work an average of one day per month. If the employee's performance is substandard in any of these areas, management has recourse to action devices to correct the deviation. In this case, appropriate action devices might be counseling sessions, a reprimand, or a short layoff.

While the basic concept of control is easy to understand, it is important to comprehend the various *types* of control that can be exercised. In this area, there are two major distinctions: feedback and feedforward control (Filley, House, and Kerr 1976), and control of organizational members and organizational subsystems (Ouchi and Maguire 1975).

Feedback and Feedforward Control

Feedback control uses information from events that have already occurred to make corrections for the future. When management uses feedback control, an *error* in the system is the signal indicating that corrective action is appropriate. A thermostat represents this kind of control, for it does not actuate a correction until the temperature in a room falls below the desired level or standard. Management frequently monitors the performance of factory workers by means of feedback control. Inspectors evaluate the finished goods factory workers produce; if they determine that the quality of these goods is below a preestablished standard, they return them to the workers, who are then required to redo the job.

Feedforward control anticipates or predicts deviations from standards even before they occur. Hence managers can use action devices to correct deviations even before an actual error is spotted. For example, managers might automatically increase their levels of inventories as soon as sales volume rises to some predetermined level, preventing inventories from running out. Feedback control cures problems; feedforward control prevents them.

Organizations employ both types of control. Feedback control is much more common than feedforward control, since feedforward systems are much more difficult to develop. In some situations it is possible to develop an overall system that combines feedback and feedforward control. Feedback control in a factory might indicate that managers should hire additional workers if more than 3 out of every 100 units prove defective. By adding workers, managers can effectively reduce the number of defective parts in future operations. Hence feedback control is directly linked to feedforward control.

Control of Members
and Subsystems

Another important distinction involves the difference between control of organizational subsystems and control of organizational members. Managers frequently attempt to control the organization's major subsystems by means of control techniques integrated with one another. For example, top management may allocate a specified budget to each of its ten major subdivisions. When a particular subdivision exceeds its budget by a significant amount, that deviation indicates a problem exists that should be analyzed.

Top management also wants to control organizational members so they will perform at a satisfactory or superior level. If members perform in a superior manner, the organization should be able to accomplish its goals. Top management exercises this control by means of promotions, salary increases, demotions, and so forth.

Combinations of Control

Of course, control of organizational subsystems and control of organizational members are not independent of one another. In fact, they influence each other so strongly that a problem with one may be corrected by changing the other. When employees do not perform at a satisfactory level, management frequently changes the control systems that govern the behavior of the entire organization or its major subsystems. Similarly, if a particular subsystem is ineffective, management may combat the problem by tightening its control of organizational members by demoting or firing some individuals. However, these two types of control are more often carried out in different ways and therefore are treated separately in this chapter.

Ideally, organizations might like to use only feedforward control of subsystems and members. They would like to avoid errors, which is possible when feedforward control is employed. However, it is simply not practical to use only feedforward control. For instance, management might not want to make any changes in its control systems until it determines the company's profits (feedback control). At present, most organizations find it both desirable and feasible to use a mixture of feedback and feedforward control in controlling subsystems and members.

The remainder of this chapter focuses on both the control of organizational subsystems and the control of organizational members. In this discussion of various control techniques, either feedback or feedforward control is specified when possible.

Control
of Organizational
Subsystems

The control of organizational subsystems is more directly related to planning than is the control of organizational members. If an organization, or any of its major subsystems, is operating in an ineffective fashion, the entire planning apparatus and the organization's very existence are jeopardized. Such outcomes do not typically occur if only one or a few individuals are functioning ineffectively. Thus management is vitally interested in the control of its financial systems, production systems, and so forth. All of these systems are interrelated in that a failure in one of them frequently spreads to other areas in the organization.

Budgets

One typical means of control is an organization's budget, which is a detailed listing of the resources or money assigned to a particular project or unit. Usually top management approves the various budgets that guide the activities of the major operating divisions of the organization. Budgets normally represent feedback control. If an operating division exceeds its budget, an error is assumed to have occurred and the division must justify the increased expenditures to top management. If the division fails to justify the deviation, top management may take corrective action, such as deciding that the probable profitability of this division is lower than that of other divisions and decreasing the amount of money allocated to it. Or top management may decide to increase the budget of any operating division that has not exceeded its estimates and has been profitable for three consecutive years if it is likely that this trend will continue.

Although top management normally approves a proposed budget, the operating division usually constructs its own. Some of the factors the operating division uses to construct a budget include previous and expected sales figures and production costs. Whatever the method used, top management must closely watch the construction of budgets and their use.

In recent years, some companies have employed budgets as feedforward control mechanisms. These companies do not establish only one rigid budget that is monitored at the end of a reporting period to ascertain whether it has been exceeded. Rather, the budget is flexible in that it can be changed within a reporting period if economic conditions indicate a new approach is warranted. Hence errors can be corrected even before they occur. For example, Emerson Electric Company of St. Louis has been highly profitable for several years, at least in part because it has developed a feedforward budget control system (*Forbes*, 1970). At Emerson there are three budgets: (1) a budget based on the division's reaching its anticipated sales volume, (2) a budget to which a division can retreat if sales slip 10 percent below expectations, and (3) a budget to be used if the market collapses completely. This approach to control allows the company to respond quickly to its problems. If plans do not work out successfully, the company can change its direction and budget with a minimum of difficulty.

Standard Costs

Planning and control techniques such as budgets require reliable data to be useful. One data source for both planning and control systems is past experience. Knowing how much something cost in the previous fiscal year is an obvious way of predicting how much it will cost this year. However, these historical costs do not always accurately reflect the current situation. Management has found historical costs to be of limited value during the past few years because of the high rate of inflation. In addition, inefficiencies or unique situations that affect historical costs may limit their usefulness as a basis for predictions.

To provide itself with more reliable data for its control systems, management frequently constructs a standard cost system. *Standard costs* are estimates of a company's resource requirements for producing its product, expressed in dollars. They incorporate past costs, suppliers' estimates, industry data, engineering estimates, and any other available information to evaluate what the company's costs should be in an ideal situation. Standard costs provide a basis for budgeting and for other control techniques to be discussed in this chapter.

Types of Costs. To understand the concept of a standard cost system, it is important to review the concepts of fixed and variable costs. *Fixed costs* are recurring expenses that are relatively stable over time and are not directly related to level of output. Some examples are property taxes, building insurance, salaries of staff personnel, and rent. *Variable costs* change with the level of output; they are often one-time expenses, or at least they change each time they occur. Some prominent examples are the materials and labor a company needs to produce its final product.

Overhead represents any costs that cannot feasibly be identified as relating to units produced, such as the cost of electricity and the salaries of clerical personnel. Some overhead costs are fixed; some are variable. For accounting purposes, these expenses may be divided into fixed and variable or apportioned between the two categories. Past experience generally guides the manager in his or her treatment of these categories. A popular way of apportioning them is to divide the annual overhead costs by the number of units produced and arbitrarily assign a proportion of the costs to each unit.

An Illustration. A typical standard cost analysis of bronze candle holders for Cumberland Industries is shown in Table 6.1. The cost of providing materials for one candle holder is $2.61; labor, $3.39; and overhead, $8.57. Hence the total standard cost per candle is $14.57. Table 6.1 represents a monthly status report for the candle holder. Inspection of the totals shows that the cost of the candle holder during July was $14.60, which is three cents higher than budgeted. Such an excess is called an *unfavorable variance*. Management would probably not become upset over a three-cent unfavorable variance in itself. However, closer inspection of Table 6.1 reveals that it took an 88-cent favorable variance in overhead to offset most of a 58-cent unfavorable variance in labor and a 33-cent unfavorable variance in materials. It is now apparent that management must initiate some corrective action.

Table 6.1 indicates that the 33-cent unfavorable variance in materials is due entirely to item 001 (the bronze casting); the 58-cent unfavorable variance in labor occurred because of an increase in the time necessary to complete the grinding operation; and the 88-cent favorable variance in overhead resulted because expected levels of production were exceeded in July. The next steps in using the Standard Cost System Status Report are to determine the causes of the variances and to take any corrective action that seems appropriate.

In this case, management might discover that the unfavorable variance in bronze casting (item 001) was attributable to pilferage in the warehouse. Workers were apparently stealing the bronze castings and selling them for scrap. Although management never caught the culprits, they instituted closer controls by tightening the security system. Hence management corrected a theft problem that probably would have gone undetected without the benefit of a standard cost system.

Management then evaluated the unfavorable variance in the grinding operation and determined that the wheel used to grind the candle holder was too fine. The industrial engineering department recommended that a coarser wheel should be installed; this would reduce the grinding time from a standard of 0.20 hour to 0.15 hour, without affecting the polishing operation. The result of this evaluation was the elimination of the unfavorable variance and the identification of an efficient method for grinding the candle holder.

As this example suggests, the standard cost system can be extremely useful

Table 6.1 Costs for Bronze Candle Holder

Cumberland Industries Monthly Standard Cost Status Report for July

1. Materials (variable costs)

Item	Standard Cost	Actual Cost	Variance
001	$ 2.50	$ 2.83	$ 0.33 UF
002	0.05	0.05	0.00
003	0.05	0.05	0.00
004	0.01	0.01	0.00
Totals	$ 2.61	$ 2.94	$ 0.33 UF

2. Labor (variable costs)

Dept.	Hourly Rate	Hours Standard/Actual		Cost Standard/Actual		Variance
Grinding	$ 5.80	0.2	0.3	$ 1.16	$ 1.74	$ 0.58 UF
Polishing	5.90	0.3	0.3	1.77	1.77	0.00
Inspection & packaging	4.60	0.1	0.1	0.46	0.46	0.00
Totals				$ 3.39	$ 3.97	$ 0.58 UF

3. Overhead (monthly costs)

Item	Standard	Actual	Variance
Fixed cost	$15,000.00	$15,000.00	$ 0.00
Units produced	1,750	1,950	200 F
Fixed cost ÷ units produced	$ 8.57	$ 7.69	$ 0.88 F

4. Summary

Category	Standard	Actual	Variance
Materials	$ 2.61	$ 2.94	$ 0.33 UF
Labor	3.39	3.97	0.58 UF
Overhead	8.57	7.69	0.88 F
Totals	$14.57	$14.60	$ 0.03 UF

Note: A favorable variance (F) indicates that the actual costs were less than the standard or anticipated costs; an unfavorable variance (UF) signifies that the actual costs exceeded the standard costs.

for pinpointing problems that might otherwise go undetected. This enables management to focus its efforts on areas in need of corrective action. A standard cost system represents feedback control, for it attempts to correct a deviation after rather than before it has occurred. In addition, standard costs are useful to a manager making decisions in the areas of pricing and planning as well as controlling. Having an accurate idea of product costs helps the manager make optimum pricing decisions; knowing the probable cost of materials and labor requirements provides information for planning future needs as well as for scheduling the use of existing facilities.

But the major reason for using standard costs is to control resource consumption and costs. If a company or unit begins to lose money, management can immediately discover the source of the problem by examining the deviations from standard costs in the areas of material, labor, and overhead. However, a compulsive use of standard costs may result in ineffective performance throughout the organization, as supervisors and managers may begin to be concerned only about staying within the acceptable ranges established by the system. It is important to remember that many factors affect costs, and these factors often change. Hence management should employ standard costs as general guides rather than as specific criteria to punish supervisors and managers who may sometimes deviate from standards because of factors over which they have little, if any, control.

Management Information Systems

A *management information system* is any way of collecting data that will help the manager perform his or her job efficiently or effectively. In many organizations, each staff group provides the line officers with a separate report on operations in its own area. The personnel department may issue a report that contains information on turnover, absenteeism, and lateness; the training department may file a report that lists the dollar amounts spent for training employees and executives; and the engineering department may provide a set of standard and actual costs. The line manager must examine each report independently. However, it is possible to combine reports so the line manager can analyze related sources of information. Thus the training report could be combined with the personnel report. In today's world, many management information systems are computer based, which means that a large number of reports can be generated easily. Because of the flexibility and capability of the computer, it is relatively easy to centralize and combine related management reports. However, the essence of management information systems is the collection of relevant data regardless of the means used to gather them.

The management of a branch-banking system might construct a management information system with four distinct parts: financial information, personnel information, performance information, and customer information (see Table 6.2). Management would collect information in each branch. In this way, it would be possible to compare all the branches on all four dimensions. Ideally, all of this information would be housed within a central office so it could be obtained easily by top management.

Such a management information system clearly can become very complicated, for the number of specific factors being measured is often quite large. It is up to an individual manager to pinpoint the factors he or she considers most

Table 6.2   Strategic Factors in a Management Information System

for a Branch-Banking System

1. Financial Information
   - Percent of change in net income
   - Percent of change in dollars for various types of deposits and accounts (for example, time deposits)
   - Percent of change in number of various types of customers (for example, time deposit customers)

2. Personnel Information
   - Percent of change in absenteeism
   - Percent of change in employee turnover

3. Performance Information
   - Amount of money lost because of inefficiency and theft

4. Customer Information
   - Complaint letters
   - Marketing surveys

Note: Data tabulated by branch for one year's performance.

important. Usually top management will become concerned about the effectiveness of one of its units if it is significantly inferior to the others on several measures of performance. However, sometimes managers focus only on a few measures, such as the percent of change in net income and the rate of employee turnover. In addition, some managers rely heavily on information that is highly subjective, such as complaint letters that can serve as a barometer of feelings toward the organization.

In general, a management information system represents feedback control, since the data are historical. Obviously, a management information system is helpful only if the data upon which it is based are accurate. Occasionally, lower-echelon managers will deliberately alter data to insure their operations are placed in a favorable light. In such instances, a management information system can actually create inefficiency, for the manager must make decisions based on erroneous data.

Machine-Controlled Systems

In some situations it is possible for a machine rather than a human being to control the work processes. For example, the worker in an oil refinery never sees the oil that is flowing through the organization. Rather, he or she sits before a series of dial controls that monitor the flow of materials. If a problem occurs, it is registered on the dials.

Typically machine-controlled systems reflect feedforward control. The dials register a warning signal; the workers attempt to correct the situation before any materials are damaged. Machine-controlled systems are becoming popular because many work processes can be largely or totally automated. Under such circumstances, the worker becomes an agent or action device of the machine who reacts to warning signals provided by the automated system.

Attitude Surveys

A control mechanism that can be used in any organization, regardless of its size, is the *attitude survey* (see chapter 7 for a closer look at specific types of attitude surveys). An organization might survey its employees by asking them about their working conditions, their supervisors, or any other related aspects of the job. Usually such a survey involves the distribution of a questionnaire, preferably on a yearly or biyearly basis. Management can then pinpoint areas that need improvement by examining attitude changes over time. Thus, if 80 percent of the employees in 1975 believed their supervisors were effective, and only 30 percent in 1976 are of the same persuasion, management should examine the reasons for this change of heart.

While questionnaires are the most common way of measuring employee attitudes for control purposes, interviews provide another approach. The major advantage of a questionnaire survey is that a great amount of information can be collected in a short time. The major advantage of the interview is that it provides a wealth of detail. Generally, management is on firm ground in recommending a particular course of action if the questionnaire data and interview data both indicate it is desirable.

Management Audit

The *management audit* is a control technique that assesses the overall quality of management through the use of several methods such as questionnaires, interviews, and the analysis of "hard" data elements (turnover, productivity, and so forth). Frequently the management audit focuses on one major operational component of an organization's activity. For example, the U.S. General Accounting Office monitors the financial and accounting practices of government agencies. However, the management audit can be comprehensive. The American Institute of Management has developed a questionnaire with 301 items that focus attention on the following organizational issues: economic function, corporate structure, strength of earnings, fairness to stockholders, research and development, directorate analysis, fiscal policies, production efficiency, sales vigor, and executive evaluation.

Because of its scope, the management audit is not as precise as most of the other control techniques discussed in this chapter. Still, it can uncover problems that would otherwise go undetected. In general, this technique is effective at identifying extremely poor or extremely good management practices.

Financial Statements

Managers typically use their financial statements as control mechanisms. The *income statement,* which is a detailed listing of sources of revenues and expenses, profiles the financial operations of the organization for a given year. If top managers determine that a particular expense is too high, they can take corrective action. For example, they might decide that salaries are too high and put a freeze on hiring or salary increases.

The *balance sheet* is a detailed listing of the assets an organization owns and the financial liabilities it has incurred. If the organization determines that its financial assets are not sufficient to meet its liabilities, it may need to rectify the situation by selling assets.

Recently, some organizations have attempted to develop *human resource accounting systems.* Basically this type of accounting measures the organization's employees in terms of replacement costs, selection costs, training costs, and the like. A large insurance company calculated the replacement costs of each employee and manager throughout the organization, and found these costs ranged from $6,000 to $185,000. If the top managers in this organization notice they are depleting their human resources because of excessive turnover, they can initiate corrective action by raising salaries, developing new training programs, and taking other steps to hold their employees.

Under normal circumstances, financial statements represent feedback control. Corrective action is not initiated until after the construction of the income statement or the balance sheet, both of which reflect past activity. Financial statements are important precisely because they are indicative of the organization's overall economic well-being. They provide a framework for planning future financial outlays and controlling or correcting past inefficiencies.

Control
of Organizational
Members

In controlling individuals, as in controlling organizations, it is first necessary to establish quantifiable standards against which the performance of employees is compared and measured. In some situations, it is relatively easy to develop these standards. For example, industrial engineers may determine that the average factory worker should produce at least 100 units of a particular item per day. However, management frequently cannot quantify performance standards with such precision, especially for white-collar and managerial employees whose activities do not lend themselves to close monitoring. Still, it is always possible to develop some standards against which performance is measured. In addition, it is possible to mold a comfortable fit between the individual and the organization through the proper use of job orientation, training, and selection techniques.

Selection

Figure 6.1 contains a model that management frequently follows to control the behavior of individuals in organizations. The first step in this model is the selection of qualified individuals. Management can control hiring by such means as devising an application form with questions known to have a bearing on subsequent performance, interviewing candidates to be sure the individual's personality as well as his or her background suits the job's requirements, and developing an ability test that accurately measures whether an applicant can actually perform the work in a satisfactory manner.

One well-known selection technique is the *weighted application blank,* which compares the background factors of an applicant to those of workers already hired (see Table 6.3). To create a weighted application blank, management divides its workers into two equal groups, one low and one high on some measure of performance or productivity. Management then ascertains the percentage of workers in a given category—such as 12 years of education—who fall in the high group. For instance, 33 percent of the workers who have only graduated from grade school are in the high group. This percentage is rounded off and becomes a weight. All of the other educational categories are similarly weighted. The same procedure is used for other background factors, such as marital status, work experience, military service, and grades in school. Management then hires workers who obtain a high score when their application blank is weighted by this procedure. Hence the personnel office increases its likelihood of hiring high performers. In this sense, management is exercising feedforward control, for it has excluded individuals from the organization who would probably be poor performers.

Job Orientation

After an individual has been hired, he or she goes through a period of *orientation*—becoming familiar with the nature and duties of the job and getting a

Figure 6.1   A Model for Controlling Organizational Members

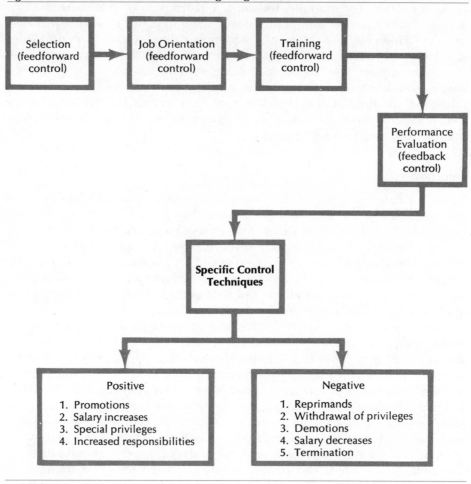

feel for the company. Many organizations provide actual job orientation programs, typically lasting one or two days, for new employees. These programs are intended not only to help employees become efficient as quickly as possible, but also to give them a positive attitude about the new job and the company. It is to the company's benefit to do this, for some research indicates that individuals who have received job orientation are more satisfied and less likely to quit than those who do not (Marion and Trieb 1969). Even an employee's interest in an organization is influenced by the job orientation he or she receives. Miner and Heaton discovered that employees who participated

Table 6.3 Weighting an Application Blank

Education	Number of Workers in Low Productivity Group (N = 100)	Number of Workers in High Productivity Group (N = 100)	Percentage of Workers with This Factor in High Group	Weight on Application Blank
Grade school	10	5	33	3
High school incomplete	8	15	73	7
High school graduate	10	20	67	7
College incomplete	20	30	60	6
College graduate	47	25	33	3
Graduate work	5	5	50	5

Note: First, a sample of workers is divided into two groups on the basis of their comparative productivity. Each weight is based on the percentage of workers in the high category, rounded off. The higher the total weighted score for all items—education, previous work experience, age, and so forth—the more desirable the job applicant.

in job orientation sessions tended to read company publications more than those who did not (Miner and Heaton 1959).

Like selection, job orientation is a form of feedforward control. The organization eliminates potential problems even before they occur by answering the individual's questions about job duties, allowing him or her to express reservations, and providing a gradual introduction to the work. Job orientation thus can be an effective control technique.

Training

A new employee typically learns more specific job-related information in some kind of training program. Virtually every large organization conducts formal training for its employees. For lower-echelon employees, the training is very specific and usually takes only a few days to complete. Many organizations also sponsor management training programs that can be one or more years in duration. The management trainee usually rotates through various departments of the organization so he or she can understand all aspects of the work.

Depending on the kind of work, a training program may consist of lectures, actual projects, films, or various other kinds of presentations. Although the employee probably will eventually deviate in some ways from this ideal pattern once he or she gets used to the work, the training provides a set of general and specific guides to follow in order to carry out the job successfully.

Although some training is usually done when a person starts a new job, training or retraining can take place at any time during an individual's tenure with an organization. Some of it may be general and not related specifically to one job. Hence training can be viewed as an ongoing process that helps an individual develop his or her general capabilities over a period of years. This approach seems to be especially appropriate for managers, as a survey of 1,666 federal government executives indicated they overwhelmingly favored receiving such training (Gannon 1975). In particular, these government managers wanted training in human relations and management science.

In the United States, training has been emphasized, for both lower-echelon employees and managers. A 1961 survey of 2,571 firms indicated that from one-third to one-half sponsored some type of in-plant training. The size of the organization seemed to be the most important factor—255 of the 277 firms with 10,000 or more employees operated training programs for at least some of their employees. In addition, more than half of these larger firms sponsored training programs for their supervisors and executives (Serbein 1961). This interest in training seems to be increasing, for a more recent survey of business firms and government agencies indicated that 75 percent sponsored management development programs (Campbell et al. 1970).

Normally, training represents feedforward control, for top management is attempting to minimize errors on the job that would otherwise occur. Sometimes training relates to feedback control if an ineffective employee undergoes it to improve his job performance. Although training will not eliminate all problems of the control of the individual, it is a useful supplement to selection and job orientation.

Performance Standards

As was stated earlier in this chapter, one crucial aspect of control is setting clear, measurable goals for employees. During the training sessions, the new employee should be made aware of the standards by which his or her performance will be evaluated. Ordinarily each employee is rated by several types of standards. Some involve work habits and attitudes: Is the employee often late for work? Does he or she get along well with other workers? Other standards involve the amount and quality of the person's work.

If the employee's job is to produce units of a standardized product, one measure of his effectiveness may be the number of units he or she produces in a given time. Research suggests that individual piece-rate systems in which each employee is paid only for the number of units he or she produces are more effective than group piece-rate systems in which each employee is paid for the average number of units produced by the group (Vroom 1964). However, although productivity is higher under an individual piece-rate system than a group piece-rate system, conflict and tension among members of the work group are higher as well. Some employees feel management may raise the level of productivity to inhuman standards and then decrease the amount of money a worker is paid for each piece; other employees focus on the number of units they are producing rather than their quality; and still others begin to resent the "ratebusters" who produce more units than anyone else. These actions may have a negative impact on the organization in the long run, in the form of decreased productivity, increased absenteeism, and high turnover. Thus, even when the work is highly standardized, it is important to evaluate periodically the impact of performance standards on employees' attitudes and behavior.

At the upper organizational levels, or in companies where employees do not produce a standardized product, it is difficult to use specific measurable standards of performance. However, performance can be evaluated in terms of how well the individual is handling his or her specific responsibilities, duties, and programs. Admittedly, the superiors of an employee who does not produce a standardized product render a judgment about his or her performance that is somewhat subjective. For this reason, it is preferable to have two or more superiors evaluate the employee's performance.

As suggested by this discussion, the use of performance standards represents feedback control. Management does not evaluate the performance of an individual until he or she has been working in a particular job for a specific period. In this sense, the use of performance standards is radically different from selection, job orientation, and training, all of which can be employed as feedforward control mechanisms.

Once an individual has been hired and trained, and his or her performance evaluated, it is to management's advantage to encourage successful performance and try to change behavior that is less than productive. To accomplish these objectives, management has recourse both to positive and negative control techniques.

Positive Control Techniques

Promotions and salaries are two of the well-known positive control mechanisms management uses to reinforce superior performance. Normally, if an individual is performing in an effective manner, he or she will periodically receive a salary increase and/or promotion. Ideally, it is preferable to give the individual both a salary increase and promotion, since he or she will typically be motivated to continue to perform in an outstanding manner if given increased responsibilities.

In some organizations, promotions and salary increases are quite uniform and open. For example, there are 18 grades through which a white-collar employee can progress in the federal government, and the top salary is $37,800 per year. Every employee knows the approximate salary of every other employee, for individuals' grade levels are public knowledge.

This openness is not common in the private sector. Rather, salary information is usually kept secret, especially in the managerial ranks. In addition, the salary range is quite wide, as top managers may be paid well over $100,000 a year. Probably the major reason for secret salary scales is that individuals cannot resent wide ranges and discrepancies if they are not aware of them. At the same time, the organization can handsomely reward a high-performing individual to reinforce his behavior.

Management can also reward an employee by delegating new responsibilities to him or her, which will make the work more interesting and rewarding. Another positive control mechanism is giving effective performers special privileges. An afternoon or a day off, a long lunch hour, or a few extra rest pauses cost management little or nothing, and they can do a lot to keep an employee's morale high. Often just a word of approval or encouragement for a superior performance is an effective reinforcement. There are many ways to reward people, and the perceptive manager will gear the techniques he or she uses to the particular employees involved.

Negative Control Techniques

When individuals fail to perform satisfactorily, management can attempt to change their behavior by using negative control techniques. Usually a manager's first course of action in dealing with an unsatisfactory employee is a simple reprimand. At this point, it is a good idea to make sure the employee knows what is expected of him or her and in what specific way he or she is failing to meet these expectations. If no change occurs, special privileges can be withdrawn; for example, the employee is no longer allowed to take five extra minutes for lunch without being docked. If the employee still fails to improve his or her behavior, stricter measures such as a demotion or salary reduction may put the employee on notice that his or her behavior is very unacceptable to management.

If there seems to be no way to make an unsuccessful employee change his or her behavior, management may resort to firing the employee. The *threat* of dismissal is sometimes effective as a control technique; but actually firing someone is not so much a control mechanism as simply a way to get rid of the problem. Still, firing one person may work as a control on other ineffective performers, for it places them on notice that they must change their behavior or meet the same fate.

Summary

Control is the monitoring of plans and the pinpointing of significant deviations from them. It involves establishing a standard or set of standards, using monitoring devices to measure performance, comparing the measurements of different monitoring devices to be sure the current state of the system is close enough to the ideal state, and using action devices to correct any significant deviations from plans. Feedback control, which is the correction of an error in a system after it has occurred, is different from feedforward control, which results when management can anticipate or predict deviations from standards or errors before they occur. In addition, control of organizational subsystems is different from the control of organizational members, although they overlap. Usually, the most effective form of control involves both feedback and feedforward control to monitor organizational subsystems and organizational members.

In controlling organizational subsystems, management has recourse to several techniques. These include budgets, standard costs, management information systems, machine-controlled systems, attitude surveys, management audits, rules, and financial statements. To control organizational members, management can refine the selection process so ineffective performers are not even hired. In addition, management can develop job orientation and training programs. All three techniques—selection, job orientation, and training—reflect feedforward control. Feedback control is exercised after an individual's performance is evaluated. Positive control techniques are promotions, salary increases, increased responsibilities, and special privileges. Some of the most important negative control techniques are reprimands, withdrawal of privileges, demotions, salary reductions, and termination.

Discussion Questions

1. What are some of the problems Cumberland Industries might have encountered in establishing standard costs for the bronze candle holders described in this chapter (see Table 6.1)? Can an excessive emphasis on standard costs ever *reduce* profits? Why or why not?

2. Describe a situation in which either feedback or feedforward control could be used effectively in an organization.

3. In what ways does the control of organizational members overlap with the control of organizational subsystems? Can these two types of control ever be independent of one another? Why or why not?

4. If planning and control represent opposite sides of the same coin, why are they treated separately? Can planning take place without control? Why or why not? Can control occur without planning? Why or why not?

5. What is the relationship between training and performance standards for employees? Between negative control techniques and performance standards?

6. How can management control the behavior of employees when they are members of a strong and militant union?

7. How can a nonprofit organization such as the March of Dimes control the behavior of its members who volunteer to work without pay? How can a church control the behavior of its members?

Critical Incidents

NOTE: *These critical incidents can be used by the whole class with the case observational method (see Appendix), or used for thought and discussion by individual class members.*

1. A dean of a college tended to be very concerned about administrative details. She called frequent meetings, appointed numerous task forces, and even checked to see that the professors were in their offices during the assigned office hours.

Questions: What kind of control is this dean exercising? Under what circumstances would this kind of control be successful in a college? Under what circumstances would it be unsuccessful?

2. A medium-sized manufacturing firm employs a large number of lower-echelon factory workers. To measure the performance of the operating divisions, the firm uses a standard cost system. Management has recently noticed the actual costs of many items far exceed standard costs, that is, the variances are very unfavorable. The main reason for the unfavorable variances seems to be that many workers are stealing these items. Some possible solutions to this problem include: a tight inspection system when employees enter and leave the plant; an open and frank discussion with employees and their leaders, who would then be asked to suggest a solution; the installation of TV cameras throughout the plant so every employee would be monitored from a central office.

Questions: Which approach do you favor? Why? What are some other possible approaches that can be used to solve this problem?

3. A top manager in a medium-sized company found it difficult to attract job applicants for managerial positions. Qualified applicants were generally attracted to large companies. In addition, his rate of managerial turnover was quite high. To attract job applicants, he began to emphasize the strong points of his organization such as: (1) a great amount of responsibility immediately after being hired; (2) the potential of learning the business quickly, since they would be involved in all of the operations. He evaded any questions from an applicant that might compare his company unfavorably with larger companies, such as questions on stock options and fringe benefits. He reasoned that the company's advantages would outweigh the disadvantages for the applicant in the long run. More importantly, even if job applicants became disillusioned and left after a few years, he still would have had the benefit of their abilities.

Questions: Do you agree with this approach? Why or why not? What problems would you expect this manager to have in training and controlling subordinates hired in this way?

Suggested Readings

Emery, James. *Organizational Planning and Control Systems.* New York: Macmillan, 1969, 166 pages, paperback.

Emery provides a general introduction to the areas of planning and control. He shows how these two concepts are related.

Gouldner, Alvin. *Patterns of Industrial Bureaucracy: A Case Study of Modern Factory Administration.* New York: Free Press, 1964 (originally published in 1954), 278 pages, paperback.

   Gouldner presents a fascinating case study of a gypsum mine. He describes in detail the reactions of both the white-collar workers in the plant and the miners to a new and tight system of control.

Lawler, Edward, and Rhode, John. *Information and Control in Organizations.* Pacific Palisades, Calif.: Goodyear, 1976, 217 pages, paperback.

   A behavioral scientist and an accountant worked together to write this short introduction to the area of control.

Organizational
Change and
Development

7

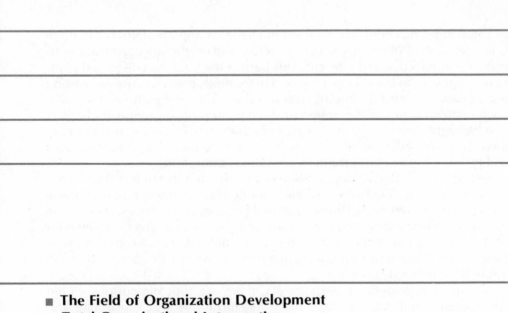

- **The Field of Organization Development**
- **Total Organizational Interventions**
- **Complex Issues Facing O.D.**

Performance Objectives

1. To understand organization development (O.D.) as the introduction of planned and systematic change into an organization within the dimensions of organization design and behavioral processes.

2. To be able to describe the techniques of O.D. and the kinds of interventions used to introduce changes into an organization.

3. To be familiar with four large-scale O.D. programs that primarily focus on changing an entire organization: Blake and Mouton's managerial grid, MAPS, system 4, and questionnaire data banks.

4. To be able to discuss some of the complex issues in the field of O.D., such as the role of the O.D. consultant.

163

Throughout this book, the concept of change is important. In part II, there was a description of various ways to structure and restructure organizations to make them effective and efficient. This part of the book has discussed planning as it relates to the change process. For example, managers use forecasting techniques to predict the future, to adjust their goals and plans, and to make appropriate changes in the design of the organization. Subsequent chapters also highlight the concept of change. For instance, managers sometimes alter their styles of leadership in order to influence the attitudes of subordinates and increase the level of productivity in the organization.

All this is to say that an organization is not static but dynamic. Even when it is successful, it is constantly changing in one way or another. Not all these changes are desired ones. Further, external environmental forces, such as the intensity of competition and the passage of laws, directly affect the activities of the organization. If the organization is to succeed, its managers must respond to such forces by introducing planned and systematic changes that will insure its continued success.

As our management model suggests, there are four dimensions within which managerial activities take place: organization design, planning and control, behavioral processes, and decision making. This chapter focuses on *organization development (O.D.)*, a relatively new area in management. O.D. deals with the introduction of planned and systematic changes into the organization within the dimensions of organization design and behavioral processes; however, its main thrust is planning. Because management must introduce the changes in a planned and systematic fashion, this book treats O.D. as a subdivision of planning and control.

In this chapter, a detailed description of O.D. is followed by a comparison of four large-scale techniques for changing an entire organization. The chapter ends by discussing some of the complex issues within the field of O.D.

The Field
of Organization
Development

Many writers have attempted to define organization development. According to Wendell French and Cecil Bell (1973), O.D. is a program for introducing planned and systematic changes into an organization. In addition, O.D. specialists rely heavily on behavioral science techniques, such as questionnaire surveys and interviews, when they introduce changes. Typically, members of the organization must actively collaborate with one another in the introduction of changes. However, they usually rely upon the advice and direction of a professional change agent—the *O.D. consultant.*

In introducing changes, the O.D. consultant places special emphasis on the activities of work groups and the interactions among them. This emphasis is logical, for the O.D. consultant normally redesigns the organization so work groups can coordinate their efforts more effectively. He or she also attempts to change the behavioral processes within and among work groups so the overall level of productivity in the organization increases. As these descriptions imply, O.D. is frequently a long-term program that may require several months or even years before the changes are successfully completed. An O.D. consultant might have to work with two departments that are having difficulty coordinating their work for several months or years before he or she irons out the problems to management's satisfaction.

Steps in O.D.

Organization development comprises three steps: diagnosis, intervention, and maintenance. Management must first recognize that a problem exists, at which time it will normally use an O.D. consultant to *diagnose* it. The consultant may examine standard management reports and use techniques such as the unstructured interview, the questionnaire survey, and group discussion sessions.

Once the O.D. consultant and members of the organization diagnose the problem, the actual *intervention* takes place. That is, the consultant and members of the organization introduce the changes. For example, two departments such as sales and production may decide they can coordinate their work better if they establish a permanent task force to monitor relations between them and straighten out any problems before they get out of hand. The consultant assists in reaching this decision and in setting up the task force.

After the intervention takes place, the O.D. consultant must ensure that the organization does not slip back to its original position. Hence he or she focuses on the *maintenance* of these changes. The consultant may meet periodically with members of the task force and help them iron out any difficulties that could hinder their effectiveness, such as a half-hearted commitment to the recommendations of the task force by members of the sales department.

Specific Techniques

O.D. consultants usually rely on behavioral science techniques both to diagnose problems and to bring about changes in an organization. Three of the most important techniques are the unstructured interview, the questionnaire survey, and the conference or group discussion.

Interviews. An O.D. consultant's first task is to seek information that will provide him or her with a deep understanding of the organization and its problems. For this purpose, he or she normally conducts private, unstructured interviews that allow an individual manager or employee to express himself or herself freely. In the *unstructured interview,* the O.D. consultant merely provides the manager or employee with general questions designed to elicit information. Hence the manager rather than the consultant controls the pace of the interview.

Such interviews are extremely helpful, for the O.D. consultant learns a great deal about the organizational problems in a relaxed manner. He or she can then use this information in helping management decide on and implement changes. In one instance, an O.D. consultant examining the causes of excessive turnover among keypunch operators in a large organization conducted several unstructured interviews with the employees, during which he discovered that they had an inaccurate idea of how their performance was being measured. Management was using a somewhat complicated formula that took into consideration both the number of cards punched and the number of errors per card. Some of the keypunch operators even said they were thinking of quitting because of the "unfair" method used to measure their performance. The O.D. consultant brought these facts to the attention of the managers, who scheduled a meeting with the employees to discuss and correct this problem. Because of these discussions, management changed its method of measuring employee performance, and the turnover rate declined significantly.

Questionnaire Surveys. Questionnaires are a popular technique for obtaining information (see p. 149). Like unstructured interviews, an anonymous and confidential questionnaire survey provides the O.D. consultant with a wealth of information that cannot be obtained easily in a group situation where individuals may be somewhat afraid to speak out openly and honestly. In organization development, the questionnaire survey is a valuable instrument, for it allows members of the organization to express themselves on a large number of job-related issues such as salaries, supervision, and working conditions. Management can use the data from the questionnaire survey to pinpoint problems.

O.D. consultants frequently employ the questionnaire survey in combination with the interview and group discussions. The consultant thus obtains information from three different sources. If he or she identifies the same or similar problems with each of these three methods, the consultant is on firm ground when recommending changes within the dimensions of organization design and behavioral processes.

Group Discussion Sessions. Once the consultant has become familiar with the nature and problems of the organization, he or she will often use group discussion sessions or conferences as part of the actual intervention. *Group discussions* are an outgrowth of sensitivity training, an approach created by psychologists to help individuals increase their self-awareness and improve their ability to relate to other people. All members of a sensitivity group contribute to each other's development. Although a psychologist is present as group leader, he or she plays a passive role most of the time. The idea of a sensitivity group is for all members to express themselves freely on a variety of issues having to do with interpersonal relations. Gradually the psychologist intervenes in the group discussion to nudge its members toward insights that should prove helpful to them. Each member thus becomes sensitized to his or her own strengths and weaknesses. Members gain insight into themselves, and change any attitudes that negatively affect the way they relate to others.

In recent years, sensitivity groups have become popular as a training forum for managers; such groups are known as *training groups (T-groups)*. However, there are several disadvantages to the use of T-groups in management. If a group leader is inexperienced and lacks adequate training, he or she may be unable to control the often highly emotional climate in the group. In addition, T-groups have been attacked on the ground that they encourage too much freedom of expression. Some members may severely criticize others, with destructive rather than constructive results. Perhaps the most serious accusation against T-groups, though, is that their positive effects often end when the group disbands. A manager who has learned to be sensitive to the other managers in a T-group does not necessarily carry this over to his or her own work situation.

O.D. consultants consequently have moved away from T-groups toward the conference approach. A *conference group* is brought together only for the purpose of attaining organizational objectives, not for personal insights. While the group members are encouraged to be open and frank, the O.D. consultant normally does not allow them to attack one another. For example, an O.D. consultant may bring together two departments that are not able to coordinate their work effectively. After some general discussion, the consultant may ask the members of each department to go into a separate room and develop a list of major problems blocking cooperation and coordination. He or she may also request each department to develop another list of the feelings its members possess about the other department. After a few hours, the two groups meet and share their lists, which then become the basis for discussion. Through these discussions, guided and controlled by the O.D. consultant, the two departments normally can solve their own problems.

The U. S. Postal Service sponsors a highly successful O.D. program that relies heavily on a conference method that is purposely nonthreatening. In the group sessions, the O.D. consultant asks individuals to attack the problem at hand rather than one another. The Postal Service attempts to bring about planned and systematic change in the 50 largest post offices by means of this approach. During a series of conferences in a major post office, the middle and top managers decided they could dramatically increase productivity if they could only increase the speed of the stamp-processing machine. These managers then reengineered this machine, a change that now saves the Postal Service $4 million a year in all of its post offices.

General Types of Intervention

Organization development usually attacks organizational problems of two general types: structural and process. A *structural* intervention involves altering the actual structure of the organization so that individuals relate to one another in a new and different way. For instance, the organization may decide to collapse ten departments into five. A *process* intervention changes the attitudes and the behavioral processes in organizational life without altering the structure in any way. Group discussions are a process intervention: if they indicate that the head of a particular department is too insensitive to the feelings of others, he or she should react by becoming more considerate.

Structural Interventions. Some examples of structural interventions are the introduction of a new technology, changing the work schedule from eight hours a day for five days a week to ten hours a day for four days a week, and developing a new system for communicating information among departments in an organization. Typically, a structural intervention directly affects the behavior of organizational members, since they must relate to one another in a new and different fashion. Ideally, these new behavioral relations will create more favorable attitudes among members of the organization and a higher level of employee performance.

One well-known structural intervention took place in a large restaurant chain (Whyte 1948). The problem was that waitress turnover and absenteeism were excessive. Moreover, many waitresses were antagonistic toward one another, since they were competing for tips from customers. In some instances, waitresses argued openly with each other and even broke down crying because of the pressures and tensions.

This situation might seem to call for a process intervention, with members of the organization coming together for group discussions to iron out the problem. However, the O.D. consultant believed the basic cause of the problems was structural: the relationships between the short-order cooks and the waitresses. In the restaurant, the waitresses verbally gave their orders to the cooks, who unconsciously resented taking commands from women. To reestablish their own authority, the cooks began to play favorites: Only waitresses who were properly respectful were given good service. Naturally the favored waitresses received better tips from the customers, for the food they served was hot and well-prepared.

This problem was eliminated by means of one small structural change: A spindle on which written orders were placed was positioned between the waitresses and the cooks. The time at which each order was placed was noted on the order slip; the cooks had to take the slips in order and so could not play favorites. Over time, the problems in the restaurant began to fade away, for the status of the cooks was no longer a factor in their work.

Process Interventions. In a process intervention, the O.D. consultant does not attempt to change the structure of the organization. Rather, the focus is on the dynamics of organizational life or the attitudes of members of the organization. The consultant attempts to change these attitudes so organizational objectives can be accomplished more successfully. For example, he or she may ask each member of a work group that is performing at a substandard level to write a narrative profile of the group's behavior. These profiles become the basis of extended discussions. Through these discussions, the consultant seeks to change the attitudes of members of the work group who are inhibiting performance.

Normally a process intervention is accompanied by some structural changes or a structural intervention. Management might try a process intervention to deal with a work group that is producing at a substandard level. During the intervention, the work group members may decide that some structural changes must be made: adding an integrator to coordinate their work with other work groups, introducing new machinery, redesigning the existing machinery, or placing workers closer together so they can communicate more effectively. Thus an organization often uses structural and process interventions simultaneously. Gaines Food has created an experimental plant in Topeka, Kansas that consists only of a small number of workers so that they can relate to one another in an optimal fashion; this represents a structural intervention. In addition, these workers meet periodically to iron out difficulties, to elect their supervisors and managers under a participatory system supported by top management, and to establish goals they seek to attain; these activities primarily reflect a process intervention.

Specific Types of Intervention

Among O.D. consultants, process intervention has received much more attention than structural intervention. Usually it is difficult to change the structure of an organization. More importantly, a process intervention frequently results in a structural intervention, as in the case of the process intervention in the Postal Service that resulted in the redesign of the stamp-processing machine. Some major types of process interventions are team building, intergroup interventions, and total organizational interventions. However, these can also represent structural interventions, as will be described shortly.

Team Building. This technique focuses on the operations of only one group. When members of a group are unfamiliar with one another or are having difficulty coordinating their work, an appropriate process intervention involves meetings of the members to strengthen their identity as a group. The goal is to build the group into a team. The group or unit should hold its meetings away from the worksite if possible, to avoid outside interferences.

At the initial meetings, group members diagnose the problems they face. One popular strategy is for the O.D. consultant to ask all members to write down five problems they consider detrimental to the functioning of the group. Each member then reads his or her list aloud, after which each problem is discussed in detail. Members then develop a final list of problems that all of them wish to attack.

After diagnosis, the group typically goes through several sessions during which they discuss possible solutions to these problems. Members also attempt to define their relationships to one another as they apply to the solution of these problems. The discussions should not become personal or vindictive in nature, as only job-related factors are covered. After the major problems of the group have been ironed out, members may meet periodically to ensure that they do not arise again.

If the O.D. consultant decides the group is too large to interact and work effectively, he or she may recommend that it be split into two groups that function independently in the organization, even though he or she has not conducted group discussion sessions. In this instance, the team-building intervention is structural.

Intergroup Interventions. When there is a great amount of tension and friction between two or more groups, an intergroup process intervention becomes appropriate. Many of the techniques employed in team building can also be used in intergroup interventions; the major difference is that more than one group is involved. Sometimes each group is asked to develop a list of strengths and weaknesses of the other group or groups. These lists become the basis for the diagnosis of problems.

Another popular intergroup approach is the *organizational mirror*. One group sits in an inside circle and is surrounded by the other group or groups. Members of the outside group discuss their general feelings about the strengths and weaknesses of the inside group, which is not allowed to participate in the discussion. Positions are then changed, and the inside group moves to the outside, where the exercise is repeated. After all groups understand how they are perceived by one another, they attempt to diagnose their problems and develop solutions.

Like team building, a structural intergroup intervention can be used as an alternative to a process intergroup intervention. For example, if two departments are unable to work together effectively because of the antagonistic relations between their two superiors, top management may put one individual in charge of both departments.

Why Efforts at Change Fail

... I reviewed my notes from thirty-two major reorganizations in large organizations in which I played some consulting and research role. I did not find one that could be labeled as fully completed and integrated three years after the change had been announced (and in many cases had gone through several revisions). That is, after three years there were still many people fighting, ignoring, questioning, resisting, blaming, the reorganization without feeling a strong obligation personally to correct the situation.

... I believe the reasons for this long delay are embedded in the change strategy typically used by management. ... The basic strategy has been for the top management to take the responsibility to overcome and outguess the resistance to change. This strategy does tend to succeed because management works very hard, applies pressure, and, if necessary, knocks a few heads together (or eliminates some). However, as we have seen, the strategy creates resisting forces that are costly to the organization's effectiveness, to its long run viability and flexibility, as well as to the people at all levels.

Chris Argyris, "Today's Problems with Tomorrow's Organizations," *Journal of Management Studies* 4, no. 1 (February 1967):53.

Total

Organizational

Interventions

Team building and intergroup process interventions rely primarily on group discussions to diagnose problems and develop solutions to them. In some situations, top management may decide to change the entire organization or a major operating division rather than just one group or a few groups. Usually top management makes this decision when the organization or operating division is performing at a substandard level or losing money.

When an entire organization is changed by means of a process intervention, a variety of techniques are employed, including group discussions, questionnaire surveys, interviews, and analysis of individuals' official job descriptions. In addition, the process intervention is usually followed by a structural intervention, such as reducing the number of departments or using integrators to coordinate work among departments. It is also possible to use a structural total organizational intervention without a process intervention. For example, management might redefine all the jobs in the organization without going through any group discussions with the employees.

As this description suggests, the total organizational intervention requires a large expenditure of time. In fact, some O.D. consultants now argue that the change process should be continuous (Kilmann 1975). One way of doing this would be for top management to sponsor a yearly questionnaire survey to identify and eliminate any minor problems that could eventually become major. This continuous effort would allow management to develop new approaches to internal and external environmental changes as they arise.

The Managerial Grid

The grid approach to O.D. has been developed by Robert Blake and Jane Mouton, and it is representative of a process intervention. Initially, Blake and Mouton attempt to change the individual leadership styles in an organization only in one group. They then strive to change the patterns of leadership among groups that must coordinate their work. Finally, they attempt to change the patterns of leadership throughout the organization (Blake and Mouton 1964 and 1969). According to Blake and Mouton, the total organizational intervention requires three to five years to complete.

Blake and Mouton begin their change efforts by focusing on the two basic aspects of leader behavior: concern for production, or *task orientation,* and concern for people, or *consideration* (see pp. 228–234). Each of these aspects is measured on a scale that ranges from 1 (low) to 9 (high). Blake and Mouton have classified leadership into five styles. The 1,1 leader is neither task oriented nor considerate; the 1,9 leader is very considerate but not task oriented; the 9,1 leader is very task oriented but not considerate; the 5,5 leader is somewhat task oriented and somewhat considerate; and the 9,9 leader is both very task oriented and very considerate (see Figure 7.1).

Figure 7.1   The Managerial Grid

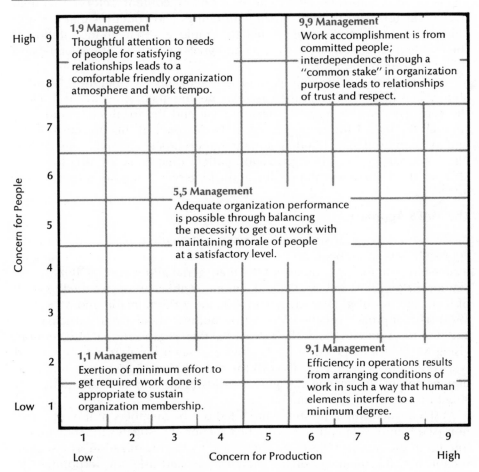

1,9 Management
Thoughtful attention to needs of people for satisfying relationships leads to a comfortable friendly organization atmosphere and work tempo.

9,9 Management
Work accomplishment is from committed people; interdependence through a "common stake" in organization purpose leads to relationships of trust and respect.

5,5 Management
Adequate organization performance is possible through balancing the necessity to get out work with maintaining morale of people at a satisfactory level.

1,1 Management
Exertion of minimum effort to get required work done is appropriate to sustain organization membership.

9,1 Management
Efficiency in operations results from arranging conditions of work in such a way that human elements interfere to a minimum degree.

Concern for People — High 9, 8, 7, 6, 5, 4, 3, 2, Low 1

Concern for Production — Low 1 2 3 4 5 6 7 8 9 High

The Grid®. From R. R. Blake and J. S. Mouton, *The Managerial Grid*, p. 10. Copyright © 1964 by Gulf Publishing Company, Houston. Reprinted by permission.

The 1,9 leader tends to abdicate his or her role as a decision maker, to smooth over difficulties and problems between individuals and subordinates, to desire a "happy" organizational climate, to motivate subordinates primarily by means of hygiene factors, and to provide praise as a substitute for a genuine rating of performance. Under these circumstances, the employee's commitment to the organization is limited mainly to social activities, such as always attending formal functions. Under the fifth style, 9,9, the leader bases his or her decisions on a consensus among members of the group, confronts and resolves problems, desires an organizational climate based on trust and acceptance, motivates subordinates by means of job content factors rather than hygiene factors, and provides them with ratings and criticisms that are specific, spontaneous, and candid. Hence the employees share in the solution of the problems and integrate their work and goals with those of the leader and the organization.

Although there are exceptions, managers generally feel that the 9,9 leadership style is ideal. Whatever the case may be, the major objective is to close the gap between the actual leadership style and the ideal leadership style through the use of the managerial grid. To accomplish this objective, Blake and Mouton used team building and intergroup process interventions. When all of the managers in the organization pattern their behavior after the ideal style for their situation, total organizational intervention is completed.

The MAPS Approach

As the preceding discussion implies, a major strength in Blake and Mouton's approach is their emphasis on the importance of gap analysis in changing leadership style through the use of the managerial grid. Recently, Bill McKelvey and Ralph Kilmann have derived a more flexible approach from the work of Blake and Mouton (McKelvey and Kilmann 1975; Kilmann and McKelvey 1975). This approach is called *MAPS* (for multivariate analysis, participation, and structure), and it is basically a structural total organizational intervention. Using MAPS, the O.D. consultants strive to match the personal needs and work preferences of individuals with the tasks that must be completed. Both dimensions of the managerial grid—consideration and task orientation or structure—are considered valuable.

MAPS begins with a questionnaire filled out by members of the organization (see Figures 7.2a and 7.2b). The first section investigates the individual's interest in the various tasks to be completed by the organization. The second section lists the members of the organization and asks the respondent to select the individuals with whom he would like to work. By means of a complex statistical analysis, individuals are matched to tasks in terms of their

Figure 7.2a   The MAPS Questionnaire

Exhibit I. An Illustration of Section 1 from the MAPS Questionnaire

Please indicate how much you would be interested in participating in either all or a portion of each of the following organizational tasks:

	Not at all.	Much below average.	Below average.	Average.	Above average.	Much above average.	Of prime interest.
Acquaint or sell customer on proposed system job	___	___	___	___	___	___	___
Furnish technical support in meetings with customer	___	___	___	___	___	___	___
Attempt to influence customer specifications	___	___	___	___	___	___	___
Participate in specification review with customer	___	___	___	___	___	___	___
Prepare detailed system description	___	___	___	___	___	___	___
Determine if all customer obligations have been met	___	___	___	___	___	___	___
Recommend design changes to simplify, reduce cost, and standardize	___	___	___	___	___	___	___
Coordinate new assemblies to utilize standard parts	___	___	___	___	___	___	___
Identify new product opportunities	___	___	___	___	___	___	___
Develop new product sales promotion and literature	___	___	___	___	___	___	___
Introduce new products to the customer	___	___	___	___	___	___	___

and so on . . .

---

preferences both for specific types of work and for other organizational members with whom they would like to work. If they become unhappy with their new assignments, they are typically allowed to change them. In its responsiveness to individual preferences, MAPS seems to be superior to the managerial grid.

Figure 7.2b The MAPS Questionnaire

Exhibit II. An Illustration of Section 2 from the MAPS Questionnaire

Listed below are all the participants in this analysis. With regard to the task items which you endorsed in Section 1, please indicate *how much you would like to work with each individual listed.*

For those individuals whom you are not familiar with, mark the category designated "don't know the person." Such a response is better than a guess. When your name appears, please mark your response toward the "none I'd like more" category for statistical purposes and to preserve your anonymity.

	Don't know the person.	Not at all.	Much below average.	Below average.	Aver-age.	Above average.	Much above average.	None I'd like more.
John Doe	___	___	___	___	___	___	___	___
Bill Green	___	___	___	___	___	___	___	___
Sam Jones	___	___	___	___	___	___	___	___
Jim Smith	___	___	___	___	___	___	___	___
and so on . . .	___	___	___	___	___	___	___	___

From Ralph Kilmann and Bill McKelvey, "The *Maps* Route to Better Organization Design." © Copyright 1975 by The Regents of the University of California. Reprinted from *California Management Review* Vol. XVII, No. 3, p. 29 by permission of the Regents.

Sometimes the results of this program are initially puzzling, but in retrospect they are understandable. For example, Kilmann designed his graduate class by means of MAPS. He broke the class into different groups on the basis of questionnaire responses, such as leadership (the group that directed the assignments), administration, collection of data, data analysis, and writing reports. Kilmann, although he was teaching the class, was assigned by MAPS to the data analysis group. This assignment, although unusual, was logical in that he happened to be the most research-oriented individual in the class. In addition, he liked data analysis. Hence his personal needs and preferences for particular tasks were matched correctly to the work of the organization.

System 4

At the University of Michigan, Rensis Likert and his associates have developed another process approach to total organizational intervention. According to Likert (1967), there are four basic styles of management or leadership: exploitive-authoritative, benevolent, consultative-democratic, and participative-

Figure 7.3 Likert's Four Systems of Management or Leadership

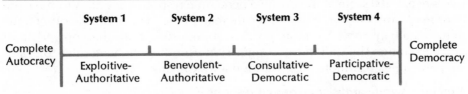

Based on Rensis Likert, *The Human Organization* (New York: McGraw-Hill, 1967).

democratic. These four styles range along a continuum extending from complete autocracy, in which subordinates have no voice whatsoever, to complete democracy, in which the employees are actively involved in the major decisions that influence the organization's success (see Figure 7.3).

According to these researchers, the participative-democratic system—*system 4*—is ideal. Under system 4, managers express complete confidence and trust in their subordinates, obtain the ideas of their subordinates and try to implement them if feasible, delegate a great amount of responsibility to their subordinates, and use group decision making as much as possible. To pinpoint problems these researchers assess an organization's managerial system by means of a standard questionnaire—The Survey of Organizational Effectiveness. Typically, there is a gap between the current system and the ideal system (system 4). The objective of the O.D. intervention is to move the organization from its current management position toward system 4.

Questionnaire Data Banks

In recent years, another important approach to the total intervention has been created: the questionnaire data bank. For the data base, managers in a large organization periodically study the attitudes of the employees by means of a questionnaire survey. Once a large number of questionnaire results has been programmed into a computer, this information can serve as a basis for several types of comparisons, such as: unit A versus all other units, lower echelon blue-collar workers in unit A versus all other lower echelon blue-collar workers in the data bank, and so forth.

To examine an organization in this fashion, it is necessary to collect several thousand questionnaires. Some companies such as RCA and government agencies such as the Navy Department have developed data banks that include well over 100,000 questionnaires.

The U.S. Civil Service Commission uses this approach when it analyzes the personnel practices of government agencies. The raw data are converted into percentiles, which compare a specific unit to all other units in the data bank in terms of a 0–100 scale. If the positive percentile response of unit A to the issue of promotions is 10, this would indicate that, in comparison to the other units in the data bank, unit A is more positive about promotions than only 9 out of every 100 units. The staff of the commission uses the following rules to evaluate percentiles (Gannon 1973; Gannon and Kopchik 1974):

1 to 15: a significantly unfavorable response

15 to 30: borderline unfavorable response; should be interpreted in relation to the overall pattern of responses

30 to 70: typical or average response

70 to 85: tending to be more favorable than average; should be related to the overall pattern of responses

85 to 100: a response significantly more favorable than average

When the O.D. consultant uses the questionnaire data bank, he or she must supplement it with other techniques to complete a total organizational intervention, for example, unstructured interviews, an investigation of "hard" data elements such as the actual rates of turnover and absenteeism, and an investigation of performance ratings.

This process approach to total organizational intervention is somewhat similar to Rensis Likert's system 4, for a norm has been established in both instances. However, the O.D. consultant makes no assumptions about "the ideal organization" or the gap between the current and the ideal organization when using the questionnaire data bank. Rather, he or she merely uses the questionnaire results to compare a specific subunit to all other subunits to identify problems within it.

Complex Issues

Facing O.D.

It is relatively easy to highlight the advantages and strengths of O.D., for its goal of bringing about planned and systematic changes within the dimensions of organization design and behavioral processes is almost necessarily a desirable one. However, the field of O.D. is faced with a number of significant problems and complex issues in implementing this goal. While these problems can usually be overcome, they require constant attention if O.D. is to be successful.

Familiarity and Dependency

In O.D., a consultant who is experienced with the process must design and guide the intervention that takes place. Sometimes he or she is not employed by the organization; the organization only employs the individual as a consultant. This has the advantage of providing the organization with a fresh outlook on its problems. However, it also means the changes are being implemented by someone who probably is not too familiar with the distinctive problems of the organization. Before the consultant can effectively guide the intervention, he or she must spend a significant amount of time becoming familiar with its unique characteristics.

An organization may also set up a separate division that lends its services to the various operating divisions that request its help. General Motors recently established an O.D. division that employs 140 professionals. The major advantage of this approach is that the O.D. consultant is familiar with the distinctive problems of the organization even before he or she visits the operating division that has requested help. The major disadvantage is that the consultant, as a member of the organization, may avoid recommending courses of action that seem risky and might harm his or her chances for promotion.

A related problem is that members of the organization may become too dependent upon the O.D. consultant. They may even reach a point where they will not undertake any changes without his or her advice. Moreover, the consultant may encourage this dependency, especially if he or she is an outsider whose fee will be terminated when the specific problem has been solved. Given these issues, the management of an organization should closely monitor both the effectiveness of the intervention and the activities of the O.D. consultant.

Time and Measurement

A major problem sometimes associated with organization development is time. Blake and Mouton argue that three to five years is required to complete a total organizational intervention. Even team building takes time, for the group must meet several times before it can diagnose and solve its problems.

Recently, O.D. consultants have directed their attention to this problem, and they have made some progress. The MAPS program can be employed as a total organizational intervention within the space of several months. An organization can also use questionnaire data banks on an annual or biannual basis to identify emerging problems. In this sense, the intervention is continuous.

Another problem is that it is very difficult to measure the success of an O.D.

intervention precisely. Organizations are not scientific laboratories in which it is possible to control all factors in the study and identify the causal relations among them. This problem is particularly acute if the intervention requires several months or years, during which the consultant introduces many changes in the organization. In this case, it may not even be possible to pinpoint the specific change or changes that seem to be creating the improved performance in the organization. Moreover, it is always possible that performance would have improved as a natural course of events even if the O.D. intervention had not taken place.

Still, performance usually can be measured in a general but convincing manner. For example, a large industrial organization sponsored a total organizational intervention that lasted five years, during which net income increased 100 percent. Just this relationship convinced top management that the intervention had been very successful and well worth the investment.

Ethics

Typically an O.D. intervention requires members of the organization to be candid with one another, for problems need to be identified. In addition, members must actively participate in defining and solving problems. However, it is often difficult for them to be open with one another, for they fear their remarks will come back to haunt them. One O.D. consultant who conducted 50 interviews with employees in an insurance company was normally greeted with hostility and remarks like "Are you a management spy?" Further, even though the O.D. consultant promises to treat the information confidentially, the employee still has reason to be wary. An O.D. consultant may obtain information during an unstructured and confidential interview that he or she then uses during a group session. Even if the consultant does not mention the source, the individuals in the group may recognize it purely on the basis of the specific information presented.

Unfortunately, a small number of O.D. consultants have engaged in unprofessional behavior. In one celebrated instance, an O.D. consultant who was involved in redesigning a critical government agency supposedly began to leak information to the press because he became so frustrated in his attempts to change it. His effectiveness was seriously impaired by this action, as members of the organization could no longer trust him to keep the information they supplied in confidence. Another O.D. consultant introduced a job enrichment program into a large government agency, after which he made several speeches openly deploring the agency's managerial practices.

The problems of trust, participation, and confidentiality are difficult to resolve. Perhaps the only solution lies in the patience and skill of the consultant as he or she slowly tries to win the trust and confidence of organizational members. While such trust is sometimes difficult to win, it is essential to an effective job.

Some O.D. consultants are attacking these problems by suggesting that professional standards be established for individuals who want to practice in this area. They recommend that a certificate in O.D. be awarded to qualified individuals, as is the case in many professions (such as the C.P.A. in accounting). Although such licensing might restrict the range and type of service O.D. consultants could offer, it should eliminate marginal individuals.

Summary

To grow and prosper, organizations must continually respond to changing conditions. The most effective way to do this is for management periodically to introduce planned and systematic change into their structures. Organization development attempts to accomplish this objective within the dimensions of organization design and behavioral processes. To do this, O.D. consultants follow three steps: they identify problems (diagnosis), make changes (intervention), and ensure that the effects of the changes will last (maintenance). To gather information, the consultant typically employs behavioral science techniques such as questionnaire surveys, unstructured interviews, and group discussion sessions or conferences. O.D. consultants attempt to involve the members of the organization actively in the change process, and they focus on the interactions that take place within and among groups.

There are two major types of interventions: structural and process. The structural intervention actually changes the organization's design so that individuals relate to one another in a new and different fashion; for example, integrators might be introduced to coordinate the work of two departments. The process intervention attempts to change the attitudes of organizational members. Typically, a process intervention results in some structural changes in the organization.

There are three specific types of interventions, each of which can be either structural or process. Team building focuses only on cohesiveness within a single group; intergroup interventions strive to bring about changes in relations between two or more groups; and a total organizational intervention seeks to effect changes throughout the organization.

Blake and Mouton's managerial grid is an example of a process total organizational intervention. The main purposes are to pinpoint the difference between the actual and ideal style of leadership for a given situation, and to help managers pattern their behavior after the most effective leadership style. MAPS is a structural total organizational intervention. Individuals select the tasks on which they would like to work and the employees with whom they would prefer to work. The Michigan approach, another process total organizational intervention, emphasizes that system 4—participative-democratic management—is ideal. Some large companies and government agencies undertake process total organizational interventions by using a large questionnaire data bank and related techniques such as unstructured interviews and conferences to pinpoint problems that require attention and correction.

Typically an intervention is guided by a professional O.D. consultant, who brings objectivity as well as expertise to the task. However, because an O.D. consultant needs to be familiar with the distinctive characteristics of the organization before he or she can guide and monitor an intervention, many large companies and government agencies have created their own O.D. departments.

O.D. involves several potential problems. Sometimes members of an organization become too dependent upon their consultant. Also, an organization must invest a great amount of time and money in O.D., even though it is sometimes difficult to measure the impact of changes on the performance of the organization. Finally, there are some ethical problems in this area, for the consultant must treat information he or she obtains from organizational members confidentially, and he or she should be qualified to undertake this kind of work.

Discussion Questions

1. Why is it difficult to measure the success or failure of an O.D. program? How would you try to overcome this difficulty?

2. Four total organizational interventions were discussed in this chapter: the managerial grid, MAPS, system 4, and questionnaire data banks. Which program(s) would require the smallest investment in setup costs? Which program(s) would take the longest to complete? Is it possible to make each of these programs continuous?

3. Suppose you were in charge of a task force set up to develop a program to certify O.D. consultants. What kind of educational and professional background would a person need to obtain a certificate in O.D.? Would you establish a training program that an individual would have to take to obtain this certificate? If so, what topics would be treated in it? If not, why not?

4. Is it necessary to use an O.D. consultant when major changes such as those described in this chapter are introduced into an organization? Is it always necessary for management and other organizational members to take part in an O.D. intervention? Why or why not?

5. What is the major difference between T-groups and the conference approach? Which would you expect to be more effective in bringing about organizational changes? Why?

Critical Incidents

NOTE: *These critical incidents can be used by the whole class with the case observational method (see Appendix), or used for thought and discussion by individual class members.*

1. The management of a large company decided to reorganize its research and development division. There are 500 employees in this division, most of whom are either scientists or engineers. In recent years, the division has had problems coordinating its research efforts. These problems have adversely influenced the company, for the division has not developed an adequate number of new products. At the same time, competitors have begun to increase their share of the market because they have been able to create high-quality products.

Questions: Of the four total organizational interventions discussed in this chapter, which would you select to redesign this organization? Why?

Would your answer be different if the organization were involved in industrial work that required the use of a large number of lower echelon, blue-collar workers who were members of a strong union? Why or why not?

2. A top government executive was recently appointed head of his agency. The management of this agency had been performing its work well; in fact, this agency was frequently cited for the superior quality of its management.

Still, the new head wants to introduce some major changes he hopes will improve an organization that is already excellent. This is a regulatory federal government agency that employs a large number of professionals, many of whom possess advanced degrees.

Questions: What kind of strategy should this executive adopt? What should he do if some of the key managers in this agency resist the changes he introduces?

3. A number of years ago, Bell Telephone introduced the dial phone in the United States. This was a radical change from the manual system in which all calls were placed through an operator. Top management knew the change would be accompanied by a reduction in force and the retraining of operators. The dial system had a direct impact on the work and life of thousands of employees within the Bell System.

Questions: How could Bell Telephone have gone about introducing the dial system so it would cause a minimum of difficulty for its employees? What steps might it have taken to reassure the employees who feared the new system? What should it have done if the employees generally resisted retraining?

Suggested Readings

Beckhard, Richard. *Organization Development: Strategies and Models.* Reading, Mass.: Addison-Wesley, 1969, 119 pages, paperback.
  Beckhard outlines various methods of organization development. He then describes five organizational situations in which these methods were successfully used.

Blake, Robert, and Mouton, Jane. *Building a Dynamic Corporation through Grid Organization Development.* Reading, Mass.: Addison-Wesley, 1969, 120 pages, paperback.
  Blake and Mouton provide a full description of the managerial grid.

French, Wendell, and Bell, Cecil. *Organization Development: Behavioral Science Interventions for Organization Improvement.* Englewood Cliffs, N.J.: Prentice-Hall, 1973, 207 pages, paperback.
  This book is an overview of the field of organization development.

III CASE STUDIES

Monitoring the Performance of Bank Tellers

In chapter 1, there is a description of a large branch-banking system. Most of this system's employees are tellers who provide direct and face-to-face service to the customer in the 180 branch banks. During the middle 1960s, this banking system began to experience abnormally high turnover among the tellers; in 1967, 40 percent of all tellers left their jobs, including 60 percent of the tellers who had been there less than one year. Since personal and accurate service to the customer is vital in this kind of organization, top management became very concerned about this problem.

Top management had attempted to use feedforward control to minimize employee problems by sending newly-hired tellers to a two-week training course, where they learned the ideal way of performing their work. However, once they were working in a branch, the tellers immediately confronted a dilemma—speed versus accuracy. In the training school, the instructors stressed that accuracy was more important than speed because of the nature of the work. But because many of the local branches were understaffed, the branch managers and the experienced tellers taught the newly-hired tellers shortcuts that enabled them to work faster.

The problem of speed versus accuracy brings into focus another dilemma, that of measuring the tellers' performance. Promotions and pay increases are supposedly related to the size of each teller's difference account, which is the amount of money for which he or she cannot account. The difference account, however, is a function of the amount of trade the branch has, managerial practices, and many other factors. Thus one teller may do twice as much as another teller but have a slightly worse difference account. When an opportunity for promotion arises, the officers tend to turn down the speedy and hard-working teller if his or her difference account is high. Further, while the

Note: These cases can be used by the whole class with the case observational method (see Appendix), or used for thought and discussion by individual class members.

TABLE 1   Rankings by Employees of the Factors Considered

Important for Promotion (N = 437)

	Most Important[a] (in percentages)			Least Important (in percentages)		
	1	2	3	4	5	6
Good relations with customers	6.8	10.3	19.9	19.9	21.0	22.0
Speed in doing work	1.6	11.4	22.0	23.9	22.9	17.2
Recommendation by right person	12.6	17.4	7.1	5.9	17.4	39.8
Cooperation in finishing work	3.6	10.7	23.6	31.1	21.5	9.4
Accuracy in doing work	35.6	32.5	17.8	9.8	3.7	0.5
Education	39.8	17.7	9.6	8.4	13.5	11.1

[a] Percentages calculated by column.

From Martin J. Gannon, "Employee Perceptions of Promotion," *Personnel Journal* 50, no. 3 (March 1971), p.215. Reprinted by permission of Personnel Journal, Inc. Copyright March 1971.

officers may reward effective tellers with small salary increases and praise, they frequently try to delay their promotions because they process the work so quickly. Hence these tellers are sometimes locked into their jobs purely because they are so efficient.

The bank's management hired a consultant to examine the problem of promotion. This consultant conducted several unstructured interviews with tellers, during which they frequently mentioned six factors they perceived as important in managers' evaluations of their work. Tellers must cooperate with one another: they share the workload by asking customers to step over to their windows when another teller is very busy, by helping each other to balance the books at the end of the day, and by spending time aiding the new tellers. Accuracy in doing the work, as reflected in the difference account, is also a major item, as is speed. Another factor is education: the more education, the better the chance for promotion. In some branches, getting along well with an influential superior may lead to a promotion. And, because they work directly with the public, good relations with customers are important.

The consultant then asked all 437 tellers in the system to complete a short questionnaire on which they rank-ordered these six items (see Table 1). The tellers felt that two factors were of overwhelming importance for promotion—68.1 percent of the tellers ranked accuracy as either first or second and 57.5 percent ranked education as first or second. From the tellers' perspective, speed, or its equivalent, hard work, is not as likely to be rewarded in this system. Helping other employees and managers also is of less significance, as is good relations with customers.

Questions. How can top management develop a better control system for the performance of tellers? What other factors should top management use to evaluate the performance of tellers? What can the bank do about the dilemma of speed versus accuracy? In what other kinds of jobs would this issue be important?

The New Engineers

The Organic Chemicals Division of a major chemical manufacturer operates a medium-size plant in a major eastern industrial center. The plant employs about 350 blue-collar workers and about 90 white-collar workers, 30 of whom are graduate engineers. The facility mainly produces organic intermediates and insecticides. Much of the equipment at the plant is old and outdated, but about 25 percent of the processes use modern technology (either continuous or semicontinuous).

Entry-level positions for engineers are located in the Process Engineering Section (see Figure 1). This section is usually composed of six to eight engineers under the direction of the process superintendent. Each of the engineers reports directly to the process superintendent; there is no distinction between junior-level and senior-level engineering positions. Since there is no management hierarchy in the section, there is little chance for advancement; upward mobility for aspiring engineers generally means moving into the production department at the unit supervisory level.

Description of the Job

The work performed by the engineers in the Process Engineering Section falls into two broad categories, process improvement and new process start-up.

Process improvement work consists of becoming familiar with unit processes used for production, evaluating the effectiveness of these production methods in light of current technology, experimenting with process changes both in the laboratory and in actual production processes, and making recommendations aimed at increasing yields or improving the profitability of an operation in some other way. Each newly employed engineer is given a few processes to study in any manner he deems appropriate, subject of course to any limitations imposed by the unit supervisor whose process he is studying. These limitations are sometimes substantial, since unit supervisors are concerned with production schedules and are often reluctant to permit experimentation which might interfere with their schedules. The troubleshooting aspect of these assignments requires the engineers to apply the knowledge they have acquired during process study to actual production problems when production department personnel are unable or too busy to work on processing breakdowns. The engineers are free to work at their own pace; they are seldom under any pressure to produce immediate results. Since the engineer's role is often rather undefined and effectiveness is rather difficult to evaluate, there is no formal performance appraisal program. Consequently, there is no significant link between performance and pay. Information about progress on

Figure 1 Schematic Diagram of Organization Structure

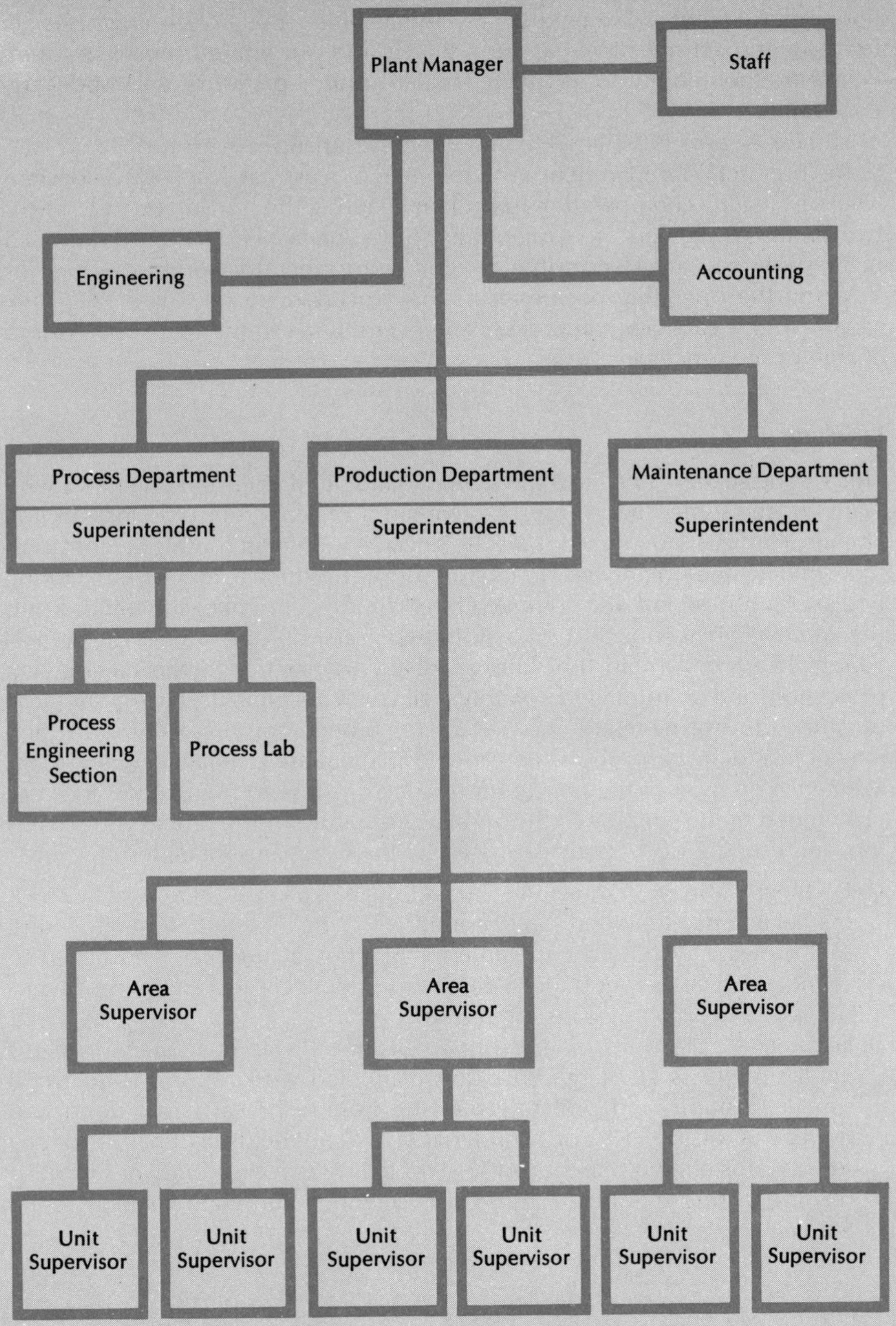

```
                    ┌──────────────┐      ┌──────────────┐
                    │ Plant Manager│──────│    Staff     │
                    └──────────────┘      └──────────────┘

┌──────────────┐                          ┌──────────────┐
│ Engineering  │                          │  Accounting  │
└──────────────┘                          └──────────────┘

┌──────────────────┐  ┌──────────────────────┐  ┌──────────────────────┐
│ Process Department│  │ Production Department │  │ Maintenance Department│
│   Superintendent  │  │   Superintendent      │  │   Superintendent      │
└──────────────────┘  └──────────────────────┘  └──────────────────────┘

┌──────────┐ ┌──────────┐
│ Process  │ │Process Lab│
│Engineering│ └──────────┘
│ Section  │
└──────────┘

┌──────────┐        ┌──────────┐        ┌──────────┐
│   Area   │        │   Area   │        │   Area   │
│Supervisor│        │Supervisor│        │Supervisor│
└──────────┘        └──────────┘        └──────────┘

┌──────────┐┌──────────┐ ┌──────────┐┌──────────┐ ┌──────────┐┌──────────┐
│   Unit   ││   Unit   │ │   Unit   ││   Unit   │ │   Unit   ││   Unit   │
│Supervisor││Supervisor│ │Supervisor││Supervisor│ │Supervisor││Supervisor│
└──────────┘└──────────┘ └──────────┘└──────────┘ └──────────┘└──────────┘
```

various projects is generally transmitted upward through informal conversations or infrequent staff meetings. In summary, then, the process engineers are free to approach problems as they see fit and are limited mostly by their creativity, their ability to sell their ideas to unit supervisors, and budgetary constraints.

Process engineers assigned to new process start-ups are essentially on loan to the production department until the new process has reached the desired level of capacity and operational regularity. During the start-up period, one or two process engineers are assigned as shift supervisors on the evening and night shifts and are responsible for correcting operating problems and instructing the operating personnel in the procedure to be followed. While serving in this capacity, the process engineer reports to the unit supervisor in charge of the process.

Problems

This setting seems to be ideal for recently graduated chemical engineers who want to get some "hands-on" experience and learn the workings of the chemical industry. On the contrary, however, it is difficult for this organization to assimilate new engineers into its structure as productive employees. During one six-month period, the company hired four recent college graduates into the Process Engineering Section; within two years, all four had left the organization. The four all had the skills necessary to practice in the engineering profession, and performed reasonably well when assigned to start-up projects, but they did not generate many ideas for process improvement, and their overall productivity level was considered inadequate by management. Management's opinion of the poor performance of these four engineers was not unfounded or attributable to the ambiguous nature of the process engineer's job, and it might best be substantiated by the following examples:

1) Engineer B, the second to enter the section, had a keen interest in the stock market and had inherited some money, which he invested. When he found that he was not held accountable for his time at the plant, he began to spend as much as four hours a day performing technical analyses of security issues in which he was interested.

2) Engineer C, the third of the four to be hired, was near the top of his graduating class at a large state university, had worked for one year in a similar position, and probably had the best technical background and training of the four. He also found that he was not held accountable for any results. This engineer spent nearly all of his time in the library or his office reading technical journals and solving scientific and mathematical "brain teasers."

The situation eventually became intolerable to upper management, so they demoted the process superintendent to a position in the production department and replaced him with an engineer from outside the company. By the time this change was made, one of the four engineers had been fired, one had resigned, and the other two were actively searching for new jobs, which they both found within six months.

Questions.   Suppose you are an O.D. consultant hired to examine this situation and introduce major changes that would eliminate these problems. What kinds of changes would you make? How would you go about introducing them? How is planning related to control in this case? Are behavioral processes or organization design more important in explaining the behavior of these engineers? Would you use team building, intergroup, or total organizational intervention? Why or why not?

■ Even when an organization is designed ideally and its systems of planning and control are excellent, it is quite possible that problems will arise if the behavioral processes are not functioning smoothly. *Behavioral processes* is a general term for the interpersonal and group relationships that establish a basis for completing work in the organization.

Why is the production department so slow at keeping the marketing department informed about new products? Is George in production still mad at Tony in marketing for running into his car in the parking lot? Or is it because the secretary of George's assistant can't send a memo to the secretary of Tony's assistant without routing it through half a dozen people? Problems that might seem too human, too trival, to worry about have been known to bring a whole organization to a grinding halt.

Although the design of the organization is static, behavioral processes are dynamic, for they are the interactions of the organization's members that move the organization toward its goals. They may be hard to measure, or even sometimes to identify, but they are always important. Behavioral processes—motivation, leadership, group behavior, and communication—constitute the third essential dimension in the integrated model of management proposed in this book.

BEHAVIORAL PROCESSES

IV

Motivation

8

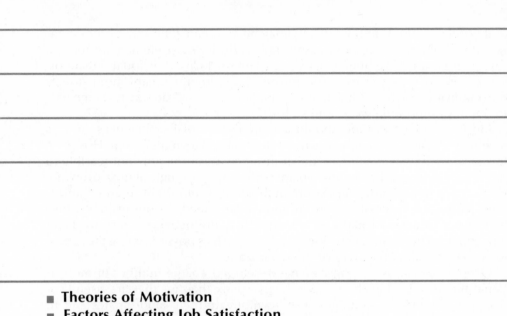

- **Theories of Motivation**
- **Factors Affecting Job Satisfaction**
- **Motivating Various Types of Workers**

Performance Objectives

1. To understand how a manager motivates his or her subordinates to behave in a way that will move the organization toward its objectives.

2. To be familiar with some useful theories of human motivation within the broad framework of expectancy theory.

3. To be aware of the importance of job satisfaction, the factors that influence it, and its relationship to motivation.

4. To understand the motivational differences that exist among various types of workers.

It is difficult, if not impossible, to imagine an organization that is not composed of human beings. An *organization* is, in its most elementary form, a system of cooperative human activities (Barnard 1938). Individuals create organizations to accomplish specific purposes. In turn, the organization attracts other individuals who wish to become members so they can satisfy their needs for money, interesting work, and so forth.

Ideally, the organization should accomplish all of its objectives, and its members should satisfy all of the needs that have drawn them to it. However, this ideal is rarely if ever attained. For instance, it is ordinarily not feasible to promote every member of the organization, even though almost everyone wants a promotion. For this reason, motivation is important in an organization. *Motivation* basically means an individual's needs or desires that cause him or her to act in a particular manner. It is the manager's task to direct individuals so they can satisfy their needs as much as possible while they strive to accomplish the objectives of the organization.

Over the years, psychologists have developed a large number of motivational theories. In this chapter, we focus on six theories that are useful for managers attempting simultaneously to motivate their subordinates and to accomplish organizational objectives. All of these theories can be seen as logically related to one another if they are viewed within the context of expectancy theory, which is a broad approach to the problem of motivation. This chapter begins with a treatment of expectancy theory, followed by a discussion of the other relevant theories of motivation. Some practical implications of motivation are then highlighted by means of an analysis of types of work and job satisfaction.

Theories

of Motivation

For many years, managers were not very interested in the area of motivation. They generally accepted Frederick Taylor's rather simplistic approach to motivation: Individuals are primarily motivated by economic factors, and they will normally increase their efforts if they receive additional money (see chapter 2). However, psychologists have demonstrated that motivation is much more complex and important than Taylor believed. Significant theories of motivation that directly apply to the practice of management include expectancy theory, Maslow's need hierarchy, McClelland's achievement motivation theory, Herzberg's two-factor theory, cognitive dissonance, equity theory, and behavior modification.

Expectancy Theory

Expectancy theory, also called performance-expectation theory and instrumentality theory, is so named because it treats motivation as a function of a person's expectations about the relationships among his or her efforts, the effectiveness of those efforts, and the rewards they obtain (see Vroom 1964). According to this theory, an individual will be motivated to produce at a high level if he or she perceives that his or her efforts will result in successful performance. This perceived link between effort and performance is called the *effort-performance linkage* (see Figure 8.1). In addition, the individual must perceive that successful performance will result in desired outcomes; this is the *performance-reward linkage*. Desired outcomes can be of two types: First, there are *intrinsic rewards* that relate directly to the work itself, that is, how interesting and challenging it is. Second, there are *extrinsic rewards* that do not directly relate to the nature of the work, for example, salary increases and working conditions.

Possibly the major advantage of expectancy theory is that the two main linkages can be expressed as probabilities. That is, interviews or a questionnaire survey can be used to measure the strength of employees' expectations that effort will lead to successful performance, and successful performance to desired outcomes. From these probabilities, management can derive a mathematical equation or function for any individual or work group that should be predictive of his or her level or its level of motivation.

However, this major advantage is also a disadvantage. For one thing, it means an employee's attitudes must be translated into exact figures and probabilities before a mathematical equation can be used to predict his or her level of motivation. Given the current state of behavioral science research, it is very difficult to reduce human attitudes to mathematical probabilities in most organizational settings.

Research evidence supports the performance-reward linkage in expectancy theory; that is, individuals do continue to perform at a high level if they obtain intrinsic and extrinsic rewards they desire. For instance, one research study indicated that production workers who were high performers tended to be significantly different from the low performers in that they believed their level of productivity directly affected their attainment of rewards (Georgopoulos, Mahoney, and Jones 1957). However, the linkage between effort and performance has not been clearly established, although some research supports this position (Cummings and Schwab 1973).

Figure 8.1   Expectancy Theory

Both the effort-performance linkage and the performance-reward linkage can be expressed in terms of mathematical probabilities, which can be used to predict an individual's or group's level of motivation.

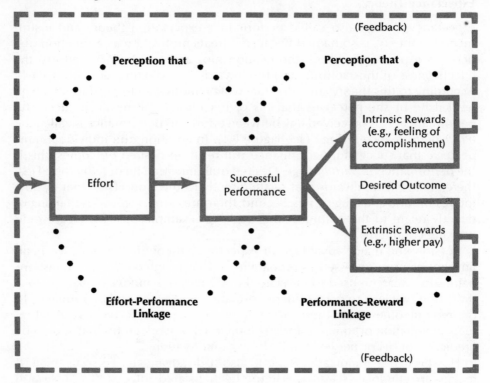

Maslow's Need Hierarchy

Individuals become members of organizations for a variety of reasons. Many of them seek work primarily because they want to satisfy their physiological needs for food and shelter. Others, however, may be sufficiently wealthy so they are not primarily attracted to an organization in this manner. Since an individual does have needs or desires he or she would like to satisfy, it seems logical that he or she would focus on some of them before even thinking about the others.

Abraham Maslow (1954) has proposed that the needs of an individual are arranged in a hierarchy, and that he or she seeks to satisfy them in a certain sequence (see Figure 8.2). After the individual's basic and elementary needs

Figure 8.2   Maslow's Need Hierarchy

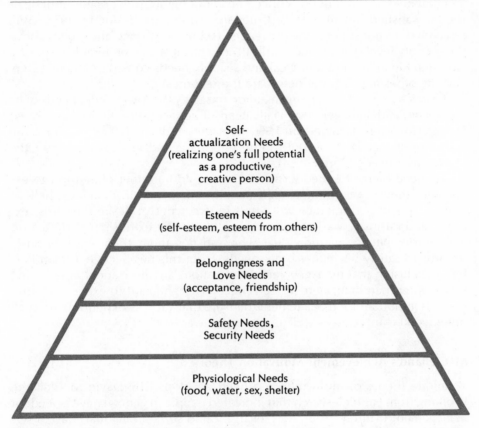

Self-
actualization Needs
(realizing one's full potential
as a productive,
creative person)

Esteem Needs
(self-esteem, esteem from others)

Belongingness and
Love Needs
(acceptance, friendship)

Safety Needs,
Security Needs

Physiological Needs
(food, water, sex, shelter)

Adapted by permission from A. H. Maslow, "A Theory of Human Motivation," *Psychological Review,* 50 (1943): 370–96, American Psychological Association.

are satisfied, he or she turns to higher-order needs. Maslow classifies needs into five types in ascending order: (1) physiological needs, for example, food and water; (2) safety needs, for example, protection against physical danger and economic disaster; (3) belongingness and love needs; (4) esteem needs, for example, the respect of fellow workers; and (5) self-actualization, realizing one's full potential as a productive and creative person or becoming what one is capable of becoming. As shown in Figure 8.2, physiological needs must be satisfied first, after which safety needs become prominent, and so forth.

Some research supports the idea that an individual must satisfy his or her physiological needs before any of the higher-order needs can be activated, and that he or she will not be concerned about higher-order needs until he or she has satisfied security needs (Cofer and Appley 1964; Alderfer 1972). Still, research does not support the existence of a hierarchy once one moves above the security level (Lawler and Suttle 1972). Thus it seems preferable to posit a two-step hierarchy: Physiological and security needs constitute the first step, and the other higher-order needs are the second step.

It is relatively easy for an organization to satisfy the lower-order needs of its employees and managers, especially in an affluent country such as the United States. However, a survey of 1,900 managers indicated they consider the higher-order needs to be both more important and less satisfied than the lower-order needs (Porter 1964).

The need hierarchy theory can be used to add another dimension to expectancy theory. According to expectancy theory, an individual must believe that successful performance will result in two types of desired rewards—extrinsic and intrinsic. Maslow's theory would say that extrinsic rewards act on lower-order needs; an individual who satisfies them then seeks intrinsic rewards to satisfy his higher-order needs. From this perspective, Lyman Porter's conclusion that managers feel organizations are more adept at satisfying lower-order than higher-order needs becomes significant to expectancy theory: It is important for management to insure that successful performance will bring workers intrinsic as well as extrinsic rewards.

McClelland's Achievement Motivation Theory

A unique theory of motivation has been developed by David McClelland. Working from earlier research that indicated people in general have a need for achievement (Murray 1938), McClelland found some individuals have a significantly higher need to achieve than others (McClelland 1961; McClelland and Winter 1969). *Need for achievement* refers to the person's inclination to strive to overcome obstacles. To measure needs, McClelland used the Thematic Apperception Test (TAT), which consists of a series of ambiguous pictures. Individuals are asked to write stories about the characters in the pictures. McClelland identified three distinct needs that are important for various types of individuals: need for achievement, need for power, and need for affiliation.

From a managerial perspective, the most important need is that for achievement. McClelland has cogently argued that managers must have a high need for achievement if they are to make their organizations prosperous. According to McClelland, this need for achievement can be learned. Thus, he attempted to instill a high need for achievement into 76 managers of small enterprises in India. During this training, the managers were taught to create high-achievement fantasies, to examine work in terms of achievement, to internalize the characteristics of high-achieving individuals, and to work to-gether in achievement-oriented groups (McClelland and Winter 1969). Achievement motivation increased significantly after the training program had been completed. Further, the experimental group of managers who had been trained were subsequently more active in an economic sense than members of a control group that did not undergo this experience.

From the vantage point of expectancy theory, McClelland's approach is significant. If an individual has a high need to achieve, it is important for him or her to believe his or her efforts will result in successful performance, and, even more, that successful performance will bring reward (achievement). If these two linkages are strong, he or she can be expected to make a significant effort to increase the probability of successful performance.

Two-Factor Theory

Several years ago, Frederick Herzberg and his associates conducted a series of interviews with 200 engineers and accountants, focusing on factors the sub-jects considered important sources of motivation (Herzberg, Mausner, and Snyderman 1959). Each engineer was asked two questions: (1) Can you de-scribe, in detail, when you felt exceptionally bad about your job? (2) Can you describe, in detail, when you felt exceptionally good about your job?

Hygiene Factors and Motivators. The results of Herzberg's investigation are reminiscent of expectancy theory. When an engineer or accountant described times he felt exceptionally bad about his job, he usually mentioned factors like pay, the technical competence of his supervisor, his relations with other employees, company policies and administration, working conditions, and job security. All these factors can be described as extrinsic; they do not relate directly to the actual work an engineer or accountant performs. These factors are associated more with the *context* of the job than its *content*. Herzberg classified them as *hygiene factors*.

However, when an engineer or accountant described times he felt excep-tionally good about the job, he talked about having successfully completed an important task, having been singled out for praise for being effective, having a sense of responsibility for his own or others' work, and getting a promotion. These factors are *intrinsic* in that they relate more to the content of the job than to its context. Herzberg termed such factors *motivators,* for they are apparently able to move people to complete their work efficiently.

According to Herzberg, hygiene factors are independent from motivators. Hygiene factors can make a worker dissatisfied, but they do not contribute significantly to his or her sense of satisfaction with a job. Motivators affect the individual's sense of intrinsic satisfaction, but not dissatisfaction. According to Herzberg, an individual who becomes too dissatisfied with hygiene factors such as pay or relations with other employees generally will try to escape from the work environment by coming in late or not at all, and eventually quitting. However, hygiene factors do not significantly influence the individual's level of productivity. Motivators, on the other hand, act directly upon the individual's level of productivity, even though they do not tend to affect such factors as lateness, absenteeism, and turnover.

Other investigators who have attempted to replicate or duplicate Herzberg's findings, by means of a questionnaire rather than interviews, have been unable to do so (see Campbell et al. 1970). Researchers are currently revising, trying out, and expanding his theory (see Schneider and Locke 1971). Still, even in its current form, Herzberg's theory has important managerial implications for two areas—job enlargement and enrichment, and ranking of job factors.

Job Enlargement and Enrichment. In Herzberg's theory, hygiene factors and motivators are directly linked to the issues of job enlargement and job enrichment (Herzberg 1968). According to Herzberg, *job enlargement* means increasing the number of operations an individual performs in a given job cycle. An employee on an automotive assembly line who performs five distinct operations during his or her job cycle holds a "larger" job than an employee who performs only four. *Job enrichment,* on the other hand, concerns the amount of responsibility an individual is able to exercise in his or her work environment.

According to Herzberg's theory, job enlargement is related to hygiene factors, for the context of the work rather than its content is involved. Some research on automobile workers supports this theory. Their work is monotonous, but less so when an individual is allowed to perform five operations than when he or she performs only four or three (Walker and Guest 1952). Hence the tendency to escape from the work environment by means of absenteeism or termination should decrease when such a job is enlarged.

Job enrichment involves the content of the work. Because it has to do with motivators, it affects a person's positive feelings about his or her job. A professor can enrich the job of a research assistant by allowing him or her to teach a class periodically. A manager can enrich the job of an engineering draftsman by permitting him or her to perform work normally reserved for fully qualified engineers. When a job is enriched, the individual assumes responsibilities not previously delegated to him or her.

There does seem to be some empirical support for this idea (see Miner 1973; Filley, House, and Kerr 1976; and Ford 1969). In particular, the link between job enrichment, job satisfaction, and decreased turnover was borne out by a program in which American Telephone and Telegraph (AT & T) Company enriched the shareholder correspondent job in its treasury department. Not only were employees happier, but the company saved $558,000 in the first 18-month period after the job was enriched (Ford 1969). Besides decreasing turnover, AT & T's program eliminated salaries of workers performing the duties now transferred to shareholder correspondents. Other benefits to the company were difficult to measure (see Table 8.1).

However, related research indicates that job enrichment will be successful only if an individual possesses a high need for achievement (Hackman and Lawler 1971).

Ranking of Job Factors. As we have seen, individuals can be motivated by many job factors. The most important seem to be the nature of the work itself, pay, promotion, recognition when a job is completed successfully, fringe benefits, working conditions, style of supervision, relationships with coworkers, and the prestige of the company and its top management (Locke

Table 8.1   Job Enrichment at AT & T

Projected Savings, First 18-Month Period, After a Shareholder Correspondent Job Was Enriched in the AT & T Treasury Department.

1. 27 percent drop in turnover: nonsupervisory specialists	$245,000
2. Investigation and file clerks: annual salaries (force reduced from 46 to 24 clerks, three management jobs eliminated)	135,000
3. Correspondents' group: salaries (five management, four verifier jobs eliminated)	76,000
4. Stock transfer group: salaries eliminated	40,000
5. Merger of employee stock-pension unit and dividend reconciliation unit: salaries eliminated	100,000
6. Improved productivity (not priced)	?
7. Improved service indexes (not priced)	?
8. Improved tone of exit interviews (not priced)	?
9. Personnel section: job rearrangements (not priced)	?
10. Must offset half the salary of the six employees working on job-enrichment program part-time	(38,000)
	$558,000

From Robert Ford, *Motivation Through the Work Itself*, p. 44. Copyright © 1969 by American Management Association. Reprinted by permission.

1976). Researchers investigating factors in motivation traditionally have gathered data by presenting a list of job factors to an employee and asking him to rank them in terms of how important they are to him. Respondents to such a questionnaire normally rank money in the middle (Lawler 1971). From the viewpoint of Herzberg's theory, it would be more appropriate to present the employee with one list of hygiene factors and one list of motivators, which he or she would rank separately. Other researchers have refined this approach by using three or more general factors.

Cognitive Dissonance

Another factor that sometimes can affect an employee's attitude toward his or her job is cognitive dissonance. Essentially, the theory of *cognitive dissonance* holds that an individual has difficulty accepting two concepts that contradict each other (Festinger 1957). To deal with the dissonance between two conflicting ideas, a person will try to modify his or her perception of one of the ideas so it no longer contradicts the other. A college graduate who is looking for a job may be offered two equally attractive positions. After he makes his final selection, he may experience a state of dissonance, since he realizes that he has rejected an excellent opportunity. To reduce this dissonance, he convinces himself that the job he turned down was not as good as the one he took (Vroom 1966).

Managers frequently use the techniques of cognitive dissonance in marketing and selling goods. It is common for a salesman to show a customer a complete line of goods and then encourage him or her to buy the most inexpensive item, even though it is obvious the customer's taste is for a medium-priced item. This approach normally offends the customer, who experiences dissonance between the idea of spending money and the idea of himself or herself as a cheapskate. He or she frequently attempts to eliminate the dissonance by purchasing the highest-priced item (Zimbardo and Ebbesen 1969).

A manager can motivate his or her employees by using techniques derived from the theory of cognitive dissonance. If an overly confident subordinate is performing slightly below average, the manager might inform him that his performance is very poor rather than moderately poor. The subordinate may increase his level of productivity to eliminate the dissonance between his self-image and the manager's report.

Expectancy theory relates to cognitive dissonance in that an individual who perceives a dissonant relationship between successful performance and desired rewards will move to reduce the dissonance. For instance, if he thinks his

performance is high but his rewards are low, he may either reduce his performance or try to increase his rewards. Thus it is advisable for managers to
prevent dissonance between performance and desired rewards.

Equity Theory

The link just noted between expectancy theory and dissonance theory is essentially a description of equity theory. *Equity theory* holds that a person must
see a relationship between the rewards he or she obtains and the amount of
work required to get them (Adams 1965). When such a balance between
inputs and outcomes does not exist, the person will attempt to restore it by
working more or less efficiently, or by trying to obtain greater rewards. His or
her judgments of balance usually are based on how his or her situation compares to that of some other employee considered an equal.

An experienced bank teller probably would feel he or she has been treated
unfairly if a newly hired teller is making more money. He or she could respond
to this inequity in several ways: complain to the superior, express resentment
by showing up late for work or being absent, decrease his or her level of
productivity, complain to an outside friend about the situation, call all the
experienced tellers together to decide on a course of action that would
change the situation, or quit. The selection of alternatives obviously depends
upon a number of critical factors. For example, the teller will not quit if there
are no other available jobs.

Behavior Modification

Behaviorism, in psychology, is a school of thought that analyzes human beings
(and animals) in terms of their observable behavior. A behaviorist is skeptical
of attempts to pinpoint someone's unconscious reason for doing something,
or even of attempts to describe someone's mental state. Hence a behaviorist
makes no assumptions about internal states, needs, or concepts of the individual that cause him or her to act in a particular manner. For example, most of
us think of fear as an emotion. To a behaviorist, fear is a set of physical
activities: running from danger, perhaps, or just having sweating palms, a dry
throat, and shaking knees.

The behaviorist viewpoint on motivation is based on an important principle
known as the *Law of Effect:* Behavior followed by desirable or pleasant consequences will be repeated, while behavior not followed by pleasant consequences will be extinguished (not repeated). From this perspective, behavior is externally determined and learned. Early behavioral research was done

with food. No assumptions were made about the animal's feeling about food—it was simply observed that if a rat pressed a bar and was given a food pellet, the rat would learn to press the bar again and again. The food was termed a *positive reinforcement* because it strengthened or reinforced the likelihood that the response preceding it would be repeated.

Modifying Behavior. *Behavior modification* is a systematic attempt to change a person's behavior—one specific behavior—by manipulating reinforcements in keeping with the Law of Effect. For instance, behavior modification can be used to help a smoker give up cigarettes by counteracting the rewarding effect cigarettes have for him, and replacing smoking with some other activity like chewing gum.

To encourage a behavior that has never occurred, an individual should be rewarded or positively reinforced as he or she gets closer and closer to the correct behavior so that he or she will complete it. Whether the desired behavior is a new one or an old one, reinforcements are most effective if they are intermittent or irregular. Further, most behaviorists argue that only positive reinforcement should be employed. Admittedly, negative reinforcement or punishment motivates an individual immediately after it is administered. However, the individual typically reverts to the undesired pattern of behavior once the negative reinforcement is removed.

Applications in Management. In recent years, managers have applied behavior modification to their organizations. For example, Emery Air Freight provided feedback to its employees to demonstrate the discrepancies among their actual performance, their perceptions of it, and company standards (Feeney 1972). Management then rewarded employees who improved their performance. This feedback, coupled with rewards, led to a significant increase in productivity.

Behavior modification can be used to encourage (or discourage) a variety of behaviors. As suggested above, it can lead to an increase in the productivity of unmotivated workers. In addition, managers have implemented behavior modification to retrain the hard-core unemployed and to decrease the rate of absenteeism in the work force (Schneier 1974).

Although behavior modification is quite different from the other motivational approaches discussed in this chapter, it fits nicely into the framework of expectancy theory. The Law of Effect is at the core of the links among effort, performance, and reward. In particular, an individual who is rewarded for successful performance will tend to repeat it. In this sense, behavior modification is consistent with the other theories discussed in this chapter.

Factors
Affecting
Job Satisfaction

Satisfaction is the difference between the amount of some valued outcome a person receives and the amount of that outcome he feels he should receive (Porter, Lawler, and Hackman 1975). Job satisfaction is an important aspect of motivation. As the overall level of job satisfaction increases, absenteeism and turnover significantly decline (Schuh 1967). As expectancy theory suggests, productivity ordinarily is influenced positively by high job satisfaction— someone who finds his or her job rewarding is likely to work harder at it if he or she receives desired rewards. Moreover, job satisfaction affects the organization's productivity, as well as the individual's, in that it is usually the most competent employees who quit when they are dissatisfied, for it is relatively easy for them to obtain work elsewhere (Likert 1967). Consequently, it is important that managers understand the concept of job satisfaction and the information major studies in this area have provided on it.

Occupational and Organizational Level

Perhaps the most important influence on a person's job satisfaction is his or her occupational or organizational level (Locke 1976; Robinson 1969). The higher someone's position in his or her field, and specifically in the organization he or she works for, the more satisfied he or she is likely to be. This finding is not surprising, for individuals in the upper organizational levels usually have more freedom and can exercise more responsibility than those in the lower echelons. Also, their pay is higher. However, although organizational level influences job satisfaction, the relationship can work the other way as well: If an individual is very satisfied with his or her work and enthusiastic about it, it is very probable that he or she will be promoted.

Design Factors

The design or structure of the organization also appears to relate to job satisfaction (see chapter 4). For instance, the larger the subunit or work group, the lower the satisfaction of those in it (Porter, Lawler, and Hackman 1975, p. 250). Apparently the members of a small subunit can satisfy their social needs, for they are able to interact comfortably both among themselves and with their superior. As the size of the subunit increases, individuals' relationships with their fellow employees seem to become more impersonal (Ingham 1970).

Noneconomic Motivation

The evidence concerning noneconomic incentives to work is not restricted to people's reports of their motivations. The existence of "dollar-a-year men" who work with only token economic rewards and entrepreneurs who continue to work after having amassed tremendous fortunes, is well known. Furthermore, there is at least anecdotal evidence that people actually do return to work after inheriting large sums of money. [J. A. C.] Brown (1954) mentioned three workers in London factories who won large sums of money from football pools which, if suitably invested, would provide enough income to enable the men to live comfortably for the rest of their lives. In each of the cases, after a short period of leisure, the men returned to work.

Victor Vroom, *Work and Motivation* (New York: John Wiley, 1964), pp. 31–32.

The type of technology an organization uses also influences the job satisfaction of its workers (see chapter 4). Mass-production technology provides the lowest degree of job satisfaction, for the work is narrow and routinized. But when an organization such as an oil refinery uses continuous-process production, the employees exercise a great amount of responsibility and are very satisfied.

Another critical organizational design factor is the number of superiors to whom an individual must report. In organizations where the technology demands a mechanistic or rigid structure, job satisfaction is lowest among subordinates who report to more than one superior (Woodward 1965; Gannon and Paine 1974). Where the technology or the work requires an organic or flexible structure, individuals who are subordinate to two or more superiors appear to be more satisfied than those who report to only one. However, someone with multiple superiors may have to deal with conflicting assignments, which can tend to lessen his or her job satisfaction and may make the assignments too burdensome.

Further, the location of the job is related to job satisfaction. Researchers have compared the job satisfaction of individuals who work at a headquarters office and at regional offices (Paine, Carroll, and Leete 1966). Uniformly, the individuals who work in the field are more satisfied with their jobs, seemingly because they have a wider range of responsibility than their counterparts at headquarters.

Work Schedules

A person's schedule of work can also influence his or her level of job satisfaction. In recent years, a number of firms and government agencies have begun to experiment with various approaches to scheduling work. It has been estimated that 1 out of every 840 employees in the United States is on some form of the four-day week; 60 percent are working on the 4–40 schedule, that is, ten hours a day for four days per week (Wheeler, Gurman, and Tarnowieski 1972). Research on the 4–40 schedule has indicated that job satisfaction does seem to increase when the new approach is introduced (Nord and Costigan 1973). However, over time, workers in low-level and routine jobs report that fatigue increases. In addition, the job satisfaction of these workers declines after about a year, especially if they have no outside interests to fill their long weekends. This indicates that the Hawthorne Effect (see p. 41) may be responsible for the initial positive effects of the 4–40 work week; workers may simply enjoy being part of an experiment, or they may be refreshed by having a change. Later, the fatigue associated with the longer hours of work overcomes the benefits of the switch.

A second distinct method of scheduling work, *flexitime,* appears to create a high level of job satisfaction both in the short run and in the long run (Hedges 1973). Under flexitime, all employees must be present during a "core" period, for example, 9:00 A.M. to 3:00 P.M. However, the employees can begin work any time before 9:00 A.M., and their starting time determines their quitting time. An employee who starts work at 6:00 A.M. can quit at 3:00 P.M.; an employee who prefers to sleep late can begin at 9:00 A.M. and quit at 6:00 P.M. Employees seem to like having this measure of control over their work life and the flexibility to schedule their outside activities more conveniently.

Labor Market

Another factor that relates to job satisfaction is the state of the labor market. In general, when unemployment is high, workers tend to focus on extrinsic aspects of the job, such as pay and security. When plenty of jobs are available, this focus changes, for individuals are guaranteed many of the extrinsic rewards and are free to concentrate on the intrinsic aspects of their jobs, such as recognition and a feeling of accomplishment (Strauss and Sayles 1972). These findings tend to support the concept of a two-step need hierarchy; individuals must satisfy their lower order needs before they become concerned about their higher order needs.

Orientation to Work

Frequently the orientation an individual brings to work affects his or her level of job satisfaction. Charles Hulin and Milton Blood (1968) surveyed 1,900 factory workers employed in both rural and urban areas. They found that workers in rural areas were committed to the Protestant Ethic and believed in working hard to advance their careers. But factory workers in urban areas did not put much credence in the Protestant Ethic; they tended to avoid work they found unpleasant.

In a related study, John Goldthorpe and his associates (1968) analyzed the orientation to work of a sample of factory workers whose fathers had been professionals. Several of these workers had been employed in lower echelon, white-collar jobs, but they wanted to make more money, so they became factory workers. However, they did not identify with the other workers and generally disliked them. Nor did they socialize with the other workers, either on or off the job. Thus, even before coming to work, these workers had developed an orientation that made them very dissatisfied with their jobs, which were a far cry from the professional occupations of their fathers.

Motivating
Various Types
of Workers

In previous generations, the typical worker was a married male with children. Thus managers normally used motivational techniques directed at this group. Today, however, there are many types of workers: married and unmarried, female and male, old and young, with varied racial and ethnic backgrounds. Managers must find what motivates workers before they can direct them in such a way that they simultaneously fulfill their needs and complete organizational objectives.

Younger Workers and Executives

As suggested above, rural workers seem to be more attached to the Protestant Work Ethic than urban workers are. Since the United States has shifted from a rural to an urban setting since the turn of the twentieth century, it seems logical to assume the general level of faith in the Protestant Ethic has decreased among workers and executives. In fact, a long-term study of college students suggests that younger workers and younger executives do not put much stock in the idea of working hard for traditional rewards. Even in the past 15 years, the need to strive for success has significantly declined among college students (Miner 1974).

It is possible the decline of the Protestant Ethic reflects a decline in the need

"Charley, how'd you like to join the millwright gang?" the foreman called to me. He appeared to think he was offering a distinguished honor—in spite of his explanation that it paid only 2 cents an hour more. The change was accepted with indifference; surely so slight an increase in pay could not mean much of a promotion. Half an hour sufficed to prove my error. As I came by my former companions, carrying oil can and wrench, I made a veritable sensation! Every one of these old friends leaned upon his shovel and wiped the sweat and dirt out of his eyes while he exclaimed: "Hey, Boodie! Where you catch-em job? Meelwright gang? Oil can and wr-rench! No more . . . shovel! My Ga-wd!"

From that moment it was possible to talk familiarly with the first and second helpers, those experts who peer through their colored spectacles into the changing conditions of the furnace's "bath" of "hot metal" up to the instant of the "tapping." For three weeks I had puzzled why these men would have nothing to do with me. Now we were suddenly become pals! But this was not all. My elevation brought honor not only inside but outside the plant. Without doubt, if my wife had lived nearby, she would have received the congratulations of the wives of the unskilled laborers: "Your man he catch-em fine job!" And not one of them but would have observed closely, the next day, to see whether she continued to speak to them!

Whiting Williams, *Mainsprings of Men* (New York: Charles Scribner's Son, 1925), p. 56.

---

to achieve, as Miner's research suggests. If this is confirmed, managers will need to develop more programs like McClelland's to increase this need. As indicated previously, job enrichment is effective only if the individual has a high need to achieve. Probably, however, it is not the need for achievement that has changed as much as the type of goals people are interested in pursuing. Perhaps workers and managers are no longer willing to devote their lives to winning money and status and helping an organization make a profit.

If the belief in the work ethic continues to decline in the United States, it is quite possible that traditionally oriented organizations will find themselves less and less able to attract capable managers. In the long run, it may be the organizations that can convince job candidates they are interested in social goals like decreasing pollution or supporting art and education that can attract the leadership necessary to fulfill organizational objectives.

Racial Minorities

For many years, racial minorities were excluded from the mainstream of American life. However, equal employment opportunity laws now require that organizations hire a significant number of minority-group members. These laws were dramatically upheld in 1973 when AT & T agreed to provide 6,000 jobs for minority-group males, 800 of which are at the management level. Other organizations are following the same pattern. Because of these opportunities, racial minorities have become and are becoming an increasingly important force in American organizations.

As might be expected, job satisfaction of nonwhites is significantly and consistently lower than that of other employees (Weaver 1974a). Occupational level seems to be more important than race in the explanation of job satisfaction for all types of employees: Individuals in the lowest occupations are the most dissatisfied workers. So one major problem may be the extent to which members of racial minorities are treated inequitably in their search for satisfying jobs. Until this situation is significantly corrected, managers must be sensitive to the needs of these employees, especially their feelings of deprivation and inequity.

Women

A great amount of literature recently has focused on working women. Although much of the research so far has been superficial, studies of working women are important, for women clearly are going to play an increasingly significant role in American society and management. In previous generations, only a few women became managers. Today, however, many women are seeking advanced degrees in schools of management, and competing with men for the prestigious and lucrative management training positions that organizations offer. In addition, equal employment opportunity laws have required that organizations must hire more women. In the 1973 AT & T settlement, the company agreed to provide 50,000 higher paying jobs for women, 5,000 of which are at the management level.

In general, studies in this area suggest the factors that motivate men and women are identical. When men and women have interesting and challenging work that allows them to exercise a great amount of authority and responsibility, both sexes tend to respond in a positive and similar fashion (Gannon and Hendrickson 1973). However, this means women in management can expect to share men's problems as well as their privileges. As women gain entry into more and more fields and positions traditionally dominated by men, they will be increasingly subject to the same pressures as men. It is likely that women will begin to experience some of the physical and mental problems traditionally associated with managerial positions, such as high rates of heart attacks, ulcers, and alcoholism.

To compound these problems, women consistently report lower job satisfaction than men (Weaver 1974b). Like racial minorities, women have generally been excluded from the mainstream of American working life; their lower level of job satisfaction probably relates to the fact they are still treated inequitably. To minimize this problem, managers must try to distribute rewards as fairly as possible, regardless of the sex of the employee. Working women, especially those in managerial positions, must emphasize their professional standards and abilities.

Part-time Workers

In the United States, the segment of the labor force increasing at the most rapid rate is the part-time (Manpower Report of the President 1970). As of May 1974, 13,741,000 workers were classified as part-time out of a work force of 89,919,000 (*Employment and Earnings,* June 1974).

Only a limited amount of research has been conducted in this area. In general, part-time employees seem to have more limited job satisfaction needs than full-time employees. One research study suggests that part-time employees define their job satisfaction in terms of their relationships with fellow workers, whereas full-time employees emphasize such factors as the work itself, pay, promotion, and supervision (Logan, O'Reilly, and Roberts 1973).

From these findings, it appears that different motivational strategies are appropriate for part-time and full-time employees. For instance, managers might develop a promotion system for its full-time employees that motivates them to work hard for advancement. The organization might allow its part-time workers to increase their rest pause by five minutes, since they seem to respond positively when they interact with one another.

Clerical Temporaries

A unique form of temporary employment has recently developed in the United States. Specifically, *temporaries* are employees sent out by an agency to complete a particular job for a firm, after which they must wait until other assignments become available. They are officially employed and paid by the agency and not by the firm in which the task is completed. In 1956 there were only 20,000 employees in this industry; today estimates vary from 1.5 to 3 million workers. Of these workers, 70 percent are classified as clerical (Gannon 1974).

Clerical temporaries evidently seek this form of employment for three major reasons: for variety in work settings, as a stop-gap measure between permanent jobs, and in order to schedule work flexibly. Especially for married women, having a flexible work schedule is an important source of job satisfaction. In fact, research suggests that, for some married women, temporary employment actually provides more job satisfaction than full-time work, primarily because they can balance the conflicting responsibilities of home and work.

Since temporaries have no long-term interest in working for an organization, managers may have difficulty motivating them. Some traditional methods of motivating regular employees such as the opportunity for promotion have no meaning to the temporaries. Still, managers can motivate temporaries by providing a pleasant and interesting work environment, being considerate, and assigning interesting work.

Summary

Motivational theory attempts to explain the causes that propel an individual to behave in a particular fashion. Most theorists agree with the basic model of expectancy theory: An individual must perceive a link between his or her efforts and successful performance, and between successful performance and desired rewards, if he or she is to be motivated to continue and/or increase his or her efforts.

The need hierarchy theory assumes there is at least a two-step hierarchy of needs: An individual must satisfy basic survival needs before he or she can be motivated by more abstract needs. McClelland's need for achievement theory argues that some people are characterized by a high need to achieve, a valuable quality in workers and managers. How high the need is depends upon learning experiences, so it is possible to teach individuals to be high in achievement need. Herzberg's two-factor theory posits two sources of motivation—the extrinsic (hygiene) factors, and the intrinsic (motivator) factors. Cognitive dissonance theory postulates that the individual seeks to eliminate the conflict between two opposing concepts by changing or discarding one of them. Similarly, equity theory holds that individuals are motivated to act to change their situations if they believe they have been treated unfairly. Advocates of behavior modification believe in the Law of Effect—behavior that is rewarded tends to be repeated, while behavior that is unrewarded will be extinguished (not repeated).

Job satisfaction is an important aspect of motivation. Factors that affect job satisfaction include the person's occupational or organizational level, the design of the organization, the work schedules, and the person's orientation to his or her work. In the past, the Protestant Ethic was a major source of motivation, but today fewer employees and managers seem to believe in it, especially younger executives and employees. As racial minorities, working women, part-time employees, and clerical temporaries have become more significant in the American work force, it has become important for managers to tailor their motivational strategies to the particular needs that each group seeks to satisfy.

Discussion Questions

1. Assume that Herzberg's two-factor theory is completely correct. When managers install a 4—40 work week, are they trying to motivate employees by means of hygiene factors or motivators? Why? When managers install flexitime, are they trying to motivate employees by means of hygiene factors or motivators? Why?

2. Are factors such as the design of the organization and work schedules more important in explaining job satisfaction than the types of workers such as racial minorities? Why or why not?

3. Behaviorists do not like any theory that assumes actions are based on internal thoughts or feelings. Do you agree with this position? Why or why not?

4. What is the definition of motivation? Is it possible for managers to disregard motivation completely and still accomplish organizational objectives? Why or why not?

5. What is job satisfaction? How is job satisfaction related to motivation? Why is job satisfaction important for an organization?

6. John Northrup was recently fired from his job. According to the theory of cognitive dissonance, how does he probably feel about his performance in this job? How does he probably feel about the organization? Will these feelings change after he obtains another job?

Critical Incidents

NOTE: *These critical incidents can be used by the whole class with the case observational method (see Appendix), or used for thought and discussion by individual class members.*

1. At 35, Edward Jones was a very effective supervisor of 30 middle-level managers in an organization of 10,000 employees. He was considered to have great potential in the company. However, about two years ago, his marriage started to fall apart; eventually he was divorced. For the past year, his performance has been very poor. He does not complete his assignments on time; he frequently arrives late for work; and he even misses some important meetings. You know he is drinking heavily.

Questions: Assume you are his superior. What would you do in this situation? Of the theories of motivation discussed in this chapter, which would you use to increase his level of performance? Why?

2. You are the president of a small chemical company. The manager of one of your divisions has recently quit, and you want to replace him with someone with good technical knowledge as well as familiarity with the division. Three employees are possible candidates for the job. Bill Gruziak, a salesman, has been with the company for four years, but his chemistry is rusty. Herman Schultz, one of your best chemists, seems too research-oriented to make a good supervisor. Linda Kelly, the former manager's assistant, is the best qualified for the job; however, she is young and recently married, and you wonder how likely she is to stick with her career rather than start a family. State law forbids discrimination on the basis of sex, so you must avoid asking Kelly whether she plans to have children soon, or similar questions. If she doesn't get the job, she could sue.

Questions: How would you evaluate Kelly's commitment to her work? What other problems would you anticipate if you hire Kelly? How would you handle them? Which candidate would you hire?

3. You are a top government executive, a job you like very much. Because Congress put a ceiling on the amount of money that a government executive could earn, your salary was frozen at $36,000 from 1969 until 1975. During this time, many of your subordinates began to earn as much as you. In 1975 Congress changed the law so you and other top government executives would automatically receive the same percentage increase given to other employees. This year you are making $37,800 — but so are many of your subordinates. To make matters worse, there is little hope that Congress will rectify this situation by creating new salary differentials in the next decade. You are not about to quit since you would lose a significant amount of money in future retirement benefits.

Questions: What are your feelings about this situation? What will you do about these feelings? How can you motivate subordinates who are making the same or nearly the same amount of money as you are?

Suggested Readings

Ford, Robert. *Motivation Through the Work Itself.* New York: American Management Association, 1969, 267 pages, hardback.
> *AT&T applied Herzberg's theory and approach to job enrichment in a large-scale effort that Ford describes in a readable fashion.*

Schein, Edgar. *Organizational Psychology.* 2d ed. Englewood Cliffs, N.J.: Prentice-Hall, 1970, 132 pages, paperback.
> *Schein's book is a perennial favorite with students, especially if they are relatively unfamiliar with the behavioral aspects of management.*

Zimbardo, Philip, and Ebbesen, Ebbe. *Influencing Attitudes and Changing Behavior.* Reading, Mass.: Addison-Wesley, 1969, 143 pages, paperback.
> *This book is somewhat difficult but readable, and management students enjoy it. One reason for the book's popularity is its broad range of coverage, such as the application of dissonance theory to marketing and the methods a speaker can use to convince an audience. An interesting aspect of this book is the presentation and reinterpretation of the original grasshopper experiment. This book teaches the management student to examine data and problems in a critical manner.*

Leadership

9

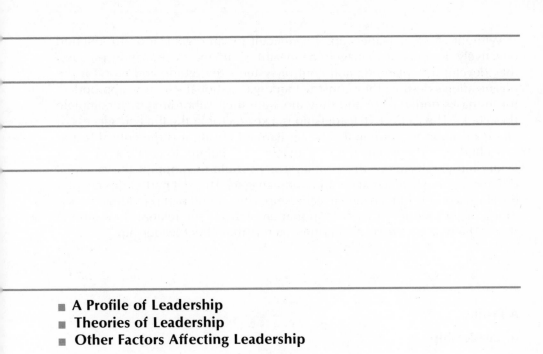

- **A Profile of Leadership**
- **Theories of Leadership**
- **Other Factors Affecting Leadership**

Performance Objectives

1. To understand the elements of and differences between task-oriented and considerate leadership.

2. To know the types of power a leader has access to, and the various roles involved in leadership.

3. To be familiar with the major theories of leadership and the relationships among them.

4. To be aware of some of the factors affecting leadership that currently are not emphasized by leadership theorists.

Without effective leadership, it is difficult for an organization to function effectively. Leaders or managers define the goals the organization pursues; they develop the planning and control systems that guide and monitor the organization's destiny; they construct an organizational structure appropriate for the tasks undertaken; and they motivate their subordinates to complete these tasks. Thus, effective leadership is a key factor in the life and success of an organization. According to Chester Barnard (1938), it is *the* critical factor.

To understand the activities of managers, it is helpful to create a profile of leadership. By means of this profile, it is possible to pinpoint the essential differences between managers and nonmanagers. The first part of this chapter develops a profile of managerial leadership. The second part provides a review of the major theories of leadership that emphasizes the relationships among them. The final part focuses on other factors that affect leadership.

A Profile
of Leadership

Obviously there are many factors involved in successful leadership. Many are difficult to measure; some are even hard to identify. In developing a profile of leadership, it is important to remember that simply being in a managerial position does not make a person a leader. What assumptions does the manager make about the behavior of his or her subordinates? What is the relationship between these assumptions and the types of power a manager may use? Finally, our profile of leadership considers the idea that being a leader is not a single role but a group of important roles that managers play in the life of an organization.

The Nature of Leadership

Until approximately 1930, there was not much interest in the area of leadership, probably because it was not really considered an important and distinctive area of study. A manager was automatically thought to be a leader. The manager did not need any formal training whatsoever in the area of leadership, for it was assumed that subordinates automatically followed his orders. For theorists such as Max Weber, a leader possessed power by virtue of his position, and power is the ability to give commands that must be accepted (Weber 1947).

Gradually the importance of leadership was recognized, at least in part because subordinates frequently disobeyed the commands of superiors. In 1938 Chester Barnard proposed a new definition of *leadership*—the ability of a superior to influence the behavior of subordinates and persuade them to follow a particular course of action (Barnard 1938). In the modern world, some subordinates openly defy their leaders or comply in a half-hearted manner with any orders given to them. Currently managers view leadership no longer as a right of office but, rather, as a skill that can and must be learned in order to motivate subordinates to be productive. However, there are different types of power a leader can employ as he or she attempts to influence subordinates.

Types of Power

According to John R. P. French and Bertram Raven (1959), there are five types of power a superior can use to persuade his or her subordinates to follow a particular course of action. When subordinates obey a superior solely because of his or her position in the organization, the superior is exercising *legitimate power*. Or a superior may influence behavior by *reward power,* persuading subordinates by means such as promotions, salary increases, and interesting assignments.

Sometimes subordinates follow the dictates of a leader because of his or her superior knowledge of the matter under discussion. For instance, engineers tend to obey a superior if he or she is more technically capable than they are. This is *expert power*. Further, subordinates occasionally will obey a superior simply because they identify with him in that they like and respect him. This is *referent power.*

Finally, the leader can force subordinates to follow the course of action outlined for them. If they do not comply, the superior can punish them. In this case, the leader is exercising *coercive power.*

Of course, a leader can employ several types of power simultaneously. Engineers may follow the commands of their superior because he or she is technically more capable and because he or she rewards them for outstanding work. Hence, both expert power and reward power come into play.

Theory X and Theory Y

Several years ago, Douglas McGregor suggested that managers have developed two distinct philosophies concerning their leadership role. These two philosophies, which he called Theory X and Theory Y, represent opposite points of view. The approach McGregor felt had traditionally dominated, Theory X, consists of the following propositions:

The average human being has an inherent dislike of work and will avoid it if he can.

Because of this human characteristic of dislike of work, most people must be coerced, controlled, directed, threatened with punishment to get them to put forth adequate effort toward the achievement of organizational objectives.

The average human being prefers to be directed, wishes to avoid responsibility, has relatively little ambition, wants security above all. (McGregor 1960, pp. 33–34.)

These propositions suggest that a manager who sees his or her role in terms of Theory X would tend to be autocratic.

What McGregor proposed as an alternative was Theory Y, which rests on an entirely different set of assumptions.

The expenditure of physical and mental effort in work is as a natural as play or rest. . . .

External control and the threat of punishment are not the only means for bringing about effort toward organizational objectives. Man will exercise self-direction and self-control in the service of objectives to which he is committed. . . .

Commitment to objectives is a function of the rewards associated with their achievement. . . .

The average human being learns, under proper conditions, not only to accept but to seek responsibility. . . .

The capacity to exercise a relatively high degree of imagination, ingenuity, and creativity in the solution of organizational problems is widely, not narrowly, distributed in the population.

Under the conditions of modern industrial life, the intellectual potentialities of the average human being are only partially utilized. (McGregor 1960, pp. 47–48.)

Generally, a manager who believes in Theory Y will allow his or her subordinates to exercise a great amount of discretion and responsibility. A manager who views subordinates in terms of Theory X will tend to use two kinds of power—coercive and legitimate. Probably he or she will employ coercive power more than legitimate power, for Theory X holds that coercion is an effective means of persuasion. The manager who follows Theory Y is more likely to use the other three types of power—reward, expert, and referent.

Managerial Roles

"The role of the manager" is really not a single role at all. Managers perform many functions or play several diverse roles in an organization. Several writers have attempted to classify these roles. One of the best-known classifications has been proposed by Henry Mintzberg, who argues that the manager performs three essential types of roles in an organization: interpersonal, informational, and decisional. He then subdivides these three major types of roles into ten distinct roles (see Figure 9.1).

Interpersonal Roles. *Interpersonal roles* refer to the relationship between the manager and others, both within and outside the organization. Within this constellation the manager plays three distinct roles: figurehead, leader, and liaison.

In the *figurehead* role, the manager acts as a symbol of the organization. Because of the manager's formal position, he or she must undertake activities designed to promote the interests of the organization. Thus he or she attends formal dinners as a representative of the organization, gives speeches that espouse the organization's position on various issues, and makes public pronouncements if the organization is attacked in the newspaper or on television. As the manager's status and position in the organization rise, he or she spends more time in activities that cast him or her as a figurehead.

However, the manager must also energize the organization and motivate subordinates so they will help accomplish the overall objectives of the enterprise. In this sense, the manager undertakes a *leader* role in the organization. As a leader, the manager's direct relationship with subordinates is his or her main focus, for he or she must influence subordinates and persuade them to follow commands. It is vital that managers at all levels in the organization perform the leader role effectively. Researchers have studied this role much more than any of the others, probably because it is essential for the success of the organization and it affects the performance of every employee.

In addition, the manager plays a *liaison* role in the organization. That is, he or she develops horizontal relationships with peers or equals in other parts of the organization or outside of it in order to accomplish his or her objectives. This web of relationships is important for the manager's work, since he or she frequently needs information, resources, and other kinds of help that can be easily obtained from peers. At the top levels in the organization, the managers typically activate the liaison role with peers who work in both their own and other organizations. At lower organizational levels, managers spend more time with peers in other parts of their own enterprises.

Figure 9.1   Ten Managerial Roles

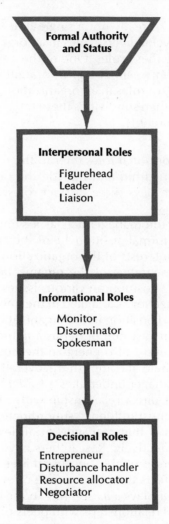

From Fig. 8 "The Manager's Roles" (p. 59) in *The Nature of Managerial Work* by Henry Mintzberg (Harper & Row, 1973).

Informational Roles. The manager is also the focal point of information in an organization. To complete his or her tasks effectively, the manager must transmit and receive information. In this area, he or she plays three distinct roles: monitor, disseminator, and spokesman.

As *monitor,* the manager is constantly trying to obtain information that enables him or her to comprehend what is taking place in the organization and outside of it. For this purpose, the manager reads reports, attends meetings, and scans business publications. More importantly, however, he or she seeks current information by talking to peers and subordinates who have a basic understanding of new developments that might affect the organization. At the top levels in the organization, managers focus on internal factors that affect the organization's effectiveness. They also scan the external environment to pinpoint factors outside of the organization that may have an adverse influence, such as new governmental regulations and new products created by competitors. At lower organizational levels, managers begin to worry more about the internal factors that may inhibit the productivity of their own subunits.

The manager also serves as a *disseminator* of information. Because of the key position he or she occupies, the manager can transmit information that will be of help to associates and, in turn, receives information that will aid him or her in completing activities. Again, managers at various levels of the organization perform this role differently. At the top levels, the manager shares information with peers in other organizations that will be of mutual benefit, and performs a similar function within his or her own organization. At lower

The Importance of Leadership

Human beings are our most precious part of civilization. What responsibility could be more important than the leadership and development of people? Without leadership, an organization is but a muddle of men and machines. Leadership is the ability to persuade others to seek defined objectives enthusiastically. It is the human factor which binds a group together and motivates it toward goals. Management activities such as planning, organizing, and decision making are dormant cocoons until the leader triggers the power of motivation in people and guides them toward their goals. The leader's act of motivation is similar in its effect to the secret chemical which turns the insect pupa into the resplendent butterfly with all the beauty that was the pupa's potential. *Leadership transforms potential into reality.* It is the ultimate act which brings to success all of the potent potential that is in an organization and its people.

Leadership is so important to group accomplishment that mankind has been concerned about it since the beginning of recorded history.

Keith Davis, *Human Relations at Work: The Dynamics of Organizational Behavior,* 3rd ed. (New York: McGraw-Hill, 1967), p. 96.

organizational levels, managers begin to emphasize the sharing of information with peers in their own enterprise.

The third informational role the manager plays is that of *spokesman*. Top managers typically transmit information to the media and other individuals outside the organization about the goals, policies, and plans of the enterprise. Typically, the top managers reserve this role for themselves, since their figurehead role makes them the logical vehicle for transmitting information to the public.

Decisional Roles. The manager also plays four decisional roles in an organization. The first is that of the *entrepreneur*. By this Mintzberg means that the manager must initiate change by searching the organization and its external environment for new products, programs, and opportunities that will insure the continued success of the enterprise. Naturally top managers perform this role. However, many other managers throughout the organization also focus on entrepreneurial activity. Production managers attempt to develop methods to decrease costs; research and development managers seek to develop new processes and products; marketing managers try to create new ways of attracting customers; and so on.

The manager also serves as a *disturbance handler* in the organization. If two organizational subunits whose activities overlap cannot work together smoothly, managers must correct the situation. In addition, the managers react to any externally generated disturbance. For instance, if the organization cannot produce its final good or service because a supplier decides to curtail shipment of raw materials, the managers must alleviate this situation. As suggested by this discussion, managers at all levels of the organization function as disturbance handlers.

The manager also serves as a *resource allocator* who apportions organizational resources of all types to various individuals and groups. In this role, the manager frequently confronts difficulties and hostilities, since resources are usually limited and scarce. Even if the organization is very affluent, it is inevitable that the manager must decide to give some individuals and groups more resources than others. Top managers usually make policy and long-range decisions in this area, for example, the decision to close a particular plant. However, the upper middle managers are frequently charged with short-range and operational activities in this area, for they allocate scarce resources to the divisions of the organization.

Finally, the manager acts as a *negotiator*. In this capacity, he or she represents the organization at major negotiations. For example, the vice-president of industrial relations puts forth management's position during contract negotiations with the union. Or, a top manager may represent the organization if a public interest group pickets it to obtain a major innovation such as the hiring of a significant number of racial minorities and women. Usually top managers perform the role of negotiator, since they have the power to commit the organization to a particular course of action.

Theories
of Leadership

As suggested by the profile of leadership, managers influence organizational activities in a number of ways, such as motivating subordinates, allocating scarce resources, and serving as a vehicle of communication. Over the years, researchers have primarily emphasized one aspect of the manager's role in their theories—the influence of leadership on the activities of subordinates. Quite a few research studies have been completed in this area, many of which have had contradictory results. In this section, the significant theories of leadership are explored for the purposes of (1) reconciling the contradictory research findings, and (2) pointing out the critical factors of leadership with which a manager should be familiar.

Trait Theory

For several years, researchers focused a great amount of attention on the traits that make leaders successful. This research is usually classified under the "Great Man" theory of leadership, because it assumes the leader is quite different from the average person in terms of personality traits such as intelligence, perseverance, and ambition. Unfortunately, research in this area tended to be obscure and contradictory. Several writers developed lists of leadership traits that were quite different from one another.

One problem in these studies was that researchers did not have any way in which to measure traits accurately. Recently, however, Edwin Ghiselli (1971) developed a short self-description inventory that has succeeded in measuring the traits of individuals. Comparing successful and unsuccessful managers, Ghiselli found that the most important trait for successful managers is supervisory ability, followed closely by the desire for occupational achievement. Other important traits are intelligence, self-actualization (the desire to reach one's potential), self-assurance, and decisiveness.

A more lasting problem with the research in this area is that trait theorists have not considered the situation or environment in which leadership takes place. Specific traits may be predictive of successful leadership in one type of organization but not in others (Fiedler 1967). For example, an autocratic individual may be successful as a director of a prison but not a welfare agency.

Still, the work of Ghiselli over the past 25 years does suggest that certain traits are critical to a manager's success as a leader. In an overall profile of managerial success, one dimension is the personality traits of the individual (see chapter 16). Trait theory is relevant, and it will probably become even more important as researchers identify the traits related to success within specific organizational settings.

The Ohio State Studies

In 1941 the United States entered World War II. This country was not well prepared for this gigantic war and experienced great difficulty in transforming its civilian economy into a war economy. In addition, the United States did not have a large number of experienced leaders who could direct this transformation at home or lead the military into battle abroad. This problem was especially pronounced in the battlefield, for the American military was relatively unfamiliar with modern warfare and the kinds of leaders it required. At least partially because of these problems, interest in the study of leadership increased immediately after the war was over. Two important and long-term independent studies, undertaken at the University of Michigan and The Ohio State University, came up with findings that were highly similar (Likert 1961 and 1967; Stogdill and Coons 1957). Because the Ohio State studies were more intensive and more exhaustive than the Michigan studies, they have been selected for discussion here.

In the Ohio State studies, managers completed a questionnaire focused on the behavior of leaders. It contained lists of statements developed to cover all aspects of each job under investigation. One questionnaire item might be, "He is capable of performing all the jobs of his subordinates." Initially, the researchers worked with a questionnaire of 1,800 items, which was eventually reduced to 150 items and administered to managers in a variety of positions.

According to the Ohio State studies, leader behavior has two major dimensions: the initiation of structure, or task orientation; and consideration. *Task orientation* concerns the degree to which the leader gives structure to his or her subordinates' work by assigning them definite tasks, specifying the procedures they are to follow, clarifying his or her expectations of them, and scheduling their work. *Consideration* refers to whether the leader constructs a supportive environment for his or her subordinates by being friendly and approachable, showing concern about the personal welfare of the group and its members, and providing advance notice of any changes that are going to take place. Statistically, task orientation and consideration are independent of each other. However, an individual can be task oriented and considerate simultaneously.

The early research on these two dimensions indicated that: (1) as a leader's consideration increased, employee turnover and absenteeism declined; and (2) as task orientation increased, employee performance rose. These findings are intuitively logical, in view of the theories of motivation described in chapter 8. However, some contradictory results began to emerge. In some instances, an increase in consideration was accompanied by an increase in turnover and absenteeism. Similarly, as task orientation increased, sometimes employee performance declined.

Much of modern leadership research has focused on these contradictory findings. Perhaps the most significant contributions in recent years have been made by two individuals, Fred Fiedler and Robert House.

Fiedler's Contingency Approach

The major significance of Fiedler's theory is that he went on to add the organizational environment or situation as a key element in judging successful leadership. For his studies, Fiedler asked a leader to answer a questionnaire in which he described his "least-preferred" coworker (subordinate) in terms of a series of bipolar adjectives. From these data, Fiedler developed the least-preferred coworker scale, which measures the degree of leniency with which the leader evaluates his or her most ineffective subordinate. Originally, Fiedler believed he was measuring the personality traits of the leader. However, his recent work suggests he was essentially measuring task orientation and consideration. A leader who describes his or her least-preferred coworker favorably tends to be considerate and employee centered. A leader who describes his or her least-preferred coworker unfavorably tends to be task oriented. Because Fiedler employed only one scale in his research, a leader could be high on either task orientation or consideration, but not both.

Fiedler then extended his analysis by focusing on three key situational factors:

1. *Leader-member relations*—the degree to which the employees accept the leader
2. *Task structure*—the degree to which the subordinates' jobs are described in detail
3. *Position power*—the amount of formal authority the leader possesses by virtue of his or her position in the organization

Fiedler investigated eight possible combinations of these situations in terms of whether task orientation or consideration was a more appropriate leadership style. Task-oriented leadership was successful in five situations and consideration in three situations, as shown in Figure 9.2.

According to Fiedler, a task-oriented style of leadership is more effective than a considerate style under extreme situations, that is, when the situation is either very certain or very uncertain. Task-oriented leadership would be advisable in a natural disaster, such as a flood or fire. In such a very uncertain situation, the leader-member relations are moderately poor, the task is unstructured, and the position power of the leader is weak, for very few individuals know what to do, and no one is typically appointed in any official way to be the leader. The individual who emerges as leader to direct the group's activity frequently does not know any of his or her subordinates intimately. Under such conditions, the task-oriented leader who gets things accomplished proves to be most successful. If the leader is considerate, he or she may waste so much time that the disaster could get further out of control and lives might be lost.

A similar kind of leadership is required under very certain situations. For instance, blue-collar workers generally want to know exactly what they are supposed to do. Hence their task is usually highly structured. Moreover, the leader's position power is strong if management backs his or her decisions. Finally, even though the leader may not be considerate in that he or she cannot waste a lot of time, leader-member relations may be extremely strong if he or she is able to gain promotions and salary increases for subordinates. Under such conditions, the task-oriented style of leadership is preferable to a considerate style.

The considerate style of leadership seems to be appropriate when the environment or situation is moderately certain, for example, when: (1) leader-member relations are good, (2) the task is unstructured, and (3) position power is weak. For instance, research scientists do not like a strong superior who structures the task for them, for they must follow their own creative leads in order to solve their problems. Under such conditions, a considerate style of leadership is preferable to a task-oriented style, for the leader's success depends partly on his or her good relations with subordinates.

In short, the task-oriented style is appropriate for very certain and very uncertain situations, whereas the considerate style is appropriate for moderately certain situations (see Figure 9.3). Since the style of leadership that is effective is dependent or contingent upon the situation, Fiedler's approach has been called the *contingency theory* of leadership.

There have been some criticisms of Fiedler's work, as some researchers who have attempted to verify his conclusions in different organizational settings have been unable to do so (Graen, Alvares, and Orris 1970). In addition , it can

Figure 9.2   Fiedler's Contingency Theory of Leadership

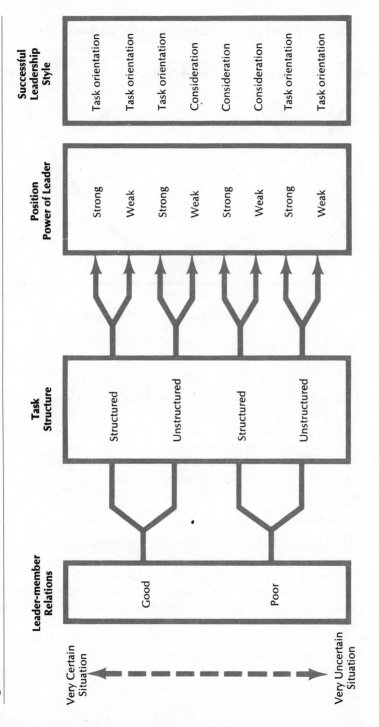

Based on Fred Fiedler, *A Theory of Leadership Effectiveness* (New York: McGraw-Hill, 1967); and Fred Fiedler, "Validation and Extension of the Contingency Model of Leadership Effectiveness: A Review of Empirical Findings," *Psychological Bulletin, vol.* 76 (1971), pp. 128–148.

Figure 9.3   Leadership Styles and the Organizational Environment

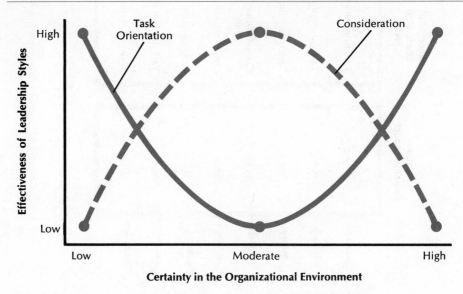

Based on Fred Fiedler, *A Theory of Leadership Effectiveness* (New York: McGraw-Hill, 1967).

be argued that a leader can be considerate and task oriented simultaneously. For Fiedler, this combination does not occur.

While these criticisms are pertinent, Fiedler's approach has been insightful in that he has introduced the setting or organizational environment into the study of leadership. Currently he is revising his theory to take into consideration some of the criticisms that have been leveled at it.

House's Path-Goal Theory

Robert House has recently developed a theory of leadership that incorporates both the Ohio State approach and Fiedler's theory (House 1971). Further, he has introduced new elements that help clarify some of the problems researchers have uncovered in those two theories. House's theory changes the focus of the research by analyzing not only the style of leadership, but also its effect on the motivation of subordinates.

House uses expectancy theory to examine the motivation of employees (see chapter 8). According to *expectancy theory,* an individual will be motivated to produce if he perceives that his efforts will result in successful performance, which, in turn, will lead to desired rewards.

House argues that the task-oriented and considerate styles of leadership are critical only if they help increase the subordinate's perception that his or her efforts will bring about successful performance, for which he or she will receive desired and equitable rewards. In other words, the style of leadership is important only when it can influence the motivational level of the subordinates. In House's opinion, there are many situations in which the style of leadership cannot affect the motivation of subordinates.

Like Fiedler, House next concentrates on the situation or organizational environment. Previous research strongly suggests that individuals do not like to work in a situation where there is a high degree of job ambiguity, that is, where they do not know what they are supposed to do (Kahn et al. 1964). The one major exception to this generalization occurs with professionals, who typically prefer to define their work for themselves. Thus, they prefer a high degree of job ambiguity.

House concludes that a task-oriented style of leadership will be effective in an organizational environment where job ambiguity is high, since employees are seeking direction. (Again, this generalization does not apply to professionals.) In general, task-oriented leadership, by reducing job ambiguity, increases employees' perceptions that they can be successful and will be rewarded for their efforts, for they now know what they must do.

House also treats job satisfaction as a critical part of the organizational environment. If employees are unhappy, the leader may be able to change their expectancies by being considerate. In particular, a considerate leader who is patient with his or her subordinates can encourage them to believe they are capable of performing successfully, and can point out instances where successful performance has resulted in desired rewards. Through such activities, the leader can change the expectancies of employees. Hence job satisfaction in the work force (group morale) increases.

House also argues that a particular style of leadership may have some indirect consequences. Because a considerate style of leadership may increase job satisfaction and group morale in the short run, employee performance in the long run will probably rise. It is usually the most capable individuals who quit when dissatisfied; and, if they do not quit, their performance will suffer.

House shows that a leader can combine task orientation and consideration. Such a combination can improve employee performance and group morale simultaneously. For Fiedler, this combination does not occur, for a leader who is high on the least-preferred coworker scale is, by definition, task oriented; if the leader receives a low score, he or she is considerate.

While House's theory will undoubtedly be refined as research evidence is accumulated, he has constructed an approach that is extremely valuable for both the theory and the practice of management.

To summarize some of the important implications of House's theory:

1. A style of leadership cannot be evaluated without taking the motivation of subordinates into consideration. In this sense, House has combined leadership theory and motivation theory.
2. The effectiveness of a particular leadership style is related to its impact on two situational factors—job ambiguity and job satisfaction.
3. In many situations, the leader cannot significantly influence the level of employee performance or group morale. For example, the leader cannot influence performance among clerical workers if there is already a low degree of job ambiguity.
4. The leader can simultaneously influence group morale and employee performance; that is, he or she can be both considerate and task oriented.

Other Factors

Affecting

Leadership

As House's theory implies, a number of other factors besides the task-oriented and considerate styles are important in the area of leadership. So far, no one theory has included all of these factors. Some of these factors relate to the qualities of the leader, others to the subordinates, and still others to the situation. Eventually, theories of leadership will probably incorporate these factors, since they are critical to a leader's success.

Influence of Subordinates

Obviously the goal of leadership is for the leader to influence the behavior of subordinates. However, it is also possible for subordinates' behavior to affect the style of leadership a manager uses.

One experimental study investigated the way that the level of competence among clerical workers affected the style of their supervisor (Aaron Lowin and James Craig 1968). The researchers instructed some of the clerical workers to perform competently and others to make a lot of errors. However, their supervisors were not informed of these instructions. Over time, leaders who directed a group of incompetent subordinates became task oriented and inconsiderate. Leaders assigned to a group whose members were competent maintained a considerate style.

As this study indicates, subordinate behavior can influence the way a manager leads a group. It also suggests that a manager, even if he or she wants to be considerate, will tend to deemphasize this style of leadership and stress a task-oriented style if his or her subordinates are incompetent.

Short-term versus Long-term Effects

In 1955 Nancy Morse and Everett Reimer conducted a year-long field experiment on leadership among the clerical employees of an insurance agency. The Survey Research Center of the University of Michigan sponsored this research. One group of employees was managed in an autocratic fashion; that is, the superior did not allow his subordinates to participate in making any decisions that directly related to their own work. The other group's leadership was the exact opposite and stressed employee participation in decision making. At the end of the year, absenteeism and turnover were significantly greater and job satisfaction significantly lower in the autocratic group than in the democratic group. While productivity of both groups increased over time, it was significantly higher in the autocratic group than in the democratic group.

These results were perplexing, since they suggested that autocratic leadership created a higher level of productivity than democratic leadership, in spite of the negative consequences such as decreased job satisfaction. However, other researchers at the University of Michigan, notably Rensis Likert, hypothesized that time is the key factor (Likert 1967; Marrow, Bowers, and Seashore 1967). These researchers suspected that autocratic leadership generates short-run increases in the rate of productivity, just because workers are intimidated. However, productivity probably will decline in the long run, inasmuch as many of the most effective employees will either quit and obtain work elsewhere or become so dissatisfied that their productivity will decline.

To test this theory, the Michigan researchers have conducted a 15-year study of participative management in a factory. When the researchers introduced participative management, productivity did not increase immediately. However, productivity began to rise gradually after the first year and continued to do so over the 15-year period. The Michigan researchers have confirmed these findings in a study at General Motors. After participative management is introduced, productivity increases over time (as reported in Dowling 1975). Both of these studies strongly suggest that participative leadership will not create a short-term increase in productivity. However, it will result in a long-term increase in productivity, since the effective employees will tend to stay with the organization and less effective employees will be motivated to become more efficient (Likert 1967).

Personality

Sometimes a leader is successful because there is a comfortable fit between his or her personality and those of his or her subordinates. James Mullen has investigated this fit between the personalities of leaders and subordinates in a study of three sales managers in a large insurance company (Mullen 1966). These managers' offices were all consistently superior in performance and sales, but their personalities were very different. Using a standard psychological test, Mullen found that one of the managers tended to be autocratic, another democratic, and a third a mixture of both elements.

Mullen decided to examine the personalities of the subordinates by using the same standard psychological test. Generally, the subordinates of the democratic manager were highly independent. Hence they worked effectively for a manager who allowed them to define their own work. But the subordinates of the autocratic manager tended to be highly dependent, so they responded well to the dictates of their leader. Finally, the subordinates of the manager who was a mixture of democracy and autocracy wanted some direction but also some independence. Their needs consequently fit a managerial style that was both autocratic and participative.

Locals and Cosmopolitans

Leadership theories have yet to incorporate adequately the social and economic backgrounds of individuals into their frameworks. The economic position of the leaders' parents, the schools they attended, the career patterns they follow—these and related factors are important for understanding leadership, especially the degrees of task orientation and consideration that the individual manifests.

In the late 1940s, sociologists at Columbia University, under the direction of Robert Merton, studied the backgrounds of leaders in a small town (Merton 1957). When researchers asked the members of the community to identify their leaders, gradually two profiles began to emerge—the local and the cosmopolitan.

The *local* leaders usually had been members of the community since birth. In addition, they were more provincial than the cosmopolitan leaders in that they read only local newspapers and were mainly interested in the affairs of the community. Moreover, they usually worked within the community.

The *cosmopolitans* tended to work outside the community. In addition, they were usually born and raised in another part of the country. These leaders also read several magazines and newspapers that were national and international in scope. While they were interested in community affairs and partici-

The Scarcity of Effective Leaders

The successful organization has one major attribute that sets it apart from unsuccessful organizations: dynamic and effective leadership. Peter F. Drucker [1954] points out that managers (business leaders) are the basic and scarcest resource of any business enterprise. Statistics from recent years make this point more evident: "Of every 100 new business establishments started, approximately 50, or one-half go out of business within two years. By the end of five years, only one-third of the original 100 will still be in business." [George R. Terry, 1960, p. 5.] Most of the failures can be attributed to ineffective leadership.

On all sides there is a continual search for persons who have the necessary ability to enable them to lead effectively. This shortage of able administrators is not confined to business but is evident in the lack of able administrators in government, education, foundations, churches, and every other form of organization. Thus, when we decry the scarcity of leadership talent in our society, we are not talking about a lack of people to fill administrative or executive positions; we have plenty of administrative "bodies." What we are agonizing over is a scarcity of people who are willing to assume significant leadership roles in our society and can get the job done effectively.

Paul Hersey and Kenneth Blanchard, *Management of Organizational Behavior*, 2nd ed. (Englewood Cliffs, N.J.: Prentice-Hall, 1972), p. 67.

pated actively in them, they also were involved in many activities outside of town.

Gouldner's Study. One of the Columbia University researchers, Alvin Gouldner, went on to confirm that organizations are frequently directed by two types of leaders (Gouldner 1957). In addition, Gouldner showed that the two types of leaders served different functions in the organization. Gouldner's analysis, which focused on university life, indicated that two kinds of professors tend to emerge as campus leaders. The first, the local leader, is a long-service professor who is usually an excellent teacher not interested in either publishing or a national reputation. The local leader is very considerate to students and fellow faculty members, and he or she spends a large portion of time helping them. The cosmopolitan leader is research oriented and very interested in his or her national reputation. He or she is essentially task oriented and does not like to waste time. Thus, this leader typically meets with students and faculty members only to accomplish specific objectives.

Carlson's Research. In an organization, usually one individual eventually becomes the leader. To find out what kind of individual tends to become the leader of an organization, Richard Carlson studied a group of school superintendents (Carlson 1961 and 1972).

In some districts, Carlson discovered that the school superintendents tended to be cosmopolitans; that is, they had:

- served as superintendents elsewhere
- changed jobs and geographical locations several times during their careers
- developed national reputations because of their work and publications.

Other districts were headed by locals, who:

- had been promoted from within the system
- had not changed jobs or locations during their careers
- did not have national reputations.

Carlson discovered that the critical factor in which type of superintendent a school board appointed was whether the school system wanted change. If the members of a school board felt their district needed change and innovation, they generally hired a cosmopolitan. As indicated above, this type of leader is task oriented, and he or she is hired to bring about major changes.

In a school district where no major change was desired, board members preferred to promote from within the organization and appoint locals as superintendents. In such cases, the superintendents tended to be considerate and interested in satisfying the needs of their subordinates.

Carlson's research also suggests that a cosmopolitan leader frequently appoints a local leader as his or her second-in-command. This course of action is logical, for it allows the cosmopolitan to concentrate on making the changes desired by the school district, while the local leader can attend to the social and emotional needs of the other people in the organization as innovations are introduced.

These results parallel those of Robert Bales (1950), who studied the emergence of leadership in small groups whose members are not previously acquainted with one another. According to Bales, two distinct types of leaders emerge, often at the same time—the task oriented and the considerate. The task-oriented leader directs the activity of the group; the considerate leader attempts to develop a feeling of group cohesion and to satisfy the social and emotional needs of the members. Typically, one individual cannot satisfy both leadership roles. Hence the task-oriented person becomes the formal leader while the considerate individual becomes the informal leader.

Pitfalls. The efficiency and task orientation of cosmopolitan leaders, although appropriate for initiating change, may also offend people who are more accustomed to the consideration of local leaders. For instance, financial leaders in an eastern community decided to upgrade the quality of a private college located there and make it competitive with Ivy League schools. They hired a cosmopolitan leader who was given virtually unlimited financial resources. This leader hired outstanding academics throughout the United States. He forced out many of the long-term and tenured professors by giving them unpleasant teaching and committee assignments and freezing their salaries. Within five years, the leader brought about some of the desired change. However, many of the community leaders felt he was rude and offensive. They also wanted to change the name of the university to honor a major family in the community. When the cosmopolitan leader did not lend his support to this effort, the financial backers of the university withdrew their support and bestowed it upon another university in the same geographical area. The leader's position was undermined so much that he resigned before he completed his goal of transforming the university from a minor into a major school.

Summary

Leadership is an influence process: The leader must persuade or influence his or her subordinates to complete a particular course of action. To accomplish this objective, the leader has recourse to five major types of power: legitimate power, which the leader holds by virtue of his or her position; reward power; expert power; referent power, or the willingness of subordinates to identify with the leader; and coercive power. Generally speaking, a leader who depends on legitimate and coercive power believes in Theory X, the traditional autocratic view of leadership. A leader who follows Theory Y, a highly participative and democratic view of leadership, primarily relies upon reward power, expert power, and referent power.

Managers perform many roles in organizations. According to Mintzberg, three of these are interpersonal roles: figurehead, leader, and liaison. There are also three informational roles: monitor, disseminator, and spokesman. Finally, the manager performs four decisional roles: entrepreneur, disturbance handler, resource allocator, and negotiator. The most important influence on which roles a given manager plays is his or her organizational level. For example, only the top managers usually act as spokesmen for the organization.

Theorists and researchers have especially emphasized one managerial role, that of *leader,* which focuses on the relationship between the manager and his or her subordinates. Ghiselli's research suggests that successful leaders possess distinctive traits, the two most important of which are supervisory ability and the desire for occupational achievement. Other researchers and theorists have primarily considered two dimensions of leadership behavior—task orientation and consideration. According to Fiedler, a task-oriented leader will be successful in a very certain or very uncertain situation, whereas a considerate leader will be successful when the situation is moderately certain. House has expanded Fiedler's approach by emphasizing the influence of the situation and by combining leadership theory and motivational or expectancy theory. According to House, a leader can influence his subordinates only when he or she can expand their expectancies or motivational levels. House and other researchers also believe that a leader can be both task oriented and considerate.

There are several other important factors in leadership. These include the influence of subordinates, short-term and long-term effects of different leadership styles, the leader's personality, and his or her background. If subordinates are incompetent, the leader tends to become task oriented. When there is a comfortable fit between the personalities of subordinates and leader, productivity tends to be high. A participative or democratic style of management seems to have little impact on productivity in the short run, but appears to increase it in the long run.

Finally, a person's background tends to identify him or her as one of two types of leaders. The local leader stays with an organization his or her entire career, has a narrow range of interests, tends to be very considerate, and is hired or promoted when the organization does not want to make major changes. The cosmopolitan leader moves from organization to organization, has a wide range of interests, tends to be task oriented, and is typically hired to make major innovations and changes. By hiring a local leader as his or her second-in-command, the cosmopolitan leader can institute new programs while the local leader takes care of the needs of subordinates in the organization.

Discussion Questions

1. From the research discussed in this chapter, what leadership style do you think is likely to characterize a politician? A religious leader? A film director?

2. Discuss the two definitions of leadership put forth by Max Weber and Chester Barnard. Which definition do you prefer? Why? How do these definitions relate to Theory X and Theory Y?

3. What elements do motivation theory and leadership theory have in common? Would it be possible to formulate a theory of leadership without considering motivation?

4. Of the ten roles that Mintzberg discusses, theorists have emphasized one—the leader or the relationship between the leader and his or her subordinates. Do you feel this is the key role of a manager? Of Mintzberg's ten roles, which three are most important for a president of a company? For a middle manager?

5. Researchers have argued that the two major dimensions of leader behavior are task orientation and consideration. What are some other dimensions of leadership?

6. Why does House argue that a leader frequently cannot influence the behavior of subordinates? In House's theory, why is it important that a leader can be simultaneously task oriented and considerate?

Critical Incidents

NOTE: *These critical incidents can be used by the whole class with the case observational method (see Appendix), or used for thought and discussion by individual class members.*

1. Susan Nash, a very dynamic middle manager in her early forties, was recently appointed as the director of a department in a large government agency. Her superiors indicated to her that the members of this department had become somewhat lethargic and ineffective. Still, there were many effective managers and employees in the department.

During the first few months, Susan was very task oriented and initiated a great many changes in the department. However, several of her able and key subordinates became dissatisfied and quit. Top management was becoming concerned that the turnover rate was excessive. Susan seemed to be effective, for she and her subordinates successfully completed some of the new programs she had established. However, top management felt the organization might become ineffective in the long run, especially after Susan moved on to another job.

Question: What should Susan do to solve her turnover problem and still initiate change?

2. Michael Porter is a young man who was recently promoted to a supervisory position. This is Michael's first experience as a leader. He feels very strange about it, for he is now supervising many of his old friends who have begun to treat him in a different fashion. Michael is no longer invited to lunch or social activities, for his friends feel he is now representing management's interests.

Question: Assuming that Michael wants to keep the job and eventually be promoted further, what should he do in this situation?

3. Tom Nystrom recently graduated from college as an electrical engineer with highest honors. Mr. Berman, a close family friend and owner of an electronics company, recently hired him and put him in charge of a department of 20 engineers. Most of these engineers are experienced and long-term employees, and they resent the fact that Tom is their superior. This resentment has intensified recently, since they have learned about the close relationship between Mr. Berman and Tom's family. Although they are not openly disrespectful, the engineers make it plain they don't like Tom. In addition, their morale has declined significantly since Tom has arrived and some of the better engineers are looking for work elsewhere.

Tom likes his job, since it provides him with a handsome salary and a great amount of responsibility that would be difficult to obtain elsewhere at his age. Hence he is determined to solve his problem with the other engineers and keep his job.

Questions: What should Tom do in this situation? How should he motivate these engineers?

Suggested Readings

Hersey, Paul, and Blanchard, Kenneth. *Management of Organizational Behavior.* 2d ed. Englewood Cliffs, N.J.: Prentice-Hall, 1972, 209 pages, paperback.
   The authors present a "life cycle theory of leadership," which fits into the framework developed in this chapter.

Likert, Rensis. *The Human Organization.* New York: McGraw-Hill, 1967, 258 pages, hardback.
   Likert's basic thesis is that a participative style of leadership is superior to others. This book is somewhat oversimplified, but students consistently

*enjoy it, especially if they have had limited exposure to behavioral applica-
tions in management. Two important ideas in this book are: While tight
supervision may produce immediate results and increase productivity, in
the long run morale will decline and the best individuals will seek work
elsewhere, thus causing a downturn in productivity; and, employees are
assets, just as physical objects are, and they should be represented on the
balance sheet.*

Miles, Raymond. *Theories of Management.* New York: McGraw-Hill, 1975, 240
pages, hardback.

*Miles puts forth the view that managers use three theories of management,
even if they do not openly recognize the fact. They are the traditional
model, the human relations model, and the human resources model. This
book is very similar to Likert's, but easier to read, since it was written
specifically for practicing managers.*

Group Behavior

10

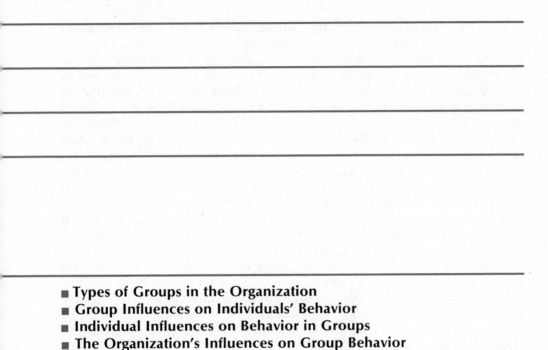

- ■ **Types of Groups in the Organization**
- ■ **Group Influences on Individuals' Behavior**
- ■ **Individual Influences on Behavior in Groups**
- ■ **The Organization's Influences on Group Behavior**

Performance Objectives

1. To be able to identify important kinds of groups that exist in organizations: problem-solving and creative groups, and zero-sum and nonzero-sum groups.

2. To be aware of the influence groups exert on the behavior of individuals, the influence of individuals on groups, and the organization's influence on the groups within it.

3. To understand how the groups within an organization can enhance and can impede the organization's efforts to achieve its goals.

245

From the point of view of management, an organization is a group of two or more individuals working together or interacting to accomplish a common purpose or purposes (Barnard 1938). If an organization consists only of one individual, relying solely on his or her work for its existence, it has no need to analyze group behavior. In this vein, James Thompson has argued that an individual is indispensable in an organization only when he or she performs all of its critical functions (Thompson 1967). This happens only infrequently. In fact, it is rare even for an organization to consist of a single group. Most organizations are composed of a series of interrelated groups striving to accomplish the overall objectives of the enterprise. Many of these groups are formal in that the organization has designed them for specific reasons. In addition, a large number of informal groups spontaneously arise in organizations for a variety of reasons, such as members' common backgrounds and interests, their interest in sharing information that is mutually advantageous, and even their need to resist managerial pressure and demands.

Typically, group behavior is very complex and difficult to understand. The tone of a leader's voice at a meeting may result in activities among subordinates that he or she did not openly command; individuals will privately champion a particular point of view but oppose it vociferously in a group meeting; some individuals try to dominate others in group situations; and one group may simply refuse to work with another group, even though its members cannot articulate all the reasons for this stance.

However, effective interaction between individuals and groups is critical to an organization's success. When misunderstandings or disagreements arise among organizational members, they are bound to interfere with the organization's overall efforts to achieve its goals.

In this chapter there is a discussion of various types of groups that exist in organizations, group influences on the behavior of individuals, the individual influences on behavior in groups, and the organization's influence on behavior in groups.

Types of Groups
in the Organization

There are many ways to classify groups, such as formal and informal, and managerial and employee. This book has focused on some of the important types of groups in other chapters. Four types that are particularly relevant for understanding the behavior of individuals in organizations are problem-solving and creative groups, and zero-sum and nonzero-sum groups.

Problem-Solving Groups

Usually an organization establishes certain formal groups or departments that are responsible for solving particular sets of recurrent and routine problems. For example, the personnel department hires workers and attempts to eliminate sources of employee dissatisfaction that might lead to high turnover and low productivity. In addition, organizations often attempt to solve nonrecurring and nonroutine problems by creating special problem-solving groups. Temporary groups and task forces, as discussed in chapter 3, are normally established to solve particular problems. After the problem has been solved, the temporary group or task force dissolves.

Normally a problem-solving group should not contain an even number of members, for the decision can be deadlocked. In addition, it is preferable if the decision-making group is small, so competitive subgroups do not emerge. Five members are often considered ideal; this allows members of the group to work closely together and still avoid a deadlock. Although there is some disagreement about the ideal size of a decision-making group, five seems to be the lower limit and ten the upper limit for effective groups (House and Miner 1969).

During the past 30 years, researchers have analyzed the behavior of problem-solving groups in experimental situations. Typically, the researchers present a problem to a group of individuals and merely ask them to develop a solution. For nonrecurring and nonroutine problem solving that takes place when individuals are very uncertain about the best course of action, research indicates that group decisions are superior to those offered by the average or typical members of the group (Harrison 1975). This result is not surprising, for the group can filter out poor information and choices. When an individual is confronted with a problem, he or she is less able to obtain feedback that would help refine his or her approach to the solution. Also, the more possible solutions offered, the better the best of them is likely to be.

Research also indicates that group decisions are not superior to those offered by the best member of the group, at least in some situations (Harrison 1975). This result seems to occur because of the limitations and liabilities associated with problem-solving activities in a group. In some situations, members of the group stop searching for a better alternative after most of them have agreed on an acceptable solution; in other situations, even though one solution is clearly superior to others, the members may accept an inferior alternative or compromise because of the resistance of a few individuals.

Creative Groups

Problem-solving groups are good at solving most of the difficulties an organization faces. However, when novel solutions are needed for unique problems, an organization sometimes must rely upon the work of creative groups. For example, England in World War II was at the mercy of the German Air Force, which met only token resistance when it dropped its bombs. To solve this problem, the English military put together a team of the finest minds in several diverse fields such as mathematics, physics, and even social science. Through the novel ideas put forth by this team, the English military created radar, which accurately pinpointed the coming attacks of the German airplanes. The English air bombers then counterattacked so effectively they virtually destroyed the German air offensive.

Creative groups frequently try to develop new products that will sustain the organization and compete effectively with those of other enterprises. These groups also are commonly used in advertising campaigns, which often seem to make or break a product or service. Avis significantly increased its car-rental profits by directing its advertising campaign against Hertz, with the novel slogan, "We're only Number 2, so we try harder."

Usually the ideal size of the creative group is much larger than that of the problem-solving group, since the objective is to generate a large number of ideas. In general, a suitable size for a creative group would be in the range of 10 to 20. A group of more than 20 individuals may become cumbersome and unmanageable, for the same reasons mentioned for problem-solving groups.

The most effective process for a creative group to use to generate ideas is still unknown. However, some research suggests that the group should meet for a warm-up period during which the general problem is presented (Dunnette, Campbell, and Jaastad 1963). After this short presentation, the members of the group should work individually. Periodic group sessions might then be held to filter the information and narrow the range of acceptable solutions.

In the creative group, it is also helpful to include a number of individuals with diverse backgrounds. For instance, an organization that is trying to develop a new product may put together a creative group that consists of engineers, physicists, social scientists, advertising executives, and sales personnel. This heterogeneity provides the group with several perspectives in the analysis of the problem.

Zero-Sum versus Nonzero-Sum Groups

In recent years, game theorists interested in military and organizational strategies have analyzed the behavior of two types of groups—zero-sum groups and nonzero-sum groups (see Schelling 1960). In a *zero-sum* situation, one group wins at the expense of another group. For instance, a country that loses a war typically gives up many of its resources to the victor. A *nonzero-sum* situation exists when the gains of one group do not mean losses for another group. In some situations, one group will gain and the other group's position will not change; in other situations, both groups will gain.

Typically, a zero-sum situation generates a great amount of conflict between the two groups. Some conflict in an organization can be helpful, for it provides motivation for the various groups to outperform one another. However, conflict in the zero-sum situation is usually more destructive than constructive, since inevitably one group must lose.

To study conflict in a zero-sum situation, Muzafer Sherif and his associates (1961) constructed an experiment in which two groups of boys at a camp competed in sports and other activities. By the end of this competition, the winning group was even more cohesive than previously. Members cooperated with one another and were complacent about the superiority of their group to the losing group. In the losing group, members began to deny or distort their situation with complaints such as, "The judges were biased." Because their leader blamed group members for the losses, the group tended to splinter, fights broke out, and unresolved conflicts came to the fore. Although members of the losing group refused to consider themselves inferior to the winners, they were not supportive of one another.

To eliminate the conflict between the two groups, Sherif tried a number of tactics, such as lectures from counselors and even introducing a third group as a common enemy. Nothing worked. Apparently, once groups see each other as a source of frustration, a threat, and an obstacle to their goals, antagonism tends to be perpetuated by acts of renewed hostility. Neither group would give up its stereotyped view of the other. Finally, Sherif established a series of goals that could be attained only if both groups cooperated. In one instance, all the boys had to work together to move a camp truck stuck in the mud. Gradually, as the two groups had to depend on each other for help in reaching their goals, the antagonism between them died down.

As this experiment indicates, it is preferable if groups within the organization view themselves as supportive of one another, that is, in a nonzero-sum situation. This proves to be true in management situations as well as in experiments. The top management of a major newspaper, the *Washington Star,* seriously considered bankruptcy in 1974 because of its shaky financial position. To help top management, all of the groups within the organization went from a five-day to a four-day workweek, which reduced the wage bill by 20 percent. Top management, in turn, promised to return to the five-day workweek (which it has done) as soon as conditions improved.

Group Influences

on Individuals' Behavior

Once an individual becomes a member of a group, he or she is directly and indirectly influenced by the people, relationships, and processes within it. In general, the individual is susceptible to three sources of influence: the group as a whole, the leader, and other members of the group.

Influence of the Group Situation

In recent years, a significant number of researchers have been concerned about the *risky shift* phenomenon, which was first studied by Stoner (1961). His research indicated that individuals tend to advocate more risky positions as members of a group than they do as individuals. One possible explanation is that individuals are conservative in making decisions when the responsibility rests squarely on their own shoulders. When an individual makes a decision that is clearly his or her own, he or she is responsible for its success or

---

Group Influences on Individuals

The most casual observation of groups indicates the existence of strong mechanisms for controlling the behavior of members. This capacity of groups to direct, limit, and influence what members do gives considerable power to the group setting and to individuals who are at the center of power in the group. The use of this power can have either positive or negative consequences for the individual and society. . . .

. . . the Chinese Communists have provided an example of systematic use of group pressures to win conversion to their doctrine. [Edgar] Schein reported these practices based on interviews with repatriated prisoners of war following the Korean War. The Chinese captors used their understanding of groups as controlling agents in an attempt to break down systems of belief and attitude. They prevented the formation of spontaneous primary groups which ordinarily serve as instruments for validating and sustaining beliefs of individuals through relationships with fellow group members. By segregating those who adamantly refused to cooperate and by exerting skills in the exposition of their tenets and in the use of group pressures, the Chinese Communists were able to induce a few of this isolated group to accept communist doctrine.

Abraham Zalesnik and David Moment, *The Dynamics of Interpersonal Behavior* (New York: John Wiley, 1964), pp. 96–97.

failure. In a group situation, the individual sometimes feels he or she can advocate a risky position because responsibility for the final decision is diffused throughout the group.

However, other research indicates that the shift can be reversed; that is, the individual will advocate a more conservative position in a group than he or she would independently. In this situation, the individual may accede to the norms of the group, which are conservative.

Although the risky shift phenomenon does not seem to hold in all cases, it does indicate quite clearly that the behavior of an individual as an individual is quite different from his or her behavior in a group situation. One study that graphically supports this proposition is the "sexy picture" experiment. In this research, undergraduate males as a group could not arrive at a consensus concerning the beauty of several women whose photographs were shown to them (March and Feigenbaum 1960). However, individual ratings of these photographs before the meeting indicated that each participant strongly favored one photograph in which a very attractive girl was in a provocative position. Seemingly these males, during the meeting, suppressed their initial preferences because each believed his original choice would draw criticism from the group.

Admittedly, individuals sometimes behave independently, regardless of the situation. However, the dynamics of a group can cause significant deviations in an individual's behavior. For this reason, a manager must be aware that a commitment given privately may not be upheld in a group situation.

Influence of Group Members

Although an individual may try to escape the most obvious kinds of control exercised over him or her by other members of a group, he or she frequently abides by the norms or values the group has established. This generalization has been confirmed by many social psychologists. Perhaps the most compelling confirmation has been offered by Solomon Asch, who established an experiment in which seven of the eight group members were working with him as confederates (Asch 1951 and 1952). All eight subjects were shown four lines and told to select the two that were the same length. This was done several times, and both the seven confederates and the one naive subject invariably selected the correct answer.

On one round, the seven confederates chose an answer that was clearly incorrect. The naive subject found himself in a difficult position—should he pick what he believed was the correct answer, when it was quite clearly different from the one selected by the other members of the group? Seventy-five percent of the naive subjects, at one time or another, made an error to agree with the group decision. Only 25 percent of the naive subjects proved independent enough to choose the correct answer.

Influence of a Leader

Group members' behavior is also influenced by their leadership. Alvin Gouldner (1954) has written an extended case study on this topic. He analyzed the behavior of work groups in a gypsum plant in a midwestern city. For many years, the manager of this plant, "Old Doug," guided it in a very loose and friendly fashion. While group cohesion and job satisfaction were high, the plant was becoming inefficient. Many employees arrived late for work and left early, and their jobs were not closely monitored. After Old Doug's death, top management appointed a dynamic plant manager who imposed strict controls on the behavior of the workers in the plant. If they arrived late or left early, he punished them by docking their pay and giving them short layoffs.

While most workers disliked the new system, they put up with it for fear of losing their jobs. The solidarity of the work groups in the plant weakened significantly, for most employees began to concern themselves only with their own careers and interests.[1]

The influence of a leader on a group is especially pronounced if he or she is *charismatic*, that is, if he or she has a special personal magnetism that convinces individuals to follow directives without question or criticism. Adolf Hitler was a charismatic leader, and millions of Germans obeyed his commands willingly. In some instances, German citizens followed unpleasant orders that conflicted with their own beliefs, largely because they completely accepted the legitimacy of Hitler's leadership.

Individual Influences
on Behavior
in Groups

While groups influence the behavior of individuals who participate in them, the reverse is also true. Individuals possess distinctive characteristics that guide their activities in a group. Even if the other members are very persuasive, an individual may resist their influence purely because of these distinctive

---

[1]However, the miners who worked below the surface of the plant were able to resist the plant manager's rigid control system because of the flexible and dangerous nature of their work.

characteristics. Major factors that influence individuals in a group are their attitudes, status, culture, and need for personal space.

Attitudes

An individual's behavior in a group is strongly influenced by his or her personal attitudes. In fact, an *attitude* can be defined as a predisposition to respond to something in a particular way. Attitudes are composed of three separate elements: cognitive, emotional, and behavioral. The *cognitive* element concerns the rational processes an individual uses before he or she takes a particular course of action—his or her opinions. The *emotional* element refers to the nonrational commitment an individual makes to a particular course of action—his or her feelings. The *behavioral* element is the action the individual takes on the basis of his or her cognitive and emotional position.

A manager who understands the influence of attitudes on behavior is at a decided advantage when he or she attempts to motivate subordinates, either individually or in groups. The manager can appeal to the cognitive side of an attitude by telling subordinates they are making valuable contributions to the organization. Some companies extend this approach by giving visible recognition to outstanding work, for example, bonuses, vacation trips, and special programs or dinners during which individuals receive certificates of merit and other honors. A manager can appeal to the emotional side of an attitude by treating subordinates as personal friends, making sure that any special requests are honored, and showing a genuine interest in their career progression.

However, attitude changes may not persist if they are not reinforced on a regular basis. This problem has been highlighted by Edwin Fleishman, who conducted a human relations training program for supervisors (Fleishman 1953). He also established a control group composed of supervisors who did not participate in the training. At the start of the program, a standard human relations test indicated that the supervisors in the two groups were roughly equal in their sensitivity to the needs of others and their feelings toward others. After the program, the trained supervisors scored significantly higher than the control group on the human relations test. However, six months later, there were no significant differences between the two groups on this test. In fact, the trained supervisors proved to be *less* sensitive than they had been before the sessions. Many factors might account for this situation. But Fleishman's hypothesis was that the organizational climate to which these supervisors returned was autocratic, and thus it failed to reinforce their new attitude. He tested this hypothesis by examining the attitudes of the second-level supervisors to whom the first-level supervisors reported. As he suspected, the second-level supervisors were highly autocratic, and they pressured the first-level supervisors to act autocratically toward their subordinates.

Some of the ways a manager can reinforce desired employee attitudes have been discussed in chapter 8. With regard to an individual's attitude toward other employees, one useful technique is role playing. If two individuals are antagonistic toward each other, it may be useful for them to switch roles during a training session. By being forced to represent each other's attitudes, they can learn more about each other's viewpoints and problems. In one organization, management used this approach with white foremen who were harrassing their black workers. When the white foremen were forced to take the insults and imperious commands of the black workers role playing as foremen, they began to dislike and change their own behavior. Group discussion sessions, in which participants are free to talk about their own and others' attitudes, are also valuable.

Group Cohesion

In a discussion of difficulties arising in collective bargaining, [Benjamin] Selekman describes an incident which occurred in a men's clothing manufacturing plant. Five men joiners, who had worked together for years, carried through the complete process of sewing together the five sections of the coat. New methods were introduced by the management which required each man to sew only one section. Although they were all pieceworkers, with varying earning capacities, the five men arranged to pool their total earnings at the end of each week and to divide them into five equal parts. "They had always been friends, they explained, and so wanted to avoid any bad feelings different earnings might create among them." In this way, they resisted a program formulated by management which would serve to transform the close group into five competing individuals. Another group, including four women canvas basters, developed a comparable device for "defending their old work group integrity against the erosion of the new methods." They, like the joiners, differed from one another in speed, accuracy and earning capacity under a piecework wage plan. When there was a shortage of work, none would work unless each had a garment to sew on. "Time and again," says Selekman, "they had held up production because 'friends like us' could not let management give too much work to the speedier or better basters. So strong was their cohesiveness that when an arbitrator expressed the desire for interviews to get to the bottom of complaints, they refused to meet him unless they were interviewed as a group. None would talk except in the presence of all."

Morris Viteles, *Motivation and Morale in Industry* (New York: W. W. Norton and Company, 1953), p. 180.

Status

Another important characteristic of individuals that affects their behavior is their status in groups. Generally, people whose status is high tend to act differently in a group than those whose status is low. This proposition has received support from C. Northcote Parkinson (1957), who has studied the behavior of individuals at cocktail parties. According to Parkinson, high-status individuals usually arrive late, but they immediately walk to the center of the room to be seen by their inferiors. At the end of the evening, they leave earlier than the other guests, apparently so their exit can be noted.

The status of individuals is frequently incorporated into their job titles. In one organization, when the production manager's title was changed to vice-president of manufacturing, his status rose significantly, although his duties remained the same. The status of his subordinates also increased, even though there was no change whatsoever in their job duties (Harlow and Hanke 1975).

Once an individual attains a position of high status, he or she normally tries to maintain it. In turn, he or she frequently attempts to restrict the number of individuals who can attain a position of high status. In one large bank, the people who kept the books had low status until the organization hired computer specialists for this job. Because these specialists were highly educated and critical for the bank's continued success, they demanded the same privileges as high-status officers such as access to the executive dining room. Resistance was so great that it took several years for the computer specialists to attain a position of high status (Strauss and Sayles 1972).

Culture

The culture in which a person has been brought up is also a factor in his or her behavior as part of a group. In a large-scale study in France of a clerical agency and an industrial enterprise, Michel Crozier has shown the impact that culture has on the behavior of individuals and groups (Crozier 1964). He argues that a dominant value among Frenchmen is individualism. Even at work, the individual wants to operate in an independent manner. Individuality is such a strong cultural value that French organizations are structured to protect it. Hence French organizations tend to be highly formal, for this approach shields the individual.

According to Crozier, this excessive emphasis on formality creates a vicious cycle. Typically it is very difficult to initiate any organizational change. In fact, organizational change usually occurs as a response to a crisis and it is mandated by top management.

Crozier also analyzed the Russian culture, which is characterized by a great

amount of friendliness and warmth. However, the government is highly autocratic. Hence members of each work group are warm and friendly toward one
another, but suspicious of outsiders who may be operating as spies.

In the United States, organizations and individuals tend to emphasize specialization according to function. However, a dominant value in America is
the protection of individuals. Hence the American system is somewhat impersonal but reflective of the cultural belief that the rights of individual workers must be protected.

Personal Space

A factor that managers often overlook in setting up work groups is each group
member's sense of personal space. That is, people dislike being forced to be
too close to other people. According to Edward Hall (1968), Americans have
established an intimate zone into which a few individuals are allowed that
extends from the surface of the skin to 18 inches. In a second zone, from $1\frac{1}{2}$ to
4 feet around the person, comfortable interactions that reflect friendship and
closeness take place. The third zone extends from 4 to 12 feet from the person;
most impersonal business is conducted in this range. Finally, there is the
public zone of 12 feet in which individuals recognize one another and say
hello, but do not engage in comfortable interactions.

As Hall suggests, an individual who violates spacing rules will be disliked by
members of his or her group. Sometimes members of the group will invoke
sanctions to force the individual to conform. For example, they may simply
walk away from him or her or mention directly that he or she is out of order.

The Organization's
Influences
on Group Behavior

In addition to understanding how groups and individuals within an organization are likely to influence each other's behavior, a manager should know
what factors in the organization itself affect these interactions. In the final
analysis, it is how the actions of groups and individuals mesh with the organization that has the greatest impact on the organization's success. Some of the
major organizational influences on group behavior are the nature of the work,
the physical structure of the organization, people's organizational positions,
and their degree of participation.

The Nature of the Work

Members of a group who perform work that is boring and unskilled usually behave quite differently from those who perform skilled tasks. In fact, skill is a major determinant, if not *the* major determinant, of how workers behave in groups.

Leonard Sayles studied the influence of skill level on behavior in several hundred American industrial work groups (Sayles 1958). His analysis indicated that these work groups were of four general types: apathetic, erratic, strategic, and conservative.

In *apathetic* groups, the individuals were performing relatively unskilled, low-paid work. In addition, the work was frequently dangerous and unpleasant. Members of apathetic groups seemed to be dissatisfied, although they did not complain a great deal to management. In such groups, there was considerable friction and ineffective, informal leadership.

Erratic groups could be identified when all of the workers performed identical or nearly identical tasks. Usually this work was paced by machines. The feelings of such groups tended to fluctuate—at times they resisted management, but at other times they cooperated closely with it.

In *strategic* groups, the work was skilled and the jobs were relatively important to the functioning of the organization. Still, the workers typically had no likelihood of promotion to more desirable jobs. These groups were highly cohesive and involved in union activities, and they were characterized by a pattern of consistent grievances.

Finally, the members of *conservative* groups occupied the most esteemed positions in the plant. Their work was highly skilled and often individual, so they operated in an independent fashion. Members of conservative groups tended to be very satisfied and easily resolved their difficulties with management without the use of threats. (Figure 10.1 contains comparative profiles of the four types of work groups.)

Even on a world-wide basis, it appears the nature of the work strongly affects group behavior. Clark Kerr and Abraham Siegel (1954) analyzed the strike rates of 16 industries in 11 countries. Each industry was characterized by a definite strike rate that did not vary significantly from country to country (see Table 10.1). For example, miners everywhere tend to strike quite frequently. One reason for this outcome may be the miners' self-concept; that is, they see themselves as very masculine and aggressive (Goldthorpe et al. 1968). Or, the nature of the work in this industry may create a climate favorable to strike activity. Miners tend to be close-knit because of the danger involved in this type of work; this may lead them to strike when they believe they are being treated unfairly. While the specific reason is not certain, it is clear that particular kinds of work are related to specific patterns of behavior.

Figure 10.1   Summary of Work Group Differences

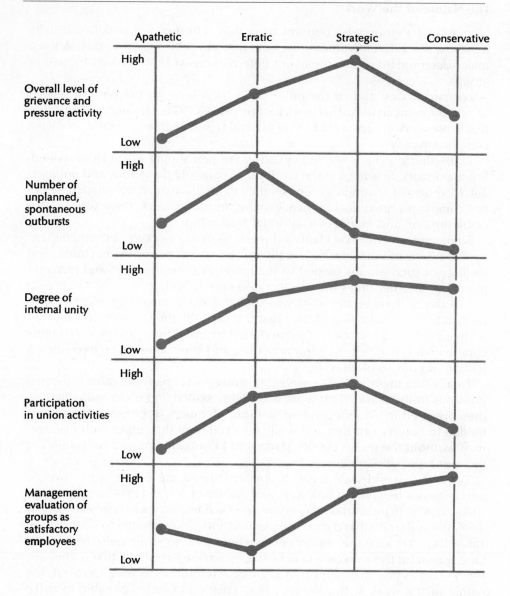

Table 10.1   General Patterns of Strike Propensities in 11 Countries

Propensity to Strike	Industry
High	Mining
	Maritime and longshore
Medium high	Lumber
	Textile
Medium	Chemical
	Printing
	Leather
	Manufacturing (general)
	Construction
	Food and kindred products
Medium low	Clothing
	Gas, water, and electricity
	Services (hotels,
	restaurants, etc.)
Low	Railroad
	Agriculture
	Trade

From Clark Kerr and Abraham Siegel, "The Interindustry Propensity to Strike—An International Comparison," in Arthur Kornhauser et al., eds., *Industrial Conflict*, p. 107. Copyright © 1954 by McGraw-Hill Book Company. Reprinted by permission.

Physical Structure

The physical structure of the organization in which interactions occur also affects group behavior, as we saw in chapter 4. As an example, the conditions necessary for unionization can be created partly by the structure of the organization.

To explore this issue, Martin Estey has compared the rise of unionism in food chain stores and department stores (in Blum et al. 1971). Historically, foodstores were not unionized, for they were too small to justify the money it would take to organize them. In addition, workers in these stores were relatively unskilled. They did not have the necessary expertise or the skilled leaders available to unionize. These conditions changed dramatically when food chains came into existence, for a large number of workers were then housed under one roof. Additionally, leadership was provided by the highly skilled meat cutters, who served as the driving wedge when unionization was attempted.

Estey found that department stores are typically not unionized, for each department is an organization unto itself. In effect, several organizations that are relatively unknown and foreign to one another exist within one structure. This lack of cohesion across departments inhibits the growth of unionism.

Organizational Position

The specific role an individual plays in an organization also affects his or her behavior in a group. An individual in a production position can be expected to support people and ideas that reflect the production view. Even if the individual disagrees with some of the production department's policies, he or she is more likely to side with another production employee than with a member of the sales or marketing department.

The importance of organizational position was established in a study conducted by Seymour Lieberman (1956), who analyzed the attitudes of a group of workers over a period of three years. At the start of the study, as indicated on a standard test, all the workers were basically antimanagement and pro-union. Later, some of these workers were promoted to supervisory positions; when retested, they were pro-management and antiunion. After a time, some of these workers were demoted because of an economic recession, and they became pro-union and antimanagement once again.

Participation

When groups or individuals are allowed to participate in decisions that bear directly on their own work, they typically react more favorably than if they feel decisions are imposed on them by management (Likert 1967; Coch and French 1948). (See chapter 7.) This generalization is particularly true when management is introducing a major change in the organization. Even if the subordinates' participation is limited, they will be more supportive of the changes than if they had not been consulted.

However, this approach may backfire if subordinates perceive it to be *pseudo-participation,* that is, if management encourages them to express themselves freely but ignores their contributions. In this situation, the subordinates justifiably feel they have been mistreated and manipulated by management. Some typical reactions are increased hostility toward management, lower productivity, and higher turnover.

Participation can also be combined with public commitment. When an individual is required to make a public commitment that he or she will pursue a particular course of action after participating in a discussion of its merits, he or she is more likely to keep it than if the commitment is private. Kurt Lewin (1958) tested this hypothesis with research designed to increase the use of meats such as beef hearts, sweetbreads, and kidneys, all of which are usually disliked by consumers. Some groups of meat buyers heard a lecture on the values of unpopular meats; in other groups, the lecture was supplemented by group discussion. Afterward, the consumers were asked to raise their hands if they were willing to try these meats. In the follow-up study, only 3 percent of the consumers in the lecture groups indicated they had served one of these meats; 32 percent of the consumers in the group that made a public commitment had served at least one of these meats.

In an organization it is not always feasible to obtain public commitment. Some individuals may be embarrassed; others may resent this technique; and some may even retaliate by following an opposite course of action. Still, the manager can use this approach in some situations. A manager who is contemplating a change from a five-day to a four-day workweek without reducing hours per week can discuss the proposed change with his or her employees and obtain a public commitment from them that they will not decrease their rates of productivity or increase their rates of absenteeism and lateness. Similarly, a manager may be able to give his or her subordinates more responsibilities and monitor them less frequently after they have participated in a discussion of the new program and made a public commitment to it.

Summary

Although group behavior is extremely complex, sufficient research has been accumulated so that some broad generalizations about it can be put forth, regarding the types of groups in the organization, group influences on the behavior of individuals, individual influences on behavior in groups, and the organization's influences on behavior in groups.

A problem-solving group may be a permanent department or a committee that deals with recurring and relatively routine problems, or a temporary group formed to deal with a specific problem. It should have an odd number of members, generally 5 to 9. Creative groups are formed to generate novel solutions to unique problems. They should range from 10 to 20 members and include individuals with diverse backgrounds so they can apply different perspectives to the problem.

In a zero-sum situation, one group wins at the expense of the other. In a nonzero-sum situation, both groups gain, or one group gains while the other group's position remains stable. To avoid the competition generated by zero-sum situations, the organization should establish goals that coordinate the efforts of two or more groups so that one of them does not benefit at the expense of the others.

There are at least three major group influences on the behavior of individuals. First, the group in entirety can influence the individual. As suggested by the risky shift phenomenon, individuals tend to behave differently as individuals than as members of a group, at least partially because of group pressures exerted on them. In addition, other members of a group can have a decisive influence on the individual's behavior. Moreover, a group leader can influence individuals' behavior so much that they will sometimes engage in activities they find reprehensible.

Individuals' characteristics also influence their behavior in groups. Frequently an individual's reactions to the pressure a group exerts are affected by his or her attitudes, status, cultural values, and desire for personal space.

The organization also influences group behavior. Perhaps the most important influence is the nature of the work. Even on a world-wide basis, workers in the same occupation manifest similar, distinctive strike rates. The physical structure of the organization is also relevant, for it frequently is a major determinant of the kinds of group activities that can take place. In addition, the type of organizational position an individual holds seems to be a major influence on the way he or she behaves in a group. Finally, an organization that allows its employees to participate in decision making, especially when major changes are contemplated, creates a climate that encourages groups to function effectively.

Discussion Questions

1. Do you agree that the risky shift phenomenon exists? Why or why not? What are some organizational implications of this phenomenon for the effective functioning of individuals and organizations?

2. Do you think zero-sum situations occur often in organizations? What are some strategies that could be used to eliminate zero-sum situations or at least minimize their impact?

3. Can a problem-solving group operate effectively as a creative group? Why or why not? What are some of the factors that distinguish problem-solving and creative groups? Which type is more important to the functioning of an organization? Why?

4. The United States was long known as a "melting pot" of immigrants of various nationalities. How do you think this ethnic diversity affects the behavior of groups in a heterogeneous workforce? How does the American "pioneer spirit" affect work groups?

5. Which factor seemed more important in bringing about unionization in food chains, the physical structure of the store or the skills of the employees? How were these two factors related? What are some other factors that might make a work group favorable toward unionizing?

Critical Incidents

NOTE: *These critical incidents can be used by the whole class with the case observational method (see Appendix), or used for thought and discussion by individual class members.*

1. As a middle manager in charge of 20 engineers, you have recently hired Ed Karetsky, a bright young man who graduated from college with highest honors. While Ed is technically competent, he finds it difficult to interact with others. In fact, Ed prefers to work independently and, if possible, only on his own projects. If he is assigned to a group project, he just does not work very hard. The other engineers have noticed Ed's behavior and, as a result, avoid him as much as possible, even to the extent of not speaking to him.

Questions: What are some possible reasons for Ed's behavior? How can you persuade him to change his behavior? How can you persuade the group to accept him?

2. The production department and the sales department in a medium-size industrial organization have traditionally been at odds with one another.

There are 1,000 employees in the production department and 80 employees in the sales department. According to the sales department, the major reason for this mutual antagonism is that the production department is operating ineffectively. According to the production department, this antagonism has emerged because the sales department frequently places unrealistic orders that cannot be filled. The situation has become so tense that the top managers in these two departments openly insult one another at executive meetings.

Question: What are some approaches top management could use to solve this problem?

3. John Kehoe is a manager who supervises 25 highly skilled, blue-collar workers. The nature of their work demands that they closely coordinate their efforts. However, two of these workers, Ed Decker and Jim Tracy, have become very antagonistic toward one another in recent months. Both have known and worked with each other for several years. However, they have never been close friends or colleagues. Their antagonism takes the form of bitter arguments about the manner in which the work is completed. These arguments have seriously damaged the productivity of the entire team, for these two individuals are critical to the overall effort.

Question: What are some approaches John Kehoe could use to solve this problem?

Suggested Readings

Crozier, Michel. *The Bureaucratic Phenomenon.* Chicago: University of Chicago Press, 1964, 320 pages, paperback.
> *This is a long and somewhat difficult book, but serious students enjoy it. Crozier focuses on the relationship between culture, bureaucracy, and group and individual behavior. An interesting aspect of this book is his comparative analysis of the kinds of bureaucracy that exist in France, Russia, and the United States (chapter 10). He also presents an insightful treatment of French entrepreneurship.*

Goldthorpe, John; Lockwood, David; Bechhofer, Frank; and Platt, Jennifer. *The Affluent Worker: Industrial Attitudes and Behavior.* New York: Oxford University Press, 1968, 206 pages, paperback.
> *Goldthorpe and his associates studied a group of workers in a prosperous industrial city in England. See the description in this chapter.*

Sayles, Leonard. *Behavior of Industrial Work Groups.* New York: John Wiley, 1958, 182 pages, hardback.

This is an excellent case study of different types of workers and the impact of technology on their behavior. It is one of the best anthropological studies of work groups, and is very readable.

Communication

11

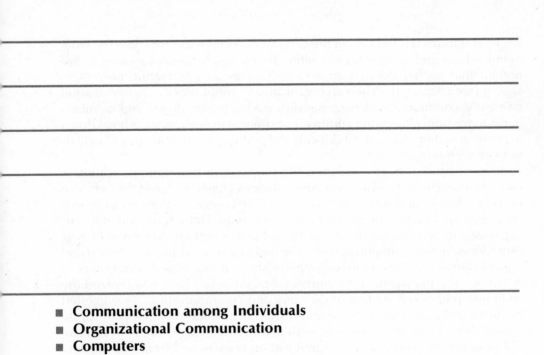

- **Communication among Individuals**
- **Organizational Communication**
- **Computers**

Performance Objectives

1. To understand communication among individuals by studying barriers to communications, communication within small groups, and the nature of managerial work.

2. To understand the functions within organizational communication of the flow of communication, overload, and the grapevine.

3. To be aware of the impact of the computer on organizational activities in different functional areas, and the typical behavioral consequences of computerizing an organization.

Organizations rely heavily on the communications that interrelate the work of individuals and groups. Jay R. Galbraith believes communication is so important that he has defined an organization as an information-processing system (see chapter 4). When an organization cannot process its information efficiently, communication becomes distorted or breaks down, and members begin to misunderstand one another. In extreme circumstances, a breakdown in communication can make it difficult and perhaps impossible for individuals to work with one another.

Research studies have supported the proposition that communication is very important in an organization. John Hinrichs (1964) analyzed the behavior of 232 managers and professionals in a research organization, all of whom communicated frequently. (Under *communication,* Hinrichs included listening, speaking, writing, and reading.) His subjects spent an average of 61 percent of their time in communication. The higher the individual's technical and organizational level, the more often he or she communicated with others.

Historically, management theorists and practitioners have emphasized the relationship between leading or directing and communication. As suggested by the model in this book, these and related behavioral processes constitute one of the four main dimensions within which managerial activities occur.

Frequently the concept of communication is examined from four distinct perspectives: intrapersonal, interpersonal, organizational, and technical (Thayer 1968). The *intrapersonal* perspective stresses communication activities within one person, such as neurological and brain processes; the *interpersonal* perspective focuses on the interactions among individuals and within groups; the *organizational* perspective looks at the flow of communications through the various formal or informal organizational channels; and the *technical* perspective centers on the design and operation of management information systems such as the installation of a new computer.

In this chapter, there is a discussion of three of these four communication perspectives: interpersonal, organizational, and technical. Since the research on intrapersonal communication is not directly applicable to management, it is not treated in this chapter.

Communication

among

Individuals

When one person communicates with others, either individually or in a group, there are many barriers that can inhibit or distort the messages he or she is transmitting. One individual may intensely dislike another person and, as a consequence, simply refuse to listen to him or her. Consequently, it is important for a manager to be aware of barriers to communication and communication breakdowns. Some research on communication in small groups and the daily activities of managers can illustrate the importance of interpersonal communication to management.

Barriers to Communication

Stereotypes (preconceived notions) can distort communications between individuals. Researchers have shown that even a hiring interviewer is strongly influenced by the match between the person he or she sees and the type of person he or she has in mind when deciding whether to hire a job applicant (Webster 1964). If the job applicant fits the requirements of the hiring interviewer's stereotype, communication between the two individuals becomes easier, and the applicant has a better chance of obtaining the job.

Cognitive dissonance, which was discussed in chapter 8, also affects communication between individuals. When an individual has a strong belief in a

---

The Essence of Communication

Almost everything a manager does involves communications, and yet it is only too easy to assume this involves no problems. After all, he has been communicating all his life. . . . But . . .

> *I thought you wanted me to start the new job after I finished what I was doing.*

> *How did I know he was serious about quitting?*

> *I discount almost everything I hear from those guys in Corporate Communications.*

> *But I was sure you meant London, Ontario.*

> *The steward thinks I am bluffing and won't fire Jones. . . .*

The basic problem in communications is that the meaning which is actually received by one person may not be what the other intended to send. . . .

Intent ————→ Expression ————→ Impression ————→ Interpretation
(Motive)   (What is said)   (What is heard)   (Meaning assigned)

George Strauss and Leonard Sayles, *Personnel* 3rd ed. Englewood Cliffs, N.J.: Prentice-Hall, 1972, pp. 205–6.

particular approach or philosophy, he or she finds it difficult to accept contradictory evidence. Instead, the individual may ignore both the evidence and its source.

Frequently, individuals fail to communicate effectively because they interpret the words they are using quite differently. Tom Burns (1954) reports that a department manager remembered giving instructions or communicating a decision on 165 separate occasions, but the subordinates could recall only 84 of the cases. In the other instances, the communication was received only as information or advice. In another situation, a manager may tell a subordinate to finish a particular job "as soon as possible." The manager expects the subordinate to comply with this command immediately. The subordinate, however, may believe the manager wants him or her to complete the task after all other work is finished.

Even symbols can create a barrier. For instance, it is quite common for college seniors looking for work to dress conservatively during hiring interviews, at least in part because they do not want to inhibit communication by wearing clothes or symbols that are too outlandish for the hiring interviewer to accept.

Additionally, the physical setting in which the communication takes place is also salient (Steele 1973). If the atmosphere is pleasant, individuals tend to relax and listen more carefully to one another. Similarly, the timing of the communication is a relevant consideration. If one individual is emotionally upset, he or she tends to distort the information he or she is transmitting or receiving. Also, the individual may be extremely tired after ten hours of work, at which time he or she is not receptive to communications.

The communication process between individuals can be improved if the sender is sensitive to the needs and values of the receiver. Both the sender and the receiver should be conscious of any symbolic meanings they are attaching to particular words, jargon, or even bodily movement. When possible, face-to-face communication is desirable, since individuals can immediately eliminate any misunderstandings that may arise. To improve communication, it is also wise for people to use simple, clear language.

One specific way to improve communication is to repeat an important message. However, if the repetition is too frequent, the person receiving the message may cease to listen carefully. Managers can supplement repetition with two-way feedback: the receiver rather than the sender can repeat the message. This allows the sender of the message to verify whether it has been correctly received. Studies indicate that two-way communication is less frustrating, more accurate, and produces greater confidence in the correctness of interpretations than one-way communication (Gibb 1964: Leavitt and Muller 1951).

Communication Networks

In the past 30 years researchers have emphasized the study of communication networks. Essentially a *communication network* is a structured arrangement of a small number of individuals who are allowed to transmit information only in a set and defined pattern. The researchers ask the members of a network under study to solve a specific problem by communicating with one another only through the unrestricted channels of communication. Researchers usually work with four communication networks: the wheel network, the chain network, the circle network, and the completely connected network (see Figure 11.1).

In the *wheel network,* one member is at the center and four or more members are each at the end of a spoke. This network is highly centralized, since the members on the spokes can communicate only with the individual at the center and no one else.

In the *chain network,* two members serve as end points; each can communicate directly only with one other person in the middle. The middle members serve as relay points to the individual in the center. In this situation, the center person communicates directly with the two middle members but not the end individuals. Thus the chain network is also centralized but not as much as the wheel network.

The *circle network* is somewhat decentralized, since each individual in it can communicate with the two other individuals next to him. Finally, the *completely connected* (all-channel) network is highly decentralized. Each individual in the group can communicate directly with every other individual in the group.

Consequences. Generally, the research on highly centralized networks, such as the wheel and the chain, suggests they are effective in solving routine problems that mainly involve collecting information (Costello and Zalkind 1963). This seems logical, for the individual at the center of the wheel and chain networks is processing and weeding out all of the information the group generates, ignoring irrelevant communications. In addition, the leadership position of the central individual in the wheel and chain networks is strong, probably because he or she has the greatest chance to influence the other members of the group. Finally, these groups structure their communication patterns very rapidly, since everyone quickly learns he or she must process information through the individual in the central position.

Decentralized networks, such as the completely connected and the circle, appear to be more appropriate when the group confronts a nonroutine or ambiguous problem. The fact that individuals can communicate directly with each other means they are freer to express opinions and to generate a large

Figure 11.1 Types of Communication Networks

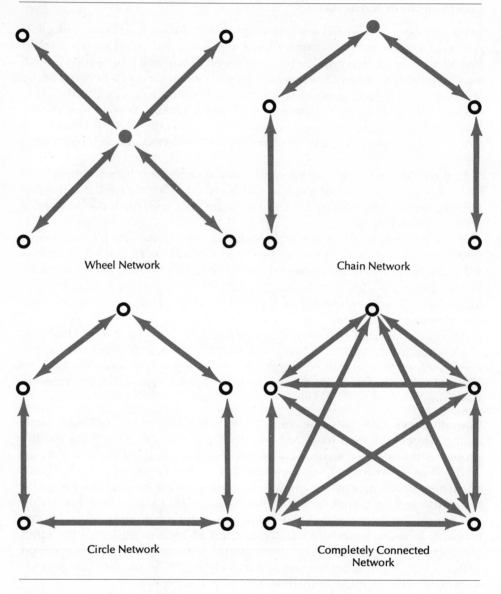

number of solutions, many of which may be very creative and innovative. In the decentralized networks, there is a higher level of satisfaction among the members of the groups than in centralized networks. This is probably because individuals are allowed to communicate with one another and to express their own points of view.

Networks in Organizations. These research findings cannot be generalized to an entire organization because of the small number of individuals who participate in a communication network. However, the manager can apply these findings to the behavior of small work groups in his or her own organization. If the work is highly structured so the members of the group must perform it in a set and routine fashion, the manager is probably dealing with a centralized network. If the manager directs the activities of a group whose work is nonroutine, he or she is probably part of a decentralized network. While all of the properties of formal network models may not always exist in actual work groups, there is some evidence that they do occur frequently. For example, unskilled employees who are doing repetitive work on the assembly line are more dissatisfied than skilled employees (see chapter 4). These unskilled employees work in centralized networks, since the pace of the assembly line allows only limited communication among individuals.

Two-Step Flow

A major role of the manager is to persuade subordinates to complete a particular course of action (see chapter 9). Consequently, it is important for managers to communicate their commands and wishes to subordinates in such a way that those directives will be accepted. Some research has indicated there is a two-step flow of communication: (1) from the original communicator to the opinion leader in a group, and (2) from the opinion leader to the rest of the group. For example, Elihu Katz and Paul Lazarsfeld (1955) discovered that the average consumer is not directly influenced to buy by relevant information and advertising. Rather, recognized opinion leaders in the community heavily influence consumers' decisions. When an opinion leader alters his or her outlook, a large number of consumers follow suit. Thus, it is important to direct advertising at the opinion leaders.

Managers can apply the two-step flow of information to communications with their subordinates and work groups. As chapter 10 indicated, there is typically an informal leader in a work group who strongly influences the attitudes and behavior of the other members. Usually an astute manager can pinpoint the informal leaders who work for him or her. The manager can then affect the performance of the group by influencing these informal leaders. For example, if the manager wants to introduce a new program that will require the organization to change some of the job responsibilities of the employees, he or she can first discuss this matter with the informal leaders. If they agree to the new plan, the probability increases that the work groups in the organization will accept it when it is presented to them.

The Nature of Managerial Work

As suggested at the beginning of this chapter, managers spend a large portion of their time communicating with others, both inside and outside the organization. In analyzing the activities that characterize managerial work, Henry Mintzberg (1973, 1975) found communication to be the most frequent and important of all of a manager's activities.

Communication is very important for several reasons. Managers work long hours at an unrelenting pace, at least partly because they must react immediately to the many and diverse problems they face. To solve these problems, managers must constantly communicate with members of their own and other organizations who can provide them with valuable, reliable, and current information.

However, because managers face a large number of various types of problems, their activities and communications tend to be brief. In Mintzberg's own study of five chief executives (1973), half of their activities lasted less than five minutes, and only 10 percent exceeded one hour. Similarly, 56 first-line supervisors averaged 583 separate activities per eight-hour shift, an average of one activity every 48 seconds (Guest 1956). In Rosemary Stewart's study of 160 British managers, the subjects worked for a half hour or more, without interruption, only about once every two days (Stewart 1967).

The Importance of Communication

The manager's work is essentially that of communication and his tools are the five basic media—mail, telephone, unscheduled meetings, scheduled meetings, and tours. Managers clearly favor the three verbal media, many spending on the order of 80 percent of their time in verbal contact. Some managers, such as those of staff groups, spend relatively more time alone. But the greatest share of the time of almost all managers is spent in verbal communication. The verbal media are favored because they are the action media, providing current information and rapid feedback. The mail, which moves slowly and contains little "live action" material, receives cursory treatment. Mail processing tends to be treated as a burden.

Henry Mintzberg, *The Nature of Managerial Work* (New York: Harper and Row, 1973), p. 171.

Oral Communication. According to Mintzberg, oral communication is of overwhelming importance to managers. When he studied the activities of five chief executives, he found that 78 percent of their time was spent in oral communication. Stewart (1967), analyzing the activities of 160 British managers, discovered they spent 66 percent of their time in oral communication. This same pattern of behavior exists at the first-line level of supervision, as indicated by Tom Burns, who reported that the foremen in a study he completed spent 80 percent of their time in oral communication (Burns 1954).

One possible reason for this pattern of behavior is that managers want to protect and bolster their power in the organization. A manager often can obtain information orally that many other managers in the organization do not possess. Oral communication is the easiest way to obtain current and live information. Managers frequently disregard information communicated through the mail and in management reports, for much of it is dated and thus of limited use.

As might be expected from this description, Mintzberg also found that managers are strongly oriented to action and dislike reflective activities. This orientation may represent the personal preferences of managers. However, it may also result because managers must respond to many problems every working day that can be handled most efficiently by means of oral communication.

Mintzberg also believes his profile of managerial work holds at all levels of the organization. While managers at different organizational levels obviously perform different activities, they constantly react to problems; they work long hours; their activities are varied, fragmented, and brief; and they tend to emphasize oral communication.

A Related Viewpoint. Although these studies indicate that managers seem to favor oral communication overwhelmingly, no manager can be successful using only this approach. Modern organizations are very complex. For instance, the following departments have been added to most organizations in the past 60 years: personnel, personnel research, management information systems, long-range planning, industrial relations, training, research and development, marketing, marketing research, and public relations. In today's organizations, a manager must rely on all sources of information and channels of communication if he or she is to be successful.

The communication policies of Alfred Sloan serve as a good example of this balanced approach (Sloan 1963). Frequently Sloan is described as the ideal manager, for he was the president of General Motors during the period when it became one of the most successful corporations in the world, as it still is.

Like other managers, Sloan relied heavily on oral communication. Once his dealers throughout the country were claiming they were holding too many cars in inventory, even though the reports at headquarters did not agree. Sloan attacked this problem directly by actually visiting a large number of dealers throughout the country. Both his talks with these dealers and their actual number of cars in stock strongly indicated that General Motors was supplying them with too many cars.

But Sloan also made considerable use of management reports in decision making. He generally prepared himself for meetings or decisions by reading relevant management reports from the many departments of General Motors. In fact, he was so systematic that he frequently wrote memoranda to himself detailing the advantages and disadvantages of various courses of action.

The message from Sloan's autobiography is clear—to be successful in the modern organization, which has become so highly complex, a manager must go beyond oral communication. A systematic approach to problems that emphasizes both oral and other forms of communication is desirable.

Organizational
Communication

While communication between individuals and within groups is of obvious significance, the flow of information through the various channels within the organization is also important. Information in an organization moves both vertically and horizontally, between supervisor and subordinate and among peers. Some of the communication is formal, but much of it is not. It is this informal web of communication in an organization that is known as the office grapevine.

Flow of Communication

Horizontal communication among equals or peers tends to predominate at the lower levels of the organization. In a study of 48 lower-echelon managers, A. K. Wickesberg (1968) showed that 67 percent of their communications were horizontal; only 33 percent were vertical, between superiors and subordinates. Among foremen or first-line supervisors, these horizontal communications primarily focus on joint problem solving and the work flow (Simpson 1959).

The communications are very specific and goal-oriented, directed at solving a particular problem. At higher organizational levels, managers have a greater variety of communications, many of which are not specifically job-related (Albaum 1964). In this way the manager is able to obtain current information on activities that may affect his or her own work.

Vertical communication in organizations is sometimes inhibited by the difference in status of the transmitter and the receiver. Also, the higher a person's status in the organization, the greater the distortion in the communications he or she receives (Barlund and Harland 1963; Cohen 1962). In some organizations, when consultants have been hired to solve specific problems, they have been unable to persuade subordinates to talk freely in the presence of their superiors. When, at the request of consultants, the superiors do not attend group sessions, the subordinates tend to be responsive and open about the organizational problems they face. This is especially true of ambitious subordinates. The more ambitious a subordinate is, the more likely he or she is to distort his or her communication to the superior (Read 1962). This distortion is particularly pronounced when the subordinate distrusts the superior (Maier, Hoffman, and Read 1963).

In some situations, the channels of communication become overloaded. The manager can sometimes solve this problem by delegating some of his or her responsibilities to subordinates. Or he or she can find a way of filtering incoming communication so that only the most important items reach his or her desk. An executive secretary, an assistant, or an entire staff could perform this function for the executive. Also, some organizations attack the overload problem by establishing an Office of the President in which two or more coequal chief executives divide their responsibilities so no one is overworked (see chapter 3). In other situations, the manager might ask his or her subordinates to complete all of the staff work on a project so his or her function would be merely to approve the final report or product. Whatever the method, the objective is to reduce the amount of communication that must be channeled through a particular organizational position.

The Grapevine

In most organizations there is an informal system of transmitting information known as the grapevine, which is independent of the formal communications system the organization establishes. Two research studies have confirmed the importance of the grapevine in organizations (Davis 1953; Sutton and Porter 1968). In these studies, the researchers planted a rumor in the organization. Several hours later they passed out a questionnaire that asked members of the organization about the rumor. In this fashion the researchers were able to find out such things as how many people passed on the rumor and how much distortion had occurred.

An important finding in these two studies is that the grapevine is highly selective. That is, members of the grapevine filter out some information because of its sensitivity. For example, only 2 of the 31 executives who had not been invited to a party given by the president of the company ever learned about it. Further, the grapevine is fast. The news that one executive had become a parent spread to 46 percent of the members of the organization within three hours.

However, only about 10 percent of the members of the organization were active transmitters on the grapevine. Most members tended to receive information, but they did not pass it on. Some individuals and groups were so divorced from the grapevine that they never received any rumors.

Unfortunately, the information provided by the grapevine is accurate in some situations but inaccurate in others. Robert Hershey (1966) studied 30 items of information transmitted on the grapevine in one organization. Of these 30 items, 16 proved groundless, 9 accurate, and 5 distorted but somewhat accurate. This may be because the greater the quantity of information on the grapevine, the less accurate it is (Rollins and Charters 1965).

Computers

Management information systems (MIS) basically are all sources of information the manager uses to make decisions (see chapter 6). In today's world, the computer serves as a major source of information and communication, for it enables the organization to generate a large number of reports in a short period, and thus to examine the problems the organization faces from many vantage points.

Initially, organizations used computers principally in the accounting area, usually for routine work such as employee payrolls and record keeping. Most organizations now use computers for this purpose. Eighty-nine percent of 408 companies, each of whom employed at least 500 individuals, reported that they applied the computer to their payroll operations; 48 percent used it to automate their pension check processing (Morrison 1969). In addition, many

Managerial Style and Communication

Gibb feels that two contrasting managerial styles influence communication in the following manner:

The Persuasion Manager Believes	*The Problem-solving Manager Believes*
1. A breakdown in communication *is* the problem.	1. A breakdown in communication is symptomatic of other problems.
2. Staff members are responsible for solving communication problems.	2. Line officers are responsible for solving communication problems.
3. Communication should be one-way from superior to subordinate.	3. Communication should be two-way between superior and subordinate.
4. Subordinates should have little, if any, involvement in developing programs.	4. Subordinates should be involved in developing programs.

Adapted from Jack Gibb, "Communication and Productivity," *Personnel Administration,* 27, no. 1 (January–February, 1964): 8–13, 45.

---

companies have extended their computer use to the areas of finance, marketing, and production scheduling.

Still, organizations have yet to realize the vast potential of the computer. Because of the computer, it is now possible to create a completely integrated MIS, linking all major subsystems in the organization (accounting, finance, marketing, production scheduling, and so forth). However, few, if any, companies have developed such a system.

According to Mintzberg, managers dislike computerized MIS because they receive dated reports that are of limited value to them when they are making decisions. In addition, the start-up costs for computer work, especially a completely integrated MIS, are quite high. The possibility of error, at least initially, increases dramatically when managers move toward a completely integrated MIS. It may take several years for staff personnel to debug the new computer programs.

Some researchers have also focused attention on the effects of computerization on employees. The computer creates more routine jobs and more skilled jobs, but jobs at the intermediate levels of skill demand are abolished (Bass 1968). For example, the computer has led to the development of the elite programming job but also the unskilled job of pressing bent IBM cards.

Supervisors spend more of their time by themselves after the introduction of the computer than previously (Whisler 1970). In addition, computer specialists have gained significant informal power because of the importance of the computer for the success of the organization (Whisler 1970; Reif 1968). The computer even affects many of the first-line workers. They communicate less with other employees and their supervisors after the introduction of the computer than previously, largely because the routine nature of their responsibilities requires them to produce a standard output within a specific period (Whisler 1970).

Summary

As modern organizations have grown more complex, the patterns of communication within them have altered. This chapter has examined communication from three distinct perspectives: the communication between individuals, the flow of communication through organizational channels, and the impact of computers on communication.

There are many barriers to communication when human beings interact with one another, either individually or in groups. For example, words mean different things to different people. Managers can help avoid breakdowns in communication by using techniques like repetition and feedback, and by being sensitive to the needs and values of subordinates.

Research on communication networks, the results of which can reasonably be generalized to small groups in the organization, suggests that centralized structures such as the wheel and the chain are effective in solving routine problems. Decentralized networks such as the completely connected and the circle seem to be appropriate for nonroutine or ambiguous problems. Further, the two-step flow of communication suggests that the manager should identify the informal leaders in his or her work group and persuade them to follow a particular course of action before appealing to other members.

Mintzberg's analysis of managerial work indicates that the activities of executives are varied, fragmented, and brief. In performing these activities, managers rely primarily on oral communication. However, the wise manager also takes full advantage of written forms of communication.

From an organizational perspective, horizontal communication tends to predominate at the lower levels in the organization. There is some distortion in vertical communication because of factors such as status differences and subordinates' mistrust of superiors. When organizational channels of communication become overloaded, management can eliminate or reduce this problem by techniques such as the delegation of responsibilities and filtering mechanisms.

Research on the informal communication network known as the grapevine suggests that it becomes inaccurate as information increases. The grapevine is also fast and selective, although only about 10 percent of the members of the organization actively transmit information.

In recent years, the computer has affected communication in organizations. Its influence has been pronounced in the accounting area, especially in the processing of routine work. However, management has extensively applied the computer to problems in other functional areas such as marketing and production, even though few, if any, companies have developed a completely integrated MIS. When the computer is introduced, computer specialists gain a great amount of informal power, some work becomes more routine, and communication among individuals tends to decline.

Discussion Questions

1. Some barriers to communications are considered in this chapter. Discuss other barriers to communication. What techniques can be employed to avoid or get rid of these barriers?

2. Compare Mintzberg's description of communication to Alfred Sloan's approach. Are they contradictory? Why or why not?

3. Can a MIS exist without a computer? Why or why not? What areas of management have been most heavily influenced by the computer? Why? What are some behavioral consequences of computerization?

4. Why have management theorists and practitioners historically emphasized the relationship between communication and leading or directing? Is the framework of this chapter consistent with this emphasis? Why or why not?

5. Why does it seem logical to generalize research results on networks and the two-step flow only to small groups but not to organizations?

6. Does the grapevine reflect communication among individuals or organizational communication? Why? What function does it serve that formal channels cannot carry out?

Critical Incidents

NOTE: *These critical incidents can be used by the whole class with the case observational method (see Appendix), or used for thought and discussion by individual class members.*

1. A large engineering company relied primarilily on government contracts for its existence. Recently the Department of Labor found that this company's wage standards for engineering draftsmen did not meet department standards. The Department of Labor directed the company to adjust its standards if it wanted to meet the specifications of the government contracts. The draftsmen expected to receive a sizable bonus because of past inequities. However, management merely added one new set of positions on the career ladder and reclassified most of the employees downward. Management did not allow any of the employees to express their opinions on this course of action. Management actually had much justification for its position, since the costs of its contracts were fixed, so the company would have lost a great amount of money if all of the draftsmen had received a bonus.

Questions: What kind of control problem is this approach creating? How would you have communicated management's decision to the employees?

2. At a large state university of 35,000 students, registration for courses is very difficult. After a mail preregistration period, most of the courses are closed because of excessive demand. During the week's registration at the beginning of the semester, there is much confusion as students try to drop and add courses. While the administration has undertaken a long-range program to change this situation, there are obviously many problems in the short run.

For example, students mill around the registration desks during this period, imploring instructors and professors on duty to allow them to sign up for closed courses. Tempers are very short. One frustrated freshman's comment after several hours of registering illustrates the feelings of the students toward the instructors and professors—"I want to meet a human being!"

Questions: Suppose you were asked to design a short, one-hour training program for all professors and instructors that would focus on communication with students during the registration period. What would be the content of this course?

Suggested Readings

Fisher, B. Aubrey. *Small Group Decision Making: Communication and the Group Process.* New York: McGraw-Hill, 1974, 264 pages, hardback.
  Fisher clearly and effectively summarizes research in the area of communication as it relates to decision making in small groups.

Haney, William. *Communication and Organizational Behavior: Text and Cases,* 3rd ed. Homewood, Ill.: Richard D. Irwin, 1973, 533 pages, hardback.
  Haney develops a distinctive conceptual framework for communication and applies it to a variety of cases.

IV EXPERIENTIAL EXERCISES

Motivation Feedback Opinionnaire

Goals

1. To learn the concepts in Maslow's Need Hierarchy.
2. To get feedback on one's use of motivational techniques in terms of Maslow's Need Hierarchy.

Opinionnaire

Directions

The following statements have seven possible responses.

Strongly Agree	Agree	Slightly Agree	Don't Know	Slightly Disagree	Disagree	Strongly Disagree
+3	+2	+1	0	−1	−2	−3

Please mark one of the seven responses by circling the number that corresponds to the response that fits your opinion. For example: if you "Strongly Agree," circle the number "+3."

Complete every item. You have about 10 minutes to do so.

1. Special wage increases should be given to employees who do their jobs very well.
   +3 +2 +1 0 −1 −2 −3

2. Better job descriptions would be helpful so that employees will know exactly what is expected of them.
   +3 +2 +1 0 −1 −2 −3

3. Employees need to be reminded that their jobs are dependent on the Company's ability to compete effectively.

+3 +2 +1 0 −1 −2 −3

4. A supervisor should give a good deal of attention to the physical working conditions of his employees.

+3 +2 +1 0 −1 −2 −3

5. The supervisor ought to work hard to develop a friendly working atmosphere among his people.

+3 +2 +1 0 −1 −2 −3

6. Individual recognition for above-standard performance means a lot to employees.

+3 +2 +1 0 −1 −2 −3

7. Indifferent supervision can often bruise feelings.

+3 +2 +1 0 −1 −2 −3

8. Employees want to feel that their real skills and capacities are put to use on their jobs.

+3 +2 +1 0 −1 −2 −3

9. The Company retirement benefits and stock programs are important factors in keeping employees on their jobs.

+3 +2 +1 0 −1 −2 −3

10. Almost every job can be made more stimulating and challenging.

+3 +2 +1 0 −1 −2 −3

11. Many employees want to give their best in everything they do.

+3 +2 +1 0 −1 −2 −3

12. Management could show more interest in the employees by sponsoring social events after-hours.

+3 +2 +1 0 −1 −2 −3

13. Pride in one's work is actually an important reward.

+3 +2 +1 0 −1 −2 −3

14. Employees want to be able to think of themselves as "the best" at their own jobs.

+3 +2 +1 0 −1 −2 −3

15. The quality of the relationships in the informal work group is quite important.

+3 +2 +1 0 −1 −2 −3

16. Individual incentive bonuses would improve the performance of employees.

+3 +2 +1 0 −1 −2 −3

17. Visibility with upper management is important to employees.

+3 +2 +1 0 −1 −2 −3

18. Employees generally like to schedule their own work and to make job-related decisions with a minimum of supervision.   +3 +2 +1 0 −1 −2 −3

19. Job security is important to employees.   +3 +2 +1 0 −1 −2 −3

20. Having good equipment to work with is important to employees.   +3 +2 +1 0 −1 −2 −3

Scoring

1. Transfer the numbers you circled in the opinionnaire to the appropriate places in the chart below:

Statement No.	Score		Statement No.	Score
10	____		2	____
11	____		3	____
13	____		9	____
18	____		19	____
Total	____		Total	____
(Self-Actualization Needs)			(Safety Needs)	

Statement No.	Score		Statement No.	Score
6	____		1	____
8	____		4	____
14	____		16	____
17	____		20	____
Total	____		Total	____
(Esteem Needs)			(Basic Needs)	

Statement No.	Score
5	____
7	____
12	____
15	____
Total	____
(Belonging Needs)	

2. Record your total scores in the chart below by marking an "X" in each row next to the number of your total score for that area of needs motivation.

	−12	−10	−8	−6	−4	−2	0	+2	+4	+6	+8	+10	+12
Self-Actualization													
Esteem													
Belonging													
Safety													
Basic													

Low
Use

High
Use

Once you have completed this chart, you can see the relative strength of your use of each of these areas of needs motivation.

There is, of course, no "right" answer. What is right for you is what matches the actual needs of your employees and that, of course, is specific to each situation and each individual. In general, however, the "experts" tell us that today's employees are best motivated by efforts in the areas of Belonging and Esteem.

T-P Leadership Questionnaire: An Assessment of Style

Goal

1. To evaluate oneself in terms of task orientation (T) and people orientation (P).

T-P Leadership Questionnaire

Name _____ Group_____

Directions

The following items describe aspects of leadership behavior. Respond to each item according to the way you would most likely act if you were the leader of a work group. Circle whether you would most likely behave in the described way: always (A), frequently (F), occasionally (O), seldom (S), or never (N).

A F O S N   1. I would most likely act as the spokesman of the group.

A F O S N   2. I would encourage overtime work.

A F O S N   3. I would allow members complete freedom in their work.

A F O S N   4. I would encourage the use of uniform procedures.

A F O S N   5. I would permit the members to use their own judgment in solving problems.

A F O S N   6. I would stress being ahead of competing groups.

A F O S N   7. I would speak as a representative of the group.

A F O S N   8. I would needle members for greater effort.

A F O S N   9. I would try out my ideas in the group.

A F O S N   10. I would let the members do their work the way they think best.

A F O S N   11. I would be working hard for a promotion.

A F O S N   12. I would tolerate postponement and uncertainty.

A F O S N   13. I would speak for the group if there were vistors present.

A F O S N   14. I would keep the work moving at a rapid pace.

A F O S N   15. I would turn the members loose on a job and let them go to it.

A F O S N   16. I would settle conflicts when they occur in the group.

A F O S N   17. I would get swamped by details.

A F O S N   18. I would represent the group at outside meetings.

A F O S N   19. I would be reluctant to allow the members any freedom of action.

A F O S N   20. I would decide what should be done and how it should be done.

A F O S N   21. I would push for increased production.

A F O S N   22. I would let some members have authority which I could keep.

A F O S N   23. Things would usually turn out as I had predicted.

A F O S N   24. I would allow the group a high degree of initiative.

A F O S N   25. I would assign group members to particular tasks.

A F O S N   26. I would be willing to make changes.

A F O S N   27. I would ask the members to work harder.

A F O S N   28. I would trust the group members to exercise good judgment.

A F O S N   29. I would schedule the work to be done.

A F O S N   30. I would refuse to explain my actions.

A F O S N   31. I would persuade others that my ideas are to their advantage.

A F O S N   32. I would permit the group to set its own pace.

A F O S N   33. I would urge the group to beat its previous record.

A F O S N   34. I would act without consulting the group.

A F O S N   35. I would ask that group members follow standard rules and regulations.

T _____   P _____

Scoring

1. Circle the item number for items 8, 12, 17, 18, 19, 30, 34, and 35.

2. Write the number 1 in front of a *circled item number* if you responded S (seldom) or N (never) to that item.

3. Also write a number 1 in front of *item numbers not circled* if you responded A (always) or F (frequently).

4. Circle the number 1's which you have written in front of the following items: 3, 5, 8, 10, 15, 18, 19, 22, 24, 26, 28, 30, 32, 34, and 35.

5. *Count the circled number 1's.* This is your score for concern for people. Record the score in the blank following the letter P at the end of the questionnaire.

6. *Count the uncircled number 1's.* This is your score for concern for task. Record this number in the blank following the letter T.

T-P Leadership-Style Profile Sheet

Directions

To determine your style of leadership, mark your score on the *concern for task* dimension (T) on the left-hand arrow below. Next, move to the right-hand arrow and mark your score on the *concern for people* dimension (P). Draw a straight line that intersects the P and T scores. The point at which that line crosses the *shared leadership* arrow indicates your score on that dimension.

**Shared Leadership Results from
Balancing Concern for Task and Concern for People**

Autocratic Leadership	Shared Leadership	Laissez-Faire Leadership
High Productivity	High Morale and Productivity	High Morale

An Interpersonal Communication Inventory

This inventory offers you an opportunity to make an objective study of the degree and patterns of communication in your interpersonal relationships. It will enable you to better understand how you present and use yourself in communicating with persons in your daily contacts and activities. You will find it both interesting and helpful to make this study.

Interpersonal Communication Inventory

Directions

1. The questions refer to persons *other than your family members or relatives.*
2. Please answer each question as quickly as you can according to the way you feel *at the moment* (not the way you usually feel or felt last week).
3. Please do not consult anyone while completing this inventory. You may discuss it with someone after you have completed it. Remember that the value of this form will be lost if you change *any* answer during or after this discussion.
4. Honest answers are very necessary. Please be as frank as possible, since your answers are confidential.
5. Use the following examples for practice. Put a check (✔) in *one* of the three blanks on the right to show how the question applies to your situation.

	Yes (usually)	No (seldom)	Some times
Is it easy for you to express your views to others?	____	____	____
Do others listen to your point of view?	____	____	____

6. The **Yes** column is to be used when the question can be answered as happening *most of the time* or usually. The **No** column is to be used when the question can be answered as *seldom* or *never*. The **Sometimes** column should be marked when you definitely cannot answer **Yes** or **No.** *Use this column as little as possible.*
7. Read each question carefully. If you cannot give the exact answer to a question, answer the best you can but be sure to answer each one. There are no right or wrong answers. Answer according to the way *you* feel *at the present time.* Remember, do not refer to family members in answering the questions.

	Yes (usually)	**No** (seldom)	**Some- times**
1. Do your words come out the way you would like them to in conversation?	____	____	____
2. When you are asked a question that is not clear, do you ask the person to explain what he means?	____	____	____
3. When you are trying to explain something, do other persons have a tendency to put words in your mouth?	____	____	____
4. Do you merely assume the other person knows what you are trying to say without your explaining what you really mean?	____	____	____
5. Do you ever ask the other person to tell you how he feels about the point you may be trying to make?	____	____	____
6. Is it difficult for you to talk with other people?	____	____	____
7. In conversation, do you talk about things which are of interest to both you and the other person?	____	____	____
8. Do you find it difficult to express your ideas when they differ from those around you?	____	____	____
9. In conversation, do you try to put yourself in the other person's shoes?	____	____	____
10. In conversation, do you have a tendency to do more talking than the other person?	____	____	____
11. Are you aware of how your tone of voice may affect others?	____	____	____
12. Do you refrain from saying something that you know will only hurt others or make matters worse?	____	____	____
13. Is it difficult to accept constructive criticism from others?	____	____	____

293

	Yes (usually)	No (seldom)	Some-times
14. When someone has hurt your feelings, do you discuss this with him?	____	____	____
15. Do you later apologize to someone whose feelings *you* may have hurt?	____	____	____
16. Does it upset you a *great deal* when someone disagrees with you?	____	____	____
17. Do you find it difficult to think clearly when you are angry with someone?	____	____	____
18. Do you fail to disagree with others because you are afraid they will get angry?	____	____	____
19. When a problem arises between you and another person, can you discuss it without getting angry?	____	____	____
20. Are you satisfied with the way you settle your differences with others?	____	____	____
21. Do you pout and sulk for a long time when someone upsets you?	____	____	____
22. Do you become very uneasy when someone pays you a compliment?	____	____	____
23. Generally, are you able to trust other individuals?	____	____	____
24. Do you find it difficult to compliment and praise others?	____	____	____
25. Do you deliberately try to conceal your faults from others?	____	____	____
26. Do you help others to understand you by saying how you think, feel, and believe?	____	____	____
27. Is it difficult for you to confide in people?	____	____	____
28. Do you have a tendency to change the subject when your feelings enter into a discussion?	____	____	____

294

	Yes (usually)	**No** (seldom)	**Some-times**
29. In conversation, do you let the other person finish talking before reacting to what he says?	____	____	____
30. Do you find yourself not paying attention while in conversation with others?	____	____	____
31. Do you ever try to listen for meaning when someone is talking?	____	____	____
32. Do others seem to be listening when you are talking?	____	____	____
33. In a discussion is it difficult for you to see things from the other person's point of view?	____	____	____
34. Do you pretend you are listening to others when actually you are not?	____	____	____
35. In conversation, can you tell the difference between what a person is saying and what he may be feeling?	____	____	____
36. While speaking, are you aware of how others are reacting to what you are saying?	____	____	____
37. Do you feel that other people wish you were a different kind of person?	____	____	____
38. Do other people understand your feelings?	____	____	____
39. Do others remark that you always seem to think you are right?	____	____	____
40. Do you admit that you are wrong when you know that you are wrong about something?	____	____	____

Total Score ☐

Scoring

Look at how you responded to each item in the ICI. In front of the item write the appropriate weight from the table on this page. For example, if you answered "Yes" to item 1, you would find below that you get three points; write the number 3 in front of item 1 in the inventory and proceed to score item 2. When you have finished scoring each of the forty items, add up your total score. You may wish to compare your score to the norms listed in Table 2.

Table 1   Response Weights

	Yes	No	Sometimes		Yes	No	Sometimes
1.	3	0	2	21.	0	3	1
2.	3	0	2	22.	0	3	1
3.	0	3	1	23.	3	0	2
4.	0	3	1	24.	0	3	1
5.	3	0	2	25.	0	3	1
6.	0	3	1	26.	3	0	2
7.	3	0	2	27.	0	3	1
8.	0	3	1	28.	0	3	1
9.	3	0	2	29.	3	0	2
10.	0	3	1	30.	0	3	1
11.	3	0	2	31.	3	0	2
12.	3	0	2	32.	3	0	2
13.	0	3	1	33.	0	3	1
14.	3	0	2	34.	0	3	1
15.	3	0	2	35.	3	0	2
16.	0	3	1	36.	3	0	2
17.	0	3	1	37.	0	3	1
18.	0	3	1	38.	3	0	2
19.	3	0	2	39.	0	3	1
20.	3	0	2	40.	3	0	2

Table 2   Means and Standard Deviations for the ICI

Age Groups	Males		Females	
17-21	Mean	81.79	Mean	81.48
	S.D.	21.56	S.D.	20.06
	N.	53	N.	80
22-25	Mean	86.03	Mean	94.46
	S.D.	14.74	S.D.	11.58
	N.	38	N.	26
26 and up	Mean	90.73	Mean	86.93
	S.D.	19.50	S.D.	15.94
	N.	56	N.	45
All age groups by sex	Mean	86.39	Mean	85.34
	S.D.	19.46	S.D.	18.22
	N. 147		N. 151	
All age groups; males and females combined		Mean 85.93		
		S.D. 19.05		
		N. 298		

■Decision making is the most crucial dimension of management. If managers consistently make decisions that are not in the organization's best interests, it does not matter if the organization is designed perfectly, if the planning and control systems are operating efficiently, or if the behavioral processes are in balance.

What must a manager know to make wise decisions? The first step is to understand the process of decision making itself. Basically, decision making is a problem-solving activity, as chapter 12 describes. It involves recognizing that a problem exists, identifying possible causes of this problem, developing alternative solutions, choosing among available courses of action, and carrying out the chosen course of action. Having identified the problem, a manager has recourse to a number of specific decision-making techniques, which are discussed in chapter 13.

DECISION
MAKING
V

The Nature
of Decision Making
12

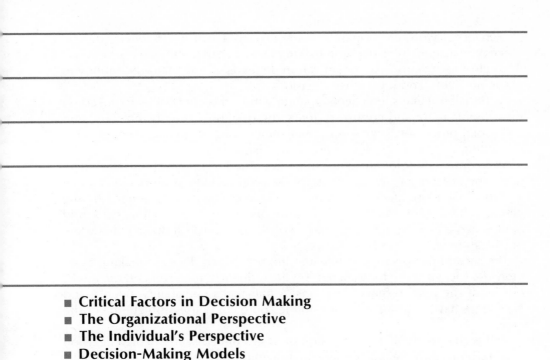

- **Critical Factors in Decision Making**
- **The Organizational Perspective**
- **The Individual's Perspective**
- **Decision-Making Models**

Performance Objectives

1. To know the steps involved in decision making as a problem-solving activity.

2. To know when to use programmed decisions and when to use nonprogrammed decisions for solving problems.

3. To be aware of both the organizational perspective and the individual's perspective on decision making.

4. To understand the differences between descriptive models and normative models of decision making.

Managerial work encompasses many diverse activities. However, the essence of management is decision making (Simon 1960). The success of everything else that occurs in an organization depends on the manager's ability to make intelligent and productive decisions.

As decision makers, managers operate within the constraints imposed on them by planning and control systems, the design of the organization, and behavioral processes. Hence the other dimensions of management provide the setting within which decision making takes place.

Like control, decision making can be examined from two distinct perspectives. The first perspective emphasizes decision making as an *organizational* activity. That is, the decisions managers make are heavily influenced by the nature of the organization in which they work. For example, managers would tend to avoid making decisions that involve serious risks if the climate in the organization were very conservative.

The second perspective stresses the importance of decision making as an *individual* activity. The focus here is on the individual manager and the methods he or she uses to make decisions. A manager's personality, talents, and experience have a strong influence on the approach to the problems he or she faces.

In this chapter there is a discussion of basic concepts, after which decision making, both as an organizational and individual activity, is examined. Finally, there is a description of models that illuminate the decision-making process.

Critical Factors
in Decision Making

The most obvious definition of *decision making* is deceptively simple: the selection of one alternative from various alternatives or courses of action that can be pursued. However, this definition is incomplete in that it fails to consider the manager's basis for making a decision. Which alternative is appropriate depends heavily on the setting within which decision making occurs. A manager may decide to give one employee a three-day layoff because the employee obviously does not care about his or her low rate of productivity. The manager may counsel another employee in a similar situation rather than lay off him or her because the employee has previously responded well to this approach. As has been noted, the setting for decision making is provided by the other three dimensions of management.

Steps in Problem Solving

Essentially, decision making takes place when an individual believes a problem exists, that is, when the gap between what is and what should be is so great that action must be taken. Thus decision making is a problem-solving activity that first involves the recognition of a problem.

For example, a manager might become concerned about his career if he has not received a promotion for three years. Perhaps the average time between promotions for managers in the organization is two years. The gap between this average length of time and the time during which he has not been promoted might eventually force the manager to conclude that a problem exists.

Looking for Causes. Once a manager recognizes a problem, he or she must identify possible causes of it. For the manager who has not been promoted for three years, some possible causes might be that: (1) the quality of his work has significantly deteriorated in the past few years; (2) his immediate superior does not like him; (3) he is doing such an outstanding job that his superior does not want to lose him; and (4) the company has no job available into which he could be appropriately promoted.

This manager may engage in a search for information by talking to his immediate superior, by comparing himself to others in the organization, and so forth. In this instance, let us assume he eventually decides the cause of his problem is his poor relationship with his superior.

Finding Solutions. At this point, the manager should develop alternative solutions to his problem. Some of these solutions could be to: (1) quit immediately and look for work elsewhere; (2) stay in the organization until he finds another job; (3) discuss the problem in a nonthreatening manner with his superior and managers at the upper levels in the organization; and (4) discuss the problem with his superior and upper managers, informing them that he will leave if he is not promoted in the near future.

Making a Choice. Given these possible solutions, the manager might decide to eliminate the alternative of telling his superior and managers that he will leave unless they promote him. Making such a threat would probably put them on the defensive so that they might be more inclined to fire him than promote him. Also, the manager might embarrass himself if he could not find work elsewhere.

This manager might decide instead to approach his superior and other upper-level managers in a nonthreatening manner. At the very least, this course of action would provide him with information that would assist him in his decision-making process. He might learn that he has identified the wrong cause of his problem, that he is in a dead-end position and will never be promoted. Or he might find out that his chances for promotion within a year are excellent.

If the manager discovers he is in a dead-end position, he might begin to search for work elsewhere. However, since it is usually best to have a job when looking for another job, he would probably stay in the organization until he could line up a new position.

This extended example of a manager's dissatisfaction with his rate of promotion includes all the steps that effective decision making usually involves: (1) recognizing a problem exists, (2) identifying possible causes of this problem, (3) developing alternative solutions, (4) choosing among alternative courses of action, and (5) carrying out the chosen course of action.

Types of Decisions

Decision making is essentially a problem-solving activity. In general, a decision maker faces two types of problems—structured and ill-structured (March and Simon 1957). A *structured problem* is one the manager can solve by means of a *programmed decision,* that is, the application of a decision rule, program, routine, or procedure that he or she has previously used to solve such problems. In some instances, a structured problem can be expressed in numbers or in terms of a numerical objective, such as minimizing costs. As we saw in the planning and control chapters, it is usually easier to deal with a problem that can be quantified than an abstract problem. For example, a manager in charge of three plants located in three different cities might want to minimize transportation costs. There are standard quantitative techniques he or she can use to solve this problem.

However, not all programmed decisions require expressing the problem numerically. Once the turnover rate among keypunch operators in a large company became abnormally high, so the top managers sponsored a questionnaire survey of the employees. This survey indicated the operators were dissatisfied with their working conditions. To solve the turnover problem, top management built a new cafeteria and redecorated the work area. Turnover subsequently declined.

Many problems are *ill-structured,* that is, the manager cannot easily apply a standard decision rule, program, or procedure that he or she has previously used to solve such problems. Rather, he or she must make a *nonprogrammed decision*—a creative response to a new problem. If a major customer of a firm quit and began to use the services of a competitor, the manager might respond by trying to win back the customer and preventing other customers from doing the same thing. The decisions he or she would make would probably be nonprogrammed, for judgment rather than a formula would be needed in reacting to the complaints of the former customer. Managers also usually must make nonprogrammed decisions when they decide to expand their organizations, for they cannot predict future conditions with complete certainty.

Uncertainty

When managers face a problem, they typically confront uncertainty. That is, a manager usually is not completely sure the decision he or she has made is the correct one until it is implemented. The issue of uncertainty is particularly acute when the problem is ill-structured, since the manager must act creatively.

However, there are many methods the manager can use to reduce the uncertainty he or she faces. For example, a manager may buy a controlling interest in the firms of his major competitors. In this fashion, he has reduced uncertainty, since the customers in this industry now must use his services. Because uncertainty is fundamental to American capitalism, some of these methods are limited or prohibited by law.

In some situations, managers from competing firms may pool their market and sales information so each firm can predict with accuracy its share of the market. This course of action sometimes involves going to excessive lengths to reduce uncertainty. This occurred during the 1950s when managers from the major electrical companies met regularly and set rates that would ensure all of them a good income and prevent customers from finding a cheaper source. The Anti-Trust Division of the Department of Justice could not prove this activity was illegal for several years. Finally, the investigators determined that the regular meetings took place in various American cities in accordance with a complex formula based on cycles of the moon. This finding eventually led to the conviction of some top managers in this industry.

In some situations, managers may practice co-optation to reduce uncertainty. *Co-optation* occurs when management attempts to influence its external environment by seeking out representatives from the community who become members of the organization. This form of compromise allows management to reduce the hostility and uncertainty of the organization's external environment, while the community representatives usually win some of the changes they have proposed.

For example, the original purpose of founding the Tennessee Valley Authority (TVA) in the 1930s was to introduce electrical power to the South. However, many of the local communities resisted the innovations proposed by this agency. Finally, the management of TVA placed several leaders of these local communities on their decision-making boards. Through the ideas and influence of these local leaders who had been co-opted by TVA, management was able to accomplish its major objective (Selznick 1949).

More commonly, managers can reduce uncertainty by training their subordinates to substitute for them when they are unavailable. In some organizations a manager is trained to handle his or her own job and that of his or her superior. If a manager is absent because of such factors as illness or a recent promotion, the organization is assured that a capable individual can complete the tasks necessary for its survival.

There are many other strategies that managers can employ when they face an uncertain situation. In all instances, the purpose is to reduce uncertainty so the factors on which management is basing its decisions can be evaluated as accurately as possible.

Limits on Decision Making

So far we have examined decision making as it would take place within an ideal organization, where a manager would be free to make and carry out whatever decision seemed most appropriate to him or her for any situation. But managers cannot make decisions in such a vacuum. Their decision-making authority is limited by their planning and control systems, the design of the organization, and the behavioral processes within the organization. These limitations suggest that managers work within an area of *bounded discretion* (Shull, Delbecq, and Cummings 1970). That is, the freedom of managers to make ideal decisions is limited by social norms, rules, and policies within the organization, and by legal restrictions and moral and ethical norms.

In modern America, the area in which management can make unregulated decisions has narrowed significantly in the past 70 years. President Baer of the Philadelphia and Reading Railroad made the following statement in 1903 in his reply to Mr. W. F. Clark who had urged him "as a Christian gentleman" to make some concessions to his workers who were on strike (Harris 1939, pp. 126–27):

> I see you are evidently biased in your religious views in favor of the right of the working man to control a business in which he has no other interest than to secure fair wages for the work he does. ... The rights and interests of the laboring man will be protected and cared for, not by the labor agitators, but by the Christian men to whom God in His infinite wisdom has given control of the property interests of the country.

A president of a company would not dare to make a similar statement today. Many restrictions now regulate the kinds of decisions that a president and his or her subordinates can make. In fact, it is currently fashionable for managers to support the concept of social responsibility. They now attempt to eliminate negative influences they might exert on society by putting voluntary controls on pollution, hiring underprivileged workers, and supporting cultural activities.

The Organizational Perspective

Probably the greatest limits on a manager's discretion in decision making are created by the nature and needs of the organization in which he or she is working. Typically an individual manager has little, if any, control over these factors. Thus it is useful to explore the decision-making process from the viewpoint of the organization. Several organizational constraints in particular are worth examining, including the goals and policies of the organization, the type of organization, the level at which a given decision is made, the time limits on decision making, the culture in which the organization operates, and the organization's learning experiences.

Goals and Policies

Top management normally establishes several goals it wishes the organization to attain. The organization then establishes policies or general guides to action that are designed to help accomplish these goals, and rules and procedures to carry out the policies (see chapter 5). These three related factors—goals, policies, and rules—impose organizational limits on the kinds of decisions managers can make.

An example of this is a bank that wanted to increase its scope of operations (see chapter 1). The bank accomplished this goal very successfully, for the number of branches increased from 20 to 180 between 1958 and 1970. The bank's major policy during this period was to attract customers by offering them a wide range of distinctive services. It then established specific rules to accord with this policy. Tellers provided specialized services such as the sale of baseball and football tickets; interest rates on savings accounts were placed at the highest level the law would permit; and long-term and "preferred" customers received special privileges such as a free safe-deposit box and having unbacked checks honored up to a limit of $500.

The branch managers attempted to carry out the policy of pleasing their customers at all costs. Some even allowed their preferred customers to cash unbacked checks that exceeded the $500 limit, since top management tacitly condoned this practice. Further, the overwhelming success and greatly increased size of the bank created decisional bottlenecks. The informal decision-making atmosphere in which all of the managers in the system knew each other was replaced by a formal and impersonal apparatus. When a branch manager wanted to develop a new program or service, he or she now had to seek the approval of more superiors than formerly. Because of this increase in formality, decisions could be bottlenecked for months, either at the regional or headquarters levels. In some instances, branch managers began to delay the start of new programs and services, primarily because they did not want to go through the prolonged procedure of gaining the approval of their superiors.

Types of Organizations

The nature of the organization strongly influences the kinds of decisions managers make. In particular, the involvement of individuals in the life of the organization is relevant, for they generate and complete the activities that sustain it. Amitai Etzioni (1961) has proposed that most organizations fall into three general types based on two factors: the kinds of power the organization uses to influence subordinates, and the kinds of involvement the organization seeks to generate among its subordinates.

Etzioni sees organizations as using three types of power to influence subordinates (see Figure 12.1). First, an organization can force its members to follow specific courses of action; that is, it can use *coercive* power, as a prison does. Second, the organization can employ *utilitarian* power, which means that the member is not rewarded if he or she does not perform what is expected; this is the case in most business firms. Finally, the organization may use *normative* power, in which case the member obeys mainly because he or she wants to be a part of the organization; one example is a religious order.

When an organization employs coercive power, the typical result is that members react to the organization with hostility, which is an *alienative involvement*. Utilitarian power usually results in a *calculative involvement*, which means members will leave the organization if they believe they are not benefiting from it. Finally, normative power frequently creates *moral involvement*. In this instance, members feel a moral obligation to obey the organization's dictates, since they have joined voluntarily.

The three types of power and the three types of involvement yield nine possible combinations (see Figure 12.1). However, power and involvement are

Figure 12.1　Etzioni's Types of Organizations

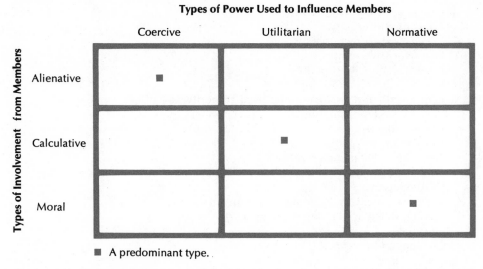

Types of Power Used to Influence Members

Based on Amitai Etzioni, *A Comparative Analysis of Complex Organizations* (New York: The Free Press, 1961).

related in most organizations, so only three types are predominant. Of course, a few organizations combine two or even all three types of power. Some labor unions use both utilitarian and normative power to gain compliance from their members. An outline of organizations according to Etzioni's typology is shown in Table 12.1.

Etzioni goes on to propose that managers should make decisions that accord with the nature of the organization in which they operate. A manager in a business firm, for instance, typically cannot employ coercive power. If he or she tries it, the members may revolt, decrease their rate of productivity, or leave the organization. On the other hand, if the manager depends on normative power, the members are likely to ignore his or her directives.

Organizational Level

Another constraint on a manager's decision-making scope is the level at which he or she is operating in the organization. According to Talcott Parsons (1960), all organizations have three levels. The first is the *technical* level, where the actual production of the organization takes place. The *institutional* level consists of the top managers who monitor changes in the external environment and define the overall goals the organization is to pursue. At the *managerial*

Table 12.1   Etzioni's Classification of Organizations

A. Predominantly *coercive* authority
   Concentration camps
   Prisons and correctional institutions
   Prisoner-of-war camps
   Custodial mental hospitals
   Coercive unions
B. Predominantly *utilitarian,* rational-legal authority: use of economic rewards
   Business and industry (with a few exceptions)
   Business unions
   Farmers' organizations
   Peacetime military organizations
C. Predominantly *normative* authority: use of membership status, intrinsic
      value rewards
   Religious organizations (churches, convents, etc.)
   Ideologically based political organizations or parties
   Hospitals
   Colleges and universities
   Social unions
   Voluntary associations and mutual benefit associations
   Professional associations
D. *Mixed* structures
   Normative-coercive—combat units
   Utilitarian-normative—most labor unions
   Utilitarian-coercive—some early industries, some farms, company towns, ships

Reprinted with permission of Macmillan Publishing Co., Inc. from Amitai Etzioni, *A Comparative Analysis of Complex Organizations,* pp. 66–67. Copyright © 1961 by The Free Press.

level, managers coordinate the organization's efforts so the production process operates efficiently. These managers at the managerial level also work with the top managers at the institutional level to accomplish the overall objectives of the organization.

Usually the problems managers at the technical level confront are routine, such as the number of units an individual worker must produce. Thus they work with a high degree of certainty, making it possible for them to complete a large number of programmed decisions. The amount of certainty is less at the managerial and institutional levels, where managers must make many nonprogrammed decisions (Figure 12.2). Examples of decisions at the institutional and managerial levels include how much money should be invested in new equipment, what actions to take in response to governmental safety regulations, and how to attract workers who are in scarce supply, such as engineers.

Time

Generally, managers in the organization work at an unrelenting pace (see chapter 11). Their activities are extremely brief, varied, and discontinuous. Based on his own work and the research of others, Henry Mintzberg concluded that this portrait of managerial work applies to all levels in the organization (Mintzberg 1973 and 1975). However, there is at least one major exception to this generalization—managers at different levels in any organization seem to spend different amounts of time on any particular decision.

In general, the higher their level in the organization, the more time managers spend on problems that require decisions (Table 12.2). At the first-line level of supervision, foremen usually face problems that can be solved within two weeks. At the institutional level of the organization, uncertainty forces managers to make nonprogrammed decisions that require much more time and thought. Fifty percent of the problems confronting top managers require at

Figure 12.2   Environmental Uncertainty, Organizational Level, and Types of Decisions

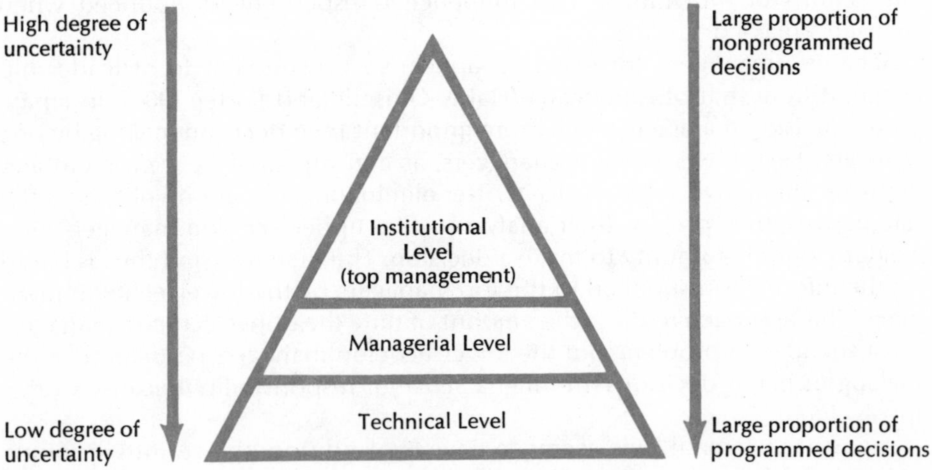

High degree of uncertainty

Large proportion of nonprogrammed decisions

Institutional Level (top management)

Managerial Level

Technical Level

Low degree of uncertainty

Large proportion of programmed decisions

Table 12.2 Time Required for Decision Making
at Different Managerial Levels (in percentages)

Time Required for Decision	Highest level			Lowest level
	Works Manager	Division Superintendent	Department Foreman	Shift Foreman
Short (0–2 weeks)	3.3%	54.2%	68.0%	97.7%
Moderate (2 weeks to 1 year)	46.1	41.4	30.4	2.1
Distant (over 1 year)	50.0	4.3	1.5	0.0
Total	99.4%	99.9%	99.9%	99.8%

From N. Martin, "Differential Decision in the Management of an Industrial Plant," *Journal of Business* 9 (1956): 251. Copyright 1956 by The University of Chicago Press. Reprinted by permission.

least one year before a final decision can be made (see Table 12.2). These findings confirm the importance of organizational level in the decision-making process.

Culture

In chapter 10, there was a discussion of how the culture of a society influences the actions of individuals. This influence is especially pronounced when managers make decisions.

Japanese managers, for instance, appear to possess a style of leadership different from that of Americans (Haire, Ghiselli, and Porter 1966). In Japan, group decision making is much more important than decision making by one manager. First, lower-echelon managers, as a group, analyze a problem and generate alternative solutions to it. After eliminating all but one or two of the alternatives, they present their analysis to the upper-echelon managers who hold the proper authority to make a decision. The final decision thus is based on the information supplied to the top managers by the lower-echelon managers. This approach reduces the amount of time the upper-echelon managers must spend on a problem. But the lower-echelon managers participate in the making of major decisions and feel a sense of responsibility because of this involvement.

Japan's managerial style seems to have evolved from the country's unique cultural problems. Japan is very small, and it does not possess abundant natural resources. To overcome these disadvantages, Japanese leaders have traditionally emphasized the belief that all parts of the society—individuals, families, groups, organizations, and the government—are closely intertwined. The obligations of Japanese managers extend not only to the firm but to all parts of the society. In return, the firm customarily guarantees the manager lifetime employment.

Group Decision Making

Although group decision making is not as prominent in the United States as in Japan, it is becoming an increasingly popular technique for dealing with complex problems. Since the complexity of the world in which organizations operate is increasing, it is more and more difficult for one manager to make important decisions independently. In fact, this complexity may eventually create a situation in which group decision making is the dominant mode in this country.

E. Frank Harrison (1975) has summarized the advantages of group decision making:

1. A greater sum of knowledge or information is brought to the decision.
2. Participating in decision making increases managers' acceptance of the final choice.
3. Because more managers are involved in making the decision, they can inform members of their units about the reasons for it. Hence the units increase their understanding of the reasons that form the basis for a decision.
4. A problem is approached in more ways and more alternative solutions are proposed.

However, group decision making also has some liabilities:

1. Members of the decision-making group may feel pressure to accept the decision supported by the majority.
2. When members of a group reach agreement on a tentative solution, they frequently refuse to look for a better approach.
3. One individual or a few individuals may dominate the group.

Learning

Just as individuals learn to respond to situations from previous experience, so do organizations. That is, managers in an organization learn to respond to a new situation or problem on the basis of what has been effective in their previous experiences. If salesmen throughout an organization have learned that their customers respond negatively to hard-selling practices, they may automatically rule out a hard-sell approach when a new product is introduced.

Learning can have negative as well as positive effects. For instance, Montgomery Ward was much larger than Sears, Roebuck at the end of World War I. Because the end of a war usually signals the beginning of a period of prosperity, the top managers of Montgomery Ward decided to expand their operations. This approach was successful for a year or two but, in 1921, a major recession occurred. As Montgomery Ward began to retrench, it started to lose many of its customers to Sears, Roebuck.

Still, Montgomery Ward continued to be successful until the end of World War II. At that time, the company had plenty of working capital that would have allowed it to expand. However, its top managers recalled their experience after World War I, when expansion hurt the company because of the recession. Hence they decided not to expand.

Meanwhile, Sears, Roebuck pursued an aggressive course of expansion. No recession occurred until 1953, when it was too late for Montgomery Ward to catch up. Thus, organizational learning had proved detrimental to Montgomery Ward, since the conditions that existed at the end of World War I were very different from those at the end of World War II.

The Individual's Perspective

Although group decision making seems to be gaining popularity in the United States, individuals still make many or most decisions independently. The typical manager makes several decisions of various types during an average work day. Moreover, it is the manager who exercises considerable responsibility and makes successful decisions who is commonly rewarded and promoted.

Managers' Biases

The decisions of managers are heavily influenced by their mental images of the world. A manager, like anyone else, develops certain stereotypes with which he or she categorizes individuals and activities. One researcher dramatized the importance of stereotypes in a study in which managers described pictures of individuals more favorably when they were called managers than when they were designated as union representatives. The group of managers who saw the pictures identified as managers described them in such terms as hard working, intelligent, and trustworthy. When the pictures were identified as those of labor representatives, another group of managers used such terms as shiftless, lazy, and untrustworthy (Haire 1955).

Even before an individual becomes a manager, he or she develops stereotypes that influence the kinds of decisions he or she will eventually make. Some of the most common stereotypes involve people's race, sex, hair style, dress, and educational background. In a striking study of stereotypes, two researchers provided a description of factory workers to 179 college students that incorporated such elements as: works in a factory, reads a newspaper, goes to movies, average height, cracks jokes, strong, and active. When given this profile, the college students described the factory worker as the "typical American Joe" who is likable, friendly, but not too intelligent. When the researchers merely added the word "intelligent" to the profile, many of the college students refused to accept this concept or deemphasized its importance (Haire and Grunes 1950). Such a stereotype is bound to influence these students when they become managers.

In addition, their own professional training and departmental identification appear to influence managers in decision making. In one study, sales executives tended to view most problems with a sales bias, regardless of their nature. Similarly, finance executives perceived the same problems in terms of finance (Dearborn and Simon 1958). Although such biases are bound to exist, it is important to be aware that they can have a strong influence on decision making.

Personality

Some individuals do not like to face a problem whose solution is very uncertain; others enjoy this situation immensely. An individual's basic personality is the most important factor that influences his or her reaction to an uncertain situation. Consequently, personality is a key determinant of decision-making styles among managers. Even the individual's willingness and desire to change jobs is partially determined by his or her personality. For example, Joan Sieber and John Lanzetta (1964) have shown that high-risk takers are more likely to accept the uncertainties of job changes than low-risk takers.

Intelligence appears to be another factor that influences an individual's decision-making style. Generally, more intelligent individuals make better decisions. In one study, the more intelligent subjects tended to find a strategy that proved to be successful and stayed with it. The less intelligent subjects did not evolve any particular strategy but tended to make their choices at random (Scodel, Ratoosh, and Minos 1959).

Decision-Making
Models

Generally, people who study decision making look at it from two points of view, normative and descriptive. The *normative model* of decision making focuses on the way managers should make decisions; the *descriptive model* emphasizes the way managers actually do make them.

Economic Man and Administrative Man

For the past 200 years, many economists have accepted the normative model that Adam Smith developed, called *economic man*. In this model, the manager is assumed to understand all of the alternatives he or she can pursue to accomplish a particular goal. From these, the manager supposedly chooses the most desirable alternative, that is, the one that will maximize some economic value, such as profit.

However, managers often deviate significantly from this normative model. Based on the actual study of managerial behavior, Herbert Simon (1976) put forth a descriptive model, called *administrative man*. According to this model, the manager cannot possibly be aware of all the alternatives he or she might pursue, nor all the goals he or she might wish to accomplish. Rather, the manager reduces the complexity of each problem so as to make a decision. Typically, the manager will examine only four or five alternatives that are minimally acceptable, and choose one of them. That is, the manager *satisfices* rather than *maximizes;* he or she chooses a solution that will be adequate rather than taking additional time and effort to find the best possible solution. In this sense, the manager *bounds reality* by limiting the number of alternatives he or she will examine to make a reasonable decision.

Charles Lindblom supports this view of decision making, for he argues that the manager "muddles his way" through a problem to find an acceptable solution (Lindblom 1959). According to Lindblom, the manager operates in steps: he or she makes a change, interprets the feedback, makes another change, and so forth. In this sense, the manager is making nonprogrammed responses to ill-structured problems that are exceedingly difficult to solve.

Vroom and Yetton Model

Recently, Victor Vroom and Philip Yetton (1973) have developed a normative model of decision making that potentially can be of enormous benefit to the manager. These researchers argue that there are five styles of decision making a manager can use, all based on the degree of subordinate participation necessary to choose an alternative. These styles are:

1. *A1 (autocratic method #1):* You solve the problem or make the decision yourself, using information available to you at the time.

2. *A2 (autocratic method #2):* You obtain the necessary information from your subordinates; you may or may not tell them what the problem is. The role your subordinates play in making the decision is clearly one of providing the necessary information to you rather than generating or evaluating solutions.

3. *C1 (consultative method #1):* You share the problem with relevant subordinates individually, getting their ideas and suggestions without bringing them together as a group. Then you make the decision, which may or may not reflect your subordinates' influence.

4. *C2 (consultative method #2):* You share the problem with your subordinates as a group, collectively obtaining their ideas and suggestions. Then you make the decision, which may or may not reflect your subordinates' influence.

5. *G2 (group method #2):* You share the problem with your subordinates as a group. Together you generate and evaluate alternatives and attempt to reach agreement (consensus) on a solution. Your role is essentially that of chairman—you do not try to influence the group to adopt your solution, and you are willing to accept and implement any solution that has the support of the entire group (Vroom and Yetton 1973).

In deciding which method to use to solve a particular problem, a manager must answer yes or no to seven questions related to the amount of information available, type of decision required, and involvement of subordinates (see Figure 12.3). The answers determine the style of decision making he or she should use. For example, the manager may face the following situation: (1) there is no quality requirement such that one solution is likely to be better than another; (2) there is not enough information available to make possible a high-quality decision; (3) the problem is not structured; and (4) the decision does not have to be accepted by subordinates to be implemented. In this instance, the manager should make an autocratic decision, method #1 (A1).

Figure 12.3   Decision Process Flowchart

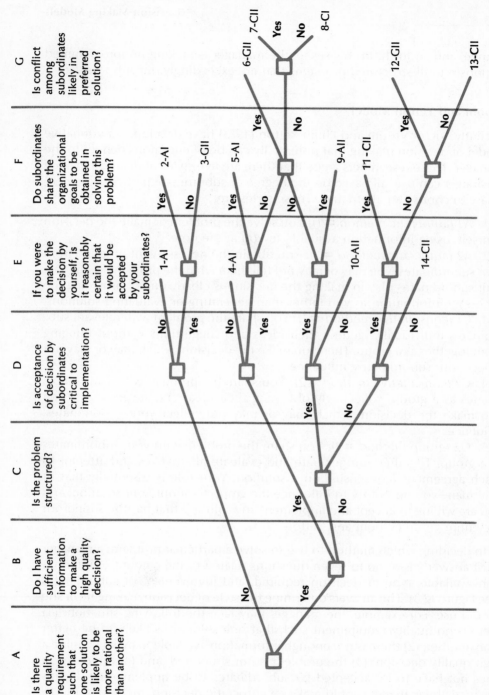

From Victor H. Vroom, "A New Look at Managerial Decision Making," p. 70. Reprinted by permission of the publisher from *Organizational Dynamics* (Spring 1973). © 1973 by AMACOM, a division of American Management Association.

In short, Vroom and Yetton have developed five styles of decision making a manager can use depending upon the problem he or she faces. This model can serve as a helpful tool for the manager who is faced with a difficult and nonprogrammed problem.

Summary

Decision making is a problem-solving activity that takes place within the setting provided by the other dimensions of management. The first step is recognizing that a problem exists; the manager must then identify possible causes, develop alternative solutions, choose among these alternatives, and implement the desired course of action.

It is useful to distinguish between programmed and nonprogrammed decisions. Managers make programmed decisions in response to structured problems. That is, the manager can attack the problem by implementing a program or routine he or she has successfully employed in the past on similar problems. Nonprogrammed decisions are a creative response to ill-structured and distinctive problems the manager has not previously encountered.

Decision making can be seen from two perspectives: organizational and individual. Organizational factors that influence the decision-making process include the goals and policies of the organization, the type of organization, the organizational level at which a given decision is made, the time limits on decision making, the culture in which the organization operates, and the organization's learning experiences. Factors that influence the individual's style of decision making include his or her personality, intelligence, and personal biases.

Finally, there are two general models of decision making—normative and descriptive. The normative model specifies the manner in which the manager should make decisions; the descriptive model portrays the manner in which he or she actually does make decisions. Simon developed a descriptive model called "administrative man." According to this model, the manager "bounds reality" and "satisfices" by examining only a small number of reasonable alternatives and selecting the most acceptable one, rather than seeking out the best possible alternative. Recently, Vroom and Yetton constructed a normative model that emphasizes the degree of subordinate participation in the decision-making process.

Discussion Questions

1. In the Vroom and Yetton model, how is leadership related to decision making?

2. What are some cultural factors in the United States that influence the kinds of decisions managers can make?

3. Etzioni classifies combat units as a mixed structure, that is, a normative-coercive organization. Why?

4. Describe some situations in an organization in which group decision making would be more appropriate than individual decision making. Explain.

5. What factors in your own personality do you think influence your decision-making ability? Can you think of a problem you and someone else analyzed differently because of personality differences? Describe the problem and the personalities.

6. Describe a problem you think would have to be solved by maximizing rather than satisficing. Now describe a problem you could solve by satisficing rather than maximizing.

Critical Incidents

NOTE: *These critical incidents can be used by the whole class with the case observational method (see Appendix), or used for thought and discussion by individual class members.*

1. For several years, a consulting company with 400 employees relied heavily on government contracts for its success. Its employees, most of whom had been with the company for several years, were very productive and loyal. However, the government decided to hire its own employees to do the work the consulting firm had been performing. Some jobs still would go to the consulting firm, but they would not require 400 employees. In fact, the firm's management estimated that the company could use only 150 employees productively.

Questions: What are some alternatives that management might pursue to solve this problem? What would you do if you were in charge of this firm?

2. During the late 1960s, many universities experienced student strikes, which sometimes led to riots. At one university, a riot broke out in the spring when the dean of a particular college was attending an important meeting in another city. The purpose of this meeting was to solidify an agreement that would provide the university with a major endowment from a business firm. Although the dean saw television pictures of the rioting at his university, his two top subordinates told him on the phone that it was not necessary for him to return, since the situation was calming down. In addition, many other administrators on campus were available to handle the problem.

Questions: Is the dean facing a structured or ill-structured problem? Why? Should the dean make a programmed decision? Why? If you were the dean, what would you do in this situation? Why?

3. A personnel researcher in a large organization was asked to do a study based on the work of some other researchers in another part of the organization. This project was very important, since it concerned the development of a form rating the career potential of managers in the organization. However, when the researcher approached the managers and researchers in the other part of the organization for the information she needed, they were evasive. Finally, the manager who had been responsible for directing the first study told her to mind her own business. According to this manager, his researchers had completed an excellent study and it was not necessary to extend it.

Questions: Does this problem appear to arise from organizational or individual factors? Why? What should the researcher do? Why?

Suggested Readings

Harrison, E. Frank. *The Managerial Decision-Making Process.* Boston: Houghton Mifflin, 1975, 341 pages, hardback.
   This is a readable and sophisticated treatment of the decision-making process. Harrison reviews the major research studies and theories in this area.

Simon, Herbert. *Administrative Behavior,* 3rd ed. New York: The Free Press, 1976 (originally published 1947), 364 pages, paperback.
   This is a classic study of actual decision making.

Walton, Clarence, and Cleveland, Frederick. *Corporations on Trial: The Electric Cases.* Belmont, California: Wadsworth, 1964, 138 pages, paperback.
   The authors have written a fascinating case study of the conspiracy among some executives in the electric industry to fix prices, and their prosecution by the government.

Decision-Making
Techniques

13

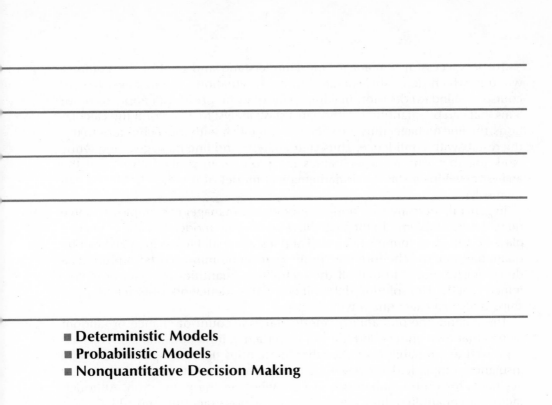

- **Deterministic Models**
- **Probabilistic Models**
- **Nonquantitative Decision Making**

Performance Objectives

1. To be familiar with major quantitative and nonquantitative decision-making techniques that managers can use to solve problems.

2. To be able to classify quantitative techniques as either probabilistic or deterministic.

3. To know when and how to use each of the techniques managers employ to make decisions.

To be successful, a manager must understand and control the complex world in which he or she operates. In many situations, the manager has recourse to standard decision-making techniques he or she can apply to problems that can be quantified. Although a staff analyst may perform the calculations, the line manager must be sufficiently familiar with the techniques to use the results with confidence. Thus staff analysts and line managers frequently work together. The manager frames the problem in general terms and the analyst develops a statistical-mathematical model of it which he or she can then solve.

In general, there are two kinds of models the manager can employ to solve quantitative problems. In the first, the *deterministic* model, the law of chance plays no role. A deterministic model applies when all factors involved can be quantified exactly. The formula "profit = revenue minus costs" represents a deterministic model in that all the factors are quantities that can be determined exactly. The solution determined by this framework of exact relationships is also an exact quantity.

The second, the *probabilistic* model, takes account of chance or random factors that exist under conditions of uncertainty. Both data and solutions are expressed as probabilities rather than certainties. For example, automobile insurance companies have developed tables that profile the probability of car accidents for various subgroups of car owners in the population. Although factors are quantified, they are recognized as not exact but "most likely."

The first part of this chapter contains a discussion of important deterministic models; the second part focuses on probabilistic models. However, managers also use many nonquantitative decision-making techniques, and these are discussed in the third part of the chapter.

Deterministic

Models

A deterministic model is typically appropriate when a manager can obtain reliable data. If a manager knows precisely what revenues are for a particular year, this enables him or her to solve problems involving revenues. Some of the most important deterministic models are break-even analysis, linear programming, capital budgeting, and inventory management.

Break-Even Analysis

Managers want to make money. To do so, they must exceed their *break-even point,* which is the level of operations where the total revenue a product brings in equals its total cost to produce. Total revenue depends on the market demand for a particular product, and this varies with the price managers ask for it. In addition, total costs vary with the number of units of a product an organization manufactures. The objective of *break-even analysis* is to determine the *optimum break-even point,* that is, where profits will be highest. This is done by taking into consideration the costs associated with each level of demand, and the demand for a particular product when the organization sets varying prices for it.

As suggested by this discussion, break-even analysis involves three steps. First, managers examine the costs of the organization to determine the relationship between cost and volume of output. Second, they determine the number of units that must be sold to cover costs at a specific price per unit. Third, they evaluate the effect of demand on profitability at various prices.

Costs. The break-even model depends heavily on the distinction between *fixed* and *variable* costs. As chapter 6 indicated, *fixed costs (FC)* are relatively stable over time; for example, property taxes and rent essentially stay the same no matter how output changes. *Variable costs (VC)* change with the level of output; for example, the materials and labor used in the production process cost more as more units are produced.

Cumberland Industries is a hypothetical firm whose sole product is bronze candleholders (see chapter 6). This firm requires $180,000 to exist even before it begins producing, since its fixed costs total $180,000. Then, an additional $6 of variable costs will be incurred for each candleholder produced. Total costs *(TC)* equal total fixed costs plus total variable costs. For Cumberland Industries, total costs for 100,000 units are $180,000 *FC* + $600,000 ($6 per unit) *VC,* or $780,000 *TC.*

Price. Without knowing the selling price of Cumberland Industries' product, we cannot determine the company's profitability (or lack thereof). To figure profitability, we must first know total revenue, from which we deduct costs. Let us assume that each bronze candleholder retails for $25. The retailer pays Cumberland Industries $15 per unit. Let us also assume there are no quantity discounts. Consequently, each bronze candleholder generates $15 revenue for Cumberland Industries. From the $15 brought in by one candleholder, Cumberland Industries must first pay the $6 variable cost. The rest of the $15 must go toward paying off the company's fixed costs, until enough candleholders have been sold to cover all of the fixed costs ($180,000). At that point, the *break-even point,* total revenue *(TR)* equals total costs, and profits equal zero.

To determine the break-even point, or the sales volume *(Q)* necessary to cover the total and fixed costs, the following formula is applicable:

$$TR = TFC + TVC$$
$$\$15(Q) = \$180,000 + \$6(Q)$$
$$\$9(Q) = \$180,000$$
$$Q = 20,000 \text{ bronze candleholders (break-even point)}$$

Demand. Let us now assume that Cumberland Industries is able to sell 25,000 candleholders per year when it charges $15 per candleholder. At this demand level, total profit *(TP)* will be the amount left over after fixed and variable costs have been paid.

$$TR = TFC + TVC + TP$$
$$(\$15)(25,000) = \$180,000 + (\$6)(25,000) + TP$$
$$\$375,000 = \$180,000 + \$150,000 + TP$$
$$\$375,000 = \$330,000 + TP$$
$$\$45,000 = TP$$

While the profit of $45,000 is good, it may be possible to generate even more. Market research into the demand for bronze candleholders indicates that annual sales would vary with prices, as follows:

Price	$12	$15	$17	$19
Annual Demand	32,000	25,000	21,000	17,000

In order to determine the price that will maximize profits, a price-demand table can be constructed, as shown in Table 13.1.

Table 13.1 indicates that Cumberland Industries will reap the highest profits if it charges $17 per bronze candleholder to retailers. Although Cumberland Industries could charge the retailers $19 per candleholder, demand would fall to 17,000, causing a decline in total profits. Hence Cumberland Industries should increase its price per candleholder from $15 to $17 in order to make the highest profits.

In general, break-even analysis provides the decision maker with an overview of the effect of price on profit that is helpful when he or she attempts to set the price of a product. Still, many other factors will influence the final

Table 13.1   The Effect of Price on Demand for Bronze Candleholders

Price	Demand	TFC	TVC	TC	TR	TP
$12	32,000	$180,000	$192,000	$372,000	$384,000	$12,000
15	25,000	180,000	150,000	330,000	375,000	45,000
17	21,000	180,000	126,000	306,000	357,000	51,000
19	17,000	180,000	102,000	282,000	323,000	41,000

pricing decisions, such as competitive conditions, trade relations, and level of capital investment. The manager must also take them into account when he or she sets prices.

Linear Programming

Linear programming is an extension of break-even analysis that is very useful in analyzing complex problems. In essence, *linear programming* focuses on either maximizing some objective function, such as profits, or minimizing some objective function, such as costs. Linear programming involves the solution of linear equations and is appropriate when the manager must allocate scarce resources to competing projects or objectives. Examples of this type of problem include finding the most advantageous product mix, allocating advertising budgets, and allocating machinery and personnel to various projects.

Suppose that Gray Industries has a division which manufactures two products, a hand lawn mower and a power mower. The hand mower contributes $20 per unit to profit after variable costs have been paid. The power mower contributes $120 per unit to profit after variable costs have been paid. Gray Industries employs two resources in the production of both lawn mowers, assembly time and testing time. The hand mower requires 1 hour of assembly time and 2 hours of testing time per unit of output; the power mower needs 5 hours of assembly time and 2 hours of testing time per unit. There is a total of 40 man-hours of assembly time and 60 man-hours of testing time available per day. Gray Industries' objective is to maximize profits. Hence the problem is to determine the number of units of each product that will maximize daily profit.

This simplified problem can be solved without the aid of a computer. However, managers typically face complex situations in which they must allocate scarce resources to several products. In addition, several resources are normally required to produce each of these products. To solve complex problems, the manager can use a standard program, *The Simplex Method,* which is available on most large computers. The Simplex Method also provides other important information such as (1) the value to the firm of additional resources the managers might want to buy, and (2) the effect that changes in product profitability and resource availabilities will have on the ideal product mix.

Linear programming is a powerful tool for managerial decision making. It has two major functions: it establishes optimal operating conditions and pinpoints areas that may need managerial attention, and it identifies the sensitivity of operating variables to changes in conditions. This information allows managers to focus attention on areas sensitive to change, where their input is most important.

Capital Budgeting

A manager relies heavily on linear programming when he or she allocates resources to competing projects. Similarly, *capital budgeting* provides a set of techniques a manager can use to evaluate the relative attractiveness of various projects in which a lump payment is made to generate a stream of earnings over a future period. Examples of capital budgeting projects include an investment in a new machine that will increase future profits by reducing costs, an investment of a sum of money into an advertising campaign to increase future sales (and profits), and an investment in research and development that will improve the product and result in increased profits due to higher sales.

Assume that Franklin Enterprises has $10,000 to invest, and three possible ways to invest it. Management can put the $10,000 into new production machinery that will save the company $3,000 per year for the next five years; it can spend the $10,000 on revised package graphics that will increase profits by $4,500 for the first two years and by $2,000 for the following three years; or it can invest in research that will result in product improvements that will increase earnings by $1,000 in the first three years and by $6,000 in the fourth and fifth years. (Obviously, these figures are estimates, but we will assume they are reliable.) All three projects have an economic life of five years.

Several issues confront the decision maker in evaluating the three projects. First, we can see that all three projects require an initial investment of $10,000 and will return $15,000 in additional earnings within five years. Second, we can see that the projects have different rates for their earning flows. Project B generates its highest earnings in the first two years, and Project C generates most of its earnings in its last two years. Project A's earnings occur uniformly over the five-year period. Finally, the three projects differ in the time needed to recover the initial investment. The time needed to recover the initial investment is called the *payback period (P)*. It can be determined by the formula $P = I/E$, in which P equals the original investment (I) divided by the annual increase in earnings (E). The payback periods for the three projects in our example are given in Table 13.2. We can see from Table 13.2 that Project B has the shortest payback period. In general, businessmen prefer the project with the shortest payback period, since they are averse to risk and like to avoid the uncertainty of long-term investments.

In essence, capital budgeting techniques provide management with a useful method for analyzing the profitability of potential investments that have dissimilar earnings characteristics. Without these techniques, it would be nearly impossible to weigh the advantages of dissimilar investments.

Inventory Mangement: The *EOQ* Model

In the quest to make money, a manager should employ his or her resources as efficiently as possible. *Inventory management* involves determining and controlling the amount of raw material an organization should keep in stock to operate effectively and efficiently. Efficient management of inventory requires balancing several conflicting goals. The first goal is to keep inventories as small as possible to minimize the amount of warehouse space and the amount of money tied up in inventories. This goal is in conflict with the need to fill all customer requirements, to maximize the number of orders placed, and to take advantage of the economies of long production runs and quantity discounts.

To solve inventory problems, the manager can use the *economic order quantity (EOQ) model*. This model can be expressed as a mathematical formula, as explained below. The solution of the *EOQ* formula tells the manager how many items he or she should purchase, and how often. In addition, it contains several assumptions the manager must understand.

The first assumption in the *EOQ* model is that consumption (or sales) occurs at a constant rate. In addition, the lead time between placing the order and receiving the shipment is assumed to be constant. Finally, both the cost of placing an order and the cost of holding one item in inventory are assumed to be known. While these assumptions may appear sweeping, fairly sizable errors do not significantly reduce the value of the *EOQ* model.

Table 13.2   The Payback Method of Capital Budgeting

	A	B	C
Investment *(I)*	$10,000	$10,000	$10,000
Annual earnings *(E)*	$ 3,000	$ 4,500 1st 2 yrs.	$ 1,000 1st 3 yrs.
		$ 2,000 last 3 yrs.	$ 6,000 last 2 yrs.
Payback period *(P = I/E)*	3.33 yrs.	2.50 yrs.	4.17 yrs.

Figure 13.1 *EOQ* **Model Under Certainty**

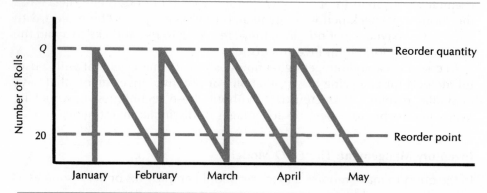

The inventory policy involves two elements—a reorder point and a reorder quantity. The *reorder point* is expressed in terms of the number of items on hand at the time the order is placed. The *EOQ* model assumes that inventory level varies as depicted in Figure 13.1. Demand rate and reorder lead time are constant and known; so the reorder point *(ROP)* is set to equal demand during lead time *(DDLT)*.

If the Winklepeck Company uses 20 rolls of plastic film a week, and it always takes one week for a new shipment to arrive after an order has been placed, the company could reorder plastic film when its inventory falls to 20 rolls. The company's minimum inventory will be zero, for the last roll is used up just before the arrival of the new shipment. Thus the maximum inventory that will occur is the reorder quantity, Q units. The average inventory is determined as follows:

$$\text{Average Inventory} = \frac{Q + 0}{2} = Q/2$$

Thus far the Winklepeck Company has determined that a reorder will be placed when the inventory level reaches demand during the lead time period, and that average inventory will be one-half of the order quantity. However, nothing has been said about the number of rolls that should be ordered.

If the cost of holding the inventory is small in comparison to the cost of placing an order (for example, paper clips), management will order the item only infrequently and in quantities that will meet operating needs for several months. But if the cost of holding inventory is very high in relation to the cost of ordering (for example, baked goods), management may order the item frequently, or even daily. Many products fall between these two extremes and can be efficiently managed by means of the *EOQ* model. The basic *EOQ* formula is:

$$EOQ = \sqrt{\frac{2\,Sr}{i}}$$

where S = annual usage

r = reorder cost
i = annual inventory cost per unit.

The economic order quantity for Winklepeck's plastic film can be determined as follows. (For ease of calculation, a 50-week year is used.)

S = Number of rolls used per year = (20 per week)
(50 weeks/year) = 1,000 per year
i = Inventory cost due to storage space, damage, and interest
on investment = $5.00 per year per roll in inventory
r = Reorder cost (cost of placing an order) = $6.25.

These numbers can then be placed in the *EOQ* formula:

$$EOQ = \sqrt{\frac{2\,Sr}{i}}$$

$$EOQ = \sqrt{\frac{2 \times 1,000 \times 6.25}{5}} = \sqrt{2500} = 50 \text{ rolls}$$

Winklepeck's inventory policy for plastic film should then be to order 50 rolls when the inventory level reaches 20.

Probabilistic

Models

As indicated previously, to use deterministic models, the manager must know the exact value of all factors in a problem. *Probabilistic models,* on the other hand, can be used for solving problems involving chance or random factors.

Managers rarely, if ever, know with complete certainty how demand will shift as the price of a product is raised. Typically, managers must make decisions under conditions of at least some uncertainty. The function of probabilistic models is to reduce uncertainty. Three important probabilistic models are the expected value model, decision trees, and simulation.

Expected Value

To understand the expected value model, it is important to comprehend the concept of *probability*, which refers to the likelihood that an event will happen. Mathematically, probability is expressed as a fraction or percentage. For example, there may be a 30 percent chance or probability that it will rain tomorrow. Some probabilities can be established empirically, by observing some phenomenon over time: flipping a fair coin several times provides data the individual can use to predict the likelihood of either heads or tails in the future. Most of the events a manager needs to predict cannot be observed so conveniently, however. In those cases, he or she can establish probability by estimating the likelihood of one event on the basis of previous similar ones. An automobile salesman might figure that a family with six children and a dog has a 0.60 probability of buying a station wagon.

When several courses of action are available and the outcome of each is uncertain, the decision maker can use probabilities to select his or her final choice. For instance, the sales level of a new room air conditioner will be related to the warmness of the summer. Sales will be $10,000,000 if the summer is hot; $7,000,000 if normal; and $4,000,000 if cooler than normal. Past experience indicates that the probability for a very warm summer is 0.3; for a normal summer 0.5; and for a cool summer, 0.2. These three probabilities add up to 1.0; that is, there are no significant possibilities besides these three. This is a necessary condition for use of the expected value technique.

The *expected value* for any event is the income it would produce times its probability. Adding the expected values of all possible events yields *expected sales*, the average level of sales that can be expected over the long run if the given probabilities hold, as shown in Table 13.3. For the air conditioner described above, expected sales for the summer are $7,300,000.

Decision Trees

Another probabilistic model for decision making is the *decision tree*. This technique is appropriate when a series of decisions must be made but the outcome of each is unknown. Hence decision trees are similar to the expected value technique in that expected values are computed in both instances.

Table 13.3 The Expected Value Model

The sales of an air conditioner will depend on how hot the summer is. Adding the expected value of each alternative yields expected sales for the summer.

Event	Outcome (Sales) × Probability =		Expected Value of Each Alternative
Hot summer	$10,000,000	0.3	$3,000,000
Normal summer	7,000,000	0.5	3,500,000
Cool summer	4,000,000	0.2	800,000
Expected sales			$7,300,000

As an illustration, let us assume that a toy manufacturer of consumer goods is in the process of deciding whether to market a new product, the Hijack Game. Management estimates that costs over the first three years will be $14 million. Revenues are projected to be either $30 million if competition does not materialize or $10 million if it does. The probability that competition will materialize is estimated to be 0.6 while the probability that it will not emerge is estimated to be 0.4.

Calculating the expected revenue associated with the production of the Hijack Game produces the following results:

$$\text{Expected Revenue} = (0.4)(30) + (0.6)(10) = 12 + 6 = \$18 \text{ million}$$

As shown in Figure 13.2, the expected profit of not marketing the Hijack Game is zero. However, the expected profit of marketing the product is $4 million ($18 million gross income minus $14 million costs). Management might reasonably decide to manufacture this product on the basis of this information.

Simulation

Because large electronic computers have become easily accessible in recent years, management can simulate complex situations in order to determine the best course of action. *Simulation* is a process of building, testing, and operating models of real-world phenomena through the use of mathematical relationships that exist among critical factors. This technique is useful for solving complex problems that cannot be readily solved by other techniques. A simulation model can be deterministic if the manager knows exactly the value of the factors he or she employs in the equations. However, simulation is essentially probabilistic, since the manager typically must estimate the future values

Figure 13.2   Decision Tree for Expected Profit on the Hijack Game

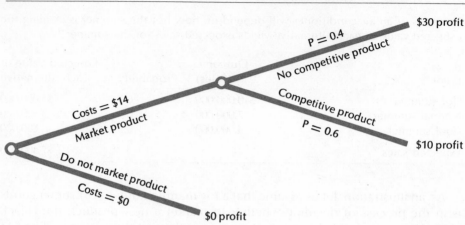

of these factors. For example, if the population of a particular region of a country has been growing at an annual rate of 10 percent for the past 20 years, the manager assumes this trend will continue for the next 50 years.

Simulation is a useful tool for evaluating problems that cannot be attacked with other problem-solving techniques. In addition, the manager can evaluate the effects of a change in his or her system or organization without actually making the change by altering the values of the factors in the model. Simulation also enables the manager to develop alternative solutions by adding factors he or she considers important.

Implications for Managers

It is often tempting for managers to assume when making decisions that the world is certain and reliable. Such an assumption is dangerous, for both conditions and outcomes are typically uncertain. Thus probabilistic models for decision making, because they reflect the state of the real world, are a valuable way for the practicing manager to analyze a problem rationally.

In addition, probabilistic models enable the manager to quantify many decisions that otherwise could not be evaluated. The manager can assess the relative impact of several courses of action based on different assumptions; and he or she can redefine probabilities and hence outcomes when conditions change. This flexibility is very valuable in actual decision-making situations. For example, a manager might select a risky rather than a conservative approach to a particular problem because its expected value is considerably higher.

However, probabilities should be used cautiously, for there is a chance that the actual outcome may be the least desirable one, regardless of its probability. For this reason, a manager should always consider the impact on the organization of the least desirable event. If it would result in bankruptcy, a more cautious approach than the one suggested by quantitative techniques is probably advisable.

Clearly, managerial judgment is critical when probabilitstic models are employed. While the use of mathematical estimates to represent real events may create the impression that there is one best solution which the manager can determine, it is usually not that simple. In the final analysis, probability techniques are not an effective substitute for good judgment, but, rather, an aid to decision making.

Nonquantitative

Decision Making

This chapter has emphasized the importance of statistical and mathematical models in the decision-making process. Still, many of the decisions managers make are nonquantitative and ill-structured. Frequently the manager cannot quantify the problem; sometimes he or she rejects the quantitative solution and relies on intuition, experience, and judgment in making a decision; and sometimes the manager uses other approaches he or she considers superior to statistical and mathematical models. In this section, there is a short description of some of the many nonquantitative techniques managers employ to solve problems.

Nonprogrammed Decisions

A *nonprogrammed decision* is a creative response to a new problem (see chapter 12). The manager cannot apply a standard decision rule, program, or routine that he or she has previously used to solve similar problems. Many managerial decisions fall into this category.

Peer Soelberg (1967) analyzed nonprogrammed decision making among graduating graduate students at the Massachusetts Institute of Technology

who were searching for full-time jobs. He interviewed one group of graduating students over a period of time in 1964, after which he developed definite
hyphotheses he wished to test. In 1965 he tested these hypotheses by interviewing each of 32 graduating students biweekly for the eight weeks when
they were seeking work.

Soelberg found the students generally stopped searching for new alternatives or jobs long before they were willing to admit having made this decision.
Usually a student had two or more acceptable job offers before he or she
ended the search. If the student had obtained a firm job offer from only one
organization during the period when he or she wanted to end the job search,
he or she tried hard to secure, and usually did obtain, at least one other
acceptable offer to have something to compare against the one alternative.

The student also tended to make a decision early in the job search by
selecting a favorite alternative, although he or she did not consciously recognize this fact. Even if a student had five or six firm offers, he or she tended to
compare only two alternatives before selecting an implicit favorite. If the two
were essentially noncomparable, the student typically compared them in
terms of only one or two criteria, which simplified the decision process.

The students generally did not experience any uneasy feelings or dissonance afterwards about their final decisions unless they had been unable to
identify an implicit favorite or had only one firm job offer at the time they
announced a decision. In these two instances, Soelberg's data suggest a student might subsequently become unhappy with the new job and initiate new
search procedures.

Soelberg's research generally confirms and extends Herbert Simon's theory
of nonprogrammed decision making (see chapter 12). The manager typically
bounds reality by examining only a few acceptable alternatives and *satisfices*
by selecting one of these minimally acceptable alternatives. Soelberg's research also suggests that a manager should systematically evaluate his or her
alternatives as early as possible in the decision process, before unconsciously
selecting an implicit favorite. Once the manager has selected this favorite, he
or she tends to eliminate all the other acceptable alternatives. And once the
manager has announced a decision, he or she will probably not change it or
search for new alternatives.

The Managerial Team

Managers must coordinate their efforts and decisions if the organization is to
be successful. Sometimes it takes years before a group of managers whose
work overlaps can develop an effective working relationship. Alfred Sloan

spent five years developing the top management team that eventually made General Motors the largest corporation in the world (Sloan 1963). At every level in the organization, it is important that managers whose work overlaps form a cohesive unit in which they know one another's problems, weaknesses, and strengths. They also must trust each other, especially when one manager in the group takes on responsibility that influences the performance of all of them.

Recently, Arch Patton (1973) undertook an investigation of the managerial problems in the federal government. One major weakness he found in many government agencies is the lack of an experienced managerial team whose members trust one another. This weakness occurs because every newly elected president has the authority to make key political appointments, such as the assistant secretary of labor, who theoretically supervise the nonpolitical heads of the agencies. However, these appointees usually stay in their positions for such a short time that the nonpolitical heads of the agencies do not especially trust them and frequently cannot work effectively with them. A cynical but experienced Washington bureaucrat knows that one presidential program will be replaced by another in a few months or years, so he or she tends to support it half-heartedly, making decisions that are sometimes in direct conflict with the wishes of the political appointee heading the program. A management team whose members have such an attitude is almost bound to be ineffective.

Unscheduled Visits

One way managers can gather nonquantitative information on which to base decisions is by making unscheduled visits to various parts of the organization. The president of one successful manufacturing company requires that his six top subordinates keep all of their key reports on top of their desks or in a visible place. He periodically visits their offices and scans all of those reports, which keeps him constantly up-to-date on activities in his organization.

In the same company, the president uses unscheduled visits to make decisions about his employees. On one such visit, the president became involved in a discussion with an employee who did not recognize him. The president asked the employee to describe his job. The employee candidly replied that he was being paid to operate a machine, but he did not understand how the operation of his machine fit into the overall manufacture of the company's final product. Because of this unscheduled visit, the president instituted a training program for his employees focusing on the relationship between each employee's work and the final product the company sold.

Summary

Managers can use quantitative decision-making techniques if the problem can be expressed in numbers. There are two general types of quantitative models—deterministic and probabilistic. A deterministic model is appropriate when all factors are exact and the law of chance plays no role in the formulation or solution of the problem. The probabilistic model includes chance or random factors.

Four of the major deterministic models are the break-even model, linear programming, capital budgeting, and inventory management. In break-even analysis, the break-even point is the level at which total revenue equals total costs. The objective of break-even analysis is to determine the optimum break-even point by taking into consideration the costs associated with each level of demand and the way demand changes as price changes. Linear programming is an extension of break-even analysis that is particularly appropriate when an organization manufactures two or more products and uses two or more resources. It guides the organization in allocating scarce resources to the products or projects so as to maximize some objective function such as profits or minimize some objective function such as costs. Capital budgeting is a way to evaluate the relative profitability of investing a lump sum in various projects. Inventory management also helps the manager to use his or her resources as efficiently as possible. Using the *EOQ* formula, a manager can determine how much raw material to keep in stock to minimize space and investment in stock, and how often and how much to reorder.

Three of the most important probabilistic models are expected value, decision trees, and simulation. The expected value of an event is its outcome (such as sales) times its probability of occurrence. Managers can determine expected sales with this model by adding together the expected values for various events or outcomes. Managers use decision trees when they must make a *series* of decisions but the outcome of each is uncertain. Simulation is a process of building, testing, and operating models of real-world phenomena.

In addition there are many nonquantitative techniques that managers use to make decisions. When making nonprogrammed decisions in response to ill-structured problems, the manager tends to accept unconsciously an implicit favorite early in his or her period of search, and to compare only two alternatives before selecting the implicit favorite. Managers whose work overlaps frequently form a managerial team that makes decisions influencing all members of the group. Managers also use unscheduled visits as a decision-making technique.

Discussion Questions

1. In what sense is a deterministic model probabilistic?

2. Discuss some situations in which capital budgeting analysis would be a useful analytical technique.

3. What are some of the advantages of simulation in comparison to other analytical techniques discussed in this chapter?

4. Overall, do managers use quantitative decision-making techniques more frequently than nonquantitative decision-making techniques? Why or why not?

5. Why is linear programming an extension of break-even analysis?

6. In Chapter 12, a distinction was made between programmed and nonprogrammed decision making. What kind of decision making is represented by the quantitative techniques described in this chapter?

7. The quantitative techniques discussed in this chapter relate directly to planning and control. Which relate most directly to planning, and which to control (break-even analysis, linear programming, capital budgeting, inventory management, expected value, decision trees, and simulation)?

Problems

1. An item costs $25, is used at the rate of 1,600 units per year, and has an inventory carrying cost of $10 per year per item. Reordering costs are estimated at $5 per order. Compute the economic order quantity for this item.

2. An item that costs $10 has an annual usage rate of 300 units and an annual carrying cost of $2 per unit. The cost of a reorder is $3. Compute the economic order quantity for this item.

3. A manufacturer of electronic calculators has annual fixed costs of $5,000,000 per year. His plant can produce 300,000 major appliances annually. If his variable cost per appliance is $150, how much must he charge to achieve his profit objective of $2,400,000, if he can sell only 80 percent of his production capacity? What would his profits be if sales were at 60 percent of capacity? At 100 percent of capacity?

4. For problem 3, market research indicates the manufacturer can sell 240,000 major appliances annually at a price of $180 or 300,000 annually at a price of $170. What price should the manufacturer set to maximize profits?

5. Bill McGowan is evaluating a new piece of equipment for his production department. The management of the engineering department estimates the cost to install and debug the equipment is $20,000. From past experience, Bill knows there is a 0.5 probability the actual cost will be 50 percent higher than the estimate, a 0.4 probability the cost will equal the estimate, and a 0.1 probability the cost will be 20 percent lower than the estimate. Find the expected cost of installing and debugging the new equipment.

6. A firm's fixed costs are $100,000 per year and variable costs are $3.00 per unit. It is estimated that the firm can sell 30,000 units per year at a price of $8.00 per unit or 40,000 units per year at a price of $6.50 per unit.

   a. What is the firm's break-even volume at a price of $8.00 per unit?
   b. Which price will maximize revenues?
   c. Which price will maximize profits?

7. The profitabilities and probabilities for a project are given below. What is the expected profit of this project?

Probability	Profit
0.25	$8,000
0.45	6,000
0.30	2,000

8. Two alternative strategies are being considered by the management of Tot-Fun Toys, Inc., for the development of a new product. Conditional profits, probabilities, states of nature, and expected profits for the two alternatives are given below. Management feels that a loss in excess of $5 million would seriously weaken the firm. Which strategy should Tot-Fun choose?

State of Nature	Probability	Conditional Profits	
		Strategy A	Strategy B
Good sales	0.3	$15,000,000	$10,000,000
Fair sales	0.4	12,000,000	6,000,000
Poor sales	0.3	−8,000,000	−3,000,000

9. Joan Rexford is considering the replacement of her eight-year-old car. She has estimated the average annual cost for the next five years of: (1) keeping the old car, (2) buying a used car, and (3) buying a new car.

If she keeps the old car, there is a 0.5 probability it will last for five years with an average annual repair bill of $300. There is also a 0.5 chance the car will deteriorate so much that she will be forced to buy a new car, which will cost $2,000 per year in combination with repairs on her old car. There is a 0.7 chance the cost of the used car will be $700 per year and a 0.3 chance it will deteriorate and have to be replaced at an average annual cost of $3,000 per year. Average annual costs for a new car will be $1,200 per year if it causes little trouble (0.5 probability) and $1,800 per year (0.5 probability) if it turns out to be a lemon. Which automobile strategy will result in the lowest expected annual cost?

Suggested Readings

Allison, Graham. *Essence of Decision.* Boston: Little, Brown, 1971, 338 pages, paperback.
   Allison applies three different organizational models or perspectives to the decisions that led to the Bay of Pigs fiasco. The emphasis is on nonquantitative decision making.

Miller, David, and Starr, Martin. *The Structure of Human Decisions.* Englewood Cliffs, N.J.: Prentice-Hall, 1967, 177 pages, paperback.
   This book contains a readable introduction to quantitative decision making.

EXPERIENTIAL EXERCISE

Group Decision Making

Goals

1. To demonstrate the forms of conflict-resolving behavior.
2. To compare and contrast the effects of individual and group decision making.
3. To demonstrate the effect of consensus methods on group problem solving.

Group Conditions

Any number of people divided into small groups of four or five.

Time required: Fifteen minutes for individual responses, thirty minutes for group consensus.

Materials needed: Worksheet for each individual, worksheet for each group, pencils, flip chart (newsprint or blackboard), marker pens or chalk.

Physical setting: Flexible seating in one large room so that small groups may work together.

Process

A. Each individual has fifteen minutes to read the story and answer the eleven questions about the story. Each person may refer to the story as often as needed but may not confer with anyone else. Each person should circle "T" if the answer is clearly true; "F" if the answer is clearly false; or, "?" if he cannot tell from the story whether the answer is true or false.
B. After fifteen minutes each small group makes the same decisions using group consensus. No one should change his or her answers on the individual worksheet.

The ground rules for group decisions are:

1. Group decisions should be made by consensus. It is illegal to vote, trade, average, flip a coin, etc.
2. No individual group member should give in only to reach agreement.
3. No individual should argue for his own decision. Instead, he should approach the task using logic and reason.
4. Every group member should be aware that disagreements may be resolved by facts. Conflict can lead to understanding and creativity if it does not make group members feel threatened or defensive.

C. After thirty minutes of group work, the exercise leader should announce the correct answers. Scoring is based on the number of correct answers out of a possible total of eleven. Each individual is to score his own individual worksheet, and someone should score the group-decision worksheet. The exercise leader should then call for:

1. The group-decision score in each group
2. The average individual score in each group
3. The highest individual score in each group

D. Responses should be posted on the tally sheet. Note should be taken of those groups in which the group score was (1) higher than the average individual score and (2) higher than the best individual score. Groups should discuss the way in which individual members resolved disagreements and the effect of the ground rules on such behavior. They may consider the obstacles experienced in arriving at consensus agreements and the possible reasons for the difference between individual and group decisions.

Worksheet

A businessman had just turned off the lights in the store when a man appeared and demanded money. The owner opened a cash register. The contents of the cash register were scooped up, and the man sped away. A member of the police force was notified promptly.

Statements about the Story

1. A man appeared after the owner had turned off his store lights.   T F ?
2. The robber was a *man*.   T F ?

3. A man did not demand money.   T   F   ?
4. The man who opened the cash register was the owner.   T   F   ?
5. The store owner scooped up the contents of the cash register and ran away.   T   F   ?
6. Someone opened a cash register.   T   F   ?
7. After the man who demanded the money scooped up the contents of the cash register, he ran away.   T   F   ?
8. While the cash register contained money, the story does *not* state *how much*.   T   F   ?
9. The robber demanded money of the owner.   T   F   ?
10. The story concerns a series of events in which only three persons are referred to: the owner of the store, a man who demanded money, and a member of the police force.   T   F   ?
11. The following events in the story are true: someone demanded money, a cash register was opened, its contents were scooped up, and a man dashed out of the store.   T   F   ?

Tally Sheet

Group Number	Group Score	Avg. Individual Score	Best Individual Score	Group Score Better Than Avg. Indiv.?	Group Score Better Than Best Indiv.?

■ Our management model posits four dimensions within which managerial activities take place. How these four dimensions fit together in actual organizations, the implications they have for the individual manager and his or her career, and their importance for the current and future practices and orientations of management are the topics of part VI. In chapter 14, there is a description of the activities of the entrepreneur who founds his or her own business and a comparison of the entrepreneur and the typical bureaucratic manager. Chapter 15 evaluates the history of the Ford Motor Company in terms of our basic model. Henry Ford, who founded the company and directed its activities for 40 years, is of interest both as an entrepreneur and as a manager. Chapter 16 focuses on specific activities and techniques that can make a manager's career successful. Finally, chapter 17 describes historical events and factors that managers should consider in assessing both the current and the future state of managerial activities.

MANAGERIAL CAREERS AND ORIENTATIONS

VI

Entrepreneurship

14

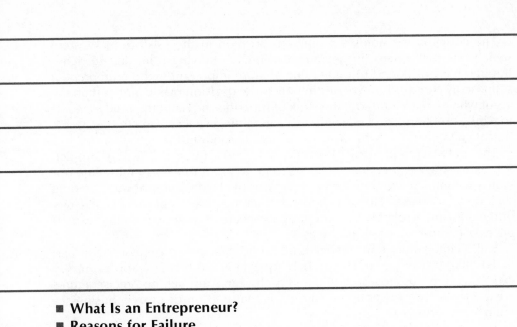

- **What Is an Entrepreneur?**
- **Reasons for Failure**
- **Contrasting Organizations**

Performance Objectives

1. To understand entrepreneurship and the various types of entrepreneurs.

2. To know the personal traits of the typical entrepreneur.

3. To comprehend the similarities and differences between corporate executives and entrepreneurs.

4. To know the most common reasons for failure among entrepreneurs.

5. To be aware of the differences among craft, entrepreneurial, and administrative organizations.

The entrepreneur holds a prominent position in the folklore of Western society. He is the hero of the American dream, moving from rags to riches through hard work and resourcefulness. More importantly, the entrepreneur supposedly controls his own destiny. He is the decision maker, rather than the agent who merely carries out the work of superiors; he is not required to report to work at set times; and he leads an exciting life, especially in contrast to the bureaucratic manager who works in a large corporation.

This is the entrepreneur as imagined by most people. The lure of such success is so great that many workers, such as automotive assembly-line operatives, minimize the boredom of their jobs by daydreaming about founding their own businesses. However, most of them never attempt to make a reality of their dreams, probably because they are aware of their own limited experience, skills, and financial resources.

Still, a large number of Americans do found their own businesses—approximately 400,000 every year. The probability of failure is high, for approximately 400,000 enterprises are also liquidated each year. Although no precise figures are available, the conventional wisdom is that two-thirds of new businesses fail by their fifth year.

This chapter begins with a profile of the entrepreneur, followed by a discussion of reasons why entrepreneurs often fail. The chapter concludes by comparing entrepreneurial enterprises to other kinds of organizations.

What Is an Entrepreneur?

Perhaps the most famous definition of *entrepreneurship* was put forth by the Austrian economist Joseph Schumpeter (1934), who argued that economic activity in a society can be viewed as a closed circle until the entrepreneur comes on the scene with a new idea or product that allows this circle to expand significantly. To Schumpeter, the entrepreneur is the critical figure in economic activity, for he combines known given resources in a way that radically alters the consumption and production patterns of society. Henry Ford is an outstanding example of the Schumpeterian entrepreneur, for he built the first all-purpose car that could be purchased by the average citizen (see chapter 15). Ford's Model T generated changes throughout society: the building of highways and gas stations, increased use of steel and other materials, and leisure activities one could pursue hundreds of miles from home.

However, only a small number of entrepreneurs influence an entire society. A broader definition of an entrepreneur would include any individual who builds a small business with at least eight employees (Hornaday and Aboud 1971). In other words, the entrepreneur is someone who creates an organization characterized by an elementary form of the bureaucratic hierarchy. Thus the owner of a "Mom and Pop" food store that has no employees would not be classified as an entrepreneur.

Usually a major distinction is drawn between a technical and a general entrepreneur. A *technical entrepreneur* has had extended technical or formal academic training, for example, an engineer or scientist. A *general entrepreneur* is one whose academic preparation is limited; he or she may not even be a high school graduate.

An entrepreneur may or may not be an inventor. Henry Ford never invented anything but, rather, combined the inventions of others to produce the Model T. Thomas Edison was an entrepreneur whose many patents formed the basis of his business activities.

Personal Traits

There are, of course, many reasons why an individual decides to become an entrepreneur. While some entrepreneurs seem to be born to running their own business from the time they start a lemonade stand in grade school, many others learn it as the protégés of older and experienced executives. In recent years, a small number of important psychological studies of entrepreneurship have been completed. Among these studies, a series by David McClelland has become prominent.

Need for Achievement. McClelland's studies, which have extended over a 25-year period, indicate that entrepreneurs are distinctive in that they have a high need to achieve and accomplish (see p. 200). Because of their need to achieve, they prefer to work with experts rather than friends when faced with a problem. Also, they tend to be long-range thinkers and planners, focusing on an overall vision of the enterprise rather than more immediate practical problems.

McClelland found that entrepreneurs prefer to undertake tasks that are accompanied by some risks. According to his findings, the entrepreneur is neither a low nor high risk taker, but, rather, an intermediate risk taker. For example, individuals who score high on a test measuring their need for achievement usually play a ring-toss game from an intermediate distance, neither so close to the ring that they never miss nor so far away that they never hit.

In a related study of 60 male entrepreneurs, John Hornaday and John Aboud (1971) generally confirmed the results put forth by McClelland. Compared to men in general, these entrepreneurs scored significantly higher on scales measuring the need to achieve, independence, and effectiveness of their leadership. They were significantly lower than men in general on scales that measured the need for supportive relationships with others. Hence the entrepreneur seems to be a self-confident loner who can withstand the criticisms of his associates.

An individual's achievement motivation appears to be set at an early age in life. Marian Winterbottom's analysis (1958) indicates that children who are urged to be successful outside their home when they are between six and eight demonstrate higher achievement motivation than those who are encouraged to be successful only in their later years. Bernard Rosen and Roy D'Andrade (1959) have also shown that parental expectations are important. In general, the parents of high-achieving children establish goals for them that are higher than those set by parents of low-achieving children. These parents also involve themselves in their children's problems and concerns.

One's Own Master. While achievement orientation is of obvious significance, related research suggests that entrepreneurs have a firm belief in their skills and abilities (Shapero, 1975). They feel their actions can change events. An entrepreneur is the master of his or her own life and refuses to believe that outside forces can decisively influence his or her success. A study of 375 college students indicated that those who planned to found their own enterprises strongly believed they were masters of their own destinies (Shapero, 1975). This feeling was not evident among other students.

Few Emotional Attachments. Another important psychological study of entrepreneurship was conducted by Orvis Collins and David Moore (1964). In this study the authors suggest that entrepreneurs frequently have difficulty forming close emotional attachments—a finding similar to that of Hornaday and Aboud. However, Collins and Moore's research indicates this may result from the poor psychological relationships they developed with their parents and, in particular, with their fathers. Because of the entrepreneur's difficulty in forming close relationships, he or she becomes deeply involved in work and transfers all hopes and feelings from human beings to his or her own business. Thus the entrepreneur treats the business almost as a living, breathing creature, and is emotionally involved with it. The long hours of work are not burdensome but exciting and enjoyable.

Collins and Moore suggest the entrepreneur cannot maintain a close emotional attachment over an extended period, even with a business firm. Hence the entrepreneur unconsciously wants the business to fail, after which he or she can begin to structure another enterprise. Although this idea seems preposterous, a definite pattern of behavior among some entrepreneurs is to found a business that is highly successful, drive it into bankruptcy, and begin again (Collins and Moore 1964). Some entrepreneurs have achieved five or more gigantic successes during their lifetimes, each followed by the failure that Collins and Moore's interpretation would predict.

Given the fact that the entrepreneur is only minimally concerned about relationships with others, he or she tends to treat subordinates in an autocratic fashion. The entrepreneur's word is law, and he will typically brook no opposition (Filley, House, and Kerr 1976).

Further, many entrepreneurs are not loyal or trustworthy. In the histories of various entrepreneurs, it is common to come across stories of industrious and loyal subordinates who, after years of hard work for an entrepreneur, were fired for unjustified reasons. Such behavior fits well with the research findings that entrepreneurs are not critically influenced by the reactions and criticisms of their peers and their relationships with other human beings.

Lack of Attention to Details. Since entrepreneurs are moved by a need for personal achievement, they often have little interest in the organizational structure of the firm (Filley, House, and Kerr 1976). Organizing, staffing, motivating—the entrepreneur treats these and other key managerial activities with disdain.

William Durant, the founder of General Motors, aptly illustrates this pattern of behavior. He essentially created General Motors by buying other companies. However, he was so unconcerned about the daily organizational activities that he did not know how many companies General Motors owned in 1920. When the company's financial backers forced Durant out in 1920, it took the accountants several months to identify all of the holdings of General Motors. Durant once remarked, supposedly in jest, that he loved to set policies—every time his door opened and closed, he had made and broken another policy. Durant even developed a novel motivational strategy when Walter Chrysler, his key production subordinate, constantly complained to him about his lack of attention to details—Durant merely raised Chrysler's salary each time he complained until Chrysler was making $500,000 a year, at which time he quit in disgust and formed his own company.

In sum, entrepreneurs are achievement oriented and believe they are masters of their own destiny. They are not very dependent upon others for emotional support and are usually highly dictatorial and unconcerned about the daily organizational problems that plague all or most firms. A profile of the entrepreneur is shown in Figure 14.1.

Figure 14.1 The Relationship between the Personal Traits and Actions of the Entrepreneur

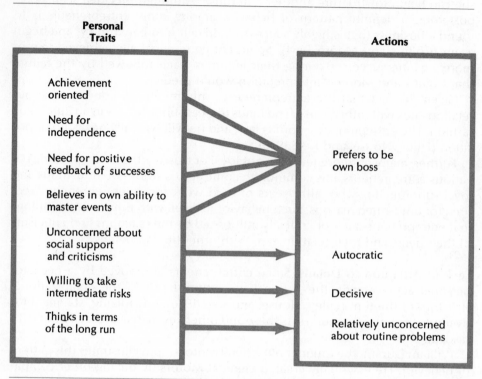

Personal Traits

Actions

Achievement oriented

Need for independence

Need for positive feedback of successes

Believes in own ability to master events

Prefers to be own boss

Unconcerned about social support and criticisms

Autocratic

Willing to take intermediate risks

Decisive

Thinks in terms of the long run

Relatively unconcerned about routine problems

The Manager versus the Entrepreneur

Obviously some of the qualities necessary for a successful entrepreneur are also required if an individual wants to become a successful manager. Why, then, do some people choose to start their own businesses while others prefer to work within existing firms?

Need for Independence. One hypothesis is that the type of individual who becomes a manager within a modern corporation is radically different from the entrepreneur in that he or she has much less need for independence. David Riesman (1950) holds that this attitude (among others) is related to the social patterns of the society at large. Traditionally, social institutions such as the school, the family, and the church teach children the values of the society so they recognize right and wrong in terms of preestablished standards. Riesman compares these standards to the gyroscope that pilots a submarine—even though the crew in the submarine cannot see water or land, they ascertain the proper direction by means of the gyroscope. Similarly, the primary institutions in a society give the individual a set of internal standards that guide him or her throughout life. But, as society has become more complex, especially in cities, institutions no longer can maintain social control. The individual's value system becomes flexible, dependent upon the peer group in which he or she operates.

Some writers, such as William H. Whyte, Jr. (1956), have used Riesman's theory to argue that entrepreneurship has declined in the United States since the 1800s. To found his or her own business, an individual must be able to take risks and be relatively unconcerned about the feelings and reactions of peers. In a small but traditional society such as the agriculturally based society of nineteenth century America, the individual learns to be independent and self-reliant, since he must eventually fend for himself. Today's giant corporations, however, typically protect their managers through handsome salaries and fringe benefits. Even the manager's old age is free of worry because of the pension benefits he or she receives. In such a setting, Whyte believes the managers are low risk takers who are very sensitive to the reactions of their peers.

Negative Experiences. More recent research suggests that successful corporation executives are willing to take risks; they seek a sense of achievement; and they will pursue a course of action they believe is correct, even if their peers are critical of them (Porter and Lawler 1968; Shapero 1975). These findings imply that the successful corporation executive is similar to the entrepreneur in terms of achievement motivation, reactions to criticisms of peers, and even risk-taking behavior. This makes it easy to understand why some corporation executives eventually found their own businesses, for they are characterized by a psychological profile similar to the entrepreneur's. But it leaves the basic question unanswered—when the psychological factors are equal, why does one individual become a corporation executive while another becomes an entrepreneur?

One major reason a corporate executive becomes an entrepreneur is that negative experiences such as being fired propel him into it. Albert Shapero (1975) interviewed 109 entrepreneurs in Austin, Texas, 65 percent of whom indicated that their sole or primary influence was negative.

Although entrepreneurs and corporation executives are similar psychologically, they do differ on one dimension—entrepreneurs believe more strongly than do corporation executives that they are masters of their own destinies, and they do not like to be controlled by forces outside of themselves (Shapero 1975). Many entrepreneurs have been fired from their jobs, after which they insist that this will never happen again. So they form their own enterprises. Some corporation executives have undergone the same experience but they are willing to put up with this lack of control. Hence they seek a similar job within another large corporation.

The Environment. Although psychological factors are important in the explanation of entrepreneurship, the external environment in which the individual operates is also relevant. This is particularly true for the technical entrepreneur. A large-scale study of technical entrepreneurship was completed by Arnold Cooper (1970), who sought to discover why some engineers and scientists become entrepreneurs while others do not. His research took place in an area around Palo Alto, California, which is known for its large concentration of entrepreneurial firms.

Cooper found that firms with less than 500 employees had a spin-off rate eight times as high as firms with more than 500 employees. Thus, according to Cooper, an engineer or scientist in a small firm was attracted to entrepreneurial activity because he or she could see how it was carried out successfully. In the larger organizations, such insights were difficult to obtain. Cooper also discovered that an individual who was thinking about founding his or her own firm learned a great deal through interactions with others in the organization who did eventually strike out on their own. Exposure to their experiences sensitized the potential entrepreneur to many of the problems he or she would encounter.

In a related paper, Albert Shapero (1975) reports that his graduate students, after interviewing entrepreneurs, were attracted to this way of life at least in part because they began to realize that entrepreneurs are not supermen. Some of the students were amazed to find out that these entrepreneurs are frequently no more, and, in some cases, much less, intelligent than they are.

The home environment also can be a decisive influence. Although only 7 percent of the nonagricultural work force in the United States claims to be self-employed, 58 percent of American entrepreneurs studied originate in families in which one or both parents are self-employed (Shapero 1975). These entrepreneurs see the independence their parents possess in their careers, and they model their behavior accordingly. Similarly, particular ethnic groups such as the Chinese and the Jews produce a disproportionate number of entrepreneurs, at least in part because the children see visible and successful examples early in life.

Reasons
for Failure

Stories about entrepreneurship tend to focus on successes rather than failures. However, the failure rate is high, as indicated at the beginning of this chapter. According to Maury Delman (1971), there are nine major reasons why entrepreneurial businesses fail. Although his list is subject to question, it does describe most of the problems that entrepreneurs generally face.

The most important reason Delman cites for an entrepreneur's failure is simply a lack of balanced managerial experience. Many entrepreneurs do not fully understand the intricacies of running a business. For instance, an entrepreneurial engineer may be skilled enough to create a valuable product, but the business can easily fail if he or she knows nothing about accounting, finance, marketing, personnel, and so forth. Moreover, some entrepreneurs enter lines of business with which they are not familiar. Then, when problems specific to the particular industry arise, they are not able to solve them.

Some entrepreneurs also underestimate the capital they need to start a new business. They frequently believe they possess enough capital to see them through the first difficult years, but then discover it is gone within the first few months. When the business fails, entrepreneurs are frequently embarrassed, since almost all of them borrow money from friends and relatives to start the enterprise. Venture capital firms or organizations that exist solely to invest in other enterprises average only 2.6 investments per year, and less than 15 percent goes to new ventures. These firms usually wait until a company proves itself before they provide expansion money (Shapero 1975).

Some entrepreneurs attempt to save money by picking an inexpensive location, only to find that the clientele they are seeking are not attracted to the organization because its location is unappealing or inconvenient. When location is critical, the entrepreneur is wise to spend enough money for a suitable one.

Another reason many entrepreneurs fail once they have started a firm is that they employ standard control procedures, such as inventory control systems and accounting systems, very ineffectively. Frequently the entrepreneur will not even know the number of items in stock. Such poor practices keep the entrepreneur from being able to plan effectively for the future, and he or she can eventually face financial losses that may lead to bankruptcy.

Some entrepreneurs put too much of their capital into fixed assets, such as furniture and office machines. This limits the working capital they have available. Hence, when opportunities arise, the entrepreneur is unable to take advantage of them. For example, a client may wish to double his regular orders, but the entrepreneur has too little free cash to fulfill the request. A similar—and major—source of failure is poor credit-granting practices. If customers do not pay their bills, the entrepreneur is forced to operate with reduced working capital. Eventually this problem can become so great that the entrepreneur may have to liquidate the firm.

When the entrepreneur creates his own organization, he frequently exists on the salary he allocates to himself. At least initially, the entrepreneur should pay himself only a small salary, for it is essential to put money into the company if it is to expand.

The entrepreneur also must be aware of the dedication to hard work that an owner-run business requires, especially in its formative years. He often will need to work long and irregular hours; he sometimes has to sacrifice family life, at least partially; and he must be willing to endure these difficulties until the business becomes sound. If the prospective entrepreneur is unwilling to make these sacrifices, he should not start a business.

Finally, even when the entrepreneur is successful, he or she may create major problems through overexpansion. When the business expands, the quality of service may decline, at least temporarily, and some of the entrepreneur's clients are likely to react negatively. Also, he may be unable to generate enough new business to pay off the price of the expansion.

Contrasting

Organizations

In a theoretical article, Warren Bennis (1966) has compared an organization to an individual in terms of psychological health. Psychiatrically, an individual is healthy if he does not distort reality, is not so rigid and fixed in his opinions that he eventually becomes paranoid, and is open and adaptable to change. Similarly, a healthy organization is one that matures to the point where it is sensitive to environmental demands and constraints, flexible and adaptive when conditions demand, and perceptive to what is actually occurring in the business world.

As we have seen, the entrepreneur tends to be a dominating individual who seeks a sense of achievement and independence, and is not very concerned about the feelings and reactions of peers. His or her influence on an organization, consequently, is not always beneficial to its health. Alan Filley, Robert House, and Steven Kerr (1976) contrasted the entrepreneurial organization to two other types of organizations, craft and administrative. The contrast among these three types of organizations provides interesting insights into the ways an entrepreneur influences organizational activities. Dimensions along which these three types of organization can be compared and contrasted include the objectives of the organization, its policy-setting procedures, leadership, work-group bonds, functional development, structure, line-staff distinction, degree of innovation, and risk-taking behavior.

The Craft Organization

A craft organization is typically small. The objectives of its owner are comfort and survival. That is, he or she seeks a comfortable pattern of living; the owner wants a business he will enjoy as well as one that will pay the bills. In this setting, he sets policies that gradually become traditions and are communicated orally and informally. Generally, the owner's leadership style is paternalistic, and he is the only leader of importance. Because the organization is static, everyone in it has a fixed role to play that is relatively permanent.

In this type of organization, the owner relies primarily on manufacturing a single product or selling one or a few items. The structure of the organization is relatively simple. There is no complex hierarchy but, rather, levels of power, the most important one being the owner's. As might be expected, all employees are involved in line activities. If specialized staff executives such as accountants are required, they are hired only on a part-time basis and for the sole purpose of housekeeping. Obviously, there is no innovation or creativity once a reasonable level of comfort has been attained. Hence the owner takes few, if any, risks that might jeopardize his comfortable way of life.

The Entrepreneurial Organization

In the entrepreneurial organization, as we have seen, the entrepreneur defines the organization's objectives in relation to his own success and achievement. He is not very concerned about objectives that would tend to help key executives structure their jobs; they must fend for themselves and react to his whims. The policies that parallel these objectives are likewise highly personal and subject to change. If the entrepreneur decides a specific policy will not help him achieve his personal objectives, he will quickly change it. If key executives disagree with his position, he tells them thay are out of order. If disagreements persist, the entrepreneur may even fire them or make life so uncomfortable they are forced to leave.

Obviously, this type of organizational structure is highly fluid, for roles are very loosely defined. Subordinates have difficulty understanding the type of behavior expected of them. Hence the bonds among members of a work group are weak or nonexistent. Whereas ordinarily the work-group members tend to follow preestablished performance standards, here the subordinates attempt to develop standards by means of constant interactions with the entrepreneur, during which they seek to find out what is important to him. The entrepreneur is, so to speak, a "field of force" around which key executives operate. Because the entrepreneur does not develop a formal organizational structure, he does not see a need for specialized staff offices. To the entrepreneur, there is little distinction between line and staff, since he *is* the organization. Consequently, he relies on all-purpose key executives whom he designates as his "assistants."

Usually the entrepreneur develops one innovation he or she hopes will prove successful. Because of the entrepreneur's energetic nature, he tends to emphasize different functional areas such as marketing or production as the innovation begins to penetrate the markets. Since he has not created a formal organizational structure in which the key subordinates can handle many activities in different functional areas, it is nearly impossible for him to devote attention to more than one functional area at a time.

Naturally this kind of organization is characterized by substantial innovation. The essence of entrepreneurship is innovation, and the entrepreneur typically emphasizes this activity, even when it affects the organization's success adversely. Because the entrepreneur is a risk taker, he or she is not bothered by operating in an uncertain environment in which the possibility of failure is great. The entrepreneur seems to be able to handle stress adequately, but frequently fails precisely because of the large number of risks he or she must assume.

The Administrative Organization

In the administrative organization, which is usually quite large, professional executives (who do not usually own the enterprise) operate in a rational, bureaucratic fashion. A small number of key executives define the organization's objectives, usually in terms of a long-run perspective. If the markets for the firm's goods and services radically alter, these executives will redefine the objectives, for practical considerations rather than personal ambitions serve as the basis of planning, design, and decision making. The organization's policies place less importance on the goals of individuals and subdivisions than on the maximum overall good of the organization. Usually these policies are written and are long term.

The leadership of the administrative organization is highly professional and impersonal. If an individual is effective, he or she is usually rewarded. The ineffective individual suffers in terms of promotions and salary increases. Problems such as nepotism and favoritism are accordingly eliminated or minimized. Individual members are oriented to the firm's objectives. The same values apply throughout the organization—the rules of behavior that eventu-

---

A Profile of an Entrepreneur

Whatever the critics say about *Mahogany*—and they have few compliments—the film has just broken Broadway theatre records held by *Jaws* and *The Godfather*. The receipts have made Berry Gordy, Jr., 45, the most powerful new director in the business. That power derives from his triple role as founder, chairman and 95% owner of Motown Industries. The company was founded in 1960, shortly after Gordy quit the Ford assembly line in Detroit. The ex-professional featherweight boxer started with $800 borrowed from his father, a Georgia-born plasterer. Motown grossed $48 million last year on the combined earnings of its record label, one of the country's largest music-publishing companies, an artists' management concern and a TV and production arm, whose only previous theatrical release was the immensely profitable *Lady Sings the Blues,* also starring Gordy's close friend and protegeé Diana Ross.

Director Gordy arranged his debut by talking the producer of *Mahogany*—one Berry Gordy—into firing Tony Richardson (*Tom Jones*) ten days after shooting began. Richardson, complained Producer-Critic-Sociologist Gordy, was "losing all the subtleties" of ghetto life and humor. The not-so-subtleties were supplied—at inflationary prices. Did Ross, doubling as her own clothes designer, require more yard goods and seamstresses to realize her visions? She got them. Did the film maker require an outdoor theater for a few atmospheric shots? He hired the 17th century theatre at Spoleto for a week and transported the whole cast and crew thither in pursuit of the desired images. Was the script not quite right? Gordy took pen in hand and wrote the line that he says encapsulates *Mahogany's* philosophical essence: "Success is nothing without someone you love to share it with." Such creativity sent *Mahogany* $1.25 million over its original $2.5 million budget . . . .

Gordy is disdainful of all criticism, personal and professional. The harsh reviews? They are merely "attacks on an uppity black." As for frequent rumors that Motown is Mob financed, Gordy counters: "We have a choice of suing people for such stories or ignoring them." Employee resentment over his dictatorial managerial style is not so easily dismissed. "If I ever wrote a book," says one Motown staffer, "I'd call it *God Is On Extension 274*—that's Berry's."

Excerpted from "Black-and-Tan Fantasy," *Time* (October 27, 1975), p. 72. Reprinted by permission from *Time,* The Weekly Newsmagazine; Copyright Time Inc.

ally lead to promotion and salary increases are specified precisely. Consequently, members' behavior is fairly predictable, and work-group bonds are strong.

The organizational structure in the administrative organization is hierarchical and rational. Rules, procedures, and goals are well-defined. In addition, line and staff are distinct, primarily because the organization is so complex that responsibilities have to be allocated as precisely as possible.

Usually the management of the administrative organization strives to routinize innovation. A research and development department is established for the sole purpose of insuring that the firm will constantly have new products at its disposal if market conditions change. In this way, the management of the firm exercises some control over its external environment and minimizes the risks it takes.

Summary

According to Joseph Schumpeter, the entrepreneur is the hero of capitalism, for he combines existing resources in a society in a way that radically alters the consumption and production patterns of the society. A broader definition of entrepreneurship includes anyone who founds a business that has eight or more employees. Entrepreneurs possess a high need for achievement, independence, and control of their own destinies. They are also autocratic and typically do not form many close emotional attachments. While entrepreneurs are long-range planners, they do not like routine work and do not give much attention to the actual details of operating an organization. They are not very concerned about criticism, and they are willing to take intermediate risks.

Both corporate executives and entrepreneurs are achievement oriented. However, the entrepreneur has a stronger belief that he is the master of his own destiny than the corporate executive does. Many individuals become entrepreneurs because of a negative experience in an established organization, for example, losing a job. Individuals also can learn to become entrepreneurs because they see examples, either at home or elsewhere, of other individuals who have successfully started their own enterprises.

The failure rate of new businesses is quite high. According to Maury Delman, the most important reason for failure is a lack of balanced managerial experience. Entrepreneurs frequently do not know how to run a business.

Finally, in comparison with craft and administrative organizations, the entrepreneurial organization is characterized by autocratic leadership, the definition of objectives in a manner that is highly personal, an inefficient organizational structure, poor social relationships, a great amount of innovation, and an uncertain external environment.

Discussion Questions

1. There is a description of Berry Gordy, president of Motown in this chapter. What kind of an entrepreneur is he—technical or general? What are some differences between these two types of entrepreneurs?

2. The major reason for failure among entrepreneurs is a lack of balanced managerial experience. Describe the kind of education and work experience that would provide an individual with a balanced managerial background.

3. If you decided to found your own business, what are some major problems you might encounter? How would you solve them?

4. Shapero (1975) has put forth a theory that the entrepreneur is a misplaced person. What do you think Shapero means?

5. Suppose you would like to found your own business, but you don't have sufficient capital. Hence you must obtain a middle management job in industry or government after college. You plan to found your own business eventually. Would you choose industry or government? Why? Would you try to obtain a job in a large or small organization? Why?

6. If Schumpeter's definition of entrepreneurship is used, are there many entrepreneurs? Why or why not?

Critical Incidents

NOTE: *These critical incidents can be used by the whole class with the case observational method (see Appendix), or used for thought and discussion by individual class members.*

1. James Tillers is a young professor of marketing at a large state university. He became a part-time consultant with a large company. Through his experiences in this company, he began to realize that some new approaches could be used to market the kind of industrial goods that the company was producing. At this point, he decided to form his own consulting company to give marketing advice to corporations on a full-time basis.

a. Should he start small and invest only a few thousand dollars, or should he immediately try to form a large consulting firm? Should he operate the firm by himself and hire consultants to help him service the clients? Or should he sell shares to three or four of his fellow marketing professors who would then be actively involved in the firm?

b. How do you think he should break into the market with his specialized service? For example, should he advertise in the newspaper?

c. What are some of the specific problems he will face in attempting to provide a specialized service to industrial companies?

2. Joseph Alucio formed a very successful scientific firm that markets a product he patented. He has one son who is now in his early twenties. This son, Edward, possesses an engineering undergraduate degree and an M.B.A. He now works in his father's company. Joseph has told Edward he will become president of the company someday. Edward has told his father he would like this position.

a. How should Joseph prepare Edward for this job?

b. What are some difficulties that may arise between father and son?

3. Susan Haggburg is a very successful corporation executive making $50,000 per year at age 35. She works in a large company in the finance area. Her work has been outstanding and her future is very bright. However, Susan has developed specialized approaches to finance that could easily be used to attract clients if she founded her own company. While she likes her current position, she does not feel she can advance much further in the company. All of the positions she would like are filled by relatively young executives who will most probably stay in them for several years.

Susan is relatively well off; she has saved $50,000. However, she would need to invest at least $25,000 of this money to get her own company started. In addition, she would need additional investments of $75,000 from other shareholders. She has people lined up who have agreed to provide the backing. If the company is successful, she will be a millionaire in a few years. However, the probability of failure is high, since she must obtain clients who need her specialized services.

a. Should Susan quit her current job and form her own firm? Why or why not? What would we need to know about Susan to predict whether she will become an entrepreneur?

Suggested Readings

Baumback, Clifford, and Mancuso, Joseph (eds). *Entrepreneurship and Venture Management.* Englewood Cliffs: Prentice-Hall, 1975, 335 pages, paperback.

> *Baumback and Mancuso have compiled an excellent set of readings on entrepreneurship, many of which are based on research findings.*

Collins, Orvis, and Moore, David. *The Organization Makers.* New York: Appleton-Century-Crofts, 1970 (originally published in 1964), 237 pages, hardback.

> *These researchers conducted in-depth interviews with 150 entrepreneurs. They provide many fascinating case studies in this book, which is heavily psychological in orientation.*

Dale, Ernest. *The Great Organizers.* New York: McGraw-Hill, 1960, 276 pages, paperback.

> *Students enjoy this book, and with good reason. It is a series of vignettes of some well-known and little-known entrepreneurs. This book is highly recommended.*

A Profile
of an Organization:
The Ford Motor Company

15

- ■ **Planning: 1903–13**
- ■ **Behavioral Processes: 1914–20**
- ■ **Organization Design: 1921–29**
- ■ **Decision Making: 1930–45**
- ■ **Reorganization: 1946–Present**

Performance Objectives

1. To interpret the history of the Ford Motor Company in terms of the management model proposed in this book, and to see how the four dimensions of management influenced one another.

2. To be aware of two related and key factors in the company's history: product development and labor relations.

3. To examine the actions of Henry Ford, both as an entrepreneur who formed the company and as the president who managed it.

4. To explore the reorganization of the company under Henry Ford II in terms of the four dimensions of management included in our model.

As the basic management model described in this book implies, the effective manager should be able to: (1) design an organization, (2) plan the organization's development and control its systems, (3) guide the behavioral processes in the organization so subordinates are motivated and satisfied, and (4) make decisions that lead toward success. Many entrepreneurs would not be effective managers, as the previous chapter indicates. To see how the dimensions and elements of the model relate to a particular entrepreneur's attempts at management, this chapter examines the career of Henry Ford, founder of the Ford Motor Company.

The history of the Ford Motor Company falls roughly into five periods (see Table 15.1). From 1903 until 1914, Henry Ford essentially emphasized the dimension of planning and control; from 1914 until 1921, behavioral processes; and, from 1921 until 1930, organization design. His activities within these three dimensions set the stage for the kinds of decisions he made during the period from 1930 until 1946. After Ford relinquished power in 1946, Henry Ford II reorganized the company. This reorganization too can be seen in terms of the four dimensions of management that make up our model.

Planning:
1903–13

Henry Ford spent his boyhood on a farm in Michigan, where he showed an interest in mechanical operations. In his early adult years he was a farmer, but he left this life to seek work in industry and eventually became the chief engineer for Edison Light Company. Still, he wanted to found his own company, and he was encouraged to do so by Thomas Edison, his close friend.

Ford's great love, which essentially reflected his interest in mechanics, was the automobile, and he was involved in the creation of several unsuccessful automotive companies. It was not until 1903, when Ford was 40 years old, that he and Alexander Malcomson and James Couzens founded the Ford Motor Company.

Strategic Planning

Henry Ford was especially ambitious during these early years. He developed a distinctive strategic plan that other car manufacturers considered impractical—an inexpensive, all-purpose car (the Model T) that could be purchased by

Table 15.1 Product Development and Labor Relations

at the Ford Motor Company

Era	Product Development	Labor Relations
1903–13 Planning	The ambitious entrepreneur a. Model T b. Mass production	Rising labor problems a. Skilled work force converted to unskilled work force b. Problems with radical unions
1914–20 Behavioral Processes	The idealistic entrepreneur (no innovations)	Benevolence a. $5 day b. Some rights for workers c. Social reforms (e.g., hiring ex-criminals)
1921–29 Organization Design	The unrealistic entrepreneur a. Model A b. River Rouge Plant	Discipline of labor a. Speed-up of assembly line b. Ford Service Police
1930–45 Decision Making	The destructive entrepreneur (no innovations)	Intolerance of labor a. Resistance to labor unions b. Continued intimidation by Ford Service Police
1946–Present Reorganization	Emergence of rational management a. Different types and styles of cars b. Annual model changes	Tolerance of labor a. Far-sighted labor policies b. Cooperation with UAW

the average citizen. There was considerable opposition within the company management to this position, as only affluent individuals could purchase the highly priced automobiles at the turn of the century. As a logically incorrect consequence, companies generally felt only expensive automobiles should be manufactured. At that time, it was common for a car to cost $10,000, which, in the current era, would be equivalent to approximately $100,000. From 1903 until 1909, the Ford Motor Company competed against other auto companies by manufacturing several makes of automobiles that appealed to different types of customers. However, Henry Ford was hard at work on the Model T, which he began to produce in 1909.

During the early years of the company's history, Henry Ford was fortunate to have the services of James Couzens, who handled the business affairs of the company with unusual skill and success. Hence Ford could concentrate on directing production, a job to his liking.

Automobiles were constructed by highly skilled workers. All or most of the parts were custom made. Henry Ford enjoyed the company of the workers, for they were proud of the cars they produced. Consequently, Ford maintained a personal relationship with his workers until approximately 1909, when the number of workers had risen to more than 1,000.

Impact of Planning

When the Model T appeared, it became an instant success. The Ford Motor Company soon became the dominating force in the auto industry. However, to produce a low-price car, Ford had to redesign his organization to cut labor costs. He could no longer afford to hire highly skilled but highly paid workers. Rather, he began to routinize the work and use unskilled workers whose wages were quite low. In 1913 Clarence Avery and William Klann, two of Ford's assistants, created the concept of the conveyor belt, which made possible the assembly line and introduced mass production. Although Henry Ford was not directly involved in the origination of the conveyor belt, he immediately recognized the merits of the new system and installed it very quickly.

However, the unskilled workers at Ford were not happy. By 1913 dissatisfaction among them had resulted in huge turnovers—there was a labor turnover of over 380 percent in 1913 alone (Ford with Crowther 1926, p. 161). Undoubtedly mass production accelerated this trend, for no longer could most workers be accorded the status of skilled employees. Moreover, during the summer of 1913, grievances began to crystallize under the leadership of the International Workers of the World (IWW), a Communist-infiltrated union that appealed to immigrants, a large number of whom worked at Ford. Although it was small, this union served as a focal point and outlet for worker hostility. Finally the country, as a whole, experienced a minor depression in 1913. Henry Ford decided to combat the rising labor problems, thus turning his attention to the company's behavioral processes.

Behavioral Processes:

1914–20

For the next few years Henry Ford focused his attention on the behavioral aspects of his organization, temporarily disregarding his entrepreneurial activities. He was genuinely concerned about his workers, so much that this period can be called an era of benevolence.

Revolutionary Personnel Reforms

On January 14, 1914, Henry Ford raised the average salary of his workers from $2.34 to $5.00 a day. Almost overnight, he became known internationally as a friend and defender of the worker. This action ended his labor problems, at least for the short run, since over 100,000 men immediately lined up for employment outside the Highland Park Plant in the freezing January weather.

There were undoubtedly business reasons for the $5 day. An end to high labor turnover was definitely a prime consideration. Ford could acquire workers who were actually energetic in the fulfillment of their obligations. He later admitted that the $5 day was one of the finest cost-cutting moves the company ever made (Ford with Crowther 1922, p. 147).

Even though Henry Ford's motives in introducing the $5 day probably involved business more than charity, the host of other beneficial acts he undertook during this era of benevolence indicated his sincere interest in his workers' welfare. In 1914 a Safety and Health Department was created and immediately began efficient operations. The year 1916 witnessed the opening of the Henry Ford Trade School, an institution in which boys could learn a trade while attending school. The popularity of this school was so great that in 1920 it had 15,000 applicants for 1,500 positions. Acceptance in the school was largely based on need.

A startling policy initiated during this period was the hiring of partially incapacitated workers, ex-criminals, epileptics, and former inmates of mental hospitals. Although no other large company had any policy comparable to this one, Ford was not afraid to take chances by employing such people. Moreover, it was a continuing program, as even in 1934 approximately 20 percent of the Ford workmen were physically disabled (Federal Trade Commission 1939, p. 639). Such farsightedness was and is highly unusual, as even today tradition militates against hiring such workers.

Other Personnel Reforms

Another innovation was the Ford Sociology Department, which advised both management and employees on matters involving employees. This department investigated Ford's workmen to determine their eligibility for the $5 wage. It also counseled the workmen on how they should budget their money to get the best possible bargains for it. Further, the department provided information to them concerning the purchase of houses and other significantly high-priced goods. This department was somewhat paternalistic, even

Unpredictable Behavior

Throughout his life, Henry Ford's behavior was somewhat unpredictable. For example, he believed World War I could be ended only if the president of the United States and the German kaiser would get together and talk the matter over thoroughly and honestly. To this end, Ford commissioned the use of a large ship that could transport President Wilson and other important leaders to Germany. Naturally the newspaper reporters, who were fond of Ford, began to write about the evolution of the Great Peace Ship. Unfortunately, the entire plan was a disaster, for the president and other key officials politely declined to set sail. When the trip finally did get underway, the passengers were a strange mixture of newspaper reporters and left-wing extremists. To add insult to injury, Henry Ford contracted pneumonia and had to get off the ship in Sweden. Ford never did talk to the kaiser about the cessation of hostilities.

Based on Allan Nevins with Frank Hill, *Ford: The Times, the Man, the Company*, vol. 1. New York: Charles Scribner's Sons, 1954.

to the extent of secretly visiting the homes of workers in order to insure that disorderly behavior did not scandalize or harm the company in any way. However, the workers generally liked its activities, for it was a major source of protection for them. As an example, after receiving their first $5-a-day pay-checks, Ford workmen were besieged at the gates of the Highland Park Plant by all types of predatory salesmen (Sward 1948, p. 61).

Under the direction of the Sociology Department, the Ford Motor Company conducted a language school for its workers who were foreign-born. Thus, Henry Ford helped in the acculturation of many individuals who otherwise would have found not only the American labor market but also the American society impersonal and almost unapproachable.

Ford also developed an employee profit-sharing system. This was one of the first important systems in which employees received extra income if the profits of the company rose. In addition, Ford opened grocery stores for his employees, which, in 1919, were selling foodstuffs 25 percent below the market prices. This action contrasted rather sharply with the company stores, still in existence, in some coal towns in the United States. Another point of interest is that the *Dearborn Independent,* the newspaper directly owned and controlled by Henry Ford, supported the union in the steel strike of 1919.

Labor, for its part, reciprocated Henry Ford's good will. In 1918 he decided to run for senator from the state of Michigan. Although he lost, one of his most ardent backers was the American Federation of Labor. Apparently the workers felt their interests could be best pursued by this man who identified with them even though he was one of the richest men in the world.

Many analysts are of the opinion that *the only major labor reforms* in the early part of the twentieth century were those carried out by Henry Ford (Commons 1935; Lippman 1961). Few other companies followed Ford's example. The National Association of Manufacturers even criticized him in their publications. The top managers of other companies considered Henry Ford a maverick and scornfully allowed him to go his own way. Considering this environment, it is remarkable that he introduced so many innovative labor policies.

Organization Design:
1921–29

As we have seen, Ford's strategic plan to manufacture a low-priced car led him to redesign his organization. The new organizational structure, which brought in mass production and the use of low-skilled workers, proved to be very effective. But when, during the 1920s, Henry Ford again redesigned his organization, he was not so successful.

Total Control

In 1919 Henry Ford bought out the other stockholders of the Ford Motor Company. Typical of the entrepreneur, he was ruthless in his dealings with them—they were not even aware of his actions until it was too late. After a bitter legal battle, Ford owned the company completely. From this time on, Henry Ford was the complete autocrat. No one impeded his progress. But what was good for Henry Ford was not always good for the Ford Motor Company.

Resistance to Change

In the early 1920s, General Motors developed its policy of manufacturing different types of cars that would attract different kinds of customers. General Motors also followed a policy of changing its models on a yearly basis. These policies were sensible, for buyers wanted variety and a range of prices from which to choose. However, Henry Ford refused to change his strategic plan—he would manufacture only one type of car.

By 1922 Ford dealers throughout the country were unsuccessfully pleading with him to make some fundamental changes in car design. Ford did not even listen to the advice of his top executives, many of whom had left the company, voluntarily or involuntarily, by 1921. This loss of managerial talent proved to be a serious problem, for many of these executives joined General Motors and helped it to become more successful than the Ford Motor Company. One who left was William Knudsen, the brilliant engineer who was largely responsible for the annual model change at General Motors. He had quit the Ford Motor Company when Henry Ford simply refused to listen to his ideas.

Still, Henry Ford did have some justification for disregarding the advice of his executives. Many Ford executives had originally objected to the manufacture of the Model T and to the $5 day wage, both radical ideas that proved to be the best business propositions the company ever made. It was mainly Ford's judgment that had lifted the Ford Motor Company to the high position it occupied in 1920. Moreover, sales continued to be high, even though there was a major business recession in 1921 and 1922.

The New Structure. Henry Ford then redesigned the work processes in the company. To save money, he introduced the speed-up. The assembly line is machine controlled; the supervisors increased its speed so the workers now performed their job cycles in much less time. The supervisors were merciless and drove the workers as hard as possible. Discipline was so strict during this period that the workers were not even allowed to talk on the assembly line. At least one long-term worker managed to avoid this rule by whispering out of the side of his mouth, only to end up with permanent facial distortions in his later years.

In the late twenties, Ford met Harry Bennett, who had underworld connections and had spent some time in jail. Henry Ford took a great liking to him and treated him like a son. Ford asked Bennett to head the Ford Service Police, a 3,000-member group that enforced the speed-up and other measures of strict discipline within the company. Some workers were physically assaulted by members of this police force, especially those who were involved in any covert union activities.

Most of the idealistic projects Ford had initiated in 1914–20 had premature funerals. Dean Marquis, dynamic head of the Ford Sociology Department, resigned in 1922 when he realized the department was no longer supporting the interests of the workers. With this resignation, Henry Ford closed down the department. The plant foremen were now virtual dictators; they could hire and fire employees with no fear of reprisal. Even the press was stifled, as William Brownell, editor of the *Ford News*, who was partial to labor, resigned in 1920 and was replaced by a pro-management spokesman.

However, Ford's treatment of his workers was consistent with his economic philosophy. Ford believed the more money management paid the worker, the more industry's products would be consumed. Industry would benefit, consequently, through the payment of high wages. Still, although Ford paid workers high wages when they did work, he felt little, if any, responsibility to them if they were laid off. He believed workers could always find jobs once industry, after a relapse, began to advance again. Ford thus allowed his workers no rights except high wages, which they could obtain only when the industrialist decided they should work.

As General Motors began to take away customers from Ford, it was consonant with his economic philosophy to regiment the workers and force them to work at an inhuman pace. Similarly, Ford's deemphasis on behavioral processes and benevolence toward workers also agreed with his overall stance.

The Great Mistake. Much of the initial success of General Motors resided in its policies of the annual model changes and its appeal to a cross-section of buyers. Another important reason was its use of federal decentralization (see pp. 72–73). Under *federal decentralization,* top management allows the divisions of the company to operate independently throughout a reporting period. At the end of the period their performance is evaluated. If an operating division has not fared well, top management can introduce changes, even to the extent of shutting it down for a year or more to make substantial physical alterations in its structure. During such a period, the financial slack is picked up by the more prosperous operating divisions.

Perhaps the most important advantage of federal decentralization is that it allows a company to respond to its problems in a flexible manner. However, Henry Ford did not opt for designing his company in this manner, at least in part because he clung to his plan of manufacturing an inexpensive, all-purpose, and durable car. Because of declining sales, Ford knew he had to produce a new car. But the fact that he still refused to change his strategic plan eventually led to disaster.

To manufacture his new car, Henry Ford made plans to build the River Rouge, a centralized plant that could produce cars with a minimum of effort. Over 100,000 men could work in this plant. All the functions necessary for the building of automobiles, from iron ore furnaces to the moving assembly line, were housed in this giant plant. In the short run, this design proved to be effective, for it allowed the company to produce the new car, the Model A, very efficiently and inexpensively. Production of the Model A began in 1927. While profits were negligible in 1927 and 1928 because of these changes, there was a sizable increase in 1929 to the extent that the Ford Motor Company outsold General Motors. It appeared as if Henry Ford would regain his position as the leader of the automotive industry, but this was not his destiny—the title was perennially won by General Motors after 1929.

In short, Henry Ford made a major mistake. Although the River Rouge was

Blind Spots

Henry Ford had many blind spots that distorted his vision of reality. For example, when he was not accepted socially by the upper classes in Detroit, Ford decided to entertain. We might have expected he would hold some gala events such as sumptuous dinners and grand balls, as was the custom at the time. Rather, he hosted square dances at his mansion, which subjected him to ridicule.

During the early 1920s, Henry Ford began to make anti-Semitic statements in public. Until this time, Henry Ford had been a close friend of the chief rabbi in the city of Detroit, whom he presented once a year with a new Model T. When Ford began to make his anti-Semitic statements, the chief rabbi returned the new Model T. Ford's resentment and inability to understand this action showed his blindness to anyone's viewpoint but his own.

Based on Allan Nevins with Frank Hill, *Ford: The Times, the Man, the Company*, vol. 1. New York: Charles Scribner's Sons, 1954.

efficient for the Model A, it was not adaptable to new models, for the entire plant had to be shut down to make alterations. It was not until 1932 that Ford introduced another new car. By that time, it was too late—General Motors now dominated the industry. Throughout the 1930s, the Ford Motor Company consistently lost money.

Decision Making:

1930–45

Our model of management suggests that three dimensions of management—planning and control, organization design, and behavioral processes—essentially provide the setting within which decision making takes place. For example, because Ford designed his organization so he could use low-skilled workers, he began to experience labor problems, which led him to decide to raise wages from $2.34 to $5.00 a day. This decision was logical, given the kind of organization Ford had built and the results he wanted to obtain.

By 1930, the way Ford had set plans, developed control systems, designed his organization, and handled his behavioral problems had created a setting that strongly influenced his decisions. As emphasized throughout this chapter, he behaved in an unpredictable fashion most of his life. However, his decisions during the 1930s and 1940s were highly predictable, at least in part because the other dimensions of management provided a setting in which he was drawn to particular courses of action.

The Hunger March

Henry Ford, who was once championed as a hero by American labor, was now viewed as reactionary. In the Great Depression of the 1930s, layoffs were inevitable in every industry. But, in Detroit, resentment was directed against Henry Ford. In March 1932, the Ford Hunger March took place. Only a few hundred individuals participated in it, and their demands were, in terms of present practices, generally reasonable (Sward 1948, p. 233):

> In behalf of the Ford worker as such, the hunger marchers demanded jobs, the right to organize, reduction of speedup, abolition of labor spies, elimination of "graft" in the hiring process, two daily 15-minute rest periods on the Ford line, a six-hour day without reduction in pay, an unemployment bonus of $50 per man and free medical treatment for Ford men and their families.

Instead of meeting a sympathetic group of Ford executives who might try to eliminate the unfavorable conditions then in existence, the hunger marchers were greeted by a barrage of bullets from the Dearborn police, who were at that time under the influence of the Ford Motor Company. Four individuals were killed and over 20 were wounded. There was, of course, a public outcry. Nevertheless, labor conditions at the Ford Motor Company became worse as the 1930s progressed.

Labor Problems

In 1933 the Ford Motor Company was again involved in a labor dispute when one of its suppliers, Briggs Company, stopped production because of a strike. The Briggs concern was, through a lease, working in Henry Ford's Highland Park Plant. Many of its employees had been working a 14-hour day for 10 cents an hour. They now demanded a 9-hour day and a daily wage of $3.60 for women and $4.00 for men. In other words, they wanted treatment equivalent to that normally practiced at the River Rouge Plant. This, however, was not to be. Partially through the support of Henry Ford, the strike was crushed.

In 1933 the National Industrial Recovery Act (NIRA) was passed. Section 7(a) guaranteed the right of employees to organize and bargain collectively through their representatives without interference, restraint, or coercion by employers. Each industry was obliged to draw up a code of rules for its treatment of workers. The automotive industry was able to insert a "merit" clause into its code whereby it had the right to hire and fire without respect to seniority. But Henry Ford was so opposed to the idea of rights for labor that he would not sign even this watered-down code of rules, although it could in no direct way influence his treatment of workers.

Although NIRA was declared unconstitutional in 1935, labor trouble plagued the Ford Motor Company through 1945. In 1934 there was a strike against speed-ups at the River Rouge Plant; it was quickly ground underfoot. The Ford workers either submitted to conditions then in existence or left. Since people were clamoring for jobs during those years of depression, submission was the usual choice.

Henry Ford, the former friend and defender of the laborer, was gradually becoming the symbol of resistance to policies that would aid workers. Allan Nevins and Frank Hill cite three major reasons for union opposition to Henry Ford and his company during the 1930s (Nevins and Hill 1963). First, Ford's original liberal wage policy had collapsed. By 1940 Ford workers were actually being paid less than employees of the other major automotive corporations. Second, Harry Bennett and the Ford Service Police terrorized the Ford workers. Third, the unions were aligned against Henry Ford because of his doctrinaire opposition to any form of labor organization.

The year 1935 was critical for labor in America, as the Wagner Act was passed at this time. It established the first national policy of protecting the right of workers to organize and to elect their representatives for collective bargaining. Although it was legally contested, the act was upheld in 1937 by the United States Supreme Court. Under the protection of the Wagner Act, the United Automobile Workers (UAW) began a systematic campaign to organize union shops throughout the automotive industry. By the end of 1937 the entire automotive industry had accepted unions without violence—except for the Ford Motor Company.

Union Organization

On May 26, 1937, the UAW began its program to unionize the Ford Motor Company. Under the direction of Walter Reuther, who subsequently became president of the UAW, the union organizers planned to distribute circulars to the Ford workers on their way home from work. It was on a bridge over a road leading to the River Rouge Plant that the Battle of the Overpass occurred. Ford Service men were eagerly awaiting the union organizers. When Reuther arrived, he was besieged by press photographers. As his picture was being taken, the Ford Service Police ordered Reuther and the others to leave the bridge. Although they started to comply, the Ford Service men attacked them. Reuther and several others ended up in the hospital with serious injuries. Even the women in the group were beaten and in need of medical care.

Time was running out for the Ford Motor Company. By the end of 1937, all

of the major automotive companies had submitted to unionization; Henry
Ford was the last resister. His tactics were many and varied. Bennett and Ford
in 1938 manipulated Homer Martin, the first president of the United Automobile Workers, into private negotiations, which they hoped would neutralize
and possibly destroy the UAW. When the executive members of the UAW
became aware of these private talks, they impeached Homer Martin and
elected R. J. Thomas as president.

Another tactic was the use of the company union or one not affiliated with
any other union. Managers can effectively control a company union, since it
has no other allies if it decides to strike. Four company unions were organized
at Ford in 1937 and, as expected, they did not help the workers.

A third tactic of significance was used against workers in the Ford plants in
St. Louis, Kansas City, and Richmond and Long Beach in California. In 1937
Henry Ford appeared to reverse his position by granting de facto recognition
to the union at these plants. This stance brought the union and its leaders into
the open. However, when the plants reopened for fall production, Bennett
fired the key union leaders.

Despite Ford's struggles, it was inevitable that the Ford Motor Company
would be unionized. By 1941 the UAW once again felt strong enough to
unionize the Ford Motor Company. All they needed was a legitimate excuse
for a strike. It came on April 2, 1941, when Harry Bennett discharged the eight
River Rouge employees who composed the grievance committee at the plant.
The workers immediately and spontaneously began to walk off their jobs.
Under the leadership of the UAW, the workers surrounded the River Rouge
Plant. They did not dare to stage a sit-down strike in the plant, for the Ford
Service men would have the advantage and overpower them. But the workers
did deny food and water to the Ford Service men until a contract was signed.
On April 11 Henry Ford agreed to recognize the union.

Transitional Period

In 1941 the major problem at the Ford Motor Company was the conversion to
wartime production. This task was primarily directed by Charles Sorenson,
who was Ford's chief line executive for 40 years. He was generally regarded as
one of the best production men in the automotive business. Although many
other executives quit the company because they could not put up with the
autocratic manner of Henry Ford, Sorenson had stayed by him both in prosperous and poor times. Nevertheless, after working approximately 18 hours
per day for two years to complete the conversion, Sorenson was fired by Henry
Ford. Even in his old age, Ford was manifesting the tendency of entrepreneurs
to destroy the most loyal subordinates and friends.

Once the Ford Motor Company had made the transition from peacetime to

Autocratic Behavior

Typical of the entrepreneur, Henry Ford was highly autocratic, even with members of his family that worked for his company. His only child, Edsel, was a sensitive individual who wanted to attend college. However, Ford wanted him to enter the business. To persuade Edsel to forego his educational ambitions, Ford made him president of the Ford Motor Company, a position he occupied from 1918 until his death in 1943. However, Edsel's power was nominal rather than substantial—Henry Ford undercut the majority of the decisions Edsel made. Even after his death, Edsel's reputation suffered, for his own son, Henry Ford II, named after him the car that was associated with a $350 million fiasco during the 1950s.

Based on Allan Nevins and Frank Hill, *Ford*, vols. 1, 2, and 3. New York: Charles Scribner's Sons, 1954, 1957, and 1963.

wartime production, it became vital in the operations of the Allied effort. Unfortunately Henry Ford was becoming senile. By 1943 he was incapable of directing his company. After Ford's death in 1947, Harry Bennett attempted to wrest control of the company away from the Ford family by claiming that a codicil attached to Ford's will named him sole heir. For about a year, no one was quite sure who was running the company. At one point John Bugas, director of labor relations, told Bennett he did not believe the codicil existed. Bennett's reaction was so angry that Bugas left the room fearing, as he later said, that he might be shot in the back by the gun-carrying leader of the Ford Service Police.

Because the operations of the company were so vital to the war effort, the government allowed Henry Ford II to leave military duty to become the active head of the enterprise. Bennett's claims that he was the sole heir to the company proved unfounded and he was forced to leave. Henry Ford II became president.

Reorganization:

1946–Present

At the end of World War II, Henry Ford II's first major act was to reorganize the company. Actually, this reorganization was suggested and carried out by a group of young executives that included Tex Thorton, Robert McNamara, R. J. Miller, and other well-known names in the history of American business.

These individuals had worked together as systems analysts during World War II. Immediately after being discharged, they came as a group in their uniforms to Henry Ford and were hired to reorganize the company. Henry Ford II concerned himself with the external aspects of being company president while this group reorganized and modernized the company. The supreme irony of this reorganization is that it parallels the policies General Motors had emphasized in 1920—federal decentralization, appealing to a cross-section of customers, and annual changes in models. Because of this reorganization, the company has once again become very successful and it now ranks directly behind General Motors.

Since 1945 the Ford Motor Company has been very progressive in its relations with its workers and the UAW. It has implemented some pioneering concepts in this area, such as supplemental unemployment benefits. If a worker is laid off, he receives 95 percent of his salary for one year through a combination of unemployment benefits and supplemental funds provided by the company.

The only major catastrophe during this period was the unfortunate manufacture of the Edsel, which resulted in a loss of $350 million. However, even this catastrophe has failed to dent the fortunes of the company and it has moved ahead steadily in spite of it. More importantly, this catastrophe consisted of an understandable series of managerial errors that were, at least in part, logically justifiable. But these human errors can be compared in no way to those generated by the autocratic stance of the elder Henry Ford.

Summary

The history of the Ford Motor Company illustrates the management model proposed in this book. From the time of the company's founding in 1903 until 1913, Henry Ford emphasized the area of strategic planning—he wanted to produce an all-purpose, inexpensive, and durable car that the average consumer could afford. This plan directly affected the design of his organization. To set a low price for the Model T, he substituted unskilled for skilled workers, and radically redesigned his organization by introducing mass production. In turn, the design of the organization decisively influenced its behavioral processes. With employee turnover at 380 percent in 1913, Ford had to focus on the behavioral processes in his organization. He was very benevolent toward his workers and implemented several revolutionary reforms. However, Ford viewed these reforms as privileges rather than rights—if he began to lose money, he believed that he, as the owner of the company, could unilaterally withdraw them.

About 1920 General Motors began to take customers away from Ford. Rather than develop a new set of strategic plans that could act as a counterforce to General Motors, Ford maintained his policy of producing only one car—the Model T. To save money and keep the price of the Model T at a low level, he again emphasized the dimension of organization design—he speeded up the assembly line and built the River Rouge Plant where he could closely control the behavior of his workers. These changes directly affected behavioral processes in the organization, for the workers now viewed Ford and the Ford Service Police as adversaries.

By 1930 Ford's activities within three dimensions of management—planning and control, organization design, and behavioral processes—provided a predictable setting in which he made his decisions from then onward. He became extremely hostile toward labor and did not introduce any major changes—either new models of cars or new designs for his organization—for the remainder of his life.

When Henry Ford II became president, he completely reorganized the company. He emphasized the importance of design by organizing his company as a federally decentralized structure; he focused his attention on developing effective planning and control systems; and he stressed the importance of behavioral processes by introducing pioneering policies in the area of labor relations. Ironically, all of these changes paralleled those introduced by General Motors during the 1920s. These changes proved to be very successful, for the Ford Motor Company has been highly profitable since 1946 to the extent that it now is the number 2 company in the automotive industry.

Discussion Questions

1. Why was the construction of the River Rouge Plant so important in the history of the Ford Motor Company? When Ford built this plant, what dimensions of management was he emphasizing?

2. During the period from 1914 to 1920, Henry Ford appeared to be very idealistic. However, his later actions seemed to contradict this stance. Why was he idealistic only during the period from 1914 to 1920?

3. Organization design and control were closely related at the Ford Motor Company, especially after the introduction of mass production in 1913 and the construction of the River Rouge Plant in 1926. How and why were they related?

4. If you were in Henry Ford's shoes in the early 1920s, what kinds of strategic plans and policies would you have developed to compete against General Motors? Why?

5. The relationship between product development and personnel-labor relations in the history of the Ford Motor Company is highlighted in this chapter. Do you feel this relationship is critical in most organizations? Why or why not?

6. When Ford converted his company to mass production in 1913, the skilled workers were replaced by unskilled workers. What kinds of personnel problems would you expect under the new situation?

Suggested Readings

Nevins, Allan, and Hill, Frank. *Ford*, vols. 1, 2, and 3. New York: Charles Scribner's Sons, 1954 (vol. 1), 1957 (vol. 2), and 1963 (vol. 3).
  The Ford Foundation sponsored this historical treatment of Henry Ford and his company. A balanced view of the man and his company, these books contain innumerable anecdotes and insights.

Sward, Keith. *The Legend of Henry Ford.* New York: Rinehart, 1948.
  Sward is a former union official who takes a decidedly negative view of Henry Ford. Many of Sward's arguments are very convincing, and they place Henry Ford in a different light from that put forth by Nevins and Hill.

Predictors of
Managerial Success

16

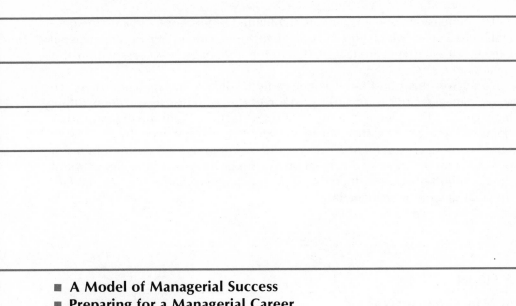

- ■ **A Model of Managerial Success**
- ■ **Preparing for a Managerial Career**
- ■ **Career Strategies**
- ■ **Periodic Assessment**
- ■ **Managerial Failure**

Performance Objectives

1. To understand how ability, motivation, and opportunity determine managerial success.

2. To know how to prepare for a successful career as a manager, and what career strategies an individual should follow to become a successful manager.

3. To be familiar with the techniques an individual can use to assess periodically the progress of his or her career.

4. To know some reasons for, and how to deal with, managerial failure.

The dimensions of management highlighted in this book indicate the general framework in which you will operate if you decide to pursue a managerial career. But what specific factors determine a manager's success within this framework?

To answer this question, it is necessary to define *managerial success*. To some managers, success means a position of power in the organization. Other managers might define it in terms of job satisfaction. From the organization's point of view, a successful manager is an effective manager. To an outside observer, a successful manager is one who occupies a high position in his or her organization and makes a large salary. Just as there is disagreement about the definition of success, there is much disagreement about the specific factors that determine managerial success.

A Model
of Managerial Success

In general, three factors appear to be essential for success: ability, motivation, and opportunity (Campbell, Dunnette, Lawler, and Weick 1970). *Ability* includes such individual characteristics as intelligence, aptitude, and knowledge. Generally, *motivation* basically means an individual's needs or desires that cause him or her to act in a particular manner. Specifically, successful managers are typified by a high need or desire to achieve (see pp. 200–201). Finally, *opportunity* refers to the specific organizational factors that enable or limit an individual's promotion. (See Figure 16.1.) For instance the top management of an organization may not promote women or minority-group members to responsible or high-paying positions.

Although all three factors are of decisive importance, the exact relationship among them is not known. It is possible that ability and motivation are related in an additive fashion: The higher the person is in each factor, the greater his or her chances for success. However, Norman Maier (1955) has argued that this relationship is multiplicative. If ability and motivation were measured on a 1 to 10 scale, an individual who scored 5 on both factors would be much more successful than someone who scored 1 and 9 (25 versus 9). This approach seems reasonable, for an individual may be only moderately high on these two factors and still be very successful. However, research supportive of the multiplicative approach is tentative and not strong, probably because other factors such as opportunities within the organization have not been taken into consideration (see Vroom 1964).

Figure 16.1   A Model of Managerial Success

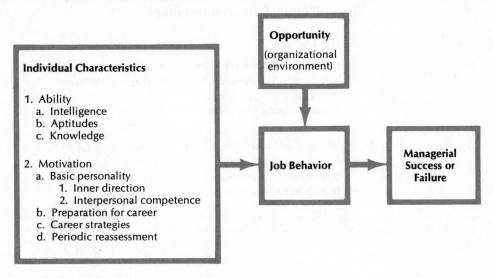

From John Campbell et al., *Managerial Behavior, Performance, and Effectiveness,* p. 11. Copyright © 1970 by McGraw-Hill Book Company. Reprinted by permission.

Ability

It is easier to assess a person's ability than his or her motivation. *Intelligence,* which is a critical aspect of ability, can be measured in a general way by means of IQ tests. For managerial success, *verbal ability*—knowledge and use of words—seems to be particularly important (Miner 1975).

Similarly, *aptitudes* or *inclinations* toward particular types of work can be evaluated by means of vocational inventory tests such as the Strong Vocational Inventory Blank. The prospective manager can use these preferences to judge which of various types of occupations he or she would enjoy most. If an individual likes to engage in business contacts, he or she would probably be successful as a sales manager or life insurance salesman (see Table 16.1). Allan Nash (1965) indicates that four specific vocational interests are related to managerial effectiveness: (1) social service, humanitarian, and people-oriented likes; (2) persuasive, verbal, and literary interests; (3) a rejection (or dislike) of exclusively scientific, technical, or skilled trades pursuits; and (4) a liking for business contact and business detail activities.

A third aspect of ability, *knowledge,* can be measured by means of standard tests or the individual's academic preparation. Both scholastic knowledge and

Table 16.1   Occupations Scoring High or Low on Two Scales
of the Strong-Campbell Interest Inventory

Scales	High Scores	Low Scores
Art scale	actors, actresses, architects, artists, interior decorators, musicians, occupational therapists, photographers	accountants, bankers, business education teachers, farmers, sewing machine operators, veterinarians
Office practices scale	accountants, bankers, business education teachers, office workers, telephone operators	anthropologists, architects, artists, photographers, writers

From David P. Campbell, *Manual for the Strong-Campbell Interest Inventory:* T325 (Merged Form), (Stanford: Stanford University Press, 1974), table 5.4, p. 42. Excerpted by permission.

the knowledge and skill that come from experience are important to an individual's success. Actual on-the-job performance tends to bring into focus the individual's specific kinds of knowledge.

Motivation

It is very difficult to measure motivation. Although many studies have been completed in this area, they do not all agree on the specific motivational factors that are critical for success. However, successful executives appear to possess a different personality profile from unsuccessful executives. Particularly, successful managers are more decisive, independent, and willing to take risks to reach their goals (Porter and Lawler 1968); and they are better at interacting with others. In fact, some research suggests that interpersonal competence may be more important than technical competence in predicting managerial success (Applewhite 1965).

Opportunity

The individual who works within an organization is limited by the kinds of opportunites available within its structure. These limitations even appear to influence entrepreneurial activities. For instance, scientific firms in the Palo Alto area that employ less than 500 employees have a spin-off rate eight times greater than firms with more than 500 employees (see p. 356). This suggests

The Life-style of Success

Men rating high in overall success report backgrounds suggesting a kind of "life-style" of success—excellent health, scholastic and extracurricular leadership in high school and college, assumption of important responsibilities rather early in life, high ambition, and active participation in religious, charitable, or civic groups.

John Campbell, Marvin Dunnette, Edward Lawler, and Karl Weick, *Managerial Behavior, Performance, and Effectiveness* (New York: McGraw-Hill, 1970), p. 197.

that the individual in the smaller firm has an opportunity to learn more about the various activities of the organization, and thus is better equipped to start his own organization.

Several researchers have studied the kind of organizational climate that is ideal for the advancement of managerial effectiveness and success. These studies have been summarized by John Campbell, Marvin Dunnette, Edward Lawler, and Karl Weick (1970), who argue that four independent factors are critical in the assessment of managerial effectiveness and success. First, the executive must be able to operate independently so he or she is responsible for his or her own activities. In this fashion the executive learns what works and what doesn't. Further, the executive must work in an organization that is loosely structured, so he or she is not constantly hounded by superiors. Moreover, the organization must reward executives handsomely if they perform exceptionally well. Finally, superiors must be considerate and supportive of the individual, even if he or she sometimes fails. In short, the four factors are:

1. Degree of independence and individual responsibility
2. Degree of structure imposed on the situation
3. Kinds of rewards
4. Consideration and support of superiors

Preparing
for a Managerial Career

To be successful, an individual should prepare for his managerial career. This preparation ideally begins long before the day he or she applies for a managerial job. The individual must first have qualifications that will convince someone he is worth hiring. Then he should offer special features that make him the best candidate for the specific job desired.

The Hiring Interview

The future manager's first meaningful contact with an organization usually takes place during one or more hiring interviews. If a job applicant appears promising, he or she is typically invited to the company for a visit and to be interviewed by several of its managers. The initial hiring interview is critical, for it serves as the basic screening mechanism for the organization.

Some research has highlighted the importance of the hiring interview. Stephen Carroll (1966) attempted to discover the factors that affect someone's initial success in obtaining a managerial position. The subjects of the research were 550 male seniors at the University of Minnesota. Only 2 of the 24 factors studied were decisive in predicting success: previous work experience in the type of job under consideration, and personal attractiveness. Carroll measured the degree of attractiveness by asking raters to evaluate photographs of the subjects in terms of a three-point scale: below average, average, and above average. The higher the candidate's attractiveness, the more successful he was at being offered a managerial position.

Even if an individual is not conventionally attractive, he or she can at least dress in a fashion that will help obtain the job. In fact, the proper outfit appears to be critical for initial success (Steinberg 1975). In one study, a young man applying for managerial positions dressed in two contrasting styles: a nondescript, lower middle-class style, and a distinctive and elegant, upper middle-class style. In the nondescript style of dress he was typically rejected for the job, but in the elegant style he was successful.

Ironically, many job candidates are not effective in the hiring interview because of a lack of experience with it. This problem can be easily overcome by simulated exercises in which the individual acts out the role of the job candidate. Such exercises are typically conducted by the career counseling center of a college or university. These exercises focus on such problems as shyness, lack of confidence, and methods for asking and answering questions.

As the discussion thus far implies, the initial impression a job candidate creates is of decisive importance. In fact, the decision to hire or not to hire is usually made within the first three or four minutes of the interview (Webster 1964). Obviously, the interviewer is heavily influenced by factors that help to create an initial favorable impression, such as attractivenesss, dress, and friendliness. On infrequent occasions, the interviewer may change his or her mind; however, the change tends to be from positive to negative rather than negative to positive.

Academic Training

It is difficult to say what kinds of academic training are most helpful for career advancement, as only limited research has been conducted in this area. Although researchers have been able to show that certain schools produce a disproportionately high number of successful managers, this does not necessarily imply a causative relationship. For example, even though a significant number of successful managers have come out of the Harvard Business School, it is possible the ability and motivation of these individuals rather than their Harvard degree explains their subsequent success. That is, it may be that people with higher ability and stronger motivation tend to apply to certain schools.

Still, research studies have consistently indicated a strong relationship between the quality of the educational institution and subsequent success. Thus an individual probably is wise to go to the best institution to which he or she is admitted, even if it involves financial sacrifice.

In today's world, it is also sensible for an aspiring manager to obtain an advanced degree that will set him or her apart from other job applicants. The master of business administration program (M.B.A.) has become popular in recent years, at least in part because it gives the type of preparation that will help the individual obtain a responsible job and perform effectively. More specifically, some types of academic majors are better than others if an individual wants to become a successful line manager. For example, with a M.B.A. in finance, an individual can aspire to the top line positions in many organizations whereas someone with a M.B.A. in industrial relations would be restricted to staff work.

A Unique Feature

The competition for managerial positions is intense. A candidate can improve his or her chances of success by developing a unique feature that only a few other applicants possess. As indicated in Carroll's study (1966), only attractiveness and some previous experience in the work under consideration were related to success during the job hunt. Accounting majors who had worked for a semester as interns obtained jobs more easily than accounting majors who lacked this experience. Similarly, a Ph.D. candidate usually can win a position at a desirable university if he or she has published one or two significant articles. The job applicant should include on his résumé any major achievement in college: managing the school paper, being a member of the debating club, and so forth. The applicant should also list jobs he has held, both while attending school and during vacations.

Training Programs

An individual can also advance his or her career by taking a position with an organization that sponsors excellent training programs. In fact, graduation from certain training programs can be as helpful or more helpful than a graduate degree in some fields. The two-year Management Training Program of the Chase Manhattan Bank is so good that managements of other banks hire its graduates. A typical day in this program is: 7:00 A.M. to 10:00 A.M., classroom instruction; 10:00 A.M. to 3:00 P.M., work in a functional area of the bank; 3:00 P.M. to 5:00 P.M., classroom instruction; and two or three hours of homework. At one point, the top management of Chase Manhattan considered eliminating this program, primarily because most of its graduates were lured away by other banks.

Assessment Centers

In recent years, some companies have created *assessment centers* to help them evaluate job candidates' managerial potential (see Howard 1974). The concept of an assessment center was drawn from the activities of the elite SS in Germany during the 1930s. To select the best applicants for this military force, its management put the candidates through a series of simulated exercises, group discussion sessions, and extended psychological interviews. Psychologists then evaluated a person's overall potential as an SS officer.

The major objective of the assessment center is to predict a person's potential within a specific organization. Thus each center should be tailored to the needs of the organization sponsoring it. However, the assessment center typically involves some exercises that measure the individual's ability to function under pressure. In the in-basket training exercise, the individual is informed that he or she is to take the place of the superior, who has been hospitalized. He or she is then assigned to the superior's desk and told to handle all business matters in the in-basket. Usually a telephone is provided with a list of numbers the individual can call as he or she attempts to solve problems. A time limit of three or four hours is fixed so the individual's ability to function under presssure can be judged.

In the 1950s, American Telephone & Telegraph Company (AT & T) developed an assessment center that managerial trainees attended for three and one-half days. Psychologists then predicted the probable success of the trainees. The psychologists did not give their results to top management, as that might have created a self-fulfilling prophecy; that is, top management might have advanced the trainees who were rated most likely to succeed. Follow-ups during the past 25 years indicate that a person's performance in the AT & T program did to some extent predict his managerial success.

Although the organization gains in that an assessment center improves the chances of selecting effective individuals, the trainee also benefits. Early in the trainee's career, he is made aware of the chances for success within a *particular* organization: Evaluations of performance in the assessment center are given to each trainee; each learns about his strengths and weaknesses; and each obtains a general idea about the probability of succeeding in the organization. If the probability of success is low, the trainee can move to a new organization at a point in life when he is still highly mobile. Or the trainee can change his behavior to improve the chances of success if he decides to stay with the organization. Assessment centers are now also employed as development mechanisms that managers may periodically attend during their careers, to find out how well they have overcome their managerial weaknesses.

Career

Strategies

Once a person begins to work, he or she can direct his or her career by means of strategies or general plans of action. As with career preparation, only a limited amount of research has been focused on this area. Still, enough information has been collected to establish guideposts for the aspiring manager.

Job Challenge

Although the proper educational credentials are usually sufficient to obtain a job, the way the individual carries out this job is critical to whether he or she keeps it and is promoted to a better one. The first year, in particular, is very important. In the AT & T study of its assessment center, the progress of the trainees was assessed after five and ten years. If the trainees were given responsible and challenging assignments in their first year that allowed them to mature as managers, they subsequently progressed in their careers significantly faster than the rest of the sample (Berlew and Hall 1966).

Even the outside professional activities of managers during the first years of employment are related to success. Accountants in large CPA firms tend to be successful if they read several professional and trade journals in their area of expertise and regularly attend professional meetings during their first few years with a firm (Loeb and Gannon 1976). At least among accountants, such professional activities were more predictive of success than educational factors like grades in college and number of extracurricular activities.

The major implication of these studies is that the individual must be very aggressive and hard working during the early stages of his career. Sometimes an individual can be stymied in a career because he is pigeonholed in a dull job at an early date. To combat this problem, the individual should request a major change in his position within the organization or actively seek work elsewhere.

Personal Responsibility

Even the individual who obtains a challenging job may be unsuccessful if he or she is not personally responsible for some projects. If the individual is always a subordinate for projects, it is difficult for others to assess his or her potential as a leader, and he or she may be bypassed when promotions are handed out.

In one case, a staff specialist in a large organization became the informal leader in his department because he was highly knowledgeable. He spent a great amount of time on group projects on which his contributions, although of obvious importance, could not be pinpointed with accuracy. To obtain a promotion, his superiors informed him, he needed to *direct* several projects. In the long run, the top management of the organization probably damaged its effectiveness by this stance, which encouraged managers to work hard only on projects for which they were personally responsible.

Rotation and Mobility

It is common for large organizations to rotate their managers through a series of jobs so they can develop an understanding of the particular problems that occur in various parts of the system. In addition, many companies move their managers from one geographic location to another. Such moves are designed to sensitize the managers to problems throughout the entire organization.

Many times, managers do not want to be rotated or moved. Top management frequently honors these preferences. However, top management normally does not promote this type of individual the next time a good opening comes up. When a manager refuses to make any change whatsoever, he or she is normally stuck in a dead-end position.

If a manager makes wise decisions on rotation and mobility, his or her career can be considerably enhanced. In some instances, an executive will quit the company to assume a position elsewhere, only to return as a former superior's superior. Such instances suggest that the top management of the organization places a high value on mobility, even if the individual is "disloyal" enough to quit temporarily.

Specialist versus Generalist

A common pattern among managers is to begin their careers as specialists but transfer to general management as they grow older. A classic example of this type of movement can be found among engineers and scientists, many of whom begin their careers in technical positions and end them in managerial positions. There are obviously many reasons for this shift. One of the major reasons is that an ambitious individual frequently winds up in a dead-end technical position from which the only promotion is into managerial responsibility.

However, as managerial responsibility increases, the individual usually begins to lose his or her technical competence. Hence there is a trade-off between the technical specialty and general managerial responsibility: Once a technical specialist has decided to accept a general management position, he or she normally cannot return to the former work, for technical knowledge becomes outdated within a few years. Someone who decides to make a career move in this direction should be fully aware of this trade-off. If the individual fails to consider the trade-off seriously, he or she may become dissatisfied, especially when he or she dislikes the current position but cannot return to the former job.

The Protégé

When the individual is new in an organization, he or she can benefit by learning as much about the firm and the industry as possible. One way to accomplish this is to become the protégé of an older and successful executive in the organization who can teach the new employee about the organization and managerial responsibilities.

A protégé relationship can be dangerous, for the individual can become too dependent upon the senior executive. If the senior executive leaves or is displaced, his or her protégé may be left in a powerless position. Although there are obvious dangers in the assumption of the role of the protégé, the advantages are considerable. Friendship, a situation in which learning the ropes is made easy, and support when promotions are given out are but a few of the reasons why many individuals become protégés of executives who help them to advance their careers.

Special Factors

The final factors that should be considered in a career are difficult to identify with precision, since they represent a unique fit between the individual and the organization. For example, a Catholic executive may find it difficult to advance in a company dominated by Protestant executives. Or an executive may not be advanced to a high position in the organization until he or she is admitted to an exclusive yacht club frequented by the top management of the firm (Dalton 1959).

Frequently the individual has a difficult time assessing the importance of special factors, especially when he is new to the organization. If the individual discovers that these subtle standards are critical for advancement, he must attempt to meet them or forego advancement within a particular organization.

Periodic
Assessment

A wise manager will periodically monitor his or her advancement and adjustments to it. The area of periodic reassessment of a career is very murky, for it can involve many factors, such as a person's preference for staying in a particular part of the country, family pressures, and even the individual's state of health. Moreover, it is not always easy for either a manager or his or her superiors to know exactly where the individual stands. In one instance, the director of a university management development program was asked by the top management of a company to assess the capabilities of a participant being considered for a major promotion. The candidate's superiors were so unsure of his capabilities, even after 25 years, that they wanted the advice of an outside expert.

Although it is obviously difficult to reassess a career objectively, there are some standards by which such a judgment can be made.

Age-Salary Ratio

There is a definite relationship among a manager's age, salary, and success. Korn/Ferry International, a management consulting firm that specializes in finding and placing qualified managers in top positions in industry, has shown that good performers should be making approximately $40,000 per year at age 40, superior performers approximately $63,000, and top performers $95,000 (see Figure 16.2). These figures relate only to the top management positions. They do suggest, however, that the individual should identify any gap between his or her current salary and potential salary. If the manager feels the gap is too wide, he or she should attempt to change the situation by either demanding a higher salary or moving to another company. If the manager

Figure 16.2   What Top Executives under 40 Can Expect to Earn[a]

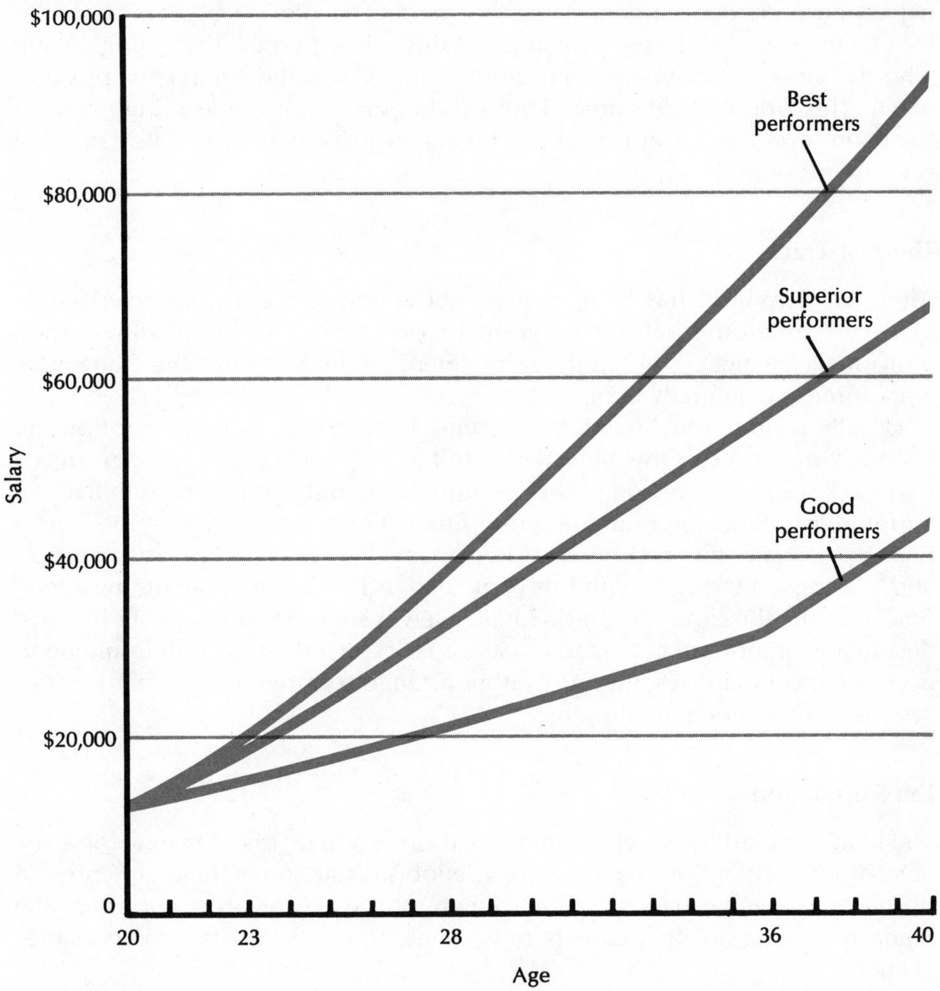

From "Young Top Management: The New Goals, Rewards, Lifestyles," reprinted from *Business Week* (October 6, 1975): 64 by special permission. Copyright © 1975 by McGraw-Hill, Inc.

[a]Data: Korn/Ferry International, based on salaries of candidates placed.

accepts the status quo, his or her rate of advancement will probably slow down considerably.

Further, the relationship between age and the number of promotions a person receives is important, even when salary is not considered. As indicated previously, the first few years on the job are critical. If the individual performs well, he or she usually advances at a rapid rate. Organizations sometimes bypass an individual later because he seems too old for a promotion. Although the law forbids discrimination against older people, the young person who has already received several promotions is in an advantageous position when other opportunities arise. Thus it is important for the aspiring manager to obtain several promotions early in his career so as to be relatively assured of subsequent ones.

The Fast Track

Although very little has been written about the *fast track,* knowledgeable observers are aware that it exists in many organizations. Specifically, certain individuals are picked for rapid advancement while the rest of the managerial work force is essentially bypassed.

Usually an individual will receive some warning signals if he is not on the fast track of success. One New York bank fed its management interns into a two-track system at the end of their six-month training course. If an individual performed well on the examination in finance and accounting, he became a high-status loan officer. Otherwise, he became a low-status operations officer and, as long as he stayed with this bank, had little chance of becoming a loan officer. When the slow-track individual receives such warning signals, he must decide how important managerial success is. If the individual is determined to become a top manager, he must either arrange to move to the fast track or seriously consider changing jobs.

Job Satisfaction

The final standard by which an individual can evaluate his or her career is the level of job satisfaction. To many people job satisfaction is the main criterion of success—which is why there are so many stories of successful or promising managers giving up their careers to become novelists, artists, or even storekeepers.

Frequently individuals are unhappy with their jobs but are reluctant to make a change, either because they fear the insecurity of unemployment or for a variety of other reasons. This approach seems to be unwise, for job satisfaction is very important to health as well as success. In this regard, Erdman Palmore (1969) conducted a long-term study of longevity. At the beginning of the study, he measured the overall physical health of the subjects. Over a period of years, job satisfaction was more predictive of longevity than either tobacco use or health at the initial examination.

If an individual is deeply dissatisfied, he or she should seek work elsewhere or change careers. In today's world, it is common to change careers during middle age. Often, however, such a change is made without the proper preparation and thought. For example, some executives decide to return to school for a few years, only to find their money has run out at the end of one year.

There are now some programs tailor-made for the middle-aged individual who decides to change his or her career. Columbia University sponsors a highly successful program designed specifically for individuals contemplating a career change. Throughout this program, counselors discuss any problems the student confronts, such as what courses to take, career possibilities, and personal problems. From all indications, a well-run career program like Columbia's can be highly successful (Entine in Sheppard and Herrick 1972).

Managerial
Failure

Even if a manager is conscious of the elements that generally lead to success, he or she is likely to face occasional career problems. A manager should be aware of the setbacks he or she may face someday, in order to avoid them if possible and deal with them effectively if they do occur. This section focuses on two aspects of managerial failure: ineffective performance and demotion.

Ineffective Performance

A manager may perform ineffectively for a variety of reasons. There may be a poor match between the manager's abilities and the needs of the organization; he may be experiencing marital or other personal difficulties; he may actually dislike being a manager. Such problems usually are damaging to both the organization and the manager's career. In some organizations, however, managers who perform ineffectively are promoted more rapidly than effective performers (Campbell et al. 1970), frequently because managers recommend their worst subordinates for promotion into another department so they can be rid of them.

Sometimes organizations function so poorly that "horror stories" are created. In one celebrated instance at a major university, some senior faculty members wanted to promote a likeable young assistant professor who had not distinguished himself in any way. To make his record acceptable to the university administration, these senior professors were able to obtain a "best teacher" award for him and the $1,000 that accompanied it. However, during the semester in which his promotion was approved, his students were signing a petition to have him fired because he skipped over 50 percent of his classes to complete his consulting assignments.

Horror stories of this type reflect badly on an organization, partly because they indicate its management is not rewarding its most effective performers. If such a horror story is only an isolated instance, an effective manager can possibly accept it as a fact of life with which he or she must live. When horror stories begin to multiply, it is time for the ambitious and effective manager to begin to think about a major change in situation.

Demotion

It is not very pleasant to contemplate demotion, but it does occur. There are many reasons why an individual may be demoted: He or she may become ineffective after a number of years on the job; a new superior may be hostile; the individual may be given increased responsibilities that he or she cannot handle; and so forth. Whatever the reason, a demotion is usually unpleasant, for the individual must confront the fact that the organization does not consider his or her services very valuable.

There are many ways to demote an individual besides firing. Changes in assignments, removal of responsibilities, and transfer to a new but inferior office are only some of the ways a demotion occurs. In many instances, a person's salary will not or cannot be touched. For instance, it is difficult to alter a person's salary in the government because of the safeguards of the merit system. But even then, a person can be effectively demoted. For example, a senior government executive made a presentation to his newly appointed superior, after which the superior made such comments as, "I can't understand what you are talking about. Does anybody in this room understand what you are talking about? Joe? Bill?" In this way, the superior made it clear to everyone that the subordinate would occupy an inferior position in the organization.

Obviously, individuals react to being demoted in different ways. Some accept it meekly; others fight it by going over the superior's head; others complain but never take any action. Whatever the reaction, managers usually find a demotion difficult to accept. Still, many receive demotions. In fact, the proportion of executives who are demoted may even be increasing, although exact figures are difficult to obtain (see Goldner 1965). It is important for a manager who is demoted to deal with the situation objectively and constructively. If the manager feels the reason is a poor fit between himself and the job, he or she should think about another job that would be more suitable. If the manager believes his or her demotion was due to company politics, it may be advisable to move to another company.

Summary

There are three factors that predict managerial success: ability, motivation, and opportunity. However, the exact relationship among these three factors is still unknown. Ability includes basic intelligence, job-related experience, and vocational interests. Motivationally, successful managers are achievement oriented, independent, and willing to take some risks. Opportunity refers to the available jobs and the chances for promotion within a given organization.

In preparing for a managerial career, the individual should attempt to obtain appropriate academic training for the position he or she seeks. In addition, he should realize that the hiring interview is very important. The individual can prepare for it with simulated exercises. Because competition for managerial positions is fierce, he should strive to develop a unique feature in order to be desirable to prospective employers. The aspiring manager also can advance his career by accepting a position with a company that sponsors management training programs or an assessment center.

Once the individual begins to work on a regular basis, he or she should guide his or her career by means of strategies or general plans of action. It is important to do well in the first years of employment. To this end, the individual should become involved in professional activities, try to complete some tasks for which he is totally or primarily responsible, and rotate through several jobs in the organization or in different geographical locations if necessary. He may benefit by becoming the protégé of a powerful sponsor. The aspiring manager also must attempt to meet any special but unwritten standards the organization has for promotion.

Periodically the manager should reassess his or her career and the rate of progress in it. Generally, there is a definite relationship among a person's age, salary, and success. In addition, there is often a fast track in an organization. If an individual assesses that his career is progressing poorly, he should strive to change the situation by demanding a promotion or seeking work elsewhere. Further, the manager should think about changing jobs if his degree of job satisfaction is very low.

Finally, managers should be prepared for the possibility of failure. Some managers become ineffective, for a number of reasons, and may be demoted. Even an effective manager may be demoted for political reasons. Although demotion is typically a painful experience, the wise manager will deal with it constructively.

Discussion Questions

1. For the ambitious and capable manager, what is the ideal organizational climate?

2. What are the major predictors of managerial success? How do these predictors relate specifically to your own career goals? How are you preparing yourself for a managerial career?

3. What is the age-salary ratio? Why is it important? When would this ratio not be important? Can you measure this ratio in an organization in which salary information is secret?

4. What seems to be the major problem when an individual changes careers? How can it be corrected?

5. What are some unique features an individual applying for a managerial job should possess?

6. Some writers have argued that the best predictor of managerial success is the individual's background or a consistent record of past successes. Do you agree with this position? Why or why not?

Critical Incidents

NOTE: *These critical incidents can be used by the whole class with the case observational method (see Appendix), or used for thought and discussion by individual class members.*

1. John Hodges is a young middle manager with a large corporation who works in finance. He has been very successful during his first three years on the job. Recently he was asked to make a major presentation on financial planning to 30 of the company's top regional officers. This presentation is very important to John, for it will expose him to a select group of influential managers who may offer him a promotion sometime.

John makes a well-prepared presentation, after which he answers some questions from the 30 managers. One of these managers is particularly hostile toward him. He begins his question by asking, "What is your definition of financial planning?"

John has only a few seconds to think of an answer. As he begins to respond to the question, the regional officer says, "Don't give me any of the academic jargon." At this point, it looks like the regional officer wants to dominate the discussion and show his superiority over John.

How should John react?

2. A representative for a large company interviews two applicants for one managerial position. The first applicant has a very strong record of past achievements. However, this applicant is not very forceful or persuasive in the interview. The second applicant is just the opposite; that is, she has an average record of past achievement but is very forceful and persuasive in the interview.

Whom should the company representative hire? Why?

3. Tom Scanlin is a young middle manager in charge of the computer operation for a medium-sized bank. Fifty male employees work in this section, most of them keypunch operators. Tom is a friendly fellow and likes to interact with these keypunch operators. In fact, he periodically takes one or more of them to lunch or out for drinks after work.

How is this practice likely to affect Tom's effectiveness as a manager? His chances for promotion?

Suggested Readings

Dalton, Melville. *Men Who Manage*. New York: John Wiley, 1959, hardback.
Dalton focuses on the activities of managers, and the means they use to promote their careers.

Hall, Douglas. *Careers in Organizations*. Pacific Palisades, Calif.: Goodyear, 1976, 236 pages, paperback.
This book summarizes research findings on career advancement, and focuses on such topics as career choice, career stages, and methods of advancement.

Jennings, Eugene. *The Executive in Crisis*. New York: McGraw-Hill, 1965, 218 pages, paperback.
This well-known consultant analyzes the psychological problems that executives face. Jennings does not present testable hypotheses, but, rather, a convincing and enjoyable series of case studies and anecdotes.

The Current and Future
State of Management

17

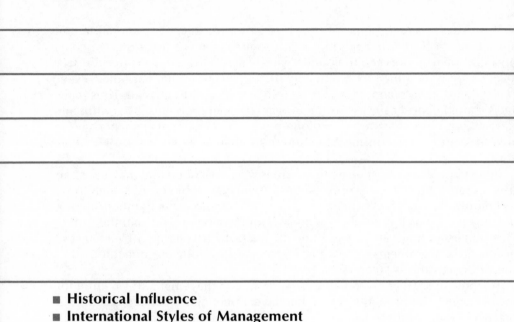

- ■ **Historical Influence**
- ■ **International Styles of Management**
- ■ **The Complex Role of the Manager**

Performance Objectives

1. To understand the historical changes in philosophy, technology, work-force mix, education, society, and organizational structures that have influenced the practice of management.

2. To be aware of how management styles differ throughout the world, and how these differences affect American managers who are sent on assignment to foreign countries.

3. To be able to discuss the complexities of the modern manager's role and the variations of it that will become more important in the future.

405

It is usually easy to pinpoint the causes of a major organizational failure after it has occurred. In fact, much of the management literature concerns organizational failures and their underlying causes. However, an after-the-fact analysis tends to come too late to help the organization that has failed, especially if its strategies and courses of action are difficult to change. Thus managers should periodically assess their organizational problems. By continually focusing on both short-term and long-term problems, management may be able to keep its position flexible enough to change when major difficulties arise.

In previous chapters, specific techniques were described that managers can use as short-term and long-term responses to major problems. Although these techniques are valuable, a manager also needs a more general understanding of management as it is currently practiced and will be practiced in the future. This understanding can provide him or her with a system to evaluate the organization's problems, especially in comparison with the difficulties that similar organizations face.

To come to such an overall understanding of management, it is helpful for the manager to know some factors that have influenced American managerial practices. Many of these factors, in addition to a variety of new ones, are still affecting the practice of management. Management education as well as management practice has felt the impact of changes that have taken place over the years. Because American managers now operate on a worldwide basis, today's manager also must be informed about international managerial styles.

This chapter examines the historical influences on the practice of management, international styles of management, and the complex role of the manager in the modern world.

Historical

Influence

Over the many years that people have been managing organizations, several types of changes have affected the practice of management. Even in the 200 years since the United States came into existence, shifts in ideas and practices have been significant. Some of the most important factors are the changes in managerial philosophy, technology, work-force composition, workers' education, social attitudes, and organizational structures.

Changes in Philosophy

The practice of management has been intimately related to basic concepts of property. Historically, the dominant viewpoint until approximately 1900 was that the owner of a company can consider employees as part of his company and therefore his property as long as they work there. This is not to say that the owner views the employees as slaves, only that his interest in them is based purely on their value as labor.

This dominant viewpoint indicated that a property owner is free to use his property in any way he desires. Hence the company owner's only obligation to employees is to pay them the going wage rate of the marketplace. Such subsidiary benefits as pension funds, vacation time, and other employee welfare measures are, in this view, inapplicable and inappropriate.

Likewise, the owner of the company does not need to worry about his customers as long as he does not visibly damage their health. If customers become dissatisfied, they can refuse to use the services of this company. The workings of the marketplace serve as the control mechanism, for the loss of a significant number of customers damages the reputation of the owner and diminishes the value of his property.

By 1900 a reaction against this philosophy had occurred. It was no longer considered reasonable for the owner of a company to view workers in the same way he or she views other property. Rather, by employing people, a person takes a certain responsibility for their welfare. He or she owes the workers those human rights dictated by society. The employer must provide the workers not only with decent wages but with fringe benefits, and he or she must not endanger their health through excessive hours of work per day or unsafe working conditions.

In the past 30 years, the concept of an owner's social responsibility has been extended to include the relationship between the company and the entire society. If a company endangers customers by producing unsafe goods, or damages the external environment by discharging harmful substances, it is not fulfilling its responsibilities to society. The federal government has established several commissions that regulate the activities of companies to guarantee that they will act responsibly. For example, the Consumer Product Safety Commission exists to insure that companies do not produce unsafe or harmful products. This commission can command a company to withdraw from the marketplace a product that is potentially or actually unsafe or harmful.

The shift in the concept of a company's responsibilities has increased managerial responsibilities as well, both to employees and to the public. Hence the role of management has changed considerably since 1900. At that time, the president of a major railroad company could proclaim openly that he had a divine right to manage as he saw fit, and he was responsible only to God (Harris 1939). Today management must fulfill many social obligations, and failure to do so can bring serious penalties under the law. Although such penalties are not always involved, they do serve as a control mechanism by sensitizing management to its obligations to employees and the general public. Thus management no longer has absolute control of its destiny and actions.

Technological Change

As the social climate has shifted, other changes have also affected the role of management. One major factor has been technological change. Since the turn of the twentieth century, the number of technological advances has been phenomenal. Cars, planes, laser beams, specialized medical equipment — these represent only a very small fraction of the technological developments that have transformed American society.

In recent years, technological changes have been introduced in many organizations at a very rapid rate. Such changes sometimes require management to redesign the organization (see chapter 7). The natural resistance of employees and managers to change is increased by an alteration in the design of the organization, for they frequently believe their jobs and status are being threatened. Hence it is critical for management, both currently and in the future, to find workable ways of introducing technological change. If management fails to make technological changes when needed, the organization's future may be jeopardized, for its competitors may use the new technology to create competitive and comparable products.

Probably the most important technological advance for the practice of management is the computer, which has revolutionized the processing of information. This industry, which is now the third largest in the United States (after the automotive and petroleum industries), increased in dollar value from $975 million to $15 billion in 1970 (McGuire 1974).

Computers enable managers to solve problems that in previous eras could be attacked only with difficulty, such as simulation and linear programming problems. However, although the computer has eased management's chores in some areas, it has created new ones in other areas. For one thing, the very availability of more information can become a burden. Many managers are overwhelmed by the large number of computer-based reports they must read. Another problem occurs when the manager is relatively unfamiliar with the operation of the computer. Being forced to rely on the help of computer specialists may restrict the use he or she can make of the computer's virtually unlimited potential.

Changes in the Work Force

For a number of years, management theorists focused their attention on industrial organizations. This was reasonable, for the management of large-scale industrial organizations was and still is crucial for the security of American society.

However, the management of nonindustrial organizations, such as hospitals and prisons, is also important. In recent years, management theorists have begun to pay more attention to nonindustrial organizations, which are increasing in number in the United States. As shown in Table 17.1, 43 percent of the employees on nonagricultural payrolls were working in the industrial or goods-producing sector of the economy in 1919. By 1975 the percentage was only 24.3.

Where are the workers who used to be in industry? Many of them have service and governmental jobs. As of 1975, 59.2 percent of the employees on nonagricultural payrolls were working in the service sector, which is the non-goods-producing sector of the economy, including hotels, barbershops, and recreational firms. In addition, 16.5 percent of nonagricultural workers in 1975 were employed in the governmental sector.

This movement of workers out of industrial jobs into service and governmental work has been accompanied by a decline in the number of blue-collar workers. In 1956 the number of white-collar workers surpassed the number of blue-collar workers for the first time in the history of the United States; by 1973 there were about 48 million white-collar workers and 28 million blue-collar workers (*Occupational Outlook Handbook* 1974–75, p. 18). In fact, the entire occupational structure of the United States has visibly changed. Although total employment is expected to rise by 24 percent between 1972 and 1985 (projected), the number of professional and technical workers should increase by 50 percent, and the number of clerical workers is expected to increase by 38 percent (see Figure 17.1).

One implication of these changes is that an aspiring manager would be

Table 17.1   Distribution of Employees on Nonagricultural Payrolls

	Goods-producing Sector	Service Sector	Governmental Sector	Total Workers
1919	43.0%	48.0%	9.0%	29,764,000
1975	24.3%	59.2%	16.5%	90,482,000

Employment and Earnings, 21, no. 9 (March 1975): 21.

Figure 17.1 Projected Percent Change in Employment, 1972–85

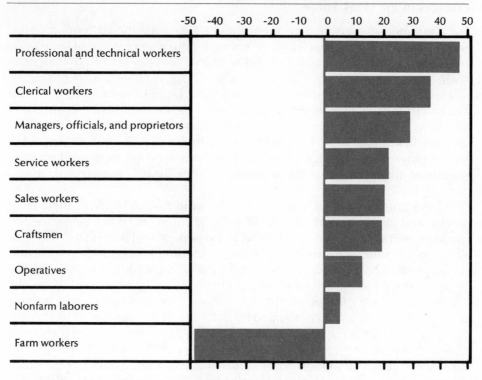

Occupational Outlook Handbook, 1974–75, p. 20.

wise to consider working in a nonindustrial area. If the current trends continue, only a small number of managers may be working in industrial organizations in the future. As these figures suggest, managers are and will be attempting to motivate a work force whose mix is quite different from that of earlier eras. Behavioral processes may become even more important than they are now, for the new work-force mix may force managers to develop novel techniques for motivating employees.

Education. As the job mix of American workers has changed in recent years, their educational level has increased significantly. In 1952 the average years of education for a worker in the civilian labor force was 10.9. By 1974 this figure had risen to 12.2 (*Manpower Report of the President* 1975, p. 264). Again, these figures indicate that the manager's job has become much more complex. He or she must now direct the work of subordinates who are better educated than their predecessors, and who thus must be led and motivated differently.

In general, today's workers tend to prefer challenging jobs (Ford 1969; Miner 1974). At the same time, they would like a great amount of independence in the fulfillment of their responsibilities. Given these preferences, management cannot expect to give orders and have them carried out without question or criticism. Rather, the modern manager must motivate members of this highly educated work force by a variety of techniques, most of which are more democratic than autocratic.

Social Change. Recent social changes, too, have both reflected and necessitated a more democratic attitude on the part of management. Groups whose role in the work force was formerly limited by traditional discrimination now have increasing access to a variety of jobs. Women, who at the turn of the century generally worked only before marriage, have become a major part of the labor force. In 1947, 31.8 percent of females 16 years of age and above were in the labor force; by 1975 this figure had risen to 45.7 percent (*Employment and Earnings*, 21, no. 9 (March 1975): 20).

Although women still tend to occupy low-level jobs in organizations, more and more of them are becoming managers. Fifteen years ago only a few determined women attempted to acquire a M.B.A. (master of business administration) degree; today, most of the major schools conduct M.B.A. programs in which at least 10 percent of the students are women. In some of the major M.B.A. programs, 25 percent or more of the students are women. The women's liberation movement has sparked this trend, and equal employment opportunity regulations have bolstered it. Under the Civil Rights Act of 1964, companies are forbidden to discriminate on the basis of race, religion, sex, or national origin in hiring or promoting. The influence of this act was dramatically illustrated when American Telephone & Telegraph Company (AT & T) settled a lawsuit in 1973 by agreeing to provide 50,000 higher paying jobs for women, 5,000 at the management level (see chapter 8).

Equal employment legislation also has been important for the advancement of racial and ethnic minorities, for they now have access to managerial positions that previously were unavailable. In the AT & T settlement in 1973, the company agreed to provide 5,000 higher paying jobs for minority-group men, 800 at the management level. As with women, only a small percentage of managers now have minority-group backgrounds, but this percentage should rise as the educational opportunities for minorities increase and traditional biases are overcome.

Changes in Organizational Structures

At the turn of the twentieth century, almost all organizations had a fairly rigid and centralized hierarchic structure. Since then, many new organizational structures have become important: the decentralized structure, project management and the matrix organization, and the conglomerate, for example (see chapter 3). In future years, the probability is high that more alternative structures will be developed to handle new problems and situations.

One direction new organizational structures might take would be in response to the growth of communications and the computer industry. According to one proposal developed by Richard P. Browne Associates of Maryland, paperwork could be telecommunicated to work centers outside of the central office. *Telecommunication* involves using electronic equipment such as videotape, television cameras, and telephones to carry work that needs to be completed to the work site from the central office. Hence managers and workers would not need to travel into the main office. If telecommunication were used on a large scale, managers might even be able to process a large part of their work in their own homes.

It is impossible to predict the specific kinds of organizational structures that will be developed to handle future problems. However, managers must guard against the excessive bureaucracy that frequently develops as an organization ages and grows in size and complexity. Organizations must be flexible and dynamic if they are to respond successfully to the pressures and problems they will encounter in the future.

During the past 15 years, a number of writers have argued that the organization of the future will be *free form* in that it will be flexible and responsive to changes. Fremont Kast and James Rosenzweig (1974) have predicted that the free-form organization will have some of these characteristics:

1. Organizations will be operating in a turbulent environment that requires continual change and adjustment.
2. Organizations will continue to expand their boundaries and domain. They will increase in size and complexity.
3. Organizations will continue to differentiate their activities, causing increased problems of integration and coordination.
4. Organizations will continue to have major problems in the accumulation and use of knowledge. Intellectual activities by all members of the organization will be stressed.
5. Greater emphasis will be placed on suggestion and persuasion rather than on coercion based on authoritarian power as the means for coordinating the activities of the participants and functions within the organization.
6. Participants at all levels in organizations will have greater influence.

7. Problems of coordination among organizations will be greater. New means for effective interorganizational coordination will be developed.
8. Computerized information-decision systems will have an increasing impact on organizations.
9. The number of professionals and scientists and their influence within organizations will increase. There will also be a decline in the proportion of independent professionals, with many more salaried professionals.
10. Goals of complex organizations will expand. Emphasis will be on satisfying a number of goals rather than maximizing any one.
11. Evaluation of organizational performance will be difficult. Many new administrative techniques will be developed for evaluating performance in all spheres of activity.

Although all these predictions may not prove correct, they serve as a basis for understanding some of the changes that will probably occur in the organizations of the future.

International Styles
of Management

In recent years, a number of American corporations have begun to operate on an international level. Today it is quite common for a corporation to own plants in several countries. If this trend continues, as it probably will, corporations may begin to lose their national identities as they extend their global activities.

An American manager operating in another country should be sensitive to the unique needs, customs, and values of the host nation. Some of these may not be immediately apparent, but it is important for the American manager to identify and respect them. Otherwise he or she may well encounter resistance that subsequently will be difficult to overcome, and may seriously hinder the organization.

In 1966 three social scientists published a research study that analyzed the management styles of 3,600 managers in 14 countries (Haire, Ghiselli, and Porter 1966). The purpose of this study was to see how managerial styles differed internationally. Such information obviously can be useful to the American executive who is operating in one or more of these countries, as many of them are quite different from the United States in important ways.

The three researchers focused on Theory X and Theory Y, which were discussed in chapter 9 (see pp. 221–222). Essentially, these theories represent autocratic management (Theory X) and democratic management (Theory Y). The managers in the study were asked to express their beliefs about four aspects of managerial leadership:

1. The average individual's capacity for leadership and initiative
2. The extent to which management should share information with subordinates
3. The degree to which subordinates should participate in management decisions
4. The degree to which management should use internal control measures such as punishment or promotion.

To compare the 14 countries, the researchers converted the raw data into standardized scores, which rank-ordered the countries on the various questionnaire items. The average standard score for all 3,600 managers was considered to be 0.00. Any score above 0.00 would be indicative of democratic values; a score below 0.00 would suggest an orientation toward autocratic values.

The analysis of the questionnaire data indicated the 14 countries clustered into five major groups on the basis of similar responses: the Nordic-European countries, the Latin-European countries, the developing countries, the Anglo-American countries, and Japan. The five clusters of countries differed significantly from one another, as shown in Table 17.2. For example, the Nordic-European managers were less positive than the other managers about the capacity of the average person to exercise leadership and initiative. However, the Nordic-European managers were about equal to the other managers in their feelings about the sharing of information and the value of employee participation (0.04 and –0.04).

An interesting finding in this study was that the managers from the Anglo-American countries were more democratic than autocratic in orientation. However, except for believing that the individual has an adequate capacity for leadership and initiative, the managers from the developing countries were more autocratic than democratic. These findings suggest that American managers will experience some culture shock when they become managers in developing countries, for their styles of management seem to be opposed to the one currently most common there.

By means of a complex statistical analysis, the researchers were also able to show about 30 percent of the differences in managerial attitudes can be explained by variations in culture. This relationship is statistically significant and quite large. The implication of this finding is that the American manager who

Table 17.2 Attitudes toward Management Practices of 3,600 Managers in 14 Countries

Positive mean values indicate attitudes that are more democratic than those of managers from other countries; negative values indicate attitudes that are more autocratic than those of managers from other countries.

	Individual's Capacity for Leadership and Initiative	Advisability of Sharing Information and Objectives	Value of Employee Participation	Desirability of Internal Control (e.g., Promotion or Punishment)
Nordic-European countries (Denmark, Germany, Norway, Sweden)	−0.24	0.04	−0.04	0.16
Latin-European countries (Belgium, France, Italy, Spain)	−0.25	0.22	0.09	0.03
Anglo-American countries (England, United States)	0.45	0.36	−0.02	−0.16
Developing countries (Argentina, Chile, India)	0.21	−0.59	−0.21	−0.18
Japan	0.39	0.04	0.44	0.04

From Mason Haire et al., *Managerial Thinking: An International Study*, p. 28. Copyright © 1966 by John Wiley & Sons, Inc. Reprinted by permission.

works outside of the United States should be very sensitive to cultural differences and attempt to adapt to the distinctive characteristics of the country in which he or she works. Many large companies conduct formal training programs for their executives to sensitize them to the problems they will face when they are sent to foreign countries.

The Complex Role
of the Manager

The managerial role has become very complex in recent years. This section describes some variations of the managerial role that are likely to become important in the future.

The Polyspecialist

Because of the complexity now associated with the managerial role, it has become more like a group of roles than a single one. The old view of a manager as a generalist, more concerned with making decisions than in becoming an expert in any specialized area, is no longer valid. Today, the successful manager must be very knowledgeable in several areas: organizational behavior, computer science, and finance, for example. Modern management education encourages this kind of background. In addition, managers frequently rotate through a variety of positions in an organization in order to increase their understanding of all its operations.

Thus it no longer seems appropriate to classify a manager as a generalist. Rather, he or she is a polyspecialist, knowledgeable in several areas. Although the manager obviously will be stronger in some areas than others, he or she must not be completely ignorant in any area.

Manager Pairs

One possibility that might materialize in the future has arisen in direct response to the problems managers face. According to Henry Mintzberg (1973 and 1975), the manager is constantly under pressure, so he or she can devote only limited attention to any specific problem. In Mintzberg's study, the managers devoted an average of nine minutes to each specific problem they faced. To compensate for this lack of time, a manager usually relies on the "instant" information he or she can obtain through personal conversations and contacts.

Since managers are not able to devote much time to researching the details of their problems, Mintzberg suggests they work in pairs. Specifically, a manager would work with a specialist who would analyze problems for him or her. In effect, the specialist would act as an organizational doctor, digging more deeply into the problems his or her partner diagnoses. The two individuals would need to work together over a period of years, since the relationship would require considerable mutual trust and understanding.

Although organizations have not yet implemented this system on a wide-scale basis, it seems likely to be a good way to make the role of the manager in an organization easier and more effective. It could help to eliminate some of the problems that have arisen from the complexity of the managerial job.

Specialized Managers for Specialized Jobs

As the structure of our economy has shifted away from industrial organizations toward service and governmental organizations, many new specialized managerial opportunities have developed. Most hospitals are now run by administrators who are not doctors, but were trained in schools of hospital administration. Professional managers also have a role to play in educational institutions and government agencies.

If an individual aspires to be a manager in a nontraditional setting, he or she might specialize in school so as to be eligible for positions that require particular qualifications. UCLA and Indiana conduct a graduate program in the management of the arts; several universities such as Cornell and Minnesota provide graduate degrees in industrial relations; and some universities now award advanced degrees in the management of specialized institutions such as prisons and churches.

Another type of specialist who may arise is the *transformation agent,* whose basic function would be to manage the vast amount of information generated by the computer (McGuire 1974). According to Mintzberg (1973 and 1975), managers frequently are overwhelmed by the multitude of reports the computer generates, supposedly to help them in their work. However, the opposite seems to occur, for the managers tend to disregard these reports, at least in part because they do not have the time to read or decipher them. One of the chief roles of the transformation agent would be to decipher and simplify these reports so they would be useful for the practicing manager.

Given the expanded scope of American business, it is also possible for an individual to become an international manager. Today it is quite common for an American manager to spend at least part of his or her career directing a corporation's activity abroad. In fact, the demand for this type of manager is so great that several schools of management and business now offer specialized programs in international subjects. Many of these programs require that the student spend an internship in a foreign country before he or she is granted a M.B.A. degree.

Education

The education of managers has been the subject of many studies over the years. From 1900 until the late 1950s, management education was very applied: Students read cases, which they analyzed and attempted to solve. These schools only emphasized the field of economics. It was not until around 1960 that other disciplines, such as operations research and behavioral science, were introduced in the management curriculum on a large scale.

However, many of the professors hired by graduate schools of management and business around 1960 tended to be interested only in their own narrow areas of expertise, such as operations research and behavioral science. Some disdained the study of the ordinary, day-to-day business and managerial problems that organizations constantly face. Hence the usefulness of their academic courses for actual managers and business operations began to be questioned (McGuire 1974). In response to the criticisms of this purely theoretical approach, schools of management are again stressing the applied aspects of management. Some schools now sponsor a 6-credit practicum for M.B.A. students. To gain this credit, the student must complete a large-scale and applied study in an organization, jointly directed by one of his or her professors and an executive of the organization.

In future years, it seems likely that management education will become somewhat more applied than it is now, narrowing the gap between management schools and managers. There probably will be no return to purely applied studies in most management schools. In short, it seems that management education has progressed from pure application through pure theory to a balanced approach that emphasizes both theory and application.

Summary

Several historical influences have significantly affected the practice of management. Until 1900, the owner of a company basically was free of any obligation except the payment of the going wage rate to his employees. Since then, the manager's obligation to his or her employees has been extended to include such subsidiary benefits as pension funds, vacation time, and other employee welfare measures. Similarly, the manager at the turn of the century had no major obligations to customers: If they did not like his or her services or product, they could go elsewhere. Today, the manager has obligations that extend to the entire society. If a company manufactures unsafe goods, or pollutes the environment, it can be punished.

Many technological changes also have affected the practices of management. The computer has revolutionized the way organizations process information. Similarly, the dramatically changed composition of the work force has become a major determinant of managerial practices: The American worker is highly educated, and he or she is more likely to work in a white-collar than a blue-collar job. Some social changes have likewise become important, including the increased participation of women in the labor force, and the entrance of both women and minority-group members into managerial positions throughout American society. All of these changes suggest that management must devise new organizational structures, such as the flexible "free-form" organization, to handle the new problems that will become important in future years.

The analysis of international management styles suggests that American managers may experience difficulty when they work in other countries. For example, American managers tend to have a democratic orientation toward subordinates, but managers in developing countries treat their employees more autocratically. This conflict between autocratic and democratic orientations will have to be resolved by any manager sent to work in a developing country.

Finally, the role of the modern manager has become extremely difficult and complex. At the same time, this complexity has helped to expand the kinds of opportunities available to an individual who wants to be a manager. A manager can be a polyspecialist, a member of a management pair, a specialist in a particular area such as hospital administration, a transformation agent, or a member of an international team, to name only a few. As the complexity of the managerial role continues to increase in the future, the variety of managerial opportunities probably will increase as well.

Discussion Questions

1. Describe the United States as you expect it to be in the year 2050. What kinds of training and education will be appropriate for the individual who wants to become a manager? Why?

2. What is a "free-form" organization? Have you ever worked in an organization that closely resembles a free-form organization? If you have, how would you compare it to more traditional organizations in terms of effectiveness?

3. Mintzberg has advanced the concept of paired managers. That is, a manager would work closely with a specialist who would analyze problems from the manager's perspective. Is this concept practical? Why or why not?

4. Several kinds of managers were described in this chapter, such as the transformation agent and the polyspecialist. What other roles or kinds of managers do you know of that have developed in recent years? What other roles might you expect to see in the future?

5. Women and minorities are entering managerial positions in increasing numbers, as this chapter indicates. Do you feel this trend will create any problems? Why or why not? What are some problems that might occur?

6. Haire, Ghiselli, and Porter's study suggests that American managers are more democratic toward their subordinates than managers in developing countries. How do you think employees in these countries will react when American managers become their superiors? Why do you feel this way?

Suggested Readings

Dunnette, Marvin (ed.). *Work and Nonwork in the Year 2001.* Monterey, Calif.: Brooks/Cole, 1973, 212 pages, paperback.
> *These predictions of the future society are put forth by social scientists. The chapters by Triandis and Bond are particularly rewarding.*

Toffler, Alvin. *Future Shock.* New York: Bantam Books, 1970, 561 pages, paperback.
> *Toffler makes several fascinating predictions about the future. Following Bennis's ideas, he predicts that the predominant organizational structure will be "adhocracy," a temporary grouping of individuals assigned to a project until it is completed, after which the organization uncouples.*

Walton, Clarence. *Corporate Social Responsibilities.* Belmont, Calif.: Wadsworth, 1967, 177 pages, paperback.
> *Walton provides a succinct overview of corporate social responsibility, and describes its historical foundations.*

VI EXPERIENTIAL EXERCISES

Coaching and Goal-Setting

Introduction

The motivation to work may be thought of as the interaction between three areas: (1) the individual as a human resource, (2) the requirements of his particular job, (3) the character of the work climate. The degree to which the individual is effective and derives satisfaction in his professional assignment depends upon the extent to which these three fit together harmoniously.

Let us examine briefly some of the factors that might be relevant in each of these three areas:

1. *The Individual as a Human Resource*   This would include his abilities, skills, experience, education, interests, interpersonal skills, attitudes, temperament, goals, and the broad area of psychological needs such as needs for achievement, status, recognition, acceptance by others, influence, and control. From these and many other factors, the individual has the potential of high performance on certain types of job requirements.
2. *The Nature of the Job and Its Specific Requirements*   It is assumed there is a range of different types of jobs for which an individual is suited, depending upon his resources. However, most of us have some awareness of the nature of work for which we think we are most suited and which "turns us on" to perform with a high degree of motivation and involvement.
3. *The Work Climate*   This can be thought of as, first, relationships between people—between you and your boss, you and your peers, or you and your subordinates. The climate has certain values and norms that characterize the atmosphere and either promote or hinder your effectiveness as an individual.

The Manager as a Coach

One of the roles of the supervisor-manager recently being emphasized is that of coach to his employees. This is of value because it helps develop the full potential of people and assures the organization that it is fully aware of its human assets; from this knowledge decisions can be made for selection, placement, assignments, rotation, career planning, promotion, and so on.

This exercise is designed to permit you to practice being both employee and coach as the roles relate to motivation and goal setting. A similar exercise has been used in industrial supervisory training in which trainees complete a questionnaire focused upon the three areas discussed in the introduction above.

Questionnaire

Part I: You as a Resource (What I bring to the job)

In answering this question, think in terms of your human resources as described in the introductory section on the previous page. Use extra sheets of paper where necessary, since little room is provided here.

1. What do you regard as some of your major strengths: abilities, work habits, needs, goals, temperament, etc. (Note: Do not try to "sell" yourself. Just state honestly how you see yourself.)

Part II: Application of Your Resources

The first question gives you an opportunity to think of your resources, which might include many assets you do not use too frequently. Now think specifically in terms of how you perform in different areas. (You do not have to confine your answers to a work situation—school, recreation, work, church, etc., are fine.)

1. What are some things you do well and would like to do more of? Why?

2. What are things you do not do so well, but would like to do better? Why?

3. What are things you have done and would prefer not to do more of? Why?

4. What are some things you have not done, but would like to do?

5. Can you recall something you have done in the past couple of years that you felt was innovative?

6. What new skill would you like to acquire in the year ahead?

7. List three brief statements that characterize you which you would like to improve or reinforce.

8. List three brief statements that characterize you which you would like to minimize or reduce.

9. What I want most out of my job is:

10. What I would like to achieve in the next five to ten years is:

Part III: The Work Climate

1. The type of relationship I want with my boss which can provide me the support I need to achieve my needs and goals is:

2. The type of work climate in which I will be most effective is:

3. Three things I do that are especially helpful for other people are:

4. Three things I would like to do better in order to be more helpful to others are:

423

Notes

1. This exercise is designed to give you the opportunity to sample an aspect of the broad area of goal setting, coaching. Obviously the times provided for this exercise are unrealistic, and the individual will probably prefer to select some aspect of the questionnaire and concentrate on it. Complete coverage is not the intent here.
2. *If you prefer to discuss questions on the topic of resources and goals not presented here, please feel free to do so.*

Role Playing: The Promotion Interview

(Students are asked not to read the case materials before participating in the laboratory exercise.)

A. Preparation for role playing.
   1. The instructor will select two players and give them their assignments at least a day ahead of time.
   2. One person is to play the role of Trudy Pearce and should study carefully "Background Information" and become thoroughly acquainted with "Special Instructions for Trudy Pearce".
   3. The other is to play the role of Jim Smith and should study carefully the "Background Information" and become thoroughly acquainted with "Special Instructions for Jim Smith".

B. Role-playing procedure.
   1. The instructor will read the "Background Information" aloud to the class, and copy the schedule of jobs held by Smith on the chalkboard.
   2. All persons not assigned a role are to act as observers.
   3. The instructor will introduce Trudy Pearce to the class and seat her at desk in front of class, indicate that Pearce has an appointment with Jim Smith, and signal Smith to arrive for his appointment with Pearce.
   4. The interview is then to be allowed to proceed to a solution or conclusion as in a real-life situation.

C. Discussion analysis with observers. (Pearce and Smith may enter discussion to evaluate correctness of conclusions reached.)
   1. Determine degree to which Pearce established a mutual interest.
   2. What use did Pearce make of various types of questions?
   3. List feelings expressed by Smith.
   4. Which feeling areas were thoroughly explored? Which not?
   5. Obtain opinions on degree to which Pearce understood Smith and vice versa.
   6. List cues which indicate there was failure to communicate.
   7. Did Pearce change as a result of the interview or was she justified in maintaining her original estimation? List reasons.
   8. How was Smith's attitude changed by the interview?

D. Repeat role playing of interview if time permits.
   1. The class is to divide into groups of three.
   2. The instructor will assign the role of Pearce to one member of each group, the role of Smith to a second member, and ask the third member to act as group leader and supervise the role playing.

3. Role playing should be terminated 10 minutes before end of the class period.
4. Group leaders will hold discussion with role players and evaluate progress made.

E. Materials for "Promotion Interview."

Background Information

The American Consolidated Chemical Company has chemical plants located in various sections of the country. The main plant is in Detroit. Important branches are at Houston; St. Louis; St. Paul; and Cleveland. All the products are manufactured in Detroit, but each of the branches specializes in making chemicals that either utilize local raw material available in the locality or have a concentration of outlets. Thus the Cleveland plant manufactures products needed in the Cleveland area, and the Houston plant manufactures products which utilize petroleum derivatives.

Since the Detroit plant makes all the products, an experienced person can be moved from Detroit to any of the other plants. When a vacancy opens up in a particular department in Detroit, it is possible to fill the vacancy by choosing someone local or by bringing in an employee from a branch that produces the product corresponding to the one made by a particular department in Detroit. Thus there has been a great deal of movement within the organization, and since the company has been expanding, opportunities for promotion have been good. Generally speaking, morale has been quite satisfactory.

Trudy Pearce is the assistant to the Works Manager of the Detroit plant. One of her duties is to keep track of the college recruits and plan their development. The company hires several college recruits each year and from these selects the employees for promotion and development in higher management positions. Pearce is about to have an interview with James Smith, a college graduate who was brought into the company 10 years ago. The following schedule shows the positions which Smith has held during his 10 years with the company.

Detroit	Dept. A	1 year	Regular employee
St. Paul	Depts. A, B, C	2 years	Regular employee
Detroit	Dept. A	1 year	Foreman
St. Louis	Depts. B, F	2 years	Foreman
Cleveland	Depts. D, E	1½ years	Foreman
Houston	Dept. G	1½ years	Foreman
Detroit	Dept. H	1 year	Foreman

Role Instructions for Trudy Pearce

Ever since *Jim Smith* graduated from college and joined the company as a college recruit ten years ago you have kept an eye on him. During his first year in the company you were impressed by his technical ability and even more by his leadership. After he'd had one year in Department A you sent him to St. Paul where they needed an employee with his training. He made a good showing and worked in Departments A, B, and C. After two years you brought him back to Detroit and made him a foreman in Department A. He did very well on this job, so you considered making some long-range plans for him. Here was a man you thought you could groom for an executive position. This meant giving him experience with all operations in all plants. To do this with the greatest ease you decided to make him a foreman in each of the eight departments for a short period of time and to get him assignments in each of the branches.

During the past two years you have had some disturbing reports. Jim didn't impress *Bill Jones*, the department head at Houston, who reported that he had ideas but was always on the defensive. Since his return to Detroit he has shown a lack of job interest, and the employees who work for him don't back him up the way they used to. You feel you have made quite a mistake in this man and that he has let you down after you've given him good build-ups with various department heads. Maybe the confidence you have shown in him and the praise you have given him during the several progress interviews have gone to his head. If so, he hasn't the stature it takes to make the top grade. Therefore, you have abandoned your plans of moving him up to superintendent at St. Paul (a two-step promotion) and think it may be best to send him to Houston where there is a job as general foreman in Department C. (Note that this is not the department in which Jones is the head). This won't mean much of a promotion because you have moved his pay up as high as you could while he was a sort of roving foreman. However, you feel that he has earned some promotion even if he hasn't lived up to your expectations. This St. Paul position is still open, but unless you are convinced to the contrary he doesn't seem up to it.

Of course, it's possible that Jim is having marital trouble. At a recent company party you found his wife to be quite dissatisfied and unhappy. Maybe she is giving Jim a rough time.

While you are waiting for Jim to arrive you have his folder in front of you showing the positions he has held.

Role Instructions for Jim Smith

You have been with the American Consolidated Chemical Company for ten years now. You joined the company on graduating from college with a major in chemistry. At the time you joined the company you were interviewed by *Trudy Pearce,* and were told that a good employee could get ahead in the company. On the strength of the position you married your college sweet-heart and moved to Detroit. You preferred the Houston and St. Paul branches but Pearce thought Detroit was the place to start. So you took your chance along with other college recruits. Because you were a good student in college and were active in college affairs, you had reason to believe you possessed leadership ability.

During your first few years you thought you were getting some place. You got moved to Minnesota and felt Pearce was doing you a favor by sending you there. After the first year you bought a home and got started on a family. During two years in Minnesota you gained considerable experience in Departments A, B, and C. Then you were offered a foremanship in Detroit, and since this meant a promotion and you had a second child on the way, you decided to return to Detroit. When you came to Detroit Pearce again saw you and told you how pleased she was with your progress.

Since this time however, you have been given a royal run-around. They tell you they like your work, but all you get are a lot of lateral transfers. You have been foreman in practically every department and have been moved from one branch to another. Other people that came to the company, even after you joined, have been made general foremen. They stick in a given department and are working up while you get moved from place to place. Although the company pays for your moves, both you and your wife want to settle down and have a permanent home for your children. Why can't people be honest with you? First they tell you what a good job you are doing and then the next thing they do is get rid of you. Take for example *Bill Jones,* the department head at Houston. He acted as if you had done him a favor to go there, but you can tell he isn't sincere. Since you've gotten to know him you can see through him. From little remarks he has dropped you know he's been saying some nasty things about you to the home office. It's obvious that the Houston man is incompetent, and you feel he got rid of you because he considered you a threat to his job.

Your wife realizes that you are unhappy. She has told you she is willing to live on less just to get you out of the company. You know you could hold a superintendent's job, such as *George Wilson* got, who joined the company when you did, and he was just an average student in college. As a matter of fact, if the company were on the ball they should realize that you have the ability to be a department head if George is superintendent material.

Pearce has asked you to come up and see her. You are a bit nervous about this interview because the news may not be good. You've felt her to be less friendly lately and have no desire to listen to any smooth manipulations. Last night you and your wife had a good talk about things, and she's willing that you should look around for another job. Certainly you've reached the end of your patience, and you're fed up with any more of her attempts to move you around just because someone is jealous of your ideas.

Appendix: The Case Observational Method

The Case Observational Method is a means by which an entire class can be involved in a small-group discussion of a case or critical incident. A five-member group chosen from the class carries out the actual discussion; the rest of the class observes and evaluates the group's performance. In this fashion, a large class can benefit from the type of analysis and give-and-take that ordinarily is possible only in small discussion sections.

To discuss a case, five members of the group sit in front of the class in a semicircle and actually carry on the discussion. (If the class is very large or the acoustics in the classroom are very poor, the group can sit in the middle of the class.) While the group is discussing the assigned critical incidents or cases, the other class members are judging its performance in terms of the criteria listed in Table 1 and Figure 1, which are explained below. Class members who

---

Table 1   A Sample Scoring for Individuals

All criteria are judged in terms of a 1 (very poor) to 9 (very good) scale, except for items 7 and 8. Three class members are assigned to each criterion. The median rather than the mean is used in the scoring.

	Thomas	Davis	Jones	Adams	Smith
1 Consideration	2	6	6	3	2
2 Task leadership	7	5	5	8	2
3 Disruption (1 = high, 9 = low)	6	1	2	8	2
4 Hiring (1 = no)	3	7	7	2	1
5 Promotion (1 = no)	2	5	5	2	1
6 Logic	1	6	6	1	2
7 Frequency of remarks	30	15	19	35	5
8 Duration of remarks (in seconds)	380	220	240	560	90

From Martin J. Gannon, "The Case Observational Method: A New Training Technique." Reproduced by special permission from the September 1970 *Training and Development Journal.* Copyright 1970 by the American Society for Training and Development, Inc.

Figure 1   A Sample Scoring for Group Characteristics

Each criterion is judged in terms of a 1 (very poor) to 9 (very good) scale. Class members judge cohesion and productivity in terms of both the overall discussion and each case or critical incident. The median rather than the mean is used in the scoring.

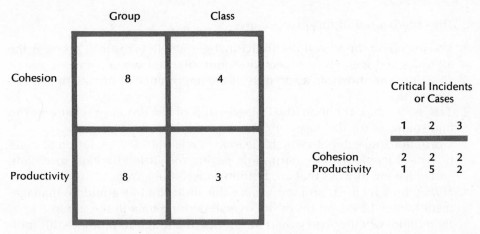

	Group	Class
Cohesion	8	4
Productivity	8	3

	Critical Incidents or Cases		
	1	2	3
Cohesion	2	2	2
Productivity	1	5	2

From Martin J. Gannon, "The Case Observational Method: A New Training Technique." Reproduced by special permission from the September 1970 *Training and Development Journal.* Copyright 1970 by the American Society for Training and Development, Inc.

are not included in the five-person group do not participate in the discussion of the critical incidents or cases, nor does the professor. However, everyone participates in the feedback discussion that takes place immediately after the group has disbanded.

Individual
Scores

Before the discussion starts, specific instructions and role assignments need to be given. An odd number of class members is assigned to each of the criteria shown in Table 1 and Figure 1. Usually three class members judge the performance of the individuals in the group on each criterion on a scale ranging from 1 (very poor) to 9 (very good). The median of these scores (not the mean) for each criterion is written on the blackboard immediately after the discussion has ended. For example, if three class members feel that Adams should be rated 1, 3, and 8 in terms of consideration, his score in this regard is 3, not 4 (see Table 1).

The criteria used in this exercise are:

1. *Consideration:* how well the individual genuinely takes into account the attitudes and feelings of others; does not interrupt when someone else is speaking; and shows an awareness of the importance of human needs and aspirations.
2. *Task leadership:* the individual's leadership of the group in its attempt to find solutions for the cases or critical incidents under discussion.
3. *Disruption:* the extent to which the individual inhibits the solution of cases or critical incidents by interrupting, paying too little attention to details, and behaving in ways that are bothersome to the group.
4. *Hiring:* how inclined you are to hire this individual as a middle management trainee based on his or her overall performance in the group.
5. *Promotion:* whether you would be confident enough to promote this individual, once hired, to a responsible middle management position based on his performance in the group.
6. *Logic:* how logical the individual is in examining factors that should be taken into consideration if the case or critical incident is to be solved optimally.
7. *Frequency of remarks:* the number of remarks the individual makes during the discussion.
8. *Duration of remarks:* the total time (in seconds) the individual speaks during the discussion period.

Scoring

for the Group

The eight criteria are used to measure how effectively each individual takes part in the group. To measure the group's characteristics as a whole, three class members are assigned to evaluate the overall productivity of the group, and another three judge its cohesion in terms of the 9-point scale. *Cohesion* refers to how well the group works smoothly together as a team. *Productivity* refers to whether the group solved the cases or critical incidents in an optimal manner by examining alternatives and then selecting the one that appeared best. After the group disbands, its members are also asked to assess its productivity and cohesion on the 9-point scale so a comparison of the group's and class's feelings in this regard can be compared. Finally, three class members evaluate the group's productivity for each case or critical incident to compare its effectiveness at different times; they also evaluate cohesion for each case or critical incident.

The Case Observational Method thus uses 12 criteria altogether, each requiring separate measurement by at least 3 class members. The theoretical class size is consequently 36, with 3 class members assigned to each of the 12 criteria. However, criteria can be dropped if the class is too small, or each class member can be assigned 2 or 3 criteria. As indicated above, it is important that the number of class members assigned to a particular criterion always be odd, for the ratings are medians rather than means or averages.

A final measurement that can easily be taken is to ask each member of the group to select the individual he or she believes is the task leader. These selections can then be placed on the blackboard in order to determine the opinions of the group members on this matter.

GLOSSARY

Age-salary ratio. The relationship between an individual's age and the salary he or she receives.

Analysis of performance. The last phase of *decision making;* a manager's assessment, once a decision is made, of how well organizational members, organizational subsystems, and the entire organization are functioning as a result.

Aptitude. A potential talent for a particular type of work.

Assessment centers. Workshops in some large companies for new managerial trainees, designed to assess a candidate's managerial potential and counsel him or her on ways to become successful in the organization. Typically, candidates are put through a series of simulated exercises, group discussion sessions, and extended psychological interviews for a few days. Their performance is normally evaluated by both psychologists and successful *line* managers in the organization.

Assets. The total property owned by an organization.

Attitude. A predisposition to respond to a certain type of stimulus.

Attitude survey. A set of questionnaires or interviews an organization uses, usually periodically, to pinpoint problems and dissatisfactions among employees.

Balance sheet. A detailed list of an organization's *assets* and *liabilities.*

Barnard's unit concept. Chester Barnard's idea that an organization should be composed of small units, each consisting of 10 or fewer members.

Barometric indicators. Historical and current economic data used to predict future trends of business activity; a *forecasting* method of *planning.*

Behavioral processes. *Motivation, leadership, group behavior,* and *communication—* the interactions between and among organizational members that enable the organization to move toward its goals. One of the four *dimensions of management.*

Behavior modification. Increasing desired patterns of behavior, or decreasing undesirable behavior, by using scientifically determined rewards or punishments.

Bounded discretion. The area within which managers are free to make decisions, limited by social *norms, rules,* and *policies* within the organization; legal restrictions; and moral and ethical norms.

Break-even analysis. A decision-making technique based on determining the point at which the income a product brings in equals the cost of producing it, at varying prices and levels of demand.

Bridge. In Henri Fayol's theory, the path by which someone in one part of a *hierarchy* can communicate with his or her equals in other sections without going through supervisors.

Budget. An allocation of specific amounts of money to various departments or groups for the purpose of controlling expenditures and monitoring activities.

Bureaucracy. A *hierarchical* organization characterized by specialized functions, adherence to fixed *rules*, impersonality, career orientation, separation of *line* and *staff*, record keeping, and rigid lines of authority.

Capital. The accumulated goods an organization possesses.

Capital budgeting. A *decision-making* technique in which a manager evaluates the relative attractiveness of various projects in which an initial lump payment generates a stream of earnings over a future period.

Capitalism. An economic system of private ownership of *capital* with competition in a free marketplace determining price, supply, and demand.

Centralization. The extent to which responsibility and authority in an organization are vested in a core executive group or office. (Contrast *decentralization*.)

Classical management. The first identifiable modern school of management. It includes *scientific management, functionalism,* and *bureaucracy*.

Closed system. A set of processes that operate in a recurring cycle and in which *feedback* provides a self-correcting mechanism. (Contrast *open system*.)

Cognitive dissonance. An uncomfortable feeling that arises when an individual perceives a conflict between two of his or her ideas or cognitions, leading the person to abandon one of the ideas.

Committee, standing. A permanent group of organizational members who meet periodically providing the organization with a stable structure by which routine or recurring activities can be handled efficiently.

Committee, temporary or ad hoc. A temporary group of organizational members formed to complete a particular objective, after which it disbands. (See *task force*.)

Communication. An exchange of information; one of an organization's *behavioral processes*. The intrapersonal perspective stresses communication within one person, such as neurological processes; the interpersonal perspective focuses on the interactions among individuals and within groups; the organizational perspective looks at the flow of information through various formal or informal organizational channels; and the technical perspective centers on the design and operation of *management information systems*.

Communication, horizontal. Exchange of information between peers or individuals at the same organizational levels; it tends to predominate at the lower levels in the organization.

Communication, one-way. A process by which one individual sends a message to another individual, with no response or *feedback*.

Communication, two-way. An exchange of information between two individuals.

Communication, vertical. Transmission of information between individuals at different organizational levels; predominant at higher organizational levels.

Communication network. An arrangement by which a small number of individuals transmit information only in a set and defined pattern for the purpose of solving a problem. Types include the wheel, circle, chain, and completely connected.

Company union. A workers' organization existing only within one company, not affiliated with any other union, and generally under the control of management.

Conference approach. A group-discussion session similar to *T-groups,* focused on the solution of a specific organizational problem. (See *organization development.*)

Conglomerate. An organization comprising two or more companies that produce unrelated products.

Consideration. One of the two key dimensions of leader behavior, involving being supportive of subordinates and constructing a friendly organizational climate.

Consultative. Sharing opinions with no obligation to act on them. (Contrast *directive.*)

Contingency theory of leadership. Fred Fiedler's theory that a *task-oriented* style of *leadership* is successful when the environment or situation is either very uncertain or very certain, and a *considerate* style is successful under moderate certainty.

Contingency theory of management. An approach that assumes the type of management that is successful depends on such factors as the kind of *technology* used to create the final product or service and the degree of external environmental uncertainty the organization faces.

Control. The monitoring of plans and the pinpointing of significant deviations from them. In some situations, the control system contains an action device that automatically corrects these deviations; in others, managers must determine what corrective action is appropriate. Both organizational subsystems and organization members must be controlled for plans to be accomplished.

Control, feedback. Diagnosis of an error after it has occurred.

Control, feedforward. Diagnosis of an error before it has occurred.

Co-optation. A method an organization uses to reduce the uncertainty it faces: Management attempts to influence its external environment by seeking out representatives from the community to become members of the organization.

Coordination. The development of cooperative relationships between individuals and groups whose work overlaps.

Cosmopolitan leaders. Managers who move from organization to organization throughout their careers and have visibility outside the organization or community.

Creative group. An informal committee formed to generate a large number of ideas for a nonroutine and distinctive problem. (See *problem-solving group.*)

Critical path. The path in a *PERT* network that requires the longest time to complete, and which thus determines the project's completion time.

Decentralization. The extent to which responsibility and authority are delegated to lower levels in the organization. (Contrast *centralization.*)

Decision making. A problem-solving activity that comes into play when the individual realizes that the gap between what is and what should be is too great. It involves recognizing a problem exists, searching for alternative solutions, evaluating these solutions, and selecting and implementing a solution.

Decision tree. A *decision-making* technique appropriate when a *series* of decisions must be made but their outcomes are unknown. (See *expected value.*)

Delphi technique. A *forecasting* technique in which the organization polls at periodic intervals a small number of experts who make predictions about long-run technological and market changes that eventually will affect the organization. (See *nominal group technique*.)

Departmentation.   Division or grouping of organizational jobs and subunits on the basis of a common characteristic, such as product or purpose, function or specialization, place or clientele.

Descriptive.   Based on actual practice rather than theory or ideals; as, a descriptive *model* of *decision making*. (Contrast *normative*.)

Deterministic.   Based on exact, known quantities; as, a deterministic *model* of *decision making*. (See *probabilistic*.)

Dimensions of management.   Four areas within which managerial activities take place: *organization design, planning* and *control, behavioral processes,* and *decision making*.

Directive.   Involving orders that are to be followed. (Contrast *consultative*.)

Econometric model.   A complex computer simulation of the entire economy used to *forecast* future levels of economic activity.

Economic man.   A *normative* model of *decision making*, developed by Adam Smith, in which the manager is assumed to understand all the alternatives he can pursue to accomplish particular goals, from which he chooses the most desirable alternative. (See *satisficing*.)

Entrepreneur.   An individual who starts a new enterprise consisting of eight or more employees. According to Joseph Schumpeter, one who combines given resources so as to radically alter the consumption and production patterns of a society.

EOQ (Economic order quantity) model.   An inventory *decision-making* method used to establish a formula for answering two questions: When should supplies be ordered, and in what quantity?

Equity theory.   A *motivational* theory that assumes an individual must see a relationship between the rewards he or she obtains (outcomes) and the amount of work he or she performs (inputs).

Expectancy theory.   A theory that assumes an individual's *motivation* is a function of two expectancies: that effort will result in successful performance, and that successful performance will lead to desired outcomes.

Expected value.   A *decision-making* technique that indicates probable profit by multiplying possible future outcomes and the probabilities of their occurrence, and summing the totals.

Fast track.   A term for the path taken by certain individuals who are picked for rapid advancement while the remainder of the managerial workforce is essentially bypassed.

Federal decentralization.   A combination of *departmentation* by product and by function, in which operating units that are largely self-contained draw personnel from functional departments as needed.

Feedback.   Information on the outcome of an action or process.

First level.   The lowest level in an organization.

Fixed costs.   Expenses that are unaffected by changes in volume of business, such as rent. (Contrast *variable costs*.)

Flexitime.   A way of scheduling work under which employees must be present during a "core" period, but can begin work any time before the core period; their starting time determines their quitting time.

Forecasting. *Planning* focused on the prediction of future occurrences that may affect the organization. Forecasts can be long-range, short-range, or rolling (integrating long- and short-range).

Functional foremanship. In *scientific management,* a system whereby each aspect of an employee's job is examined by a specialized foreman. The worker thus reports to several functional foremen.

Functionalism. An approach to management that focuses on the *functions of management.*

Functions of management. According to Fayol and other writers in the *classical management* school, the specific activities that a manager must perform (such as *planning*) to be successful.

Grapevine. An informal system of communication in an organization.

Group behavior. Interactions within and among *work groups;* one of the *behavioral processes* in an organization.

Hawthorne effect. The change in workers' behavior that automatically occurs when they are studied.

Hierarchy. The set of levels of power in an organization that makes some individuals subordinate to others in authority, earnings, and/or status.

Horizontal integration. A company's attempt to dominate a market at one particular stage of the production process by monopolizing resources at that stage. (Contrast *vertical integration.*)

Human relations. A school of management whose basic proposition is that the attitudes individuals develop in informal groups within an organization critically influence their commitment and level of productivity.

Human resource accounting system. A means of assessing an organization's employees in terms of replacement costs, selection costs, and the like.

Hygiene factors. In *two-factor theory,* extrinsic sources of *motivation,* which do not relate directly to the nature of the work (for example, working conditions), and which affect rates of absenteeism and turnover.

Income statement. A detailed list of an organization's sources of revenues and expenses for a given year.

Integrator. An employee who is neither *line* nor *staff,* but has informal power to integrate the efforts of overlapping *work groups* or units.

Intervention. The process in *organization development* by which planned changes are implemented. (See *process intervention; structural intervention.*)

Inventory management. The *decision-making* techniques managers use to determine how many items the organization should keep in stock.

Iron Law of Oligarchy. See *Michels' Iron Law.*

Job enlargement. Increasing the number of operations an individual performs in a job cycle.

Job enrichment. Increasing the amount of responsibility an individual can exercise in his or her job.

Leadership. The ability of a superior to influence the behavior of subordinates; one of the *behavioral processes* in an organization.

Liabilities.   An organization's total outstanding financial obligations.

Line.   Managers and employees directly involved in the production of the final good or service the organization produces.

Linear programming.   A *decision-making* technique that is an extension of *break-even analysis.* It is particularly appropriate when an organization manufactures two or more products and uses two or more resources.

Linking pin.   Rensis Likert's term for a member of two *work groups* whose work overlaps, responsible for coordinating the work of the two groups.

Local leaders.   Managers who normally stay with an organization or community their entire life, and who do not seek visibility outside the organization or community. (Contrast *cosmopolitan leaders.*)

Machine-controlled systems.   *Technology* in which machines rather than human beings control or monitor the work processes, as in an oil refinery.

Management audit.   A control technique that assesses the overall quality of management by means of methods such as questionnaires, interviews, and analysis of "hard" data elements (turnover, productivity, and so forth).

Management by objectives (MBO).   An organization-wide *planning* system in which top management typically defines four or five general objectives it wishes to achieve within a given period. Managers throughout the *hierarchy* refine these objectives into subobjectives for their own units. Each employee's performance is then evaluated in terms of individual objectives that relate directly to the unit's objectives.

Management information system (MIS).   Any system of data collection and analysis that will help the manager perform his or her job more effectively.

Managerial grid.   An *O.D.* approach to changing organizations; it assumes that managers should be both *task-oriented* and *considerate.*

Managerial team.   A group of managers who successfully coordinate their efforts so that they and their respective organizational units benefit.

Manager pair.   Two managers, a specialist and a generalist, who work together, the specialist digging more deeply into the problems the generalist diagnoses.

MAPS (Multivariate analysis, participation, and structure).   An approach to organization development design that allows the members of the organization to define the major task groups or units and to select the individuals most suitable for working in them.

Mass production.   Technology in which an organization spends a great amount of money on both labor and *capital* equipment.

Matrix organization.   An *organization design* that combines *departmentation* by product and function: Functional managers exercise technical authority over projects, while the product managers have responsibility for budgets and the final completion of projects. The functional managers lend employees to product managers as needed.

Mechanistic structure.   An organization having a high degree of functional specialization of jobs, a centralized *hierarchy,* formal and standardized jobs and procedures, economic sources of *motivation,* an authoritarian *leadership* style, formal and impersonal relations between individuals and groups, and vertical and *direc-*

tive communication. (Contrast *organic structure.*)

Michels' Iron Law. Michels' statement that whoever says organization, says oligarchy, or rule by the few.

Model. A simplified or concrete representation of a complex or abstract process or idea.

Motion study. *Scientific management's* analysis of the specific motions of workers at a given job, through the use of films and other devices, so as to determine what motions are necessary for the job's completion. (See *time study.*)

Motivation. The physical and mental state that propels an individual to act in a particular manner, or the deliberate creation of such a state; one of the *behavioral processes* in an organization.

Motivators. In *two-factor theory,* intrinsic sources of *motivation,* relating directly to the nature of the work (for example, interesting and challenging assignments), which affect rates of productivity.

Need hierarchy. Abraham Maslow's theory of *motivation,* which holds that the human needs are arranged in a hierarchy; the individual seeks to satisfy basic and elementary needs first, and then higher-order needs.

Nominal group technique (NGT). A *forecasting* technique in which 7 to 10 experts meet to share and discuss their ideas and predictions.

Nonprogrammed decision. A solution to a problem that cannot be found by using a standard routine or program, but demands a creative response.

Nonzero-sum situation. A competitive situation in which when one group wins, the other group also wins or its position remains unchanged. (Contrast *zero-sum situation.*)

Norm. A standard or ideal pattern, e.g., of behavior.

Normative. Reflecting a norm; as, a normative *model* of *decision making.* (Contrast *descriptive.*)

Office of the president. A system by which two or three co-equal chief executives in an organization divide the work and coordinate their respective efforts.

Open system. A set of processes whose recurring operation is influenced by outside factors. (Contrast *closed system.*)

Organic structure. An *organization design* having enriched jobs, a *decentralized hierarchy,* flexible jobs and *procedures,* economic and noneconomic sources of *motivation,* democratic *leadership,* informal and personal relations between individuals, and both vertical and lateral *consultative communications.* (See *mechanistic structure.*)

Organization design. The structure of an organization, which provides a framework for its activities and delineates lines of authority and responsibility.

Organization development (O.D.). The introduction of planned and systematic change into an organization within the dimensions of *organization design* and *behavioral processes.*

Overhead costs. Expenses that cannot be conveniently assigned as either *fixed* or *variable;* for example, electricity and the salaries of clerical personnel.

Parity principle. The idea that the amount of authority an individual possesses should be equal to his or her responsibility.

Participative management.   A system by which employees are allowed to have a voice in decisions that bear directly on their work.

Payback period.   The length of time required for the net revenues of an investment to cover its initial cost.

Personal space.   The physical area around an individual within which other people generally do not trespass.

Planning.   Specifying organizational goals and the means to be used to achieve them. There are two kinds of means: *strategies* and *tactics*.

Planning, strategic.   See *strategy*.

Planning, tactical.   See *tactic*.

Planning-programming-budgeting system (PPBS).   An organization-wide *planning* system that includes definition of objectives, analysis of anticipated costs and benefits of each program, allocation of resources to authorized programs, completion of authorized programs, and analysis of the results of each program.

Policy.   A general guide management employs to direct organizational activities.

Polyspecialist.   A manager who is neither a generalist nor a specialist, but rather is very knowledgeable in several areas.

Power.   The source of a superior's ability to persuade subordinates to follow a particular course of action. There are five types of power: legitimate, reward, expert, coercive, and referent.

Principles of management.   Certain guidelines that Fayol and other members of the *classical management* school held that a manager should follow to achieve success. (See, for example, *span of control*.)

Problem-solving group.   A task-oriented informal committee brought together for the purpose of solving a specific problem. (See *creative group*.)

Procedures.   Plans that establish a customary method of handling future activities. They normally accompany *policies*.

Process intervention.   In *organization development*, an attempt to change the attitudes of organizational members so that organizational objectives can be accomplished more successfully. (See *structural intervention*.)

Process or automated technology.   Technology in which the organization invests heavily in *capital* equipment but does not spend much money on labor.

Program evaluation and review technique (PERT).   An organization-wide *planning* technique particularly appropriate for a project that consists of a number of interrelated steps or activities, some of which must be finished before others can begin.

Programmed decision.   A solution to a problem found by using a program, routine, or procedure that has been successful for similar problems in the past.

Project management.   An *organization design* in which each subordinate is employed only for the life of a project; when the project is completed, the subordinate is either assigned to another project or let go.

Protégé.   An individual whose career is advanced by the help of an older and successful executive.

Protestant ethic.   The idea that worldly success is a necessary but not sufficient condition for salvation.

Questionnaire data banks.   Computer stores of information collected from a large number of questionnaires, used to pinpoint problems in an organization. Normally each organizational unit is compared to the *norm* or average on each questionnaire item.

Risky shift phenomenon. The finding that the behavior of individuals as individuals often is radically different from their *group behavior.* In some situations, individuals take a riskier position; in others, a more conservative position.

Rules. Specific *procedures* that individuals and operating divisions of an organization should follow to be in conformity with organizational *policies.* However, some rules are not related to policies.

Satisficing. Choosing a solution to a problem by examining only four or five alternatives that are minimally acceptable, and picking one that will be adequate, rather than taking additional time and effort to find the best possible solution. (See *Economic man.*)

Scientific management. The approach within the school of *classical management* whose proponents argue that there is an ideal way of performing any job, which can be pinpointed scientifically through *time* and *motion study.*

Sensitivity training. A group-discussion method used to give individuals insight into their strengths and weaknesses. Although a psychologist is present, the group starts off its discussions in an unstructured and "leaderless" fashion; gradually the psychologist intervenes to help members understand their attitudes and behavior.

Simulation. Building and testing models that use mathematical relationships between critical, "real-world" factors to create a facsimile of real conditions; normally done on a computer.

Span of control. The number of subordinates a manager supervises or should supervise.

Staff. Managers and employees who advise and assist *line* managers and employees, and are not directly involved in the production of the final good or service of the organization.

Standard cost system. A *control* technique that estimates anticipated costs for a particular product or level of volume.

Stereotypes. Preconceived notions about people, often based on superficial characteristics, which can distort *communication* between individuals.

Strategy. The means an organization uses to achieve its overall objectives.

Streams of management. The major schools of management have developed within two major streams, economics and behavioral science.

Structural intervention. In *organization development,* altering the structure of an organization so that individuals relate to one another in a new and different way. (See *process intervention.*)

System Four. A *total organizational intervention* stressing participative management: Managers express complete confidence and trust in their subordinates, obtain subordinates' ideas, and try to implement them if possible, delegate a great amount of responsibility, and use group *decision making* as much as possible.

Systems theory. An approach to management that assumes: (1) an organization is a system consisting of subunits that interact with one another and depend on one another; and (2) an organization is an *open system* interacting with its external environment and dependent on it.

Tactic.   The means used to attain specific objectives that relate directly to the overall objectives of an organization.

Task force.   A group set up within an organization to accomplish a specific objective, after which it disbands. It differs from a *temporary committee* in that its members are drawn from various departments in the organization interested in the outcome of the task force's work.

Task orientation.   One of the two key dimensions of leader behavior, involving focusing on initiation of structure, assignment of tasks, specification of the manner in which tasks are to be completed, and clarification of schedules.

Team building.   In *organization development,* an *intervention* focused on improving the effectiveness and efficiency of one group or unit.

Technology.   The means an organization uses to produce its good or service.

Temporary committee.   See *committee, temporary or ad hoc.*

Theory X.   The managerial assumption that human beings are lazy, avoid responsibility, need direction, and must be coerced.

Theory Y.   The managerial assumption that human beings seek responsibility and want to use their abilities.

Time study.   *Scientific management*'s method of determining the time a worker needs to complete a given job cycle, by the use of the stop watch. (See *motion study.*)

Total organizational intervention.   In *organization development,* an *intervention* focused on improving the efficiency and effectiveness of an entire organization.

Training groups (T-groups).   *Sensitivity training* groups, which can be used to train managers in interpersonal insight and relations.

Trait theory.   A view of *leadership* that assumes leaders differ from average people in traits like intelligence, perseverance, and ambition.

Two-factor theory.   Frederick Herzberg's idea that job motivation has two independent sources: *hygiene factors* and *motivators.*

Unit technology.   *Technology* in which an organization spends a great amount of money on labor relative to *capital* investment in equipment.

Unity of command.   The *principle* in *classical management* that a subordinate should be responsible only to one superior.

Variable costs.   Expenses that change with the level of output, and that normally change each time they occur, such as materials and labor. (Contrast *fixed costs.*)

Vertical integration.   A company's attempt to dominate a market by controlling all steps in the production process, from the extraction of raw materials through the manufacture and sale of the final product. (Contrast *horizontal integration.*)

Work group.   The formal group of individuals assigned to perform a particular task or function in an organization.

Zero-sum situation.   A competitive situation in which resources are finite, so that what one group wins, the other necessarily loses. (Contrast *nonzero-sum situation.*)

BIBLIOGRAPHY

Adams, J. "Inequity in Social Exchange." In *Advances in Experimental Social Psychology,* vol. 2, edited by L. Berkowitz, pp. 267–299. New York: Academic Press, 1965.

Albaum, G. "Horizontal Information Flow: An Exploratory Study." *Academy of Management Journal 7* (1964): 21–33.

Alderfer, C. *Existence, Relatedness, and Growth: Human Needs in Organizational Settings.* New York: The Free Press, 1972.

Applewhite, P. *Organizational Behavior.* Englewood Cliffs: Prentice-Hall, 1965.

Argyris, C. "Today's Problems with Tomorrow's Organizations." *Journal of Management Studies 4* (1967): 31–55.

Asch, S. "Effects of Group Pressure upon the Modification and Distortion of Judgment." In *Groups, Leadership and Men,* edited by H. Guetzkow, pp. 177–190. Pittsburgh: The Carnegie Press, 1951.

_____. *Social Psychology.* Englewood Cliffs: Prentice-Hall, 1952.

Bacon, J. *Planning and Forecasting in the Smaller Company.* New York: The Conference Board, 1971.

Bales, R. *Interaction Process Analysis.* Reading, Mass.: Addison-Wesley, 1950.

Barlund, D., and Harland, C. "Propinquity and Prestige as Determinants of Communication Networks." *Sociometry 26* (1963): 467–479.

Barmash, I. *Welcome to Our Conglomerate — You're Fired!* New York: Delacorte, 1971.

Barnard, C. *The Functions of the Executive.* Cambridge: Harvard University Press, 1966.

Bass, B. "Interface between Personnel and Organizational Psychology." *Journal of Applied Psychology 52* (1968): 81–88.

Bennis, W. "Towards a 'Truly' Scientific Management: The Concept of Organization Health," *Changing Organizations,* pp. 34–63. New York: McGraw-Hill, 1966.

"Be Prepared." *Forbes,* November 1, 1970, pp. 24–25.

Berlew, D., and Hall, D. "The Socialization of Managers: Effects of Expectations on Performance." *Administrative Science Quarterly 11* (1966): 207–233.

Blake, R., and Mouton, J. *Building a Dynamic Corporation through Grid.* Reading, Mass.: Addison-Wesley, 1969.

_____. *The Managerial Grid.* Houston: Gulf Publishing Co., 1964.

Blauner, R. *Alienation and Freedom.* Chicago: University of Chicago Press, 1964.

Burns, T. "The Directions of Activity and Communication in a Departmental Executive Group." *Human Relations 7* (1954): 73–97.

Burns, T., and Stalker, G. *The Management of Innovation.* London: Tavistock Publishing Company, 1961.

Burr, A. *Russell H. Conwell and His Work.* Philadelphia: John C. Winston Co., 1917.

Campbell, J., Dunnette, M., Lawler, E., and Weick, K. *Managerial Behavior, Performance, and Effectiveness.* New York: McGraw-Hill, 1970.

Carlson, R. *School Superintendents: Careers and Performance.* Columbus, Ohio: C. E. Merrill, 1972.

_____. "Succession and Performance among School Superintendents." *Administrative Science Quarterly 6* (1961): 210–227.

Carroll, S. "Relationships of Various College Graduate Characteristics to Recruiting Decisions." *Journal of Applied Psychology 50* (1966): 421–423.

Carroll, S., and Tosi, H. *Management by Objectives.* New York: Macmillan, 1973.

Chandler, A. *Strategy and Structure.* Cambridge: MIT Press, 1962.

Coch, L., and French, J. "Overcoming Resistance to Change." *Human Relations 1* (1948): 512–532.

Cocks, J. "Black and Tan Fantasy" (movie review). *Time,* October 27, 1975, p. 72.

Cofer, C., and Appley, M. *Motivation: Theory and Research.* New York: John Wiley, 1964.

Cohen, A. "Changing Small-Group Communication Networks." *Administrative Science Quarterly 6* (1962): 443–462.

Collins, O., and Moore, D. *The Enterprising Man.* East Lansing, Mich.: Michigan State University Business Studies, Bureau of Business and Economic Research, 1964.

Commons, J. *Legal Foundations of Capitalism.* Madison, Wisc.: University of Wisconsin Press, 1957.

Commons, J., et al. *History of Labor in the United States: 1896–1932.* New York: Macmillan, 1935.

Cooper, A. "Entrepreneurial Environment." *Industrial Research 12* (1970): 74–76.

Costello, T., and Zalkind, S., eds. *Psychology in Administration.* Englewood Cliffs: Prentice-Hall, 1963.

Cronbach, L. *Essentials of Psychological Testing,* 2d ed. New York: Harper & Row, 1960.

Crozier, M. *The Bureaucratic Phenomenon.* Chicago: University of Chicago Press, 1964.

Cummings, L., and Schwab, D. *Performance in Organizations.* Glenview, Ill.: Scott, Foresman, 1973.

Dale, E. *Planning and Developing the Company Organization Structure.* New York: American Management Association, Research Report no. 20, 1952.

Dalton, M. "Changing Line-Staff Relationships." *Personnel Administration 28* (1966): 3–5.

_____. "Conflicts between Staff and Line Managerial Officers." *American Sociological Review 15* (1950): 342–351.

_____. *Men Who Manage.* New York: John Wiley, 1959.

Davis, K. *Human Relations at Work,* 3d ed. New York: McGraw-Hill, 1967.

_____. "A Method of Studying Communication Patterns in Organizations." *Personnel Psychology 6* (1953): 301–312.

Dearborn, D., and Simon, H. "Selective Perception: A Note on the Departmental Identification of Executives." *Sociometry 21* (1958): 140–144.

Delbecq, A., Van de Ven, A., and Gustafson, D. *Group Techniques for Program Planning.* Glenview, Ill.: Scott, Foresman, 1975.

Delman, M. "Pitfalls to Avoid in Starting Your Own Business." *The American Legion Magazine 90* (1971): 24–27, 41–44, 46.

Donnelly, J., Gibson, J., and Ivancevich, J. *Fundamentals of Management,* 2d ed. Dallas: Business Publications, 1975.

Dowling, W. "At GM: System 4 Builds Performance and Profits." *Organizational Dynamics 3* (1975): 23–38.

Drucker, P. *The Practice of Management.* New York: Harper and Brothers, 1954.

Dunnette, M., Campbell, J., and Jaastad, K. "The Effect of Group Participation on Brainstorming Effectiveness for Two Industrial Samples." *Journal of Applied Psychology 47* (1963): 30–37.

Entine, A. "Second Careers: Experience and Expectations." In *Where Have All the Robots Gone?: Worker Dissatisfaction in the 70s,* edited by H. Sheppard and N. Herrick, pp. 161–165. New York: The Free Press, 1972.

Estey, M. "The Retail Clerks." In *White-Collar Workers,* edited by A. Blum, et al., pp. 47–82. New York: Random House, 1971.

Etzioni, A. *A Comparative Analysis of Complex Organizations.* New York: The Free Press, 1961.

Fayol, H. *General and Industrial Management.* Translated by Constance Storrs. London: Pittman and Sons, 1949.

Federal Trade Commission, House Document #468. *Report on Motor Vehicle Industry.* Washington, D.C.: U.S. Government Printing Office, 1939.

Feeney, E. "Performance Audit, Feedback and Positive Reinforcement." *Training and Development Journal 26* (1972): 8–13.

Festinger, L. *A Theory of Cognitive Dissonance.* Stanford, Calif.: Stanford University Press, 1957.

Fiedler, F. *A Theory of Leadership Effectiveness.* New York: McGraw-Hill, 1967.

_____. "Validation and Extension of the Contingency Model of Leadership Effectiveness: A Review of Empirical Findings." *Psychological Bulletin 76* (1971): 128–148.

Filley, A. *Interpersonal Conflict Resolution.* Glenview, Ill.: Scott, Foresman, 1975.

Filley, A., House, R., and Kerr, S. *Managerial Process and Organizational Behavior,* 2d ed. Glenview, Ill.: Scott, Foresman, 1976.

Fleishman, E. "Leadership Climate, Human Relations Training and Supervisory Behavior." *Personnel Psychology 6* (1953): 205–222.

Ford, H., with Crowther, S. *My Life and Work.* New York: Doubleday, Page and Co., 1922.

_____. *Today and Tomorrow.* New York: Doubleday, Page and Co., 1926.

Ford, R. *Motivation Through the Work Itself.* New York: American Management Association, 1969.

French, J., and Raven, B. "The Bases of Social Power." In *Studies in Social Power,* edited by D. Cartwright, pp. 150–167. Ann Arbor: University of Michigan, Institute for Social Research, 1959.

French W., and Bell, C. *Organization Development*. Englewood Cliffs: Prentice-Hall, 1973.

Galbraith, J. *Designing Complex Organizations.* Reading, Mass.: Addison-Wesley, 1973.

Gannon, M. "Attitudes of Government Executives Toward Management Training." *Public Personnel Management 4* (1975): 63–68.

_____. "The Case Observational Method: A New Training Technique." *Training and Development Journal 24* (1970): 39–41.

_____. "Employee Perceptions of Promotion." *Personnel Journal 50* (1971): 213–215.

_____. "Entrepreneurship and Labor Relations at the Ford Motor Co." *Marquette Business Review XVI* (1972): 63–75.

_____. "A Profile of the Temporary Help Industry and Its Workers." *Monthly Labor Review 97* (1974): 44–49.

_____. "The Proper Use of the Questionnaire Survey." *Business Horizons XV* (1973): 89–94.

Gannon, M., and Hendrickson, B. "Career Orientation and Job Satisfaction among Working Wives." *Journal of Applied Psychology 57* (1973): 339–340.

Gannon, M., and Kopchik, C. "The Percentile Approach to O. D. Assessment." *Business Horizons XVII* (1974): 81–87.

Gannon, M., and Paine, F. "Unity of Command and Job Attitudes of Managers in a Bureaucratic Organization." *Journal of Applied Psychology 59* (1974): 392–394.

Georgopoulos, B., Mahoney, G., and Jones, N. "A Path-Goal Approach to Productivity." *Journal of Applied Psychology 41* (1957): 345–353.

Ghiselli, E. *Explorations in Managerial Talent*. Pacific Palisades, Calif.: Goodyear, 1971.

Gibb, J. "Communication and Productivity." *Personnel Administration 27* (1964): 8–13, 45.

Gilbreth, F. *Primer of Scientific Management*. New York: Harper, 1912.

Goldner, F. "Demotion in Industrial Management." *American Sociological Review 30* (1965): 714–725.

Goldthorpe, J., Lockwood, D., Bechhofer, F., and Platt, J. *The Affluent Worker: Industrial Attitudes and Behavior*. London: Cambridge University Press, 1968.

Gouldner, A. "Cosmopolitans and Locals: Toward an Analysis of Social Roles I and II." *Administrative Science Quarterly 2* (1957): 281–306.

_____. *Patterns of Industrial Bureaucracy*. New York: The Free Press of Glencoe, 1954.

Graen, G., Alvares, K., and Orris, J. "Contingency Model of Leadership Effectiveness: Antecedent and Evidential Results." *Psychological Bulletin 74* (1970): 285–296.

Guest, R. "Of Time and the Foreman." *Personnel 32* (1956): 478–486.

Hackman, J., and Lawler, E. "Employee Reactions to Job Characteristics." *Journal of Applied Psychology 55* (1971): 259–286.

Haire, M. "Role-Perception in Labor-Management Relations: An Experimental Approach." *Industrial and Labor Relations Review 8* (1955): 204–216.

Haire, M., Ghiselli, E., and Porter, L. *Managerial Thinking: An International Study*. New York: John Wiley, 1966.

Haire, M., and Grunes, W. "Perceptual Defenses: Processes Protecting an Organized Perception of Another Personality." *Human Relations 3* (1950): 403–412.

Hall, E. *The Hidden Dimension.* New York: Doubleday, 1968.

Harlow, D., and Hanke, J. *Behavior in Organizations.* Boston: Little, Brown, 1975.

Harris, H. *American Labor.* New Haven: Yale University Press, 1939.

Harrison, E. F. *The Managerial Decision Making Process.* Boston: Houghton Mifflin, 1975.

Harvey, E. "Technology and Structure of Organizations." *American Sociological Review 33* (1968): 249−259.

Hedges, J. "New Patterns of Working Time." *Monthly Labor Review 96* (1973): 3−8.

Hellriegel, D., and Slocum, J. *Management: A Contingency Approach.* Reading, Mass.: Addison-Wesley, 1974.

Hersey, P., and Blanchard, K. *Management of Organizational Behavior,* 2d ed. Englewood Cliffs: Prentice-Hall, 1972.

Hershey, R. "The Grapevine . . . Here to Stay But Not Beyond Control." *Personnel 43* (1966): 62−66.

Herzberg, F. "One More Time: How Do You Motivate Employees?" *Harvard Business Review 46* (1968): 53−62.

Herzberg, F., Mausner, B., and Snyderman, B. *The Motivation to Work.* New York: John Wiley, 1959.

Hickson, D., Pugh, D., and Pheysey, D. "Operations Management and Organization Structure: An Empirical Reappraisal." *Administrative Science Quarterly 14* (1969): 286−309.

Hinrichs, J. "Communications Activity of Industrial Research Personnel." *Personnel Psychology 17* (1964): 193−204.

Hornaday, J., and Aboud, J. "Characteristics of Successful Entrepreneurs." *Personnel Psychology 24* (1971): 141−153.

House, R. "A Path-Goal Theory of Leadership Effectiveness." *Administrative Science Quarterly 16* (1971): 321−340.

House, R., and Miner, J. "Merging Management and Behavioral Theory: The Interaction between Span of Control and Group Size." *Administrative Science Quarterly 14* (1969): 451−466.

Howard, A. "An Assessment of Assessment Centers." *Academy of Management Journal 17* (1974): 115−134.

Hulin, C., and Blood, R. "Job Enlargement, Individual Differences, and Worker Responses." *Psychological Bulletin 69* (1968): 41−55.

Ingham, G. *Size of Industrial Organization and Work Behaviour.* Cambridge, England: Cambridge University Press, 1970.

Janger, A. "Analyzing the Span of Control." *Management Record 22* (1960): 7−10.

Kahn, R., Wolfe, D., Quinn, R., and Snoek, J. *Organizational Stress: Studies in Role Conflict and Ambiguity.* New York: John Wiley, 1964.

Kast, F., and Rosenzweig, J. *Organization and Management: A Systems Approach,* 2d ed. New York: McGraw-Hill, 1974.

Katz, E., and Lazarsfeld, P. *Personal Influence.* Glencoe, Ill.: The Free Press, 1955.

Kerr, C., and Siegel, A. "The Interindustry Propensity to Strike: An International Comparison." In *Industrial Conflict,* edited by A. Kornhauser, R. Dubin, and A. Ross, pp. 189−212. New York: McGraw-Hill, 1954.

Kilmann, R. "A Quasi-Experimental Paradigm for Organizational Development: Intervention Strategies vs. Environmental Conditions." In *Proceedings* of the Eastern Academy of Management, edited by B. Kolasa, The Pennsylvania State University, April 10–12, 1975, unpaginated.

Kilmann, R., and McKelvey, B. "The MAPS Route to Better Organization Design." *California Management Review XVII* (1975): 23–31.

Lawler, E. *Pay and Organizational Effectiveness.* New York: McGraw-Hill, 1971.

Lawler, E., and Suttle, J. "A Causal Correlation Test of the Need Hierarchy Concept." *Organizational Behavior and Human Performance 7* (1972): 265–287.

Lawrence, P., and Lorsch, J. *Organization and Environment.* Boston: Harvard Business School, Division of Research, 1967.

Leavitt, J., and Mueller, R. "Some Effects of Feedback on Communication." *Human Relations 4* (1951): 401–410.

Lewin, K. "Group Decision and Social Change." In *Readings in Social Psychology,* 3d ed., edited by E. Maccoby, T. Newcomb, and E. Hartley, pp. 330–344. New York: Holt, Rinehart and Winston, 1958.

Lieberman, S. "The Effects of Changes in Roles on the Attitudes of Role Occupants." *Human Relations 9* (1956): 385–402.

Likert, R. *The Human Organization.* New York: McGraw-Hill, 1967.

_____. *New Patterns of Management.* New York: McGraw-Hill, 1961.

Lindblom, C. "The Science of Muddling Through." *Public Administration Review 19* (1959): 79–88.

Lippman, W. *Drift and Mastery.* Englewood Cliffs: Prentice-Hall, 1961.

Locke, E. "The Nature and Causes of Job Satisfaction." In *Handbook of Industrial and Organizational Psychology,* edited by M. Dunnette, pp. 1297–1349. Chicago: Rand McNally, 1976.

_____. "Toward a Theory of Task Motivation and Incentives." *Organizational Behavior and Human Performance 3* (1968): 157–189.

Locke, E., and Bryan, J. "Performance Goals as Determinants of Level of Performance and Boredom." *Journal of Applied Psychology 51* (1967): 120–130.

Loeb, S., and Gannon, M. "Educational Factors, Professional Activity and Job Tenure among Public Accountants." *Journal of Accountancy* (April 1976): 88–89.

Logan, N., O'Reilly, C., and Roberts, K. "Job Satisfaction among Part-Time and Full-Time Employees." *Journal of Vocational Behavior 3* (1973): 33–41.

Lowin, A., and Craig, J. "The Influence of Level of Performance on Managerial Style: An Experimental Object-Lesson in the Ambiguity of Correlational Data." *Organizational Behavior and Human Performance 3* (1968): 440–458.

Maier, N. *Psychology in Industry,* 2d ed. Boston: Houghton Mifflin, 1955.

Maier, N., Hoffman, L., and Read, W. "Superior-Subordinate Communication: The Relative Effectiveness of Managers Who Held Their Subordinates' Positions." *Personnel Psychology 16* (1963): 1–11.

Manpower Report of the President. Washington, D.C.: U.S. Government Printing Office, 1975.

Manpower Report of the President. Washington, D.C.: U.S. Government Printing Office, 1970.

March, J., and Feigenbaum, E. "Latent Motives, Group Discussion, and the 'Quality' of Group Decisions in a Non-Objective Decision Problem." *Sociometry 23* (1960): 50–56.

March, J., and Simon, H. *Organizations.* New York: John Wiley, 1958.

Marion, B., and Trieb, S. "Job Orientation: A Factor in Employee Performance and Turnover." *Personnel Journal 48* (1969): 779–804, 831.

Marrow, A., Bowers, D., and Seashore, S. *Management by Participation.* New York: Harper & Row, 1967.

Martin, N. "Differential Decisions in the Management of an Industrial Plant." *Journal of Business 28* (1956): 249–260.

Maslow, A. *Motivation and Personality,* 2d ed. New York: Harper & Row, 1970.

———. "A Theory of Human Motivation." *Psychological Review 50* (1943): 370–396.

McClelland, D. *The Achieving Society.* Princeton, N.J.: Van Nostrand, 1961.

McClelland, D., and Winter, D. *Motivating Economic Achievement.* New York: The Free Press, 1969.

McGregor, D. *The Human Side of Enterprise.* New York: McGraw-Hill, 1960.

McGuire, J. "Management in the Future." In *Contemporary Management,* edited by J. McGuire, pp. 639–653. Englewood Cliffs: Prentice-Hall, 1974.

McKelvey, B., and Kilmann, R. "Organization Design: A Participative Multivariate Approach." *Administrative Science Quarterly 20* (1975): 24–36.

Merton, R. *Social Theory and Social Structure,* rev. ed. Glencoe, Ill.: The Free Press, 1957.

Michels, R. *Political Parties.* New York: Dover Publications, 1959.

Miles, R. *Theories of Management.* New York: McGraw-Hill, 1975.

Miner, J. *The Challenge of Managing.* Philadelphia: W. B. Saunders Co., 1975.

———. *The Human Constraint.* Washington, D.C.: The Bureau of National Affairs, 1974.

———. *The Management Process: Theory, Research, and Practice.* New York: Macmillan, 1973.

Miner, J., and Heaton, E. "Company Orientation as a Factor in the Readership of Employee Publications." *Personnel Psychology 12* (1959): 607–618.

Mintzberg, H. "The Manager's Job: Folklore and Fact." *Harvard Business Review 53* (1975): 49–61.

———. *The Nature of Managerial Work.* New York: Harper & Row, 1973.

Morrison, E. *Developing Computer-Based Employee Information Systems.* New York: American Management Association, 1969.

Morse, N., and Reimer, E. "The Experimental Change of a Major Organization Variable." *Journal of Abnormal and Social Psychology 52* (1956): 120–129.

Mullen, J. "Personality Polarization as an Equilibrating Force in a Large Organization." *Human Organization 25* (1966): 330–338.

———. *Personality and Productivity in Management.* New York: Temple University Publications, distributed by Columbia University Press, 1966.

Murray, H. *Explorations in Personality: A Clinical and Experimental Study of Fifty Men of College Age.* New York: Oxford University Press, 1938.

Nash, A. "Vocational Interests of Effective Managers: A Review of the Literature." *Personnel Psychology 18* (1965): 21–37.

Nevins, A., and Hill, F. *Ford: The Times, the Man, the Company,* vol. 1. New York: Charles Scribner's Sons, 1954.

————. *Ford: Expansion and Challenge, 1915–1933,* vol. 2. New York: Charles Scribner's Sons, 1957.

————. *Ford: Decline and Rebirth, 1933–1962,* vol. 3. New York: Charles Scribner's Sons, 1963.

1975 General Motors Report on Programs of Public Interest. Detroit, Mich.: General Motors Corporation, 1976, p. 8.

Nord, W., and Costigan, R. "Worker Adjustment to the Four-Day Week: A Longitudinal Study." *Journal of Applied Psychology 58* (1973): 60–66.

Ouchi, W., and Maguire, M. "Organizational Control: Two Functions." *Administrative Science Quarterly 4* (1975): 559–569.

Paine, F., Carroll, S., and Leete, B. "A Study of Need Satisfactions in Managerial Level Personnel in a Government Agency." *Journal of Applied Psychology 50* (1966): 247–249.

Palmore, E. "Predicting Longevity: A Follow-up Controlling for Age." *The Gerontologist 9* (1969): 247–250.

Parkinson, C. *Parkinson's Law.* Boston: Houghton Mifflin, 1957.

Parsons, T. *Structure and Process in Modern Society.* New York: The Free Press, 1960.

Patton, A. "Government's Revolving Door." *Business Week,* September 22, 1973, pp. 12–13.

Porter, L. *Organizational Patterns of Managerial Job Attitudes.* New York: American Foundation for Management Research, 1964.

Porter, L., and Lawler, E. *Managerial Attitudes and Performance.* Homewood, Ill.: Irwin-Dorsey, 1968.

Porter, L., Lawler, E., and Hackman, J. *Behavior in Organizations.* New York: McGraw-Hill, 1975.

Read, W. "Upward Communication in Industrial Hierarchies." *Human Relations 15* (1962): 3–15.

Reif, W. *Computer Technology and Management Organization.* Iowa City, Iowa: University of Iowa, Bureau of Business and Economic Research, 1968.

Riesman, D. *The Lonely Crowd.* New Haven: Yale University Press, 1950.

Robinson, J., Athanasiou, R., and Head, K. *Measures of Occupational Attitudes and Occupational Characteristics.* Ann Arbor: University of Michigan, Survey Research Center, 1969.

Roethlisberger, F., and Dickson, W. *Management and the Worker.* Cambridge: Harvard University Press, 1939.

Rollins, S., and Charters, W. "The Diffusion of Information within Secondary School Staffs." *Journal of Social Psychology 65* (1965): 167–178.

Rosen, B., and D'Andrade, R. "The Psychological Origins of Achievement Motivation." *Sociometry 22* (1959): 185–218.

Rue, L. "The How and Who of Long-Range Planning." *Business Horizons XVI* (1973): 23–30.

Sayles, L. *Behavior of Industrial Work Groups.* New York: John Wiley, 1958.

Schelling, T. *The Strategy of Conflict.* Cambridge: Harvard University Press, 1960.

Schneider, B., and Locke, E. "A Critique of Herzberg's Classification System and a Suggested Revision." *Organizational Behavior and Human Performance* 6 (1971): 441–458.

Schneier, C. "Behavior Modification in Management: A Review and Critique." *Academy of Management Journal* 17 (1974): 528–548.

Schoderbek, P., Kefalas, A., and Schoderbek, C. *Management Systems.* Dallas: Business Publications, 1975.

Schuh, A. "The Predictability of Employee Tenure: A Review of the Literature." *Personnel Psychology* 20 (1967): 133–152.

Schumpeter, J. *The Theory of Economic Development.* Cambridge: Harvard University Press, 1934.

Scodel, A., Ratoosh, P., and Minos, J. "Some Personality Correlates of Decision Making under Conditions of Risk." *Behavioral Science* 4 (1959): 196–210.

Selznick, P. *TVA and the Grass Roots.* Berkeley: University of California Press, 1949.

Serbein, O. *Educational Activities of Business.* Washington, D.C.: American Council on Education, 1961.

Shapero, A. "Who Starts New Businesses? The Displaced, Uncomfortable Entrepreneur." *Psychology Today* 9, no. 6 (1975): 83–86, 88, 133.

Sherif, M., Harvey, O., White, B., Hood, W., and Sherif, C. *Intergroup Conflict and Cooperation: The Robbers Cave Experiment.* Norman: University of Oklahoma Book Exchange, 1961.

Shull, F., Delbecq, A., and Cummings, L. *Organizational Decision Making.* New York: McGraw-Hill, 1970.

Shultz, G., and Coleman, J., eds. *Labor Problems: Cases and Readings.* New York: McGraw-Hill, 1959.

Sieber, J., and Lanzetta, J. "Conflict and Conceptual Structure as Determinants of Decision Making Behavior." *Journal of Personality* 32 (1964): 622–641.

Siegel, S., and Fouraker, L. *Bargaining and Group Decision Making.* New York: McGraw-Hill, 1960.

Simon, H. *Administrative Behavior,* 3d ed. New York: The Free Press, 1976.

———. *The New Science of Management Decision.* New York: Harper & Row, 1960.

Simonds, R. "Is Organization Structure Reflecting New Techniques and Theory?" *Michigan State University Business Topics* 17 (1969): 65–71.

Simpson, R. "Vertical and Horizontal Communication in Formal Organizations." *Administrative Science Quarterly* 4 (1959): 188–196.

Sloan, A. *My Years with General Motors,* edited by J. McDonald and C. Stevens. New York: Doubleday and Company, 1963.

Soelberg, P. "Unprogrammed Decision Making." *Industrial Management Review* 8 (1967): 19–29.

Steele, F. *Physical Settings and Organization Development.* Reading, Mass.: Addison-Wesley, 1973.

Steinberg, H. "Your Wardrobe is Your Weapon." *MBA* 9 (1975): 45–49.

Stewart, R. *Managers and Their Jobs.* London: Macmillan, 1967.

Stogdill, R., and Coons, A., eds. *Leader Behavior: Its Description and Measurement.* Columbus, Ohio: Ohio State University, Bureau of Business Research, Research Monograph no. 88, 1957.

Stoner, J. "A Comparison of Individual and Group Decisions Involving Risk." Master's thesis, Massachusetts Institute of Technology, School of Industrial Management, 1961. As reported in Wallach, M., Kogan, N., and Bem, D. "Group Influences on Individual Risk Taking." *Journal of Abnormal and Social Psychology 65* (1962): 75–86.

Strauss, G., and Sayles, L. *Personnel,* 3d ed. Englewood Cliffs: Prentice-Hall, 1972.

Sutton, H., and Porter, L. "A Study of the Grapevine in a Governmental Organization." *Personnel Psychology 21* (1968): 223–230.

Sward, K. *The Legend of Henry Ford.* New York: Rinehart, 1948.

Taylor, F. *The Principles of Scientific Management.* New York: Harper, 1911.

Terry, G. *Principles of Management,* 3d ed. Homewood, Ill.: Richard D. Irwin, 1960.

Thayer, L. *Communication and Communication Systems.* Homewood, Ill.: Richard D. Irwin, 1968.

Thompson, J. *Organizations in Action.* New York: McGraw-Hill, 1967.

Thune, S., and House, R. "Where Long-Range Planning Pays Off." *Business Horizons 13* (1970): 81–87.

Trist, E., and Bamforth, K. "Some Social and Psychological Consequences of the Longwall Method of Coal-Getting." *Human Relations 4* (1951): 3–38.

U.S. Bureau of Labor Statistics. *Occupational Outlook Handbook.* Washington, D.C.: U.S. Government Printing Office, 1974–1975.

U.S. Department of Labor. *Employment and Earnings 21,* no. 9 (1975): 19–21.

U.S. Department of Labor. *Employment and Earnings 20,* no. 12 (1974): 24.

Vancil, R. "The Accuracy of Long-Range Planning." *Harvard Business Review 48* (1970): 98–101.

Viteles, M. *Motivation and Morale in Industry.* New York: Norton, 1953.

Vroom, V. "A New Look at Managerial Decision Making." *Organizational Dynamics 1* (1973): 66–80.

––––––. "Organizational Choice: A Study of Pre- and Post-Decision Processes." *Organizational Behavior and Human Performance 1* (1966): 212–225.

––––––. *Work and Motivation.* New York: John Wiley, 1964.

Vroom, V., and Yetton, P. *Leadership and Decision Making.* Pittsburgh: University of Pittsburgh Press, 1973.

Walker, C., and Guest, R. *The Man on the Assembly Line.* Cambridge: Harvard University Press, 1952.

Weaver, C. "Negro-White Differences in Job Satisfaction." *Business Horizons XVII* (1974): 67–78.

––––––. "Sex Differences in Job Satisfaction." *Business Horizons XVII* (1974): 42–49.

Weber, M. *The Protestant Ethic and the Spirit of Capitalism.* Translated by T. Parsons. New York: Charles Scribner's Sons, 1930.

––––––. *The Theory of Social and Economic Organization.* Translated by A. Henderson and T. Parsons. New York: The Free Press, 1947.

Webster, E. *Decision Making in the Employment Interview.* Montreal: McGill University, Applied Psychology Centre (printed by The Eagle Publishing Co.), 1964.

Wheeler, K., Gurman, R., and Tarnowieski, D. *The Four-Day Week.* New York: American Management Association, 1972.

Whisler, T. *Information Technology and Organizational Change.* Belmont, Calif.: Wadsworth Publishing Co., 1970.

Whyte, W. F. *Human Relations in the Restaurant Industry.* New York: McGraw-Hill, 1948.

Whyte, W. H. *The Organization Man.* New York: Simon and Schuster, 1956.

Wickesberg, A. "Communications Network in the Business Organization Structure." *Academy of Management Journal 11* (1968): 253–262.

Wickstrom, W. *Developing Managerial Competence: Changing Concepts — Emerging Practices.* New York: National Industrial Conference Board, Personnel Policy Study no. 189, 1964.

Williams, W. *Mainsprings of Men.* New York: Charles Scribner's Sons, 1925.

Winterbottom, M. "The Relation of Need for Achievement to Learning Experiences in Independence and Mastery." In *Motives in Fantasy, Action and Society,* edited by J. W. Atkinson, pp. 468–471. Princeton, N.J.: Van Nostrand, 1958.

Woodward, J. *Industrial Organization.* Oxford, England: Oxford University Press, 1965.
_____. *Management and Technology.* London: H.M.S.O., Department of Scientific and Industrial Research, 1958.

"Young Top Management: The New Goals, Rewards, Lifestyles." *Business Week,* October 6, 1975. pp. 56–68.

Zalesnik, A., and Moment, D. *The Dynamics of Interpersonal Behavior.* New York: John Wiley, 1964.

Zimbardo, P., and Ebbesen, E. *Influencing Attitudes and Changing Behavior.* Reading, Mass.: Addison-Wesley, 1969.

NAME INDEX

SUBJECT INDEX

461

To the Student:

School_____ Course title _____

Please give us your reaction to the following elements of *Management: An Organizational Perspective* by ranking each element from 1 (excellent) to 5 (poor).

	1	2	3	4	5
Overall impression					
Level of difficulty					
Use of examples					
Explanation of terms and concepts					
Interest level/writing style					
Physical appearance (cover, size, etc.)					
Illustrations					
Learning aids (glossary, suggested readings, etc.)					
Critical incidents					
Case studies					
Experiential exercises					

2. Which chapter did you like best? Why? _____
   _____
   _____

3. Which chapter did you like least? Why? _____
   _____
   _____

4. Was the entire book assigned? _____ Did you read the entire book? _____

5. Did your class use the cases and experiential exercises? _____
   Which ones did you like best? _____
   Which did you like least? _____

6. Do you feel your instructor should continue to assign this book? Why or why not? _____

7. Will you keep this book? _____

8. Please add any comments or suggestions on how we might improve this book's content or format. _____

_____

_____

9. *Optional:* Your name: _____
   Address: _____
   Date: _____

10. May we quote you, either in promotion for this book or in future publishing ventures? _____

(fold here) —

Place
stamp
here

MANAGEMENT: An Organizational Perspective
College Division
Little, Brown & Co.
34 Beacon Street
Boston, MA 02106